The Audiencia of Santo Domingo in the Seventeenth Century

The Audiencia of Santo Domingo in the Seventeenth Century

Justice and Royal Authority in the Spanish Caribbean

MARC EAGLE

University of Nebraska Press
LINCOLN

The University of Nebraska Press is part of a land-grant institution with campuses and programs on the past, present, and future homelands of the Pawnee, Ponca, Otoe-Missouria, Omaha, Dakota, Lakota, Kaw, Cheyenne, and Arapaho Peoples, as well as those of the relocated Ho-Chunk, Sac and Fox, and Iowa Peoples.

Publication of this book was assisted by the History Department of Western Kentucky University.

For customers in the EU with safety/GPSR concerns, contact:
gpsr@mare-nostrum.co.uk
Mare Nostrum Group BV
Mauritskade 21D
1091 GC Amsterdam
The Netherlands

Library of Congress Control Number: 2024027756

Designed and set in Minion Pro by Scribe Inc.

For Mom and Dad

CONTENTS

ILLUSTRATIONS

ACKNOWLEDGMENTS

I am greatly indebted to quite a number of people for assistance and encouragement with a project I have been working on for over two decades. However, to my lasting shame I have forgotten to record the names of many of those who deserve thanks here, and so I ask for their pardon.

This book started life as my dissertation, ably shepherded through to completion by my committee members at Tulane University, James Boyden, Rosanne Adderley, and the late Colin MacLachlan. The research it was based on was funded by a 2001–2 Fulbright-IIE grant; I am also grateful for the support of the Fulbright staff in Madrid during that year. The great majority of the primary sources used in this book are housed in the Archivo General de Indias in Seville, and I am very appreciative of all the help its personnel have provided me over the years. I have significantly benefited from the stimulating conversation and kind words of several generations of scholars I have crossed paths with at the AGI during that time; I would particularly like to recognize Chuck Walker and Victor Uribe-Uran for presiding over *café a las once* during my Fulbright year and—together with a constellation of international scholars—creating a welcoming environment for a graduate student who initially could barely get by in Spanish. I have had the good fortune of seeing friends like Luis Miguel Glave Testino (Lucho) at the AGI multiple times since then, and in recent years Phillippe Castejón has offered very helpful information and suggestions.

Special thanks are also due to María Teresa Mora and José Gómez, with whom I lived during my 2001–2 stay in Seville. They not only made me feel like part of their family but also provided critical assistance with editing and translation and even taught me to dance Sevillanas; it has been a genuine pleasure to see them again on return trips to Seville and have them meet my own family.

I also appreciate the assistance I received at the Biblioteca Nacional and Biblioteca del Palacio in Madrid while conducting supplementary research. In the Dominican Republic, the staff of the Archivo General de la Nación and the libraries of the Academia Dominicana de la Historia and the Universidad Autónoma de Santo Domingo were extremely helpful in locating valuable secondary sources. (I'd also like to mention the late Carlos Esteban Deive, who took time to chat with me, offer me coffee, and ask gently why I was studying the Audiencia of Santo Domingo.) Even though I didn't end up using the material, Else Zayas León graciously welcomed me to the Archivo Histórico Arquidiocesano in San Juan. I also benefited from the assistance of the personnel at the Archivo Nacional and the Biblioteca Nacional in Havana.

Institutional support from Western Kentucky University in the form of New Faculty and RCAP grant funding has been instrumental in being able to carry this project through to publication. Warm thanks are also due to the members of the PCAL writing group and to my colleagues in the History Department at WKU for providing helpful comments and suggestions on drafts of several chapters.

Mark Burkholder has provided invaluable assistance and support over the years, and I especially appreciate his willingness to share data about audiencia ministers with me. María Isabel Paredes Vera got in touch with me over email and graciously shared her work with me as well, while Juan José Ponce Vázquez's recent scholarship has also been extraordinarily useful for this study. David Wheat has been an enormous help in tracking down sources, even as I am putting the final touches on this manuscript.

I would also like to thank Bridget Barry at the University of Nebraska Press for all her help and patience with this book project (and thanks as well to former UNP editor Alisa Plant for initially bringing it to Nebraska). I appreciate the care and thought that Christoph Rosenmüller (with whom I have had productive discussions about the Dominican audiencia since we were both graduate students) and the other anonymous manuscript reader put into their feedback and comments, which substantially improved the finished version. I am responsible for whatever errors or shortcomings remain.

Finally, I owe the greatest debt of gratitude to my family. My wife, Susan Eagle, who has listened to me talk about this project for far too long, has continued to provide helpful answers to a wide range of questions and has taken care of our amazing kid in both Spain and the United States while I've been occupied with research. Heartfelt thanks are long overdue to both of my parents. My father, John Eagle, passed away in 2010 and is dearly missed. My mother, Bonnie Eagle, has been unfailingly supportive throughout my life, and my scholarly career has been no exception. This book is dedicated to them.

AUTHOR'S NOTE

I have adopted a simplified and somewhat anachronistic use of "Spain," even though during this period it was what J. H. Elliott has labeled a "composite monarchy," made up of multiple kingdoms and principalities ruled by a single individual (which were listed out in formal royal decrees). However, this does echo contemporary usage; in their letters, audiencia members regularly referred to "España," in addition to using "those kingdoms" and "these kingdoms" to differentiate peninsular Spain from the Indies. I have also generally omitted titles and honorifics from personal names and standardized and modernized these names, although since most literate individuals used a consistent form when signing (despite the lack of standardization in seventeenth-century orthography), I have preserved some contemporary spellings (such as "Joseph" or "Thomás"). Due to the potentially overwhelming number of names in this book, I encourage readers to consult the appendix as necessary. I have opted to translate most quotations into English; all translations are my own unless otherwise indicated.

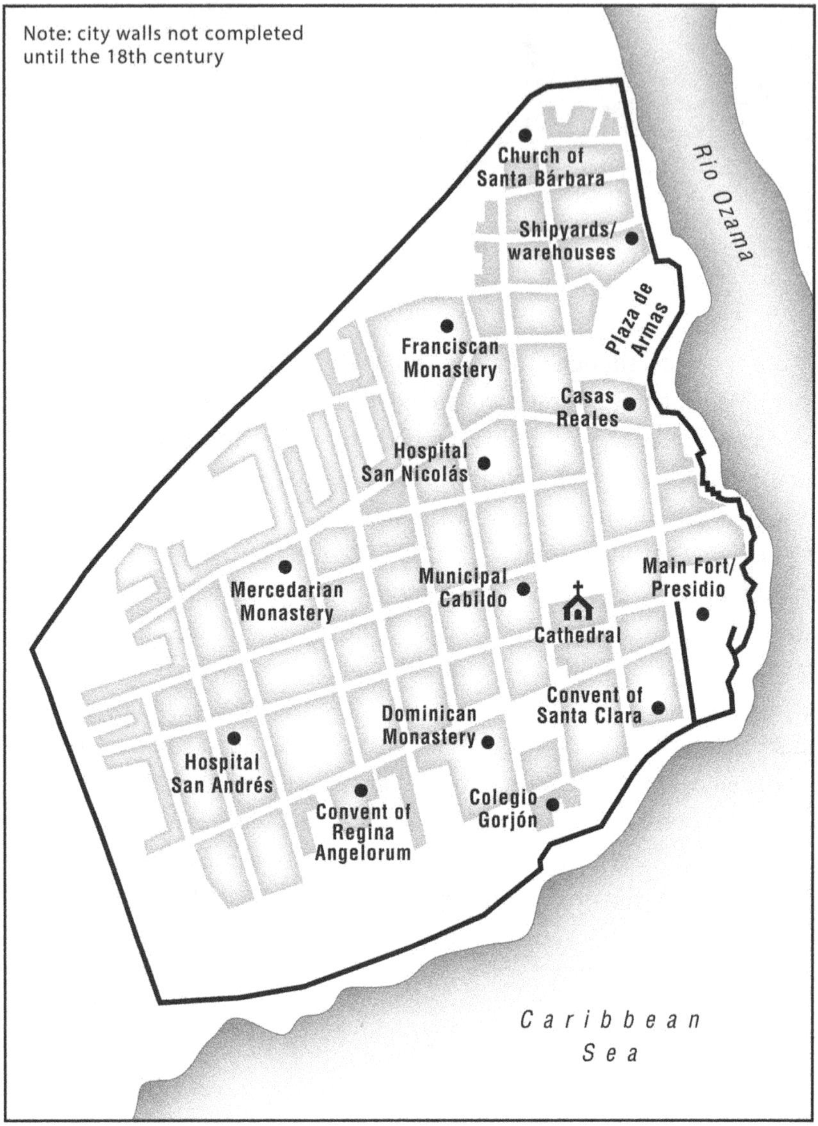

MAP 1. Seventeenth-century Santo Domingo. Map by Erin Greb.

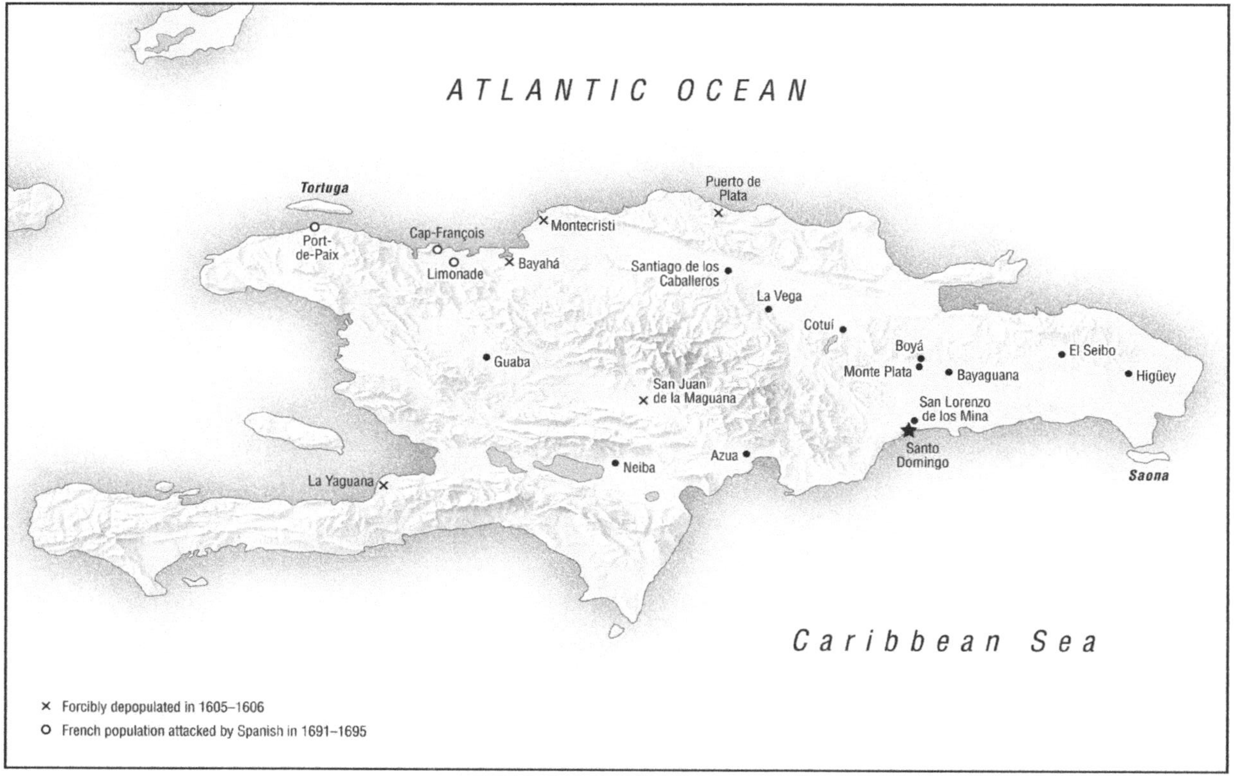

MAP 2. Seventeenth-century Hispaniola. Map by Erin Greb.

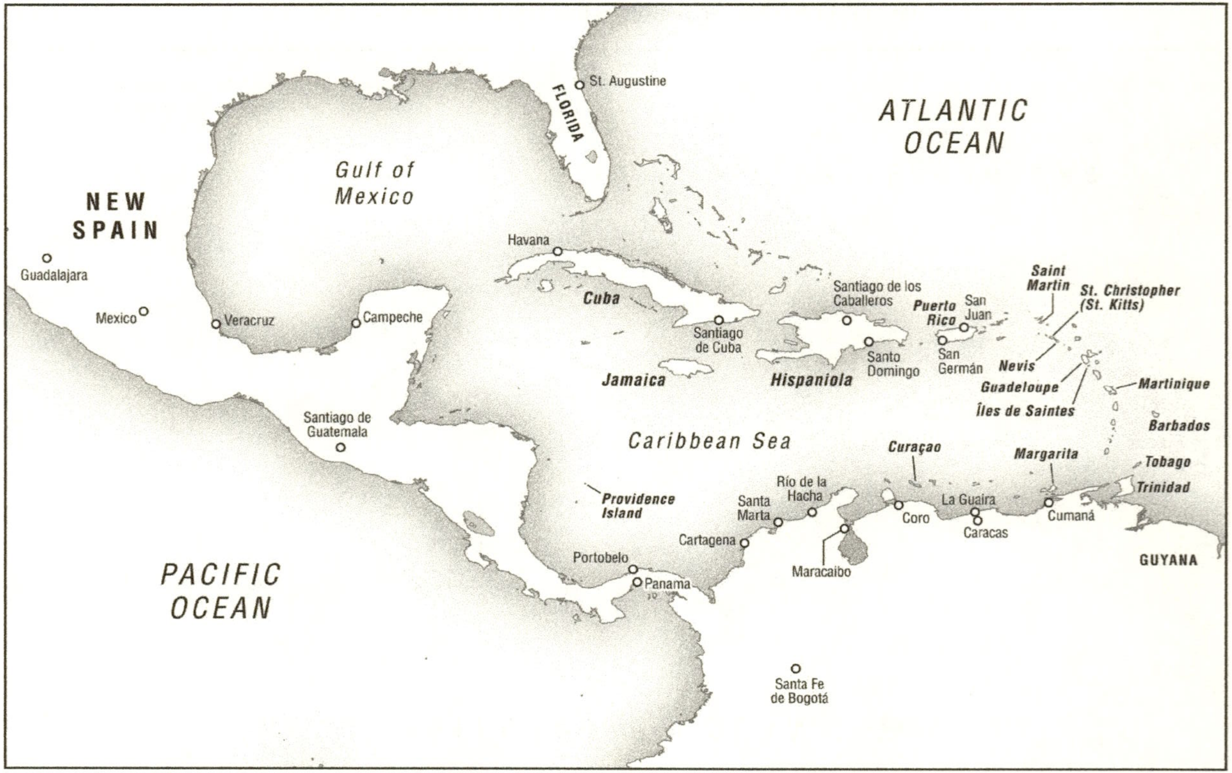

MAP 3. Seventeenth-century Caribbean. Map by Erin Greb.

The Audiencia of Santo Domingo in the Seventeenth Century

1

Introduction

Imperial Governance and the Audiencia of Santo Domingo

By the seventeenth century, the Audiencia of Santo Domingo—one of several superior courts of justice throughout Spain's overseas empire—was well known as the worst destination for an aspiring bureaucrat. In 1630 *oidor* (magistrate) Alonso de Cereceda lamented his misfortune in having to serve there, claiming he had been "proposed for the best places in the Indies, though [he] ended up with the least of them."[1] The members of the Council of the Indies acknowledged in 1658 that there was "none inferior" to it, and they described a promotion to Chile as comparable due to "the wars and discomforts of that land, in the most isolated part of Peru," but an improvement in rank and salary.[2]

Just the same, the appellate court on Hispaniola remained an integral part of the administrative structure of Spain's far-flung empire during this period. For the Spanish Crown, it performed the vital function of giving subjects in its district some form of access to royal justice while also helping supervise the Caribbean region. For the population of this district, especially in Santo Domingo itself, the audiencia represented not only a formal way to resolve disputes but also a two-way connection to the figure of the monarch through which they could seek aid and favor. For the men posted there, it provided practical experience with the challenges of embodying royal authority overseas as well as a potential stepping stone to a more prestigious audiencia. Despite the regular complaints of these men about the difficulties they faced on Hispaniola, the Dominican tribunal illustrates a durable system of overseas governance in action.

The problems Santo Domingo's audiencia ministers reported seemed to be serious ones. Although some, like internal conflicts, were not unique to this court, their complaints about foreign hostilities and the island's growing poverty and isolation reflected a dramatically different situation in the Caribbean compared to the time of the audiencia's creation in the early sixteenth century. Yet metropolitan authorities showed no interest in proposals to move the tribunal to Havana or Caracas during this time, while local elites clamored to keep it in their city; only in 1795 did the Crown relocate it to Puerto Príncipe in Cuba when Hispaniola was ceded to France by the Treaty of Basel.[3] It was not a particularly powerful or efficient institution, even by contemporary standards, but its preservation in Santo Domingo was due to something more than mere inertia or nostalgia for the island's past glories. Rather, the audiencia on Hispaniola continued to provide royal oversight for a comparatively marginalized region of Spain's overseas empire, and it met the needs of both Crown and subjects well enough to remain useful throughout this time.

This book is a study of the seventeenth-century Audiencia of Santo Domingo that uses it to better understand the practice of imperial administration under the later Habsburg monarchs up to the death of Carlos II in 1700. I have chosen to focus on the seventeenth century for two main reasons. The first is related to the audiencia's continuity across this time. The general framework of colonial administration—more properly overseas administration, since in this period the Spanish Crown officially regarded "the Indies" as kingdoms—had been established by the later sixteenth century, and the following hundred-year period was marked by relative structural stability in comparison to more substantial administrative reorganization during the Bourbon era. After the refoundation of the Audiencia of Chile in 1609, the two viceroys and eleven audiencias that constituted the upper tier of royal government overseas saw only minor alterations until the second decade of the eighteenth century, apart from a brief experiment with a new audiencia in Buenos Aires between 1661 and 1672.[4] Yet there were significant changes in both royal policies and the political situation of the Caribbean between 1600 and 1700, allowing me to examine how the Dominican audiencia maintained its role as a key piece of Spain's overseas empire. The second reason is that, although this is beginning to change, the seventeenth century has received less scholarly attention than earlier and later periods, and by focusing on it, this study can help reassess simple narratives of stagnation and decline for both Hispaniola and imperial Spain.[5]

I have also opted to write an institutional history that recognizes that the audiencia was not a self-contained entity, with the aim of connecting peninsular intentions for governance with the ways royal power was expressed and received in a local and regional context. There are numerous notable works on overseas audiencias, including the Dominican tribunal, but while older studies contain valuable insights into how audiencia ministers acted as agents of Crown control, they also tend to emphasize the corporate identity of these courts, largely divorced from the social environments in which they operated.[6] Recent decades have seen a welcome shift toward abandoning modern conceptions of the impersonal state and analyzing the ways administrative figures at all levels were embedded in the societies they were ostensibly responsible for governing.[7] While legal and ceremonial conceptions of the Audiencia of Santo Domingo as a body mattered in both Spain and Hispaniola, its members did not exist outside of the city's population; local elites in particular exerted significant influence over the court's ministers, who also depended on broader popular opinion to be able to act as representatives of the king.

Although the audiencia was principally a court of justice, this book is not intended as a work of legal history, in part because I am more interested in presenting a comprehensive portrait of the Dominican tribunal and its members during this period. However, this decision is also shaped by the lack of documentation for the great majority of the suits determined by the Audiencia of Santo Domingo during the seventeenth century. The limited number of legal processes that did end up in Spain cannot be considered representative, as most are related to investigations against royal officials or suits that involved monetary amounts sufficient to justify appeal to the Council of the Indies.[8] Even so, when read in conjunction with the enormous amount of other material preserved in the Archivo General de Indias in Seville, particularly audiencia ministers' correspondence, they can illuminate how the tribunal's procedures and supporting personnel sustained its performance of royal authority. My hope is that readers of this book will learn more not just about how this authority functioned but also about what this court provided for residents of the Spanish Caribbean and how it helped convey their perspectives and concerns to peninsular policymakers.

The fundamental purpose of the Audiencia of Santo Domingo, and the other overseas audiencias, was to put royal justice within reach of the king's subjects in the new territories of the Indies instead of obliging them to travel to Spain. However, the multiple roles the seventeenth-century Dominican tribunal played in linking the Caribbean with Madrid had evolved during the preceding century, along with the rest of the Spanish judicial system on both sides of the Atlantic. Audiencias in the Americas were not merely copies of peninsular models; rather, the tribunals in Valladolid, Granada, Galicia, Seville, the Canary Islands, and Mallorca developed concurrently with those founded in the Americas.[9] Santo Domingo's audiencia was initially created in 1511 as a court of appeals staffed by three magistrates called *jueces de audiencia y juzgado* (roughly, judges that hold hearings and judge), preceding the Council of the Indies and the Audiencia of Seville by over a decade. Although less prestigious than later incarnations, its judicial authority strengthened royal oversight of Hispaniola by counterbalancing the power of viceroy Diego Colón.[10]

This early court was not without problems, and following a 1517 *residencia* investigation reviewing their performance, its members were briefly suspended over charges of partisan behavior.[11] Yet even as Santo Domingo lost its initial role as a hub for colonizing activity, the Crown decided that this institution was an essential part of extending royal authority overseas, both because justice was seen as necessary for social order and because having multiple agents reporting to the king limited the potential for abuses. In 1527 the Crown refounded the Dominican tribunal as an "Audiencia y Chancillería Real" at the same time it established another in the city of Mexico, granting them use of the royal seal and the other privileges of the courts in Valladolid and Granada; both were issued nearly identical ordinances the following year. Across the Atlantic, the creation of a permanent, freestanding Council of the Indies in 1524 was another key step in the construction of a framework for colonial administration.[12]

This remained a trial-and-error process. The rapaciousness of the first Audiencia of Mexico convinced metropolitan authorities that the institution was useful but that they needed to select its magistrates with more care.[13] The Crown continued to set up new audiencias as it claimed and organized new territories, although those in Panama, Guatemala, Guadalajara, Manila, and Chile were suppressed or moved at least once in this time. The first Audiencia of Chile, for example, was sent to Concepción in 1565 as a check on the governors there during the conquest of the Araucanian frontier but was extinguished ten years later as ineffectual in a war zone, and the tribunal founded in Santiago in 1609 mainly provided justice for an urban population.[14] This was accompanied by an even more disorderly process of building up other secular and ecclesiastical institutions and authorities at local and regional levels, from town councils to bishoprics, so that the administrative structure of Spain's empire only gradually took on the appearance of a coherent system.[15]

In the same way the peninsular Audiencia of Granada had established judicial oversight for a recently conquered region, each new audiencia overseas helped transform new territories into recognizable kingdoms ruled by the Spanish Crown. The distance from the metropole and the complexity of colonial societies meant this was a continuing effort, which relied both on the actions of resident audiencia ministers and on the information they sent back across the Atlantic. The audiencias of the Indies performed many of the same duties as their Iberian cousins, primarily in deciding criminal and civil suits but also in occasionally auditing the accounts of the royal treasury or carrying out inspections of their provinces. The colonial tribunals could also authorize special investigations in their districts, and they provided advice and assistance to the resident governor or viceroy, who usually presided over these tribunals. Perhaps most importantly, their correspondence with Spain was one of the main ways that peninsular authorities learned about regional conditions and problems, giving overseas subjects an indirect influence over the Crown's responses.[16]

By the end of the first decade of the seventeenth century, metropolitan authorities had established eleven audiencias, in Santo Domingo, Mexico, Panama, Guatemala, Lima, Guadalajara, Santa Fe, Charcas, Quito, Chile, and Manila, representing a judicial framework that saw few major changes until well into the eighteenth century. The potential for change was always there; while the short-lived Audiencia of Buenos Aires was the only new tribunal during this time, the Council of the Indies entertained multiple proposals for creating, moving, or suppressing these audiencias.[17] Even so, council members treated them as a system, within which certain courts were organized differently or had greater relative importance. The viceregal Audiencias of Lima and Mexico were at the top of the hierarchy. Both were presided over by the viceroy and had greater numbers of magistrates divided—as in Valladolid and Granada—into two chambers, one for civil suits staffed by oidores and another for criminal matters filled by lower-ranking *alcaldes del crimen* (criminal judges); the oidores of other colonial audiencias filled both roles. Santo Domingo, Chile, Santa Fe, Panama, Guatemala, and Manila were considered "praetorian" (*pretorial*) audiencias with some measure of political autonomy because they were headed by a military officer who also held the titles of governor and captain-general. Guadalajara, Charcas, and Quito usually had jurists as presidents, at least until 1700, and were nominally "subordinated" (*subordinada*) to a viceroy.[18]

Although used infrequently, these terms corresponded to meaningful differences, and the Dominican tribunal did not experience the periodic viceregal interference that affected subordinate audiencias. In 1656 president Bernardino de Meneses protested his promotion from Santo Domingo to Charcas precisely because that court was "subject to the viceroy," which meant a reduction in the authority he had held on Hispaniola.[19] However, these categories do not fully capture the fluidity of contemporary practice. The praetorian Audiencia of Panama struggled against the Peruvian viceroy in the mid-seventeenth century over the right to name an interim president, while several military men presided over the subordinate tribunal in Charcas. Santa Fe even had separate criminal and civil chambers for part of this period.[20] In general, despite variations in the relationships between some of these tribunals, the day-to-day responsibilities of viceregal, praetorian, and subordinate audiencias were more similar than different.

The magistrates named to all of these tribunals came from the same pool of *letrado* (university-educated) candidates, who tended to value these courts according to their relative status and living conditions. In the general hierarchy of promotions for bureaucrats known as the *ascenso*, candidates might start out as *fiscal* (Crown attorney) of a nonviceregal audiencia and then become oidor in the same or a different audiencia. Better still were the posts of—in order—fiscal, alcalde del crimen, and oidor of the viceregal audiencias in Mexico and Lima, which well-connected office-seekers might be sent to directly, and a fortunate few were promoted to letrado presidents of subordinate audiencias or even royal council members back in Spain.[21] Nonviceregal audiencias also had specific advantages and disadvantages for prospective appointees, like the material wealth of Charcas or the remoteness of the Philippines. Salaries for letrado magistrates tended to reflect the status of these positions, with some exceptions; for example, fiscales and oidores in Chile, a relatively remote entry-level audiencia,

Table 1. Salaries of seventeenth-century audiencia ministers (in ducados)

Audiencia	Category	Oidor / alcalde del crimen / fiscal	President
Guadalajara	subordinate	2,000	3,500
Quito	subordinate	2,400	4,800
Charcas	subordinate	4,800	6,000
Santo Domingo	praetorian	1,600	5,000
Guatemala	praetorian	2,000	5,000
Manila	praetorian	2,400	9,600
Santa Fe	praetorian	2,400	6,000
Panama	praetorian	2,400	4,000
Chile	praetorian	3,600	6,000
Mexico	viceregal	2,133	c. 20,000
Lima	viceregal	3,600	c. 30,000

Source: Schäfer, *El Consejo Real*, 2:27–30, 119–20.

earned 3,600 *ducados* per year, more than letrado ministers in Mexico and the same as those in Lima, as an incentive to go there. Ministers in silver-rich La Plata in Charcas were paid the most, 4,800 ducados per year, largely due to the region's high cost of living. Santo Domingo offered many promotion opportunities, but its ministers were paid only 1,600 ducados, making fiscal of the Dominican audiencia effectively the lowest-status entry point to the overseas audiencia system (see table 1).[22]

The situation for president-governors (a convenient contemporary label for the presidents of praetorian audiencias, who were also governors and captains-general) was somewhat different, as they were eligible for a wider range of positions in Europe or the Indies and had much more varied career paths. Only in 1587 had Felipe II ordered that the Dominican audiencia should have a military (*capa y espada*) president, following Francis Drake's sack of the city of Santo Domingo the previous year. Throughout the following century, the Council of the Indies would consider the importance of Hispaniola for regional defense in selecting candidates for this position, which carried a substantial salary of 5,000 ducados. Yet it was not a particularly coveted post, and in 1648 Juan Bitrián de Biamonte was willing to accept 1,000 ducados less to become president of the more prestigious court in Panama.[23] For all audiencias, whether headed by a letrado, a military governor, or a viceroy, the president's notably higher salary reinforced his standing over the other ministers and signified the king's trust in the officeholder.

By about 1590, the Audiencia of Santo Domingo had reached the form it would keep throughout the seventeenth century, with only minor modifications up to 1700 and beyond. The change to a military president-governor had a lasting impact on the tribunal, not simply because presidents no longer voted in judicial decisions, but also because their perspectives differed sharply from those of letrado audiencia members. Yet metropolitan authorities intended for the overlapping jurisdictions of the court and its president to bolster royal authority in the city and island by fostering political, military, and judicial cooperation. That audiencia ministers conflicted occasionally—as happened in subordinate audiencias—was neither unforeseen nor wholly undesirable, as it reinforced the centrality of the king.[24]

For the most part, royal laws portrayed the Dominican audiencia as a cooperative enterprise, in which four oidores and a fiscal devoted most of their time to the cause of justice while also assisting the president, carrying out miscellaneous administrative duties, and representing the monarch in public functions. The oidores were to determine both civil and criminal suits, in some situations as a court of "first instance" but more importantly in appeal from decisions by other authorities in the city, island, and district, such as municipal justices, regional governors, or its own president-governor. Civil cases were further categorized by value: those involving more than 800 ducados had to be decided by three or more judges, while two were sufficient for lesser amounts. Appeals to the audiencia's sentences usually went to the Council of the Indies, although many cases were first reviewed by the audiencia itself (via *suplicación*, a type of appeal), and its decisions in local criminal matters were final. Fiscales did not vote on sentences; rather, they were to defend the Crown's interests, especially in financial matters, by bringing suits before the tribunal. Presidents were to supervise the court's public and private sessions, manage its personnel, and generally ensure royal orders were followed.[25]

The audiencia's members had a clearly structured work schedule, with morning and afternoon sessions each weekday (adjusted for summer and winter), when they were *en estrados* (in chambers); nonattendance could earn a fine of a half day's salary. On Tuesdays and Fridays, following a private mass, the ministers sat in an open session called an *audiencia pública*, during which they received petitions and pronounced sentences. Their actual sentencing decisions were made during closed-door *acuerdo* meetings on Monday and Thursday afternoons, or as needed, when they also opened letters from Spain and conferred about judicial and administrative issues. Only the superior ministers—the president, oidores, and fiscal—were allowed in the acuerdo, which was held in a separate room from the public chambers, though they might call in the *relator* (roughly, the court reporter) to present information or a notary (*escribano*) to record sentences after voting. When the superior ministers were recused from specific cases, or if business involved them or their families or allies, they were also to leave the acuerdo temporarily. All these activities took place in the *casas reales*, the building complex where the president-governors lived and where the treasury officials (*oficiales reales*) met. On Sundays and holy days, the tribunal's members represented the king by appearing publicly as a body for mass at the cathedral and by walking in religious processions throughout the liturgical year.[26]

The audiencia's magistrates had additional individual duties, which might include gathering witness testimony at the casas reales, their own lodgings, or some other location, though on occasion they sent unaccompanied notaries. The fiscal regularly cooperated with the treasury officials—for example, in their joint inspections of newly arrived ships. Presidents had military and political obligations as governors and captains-general, such as reviewing local troops or supervising the municipal *cabildo* (city council). The oidores were also differentiated by seniority. The junior oidor (*más moderno* or *más nuevo*) did less-desirable tasks, including acting as fiscal or writing reports in the acuerdo. The senior oidor (*decano* or *más antiguo*) was entrusted with reviewing accounts with the fiscal and treasury officials on Thursday afternoons but most importantly became temporary president-governor in case of the president's death or absence. All judges took turns as oidor of the week (*semanero*) to receive complaints and make limited provisions outside normal hours, subject to confirmation by the full audiencia. On Saturdays, also by rotation, two oidores examined the prison and reviewed its records for the preceding week.[27]

In his seventeenth-century treatises on the governance of the Indies, jurist Juan de Solórzano Pereira discussed the ways in which colonial audiencias differed from peninsular ones, largely because of their distance from Spain. Like their counterparts elsewhere in the Indies, the oidores in Santo Domingo also served as judges of the estates of the deceased (*bienes de difuntos*) and supervised the collection of payments throughout the audiencia's district for stamped paper, duties imposed on secular and ecclesiastical officeholders, or purchases of bulls of the *Santa Cruzada*. Most controversial was the Dominican audiencia's power to send out regional orders in the king's name and marked with the royal seal, which supposedly carried the same weight as those from the monarch. In extreme cases, they could authorize delegates, or a letrado minister, to go suppress and investigate abuses in the district (and even suspend regional governors) while awaiting further guidance from the metropole.[28]

While the portrait of the audiencia offered by peninsular legal prescriptions provides a sense of metropolitan expectations, along with clues about recurring problems addressed by new royal orders, such sources are not always a reliable guide to how the court operated in practice or how it was perceived by overseas residents. Certainly, members of the Dominican tribunal could not simply defy the king's orders for very long without consequences, not least due to their own colleagues' reports to Spain. Even so, routine correspondence together with the proceedings of official investigations make it abundantly clear that in major and minor matters, the men posted to Santo Domingo in the seventeenth century, intentionally or not, often failed to behave as metropolitan authorities wanted.

Moreover, seventeenth-century conceptions of law in the Hispanic world cannot simply be extrapolated from present-day assumptions about the ability of states to produce and enforce a coherent set of legal norms (which applies to both *ley* in the sense of written legal guidance and *derecho* in the broader sense of justice).[29] Law was not limited to regulations sanctioned by the monarch, and royal ministers overseas interpreted and applied orders in the light of what was acceptable locally together with their understanding of the "public good" and the king's intentions. Similarly, the justice produced by the audiencia was shaped to fit local conditions rather than a dispassionate application of universal rules. The seventeenth-century magistrates of the Dominican tribunal studied (and sometimes taught) civil or canon law at university but were not shackled by it: although their legal background might guide their discussions, oidores did not cite laws or precedent in rendering judicial decisions and generally were not expected to explain their sentences. Neither did litigants abide by the audiencia's declarations because they were legally correct, yet even when they complained about or appealed specific decisions, they broadly accepted the tribunal's authority to issue them.[30]

For such reasons, in this book I will rely most heavily on the correspondence between the Audiencia of Santo Domingo and the Crown to understand how the court functioned as an administrative entity during the seventeenth century. Prescriptive sources like the audiencia's ordinances, legal treatises, and the *Recopilación de leyes de los reynos de las Indias*—finalized in 1680 and printed in 1681, though manuscript versions circulated earlier in the century—were not unimportant, and Dominican magistrates consulted legal compilations and were regularly told to "keep the laws and ordinances." The *Recopilación* does capture some of the flexibility and disorder inherent in colonial administration, not just in the well-known "obey but do not comply" formula but also in regional variations or in royal orders that were ambiguous, obsolete, or contradictory; however, its superficial similarity to modern law codes can foster a fictive sense of the consistency with which royal laws were applied overseas. Peninsular instructions competed with many other considerations—including established custom, local relationships, and career or family goals—in guiding overseas ministers' actions.[31] The letters of the Dominican audiencia's ministers can provide a more direct sense of how these men perceived and carried out their duties and how they portrayed their actions, and those of their colleagues, during their time on the island.

These letters do need to be used with some caution and should be treated primarily as rhetorical tools to advance particular interests rather than reliable records of seventeenth-century events. While they do contain valuable details about contemporary conditions, they represent the perspectives of a small group of privileged men and offer limited and distorted views of the majority of the population of the island and district. They also regularly conflict with or contradict the accounts of other audiencia members, officials, or local residents. As Tamar Herzog has cautioned, I cannot hope to compare the available sources and reliably distinguish who was lying and who was not, or whether magistrates' decisions were justified.[32]

Another major problem with the audiencia's correspondence is that it generally minimizes the importance of the tribunal's supporting personnel, sometimes referred to as "inferior ministers" or "lesser officials." The Dominican tribunal could not function without lawyers (*abogados*) and procurators or legal agents (*procuradores*) to represent litigants, a relator to summarize suits for the magistrates, notaries to write and keep records of nearly all the court's proceedings, or local residents to act as substitute judges. All these men influenced the audiencia's decision-making process and helped link the court with the city's residents, but they rarely wrote directly to the Council of the Indies, and their actions and motivations are obscured by the historical record.[33] This applies to other supporting officials described in royal laws, including the bailiffs (*alguaciles*), doorman (*portero*), chancellor (*canciller*), jailer (*alcaide de la cárcel*), chaplain (*capellán*), and even the clock-keeper (*relojero*) needed to maintain an audible clock in the tribunal's chambers, although in Santo Domingo they could not always afford to keep these positions filled or pay the men who performed these duties.[34] Here I will focus most heavily on the president, oidores, and fiscal, although more research is needed into the supporting personnel of all overseas audiencias.

The audiencia's correspondence also provides relatively sparse information about its judicial work compared to its administrative role. Throughout this period, the president-governors penned a majority of the letters received by the Council of the Indies, most often as military and political leaders who occasionally reported on matters of justice, making them the loudest voices in shaping narratives about the tribunal and local and regional events.[35] However, the Dominican audiencia's connection to its president, who was both its supervisor and a quasi-independent authority with different jurisdictional boundaries, substantially expanded its involvement in managing the city and region, whether as an advisory body in the acuerdo or as a collection of royal ministers who opposed or supported their presidents. Indeed, relationships between presidents and letrados colored much of the tribunal's communication with Spain throughout the entire century.

Despite such considerations, seventeenth-century letters from the audiencia's ministers (formally addressed to the king but routed through the Council of the Indies) do capture more than just the perspectives of their authors. They often included supporting documentation, such as certifications from other officials or lengthy transcripts of judicial proceedings or acuerdo meetings. After arriving in Spain, numerous hands further annotated them with when and how they were received, summaries of their contents, marginal remarks and orders by council members and others, observations and recommendations from the council's fiscal, or draft responses. In many cases, this information can be matched with the council's consultations with the monarch (*consultas*) or copies of outgoing royal correspondence, so that these letters offer considerable insight into the discourse of colonial administration on both sides of the Atlantic. This includes regional differences and accommodations unique to the Dominican tribunal; for example, although it received general decrees encouraging the good treatment of Indians, it did not have a lawyer who acted as "protector of Indians" and rarely judged suits involving Indigenous litigants unless for commissions elsewhere in the district.[36] In general, the audiencia's correspondence captures an empire-wide process that Alfredo Jiménez Núñez has labeled "feedback," as the tribunal helped translate local and regional concerns into metropolitan policy decisions that it often became responsible for implementing within the dynamic context of the seventeenth-century Caribbean.[37]

The structure of this work is intended to progressively elaborate the ways in which the Audiencia of Santo Domingo bridged the divide between peninsular expectations and the residents of Santo Domingo and the district of the Caribbean. Chapters 2 and 3 provide a detailed chronological overview of the internal dynamics of the Dominican tribunal and key changes affecting Hispaniola and the Spanish Caribbean during the seventeenth century, which serves as a foundation for the thematic discussions in subsequent chapters. Chapter 4 examines the Dominican tribunal's relationship with other local authorities, including its own president, the treasury officials, the elite members of the municipal cabildo, and the church, primarily the city's archbishop and the cathedral chapter (*cabildo eclesiástico*). Of these, the president-governors had the most substantial impact on the tribunal's judicial and administrative duties, but while the audiencia participated in episodic struggles over jurisdiction and preeminence with most of these institutions—including particularly acrimonious conflicts with some archbishops—everyday relations tended more toward cooperation. Yet the audiencia's general inability to compel the obedience or respect of other kinds of royal agents is apparent both here and in chapter 5, covering the court's involvement in district administration. Outside the city of Santo Domingo, its effective power faded quickly, and its presence was occasional at best. The governors and cabildos of the region openly challenged the tribunal's agents, including its own magistrates, at times when they felt it was unduly interfering with local affairs. Even so, the Crown continued to use the tribunal as an indispensable component of royal oversight in the Caribbean, both as a source of magistrates for specific commissions and to counterbalance the authority of provincial officials, although not as an exclusive administrative center.

Chapter 6 examines the men who served on the Audiencia of Santo Domingo in the seventeenth century, to better understand their backgrounds, their career trajectories, and the social and family considerations that guided their actions while on Hispaniola. Although most of the tribunal's ministers pursued a variety of individual goals including promotion off the island, they and their families were obliged to make a home in Santo Domingo until the time they either departed or died. This group portrait provides necessary context for chapter 7, which explores this relationship between the audiencia and local society. Both the tribunal's superior ministers and metropolitan council members conceived of the audiencia as a conduit between the monarch and the local population, making it responsible for policing Iberian social norms and giving the tribunal's reports about Hispaniola substantial weight back in Spain. However, after arriving audiencia ministers and their families had many incentives to seek local support and quickly became integrated into the city's society, in part through the tribunal's secondary officials. Despite continual symbolic reinforcement of the tribunal's connection to royal power, ministers and locals alike understood that its ability to exercise authority was contingent on the cooperation of permanent residents, which was only rarely put to the test.

Although Santo Domingo was unique in many ways, its experiences need to be understood within a broader imperial and Atlantic setting. In the conclusion I offer some final thoughts on the Dominican court's relationship to Hispaniola and the Caribbean and on what this incarnation of the audiencia illustrates about the overseas audiencia system and imperial Spanish governance in the later Habsburg era. Despite the low prestige of the Audiencia of Santo Domingo, it drew on the same pool of jurists as other colonial audiencias and exercised similar powers and responsibilities, which included mediating between the monarch and district residents. Seventeenth-century Habsburg governance is often characterized as hidebound, but the history of the Dominican tribunal during this time reveals a persistent interest in listening to overseas concerns and seeking improvements, although severe financial constraints and a generally reactive approach to the problems of Spain's overseas empire limited their scope. Before the systematic efforts at reform under the Bourbon monarchs of the following century, the audiencia on Hispaniola was one among many mechanisms for informing and implementing a more prosaic and opportunistic process of reform.

2

Audiencias and President-Governors, 1600–1653

While Hispaniola had been at the center of colonization efforts in the early 1500s, by the beginning of the seventeenth century it was a relatively marginal part of Spain's overseas empire. Later advocates for the island romanticized a time when gold mining was the main economic activity and Spanish ships frequented Santo Domingo's port, but starting in the late 1520s the vast human and mineral wealth of central Mexico and the Andes drew Spanish inhabitants and royal attention elsewhere. Sugar production on Hispaniola was shrinking by midcentury, and the organization of the yearly fleet system in the 1560s shifted maritime traffic to Havana and away from Santo Domingo. In 1563 the city's cabildo wrote that they saw only one or two ships each year, increasing shipping costs for sugar and hides and reducing their access to enslaved Africans, and they warned that the island was in danger of being lost.[1] Local elites and royal ministers alike offered a similarly bleak view of Hispaniola throughout the following century.

However, contemporary and modern authors' emphasis on crisis and decline in Spanish Hispaniola during the later sixteenth and seventeenth centuries tends to reduce the island's history to an exceptional and inevitable downward slide all the way until the eighteenth century brought modest recovery.[2] While Spanish settlements on Hispaniola did experience serious challenges during this time—poverty, population loss, limited trade with Spain, foreign attacks, natural disasters—they were not alone. Letters from the Philippines, Panama, or Puerto Rico paint similar portraits of poverty, neglect, or the impending loss of Crown control, partly to attract a greater share of scarce resources, and need to be read in a broader imperial context.[3] As registered voyages to the island diminished in the later sixteenth century, Hispaniola's residents increasingly turned to foreign traders, which helped incentivize continued agricultural production, although peninsular authorities tried to stop what they defined as illegal commerce. The Crown's other major fear, especially after Francis Drake's 1586 sack of Santo Domingo, was the island's military vulnerability.[4] In general, metropolitan acceptance of Hispaniola's strategic importance, frequently reinforced by the audiencia's reports, ensured some royal support for its defense and the welfare of its population, which included keeping the audiencia there.

Although the Dominican tribunal experienced little structural change during the seventeenth century apart from the creation of a military assistant to the president in the 1690s—again driven by defense concerns—its personnel was in constant flux and often internally divided throughout this time.[5] In early 1601, for example, oidor Pedro Sanz Morquecho ran the court by himself as its only remaining member, following president Diego Osorio's death, oidor Juan Alcázar de Villaseñor's departure for investigations on Puerto Rico, and oidor Simón de Meneses's suspension.[6] Sharp disagreements between Sanz Morquecho and Osorio shortly before this also foreshadowed recurring conflicts among the audiencia's ministers throughout the century. While the Council of the Indies frequently had to manage such disagreements, these issues never warranted radical alterations to the tribunal, and it continued to be used to implement royal orders in the region.

In the last decade of the sixteenth century, these royal orders were frequently related to contraband trade, a problem the audiencia proved unable to solve on its own. The Council of the Indies authorized several investigations throughout the Caribbean region during this time, one of which was for Fernando Varela to verify reports of illicit commerce on Hispaniola and neighboring islands. Shortly before this, in 1593, the council also sent oidor Francisco Alonso de Villagra to carry out a *visita* (a special investigation, usually in response to news of abuses) of the Dominican audiencia, which sharpened existing tensions within the court's ranks, many of them related to ministers' local alliances.[7] Villagra eventually suspended president-governor Lope de Vega Portocarrero, though the Crown countermanded this decision in light of rumored English attacks. When Fernando Varela actually arrived in Santo Domingo in 1595, he found that the audiencia had already chosen oidor Simón de Meneses to look into contraband. Competition between the two judges led to Varela's departure from the island and a new visita into Meneses's behavior, carried out by his fellow oidor Sanz Morquecho. The testimony he gathered earned Meneses a fine of 1,000 ducados—over half his annual pay—and a permanent ban from office, mainly over mistreatment of city residents and colleagues and partiality in judicial decisions.[8]

Meneses was later permitted to seek other positions, though his punishment offered a reminder that the slow-moving yet methodical imperial bureaucracy might not prevent abuses but could call ministers to account after receiving complaints from colleagues and overseas residents.[9] Back on Hispaniola, Sanz Morquecho reported that he had been physically attacked by local residents working with French, English, and Dutch merchants while trying to investigate illicit trade on the northwest coast in 1598.[10] Around the start of the seventeenth century, then, the tribunal's correspondence reflected its involvement in the Crown's attempts to curtail foreign commerce and recurring problems with infighting, local entanglements, and abuse of office. At the same time, it also hinted at some of the ways inhabitants of the city and island could either seek advantage from the audiencia's members or limit their authority in direct and indirect ways.

The first two president-governors of the seventeenth century oversaw a major change in Spanish Hispaniola: the depopulation of the north and west of the island starting in 1605, carried out by Antonio Osorio and consolidated by Diego Gómez de Sandoval before his death in 1623. Both of these men also fought bitter battles with some of the audiencia ministers they were charged with managing, illustrating some of the ways that letrados could challenge the effective power of the tribunal's presidents. In 1601 the king confirmed Osorio, *corregidor* of Jerez de la Frontera, to fill the vacancy left by his recently deceased brother, Diego Osorio. At this time, the *Cámara de Indias*, a select group of members of the Council of the Indies, oversaw nominations for overseas positions, reflecting the efforts of Felipe III and his *privado* or favorite advisor the Duke of Lerma to exert greater control over this process.[11] Yet up to its suppression in 1609 and after the reestablishment of the Cámara in 1644, the nominees they chose for Santo Domingo were not radically different from those the full council selected, and in 1601 the Cámara noted Osorio's experience and "prudence." For its part, the council instructed Osorio to report on past conflicts between presidents and oidores but also reinforced the independence of his position by declaring that oidores should not make formal reports (*informaciones*) against him without specific royal instructions. These orders were extended to all overseas audiencias in 1604, with the stipulation that presidents could not forcibly send oidores back to Spain without Crown authorization. As the next few years showed, these measures did not resolve military-letrado tensions in the Dominican tribunal; even so, they do represent a process of ongoing negotiation about the roles and jurisdictional limits of royal ministers that was informed by practical experience.[12]

By the time Antonio Osorio arrived in fall 1602, the audiencia had three oidores, after Alcázar de Villaseñor returned from Puerto Rico and new appointee Marcos Núñez de Toledo reached the island.[13] They were joined in 1604 by Francisco Manso de Contreras, named as fiscal in 1602 but elevated to oidor before leaving Spain. Manso was the only seventeenth-century magistrate who was effectively a "native son" of the audiencia's district; although he was born in Spain, he grew up on the island of Margarita. As former *procurador general* (public advocate) of Margarita and governor of Santa Marta and Río de la Hacha, Manso had developed personal connections throughout the Caribbean region prior to becoming oidor.[14] Alcázar de Villaseñor's death in late 1602 and Sanz Morquecho's promotion to oidor of Quito in 1604 left the tribunal shorthanded, but by 1605 the audiencia had all six superior ministers, thanks to the arrival of oidores Gonzalo Mejía de Villalobos, Gaspar Narváez y Valdelomar, and Juan Martínez Tenorio along with fiscal Pedro de Arévalo Sedeño.[15]

For both the audiencia and Hispaniola, the most significant event in this period was the forcible depopulation of five towns in the northern and western parts of the island (called the *banda del norte*) in 1605 and 1606, carried out under Antonio Osorio's command. The depopulations, often labeled "the devastations of Osorio," have been a predominant theme in Dominican historiography. Scholars have seen them as the first step in the establishment of French Saint-Domingue, a key factor in the economic and demographic stagnation of the Spanish side of the island, and the root cause of the historically fraught relationship between the Dominican Republic and Haiti.[16] However, while this was a radical change for the island's population, the effects on the audiencia were limited, and audiencia members' actions during this period reveal their lack of internal unity and their potential for amplifying local discontent with Crown policies.

In mid-1603, in response to the failure of earlier efforts to end foreign trade and to recommendations made by the audiencia's ex-notary Baltasar López de Castro, the king ordered Osorio and Archbishop Agustín Dávila

Padilla to move the towns of La Yaguana, Puerto de Plata, and Bayahá inland and closer to Santo Domingo. When the archbishop died the following year, Osorio decided to act on his own. During 1605 and 1606, he and the soldiers under his command rounded up most of the residents of these places, plus those of Montecristi and San Juan de la Maguana, who Osorio felt were also involved in contraband trade, and relocated them to the newly planned towns of San Juan Bautista de la Bayaguana and San Antonio de Monte de Plata. He also compelled people living near Neiba and Azua to move.[17] This campaign faced heated opposition from many on the island, including the unwilling deportees, most of the elite families of Santo Domingo, clergy members, and oidores Manso de Contreras and Mejía de Villalobos. The audiencia was also instructed in 1603 to assist with the planned depopulations, but these two magistrates sided with local critics in arguing that the archbishop's death called into question the legitimacy of the initial commission. Osorio overrode their objections.[18]

Osorio has been vilified by some historians for the way he carried out the king's orders, which included burning down residents' houses to ensure they did not return and executing some who resisted. Yet both he and his opponents claimed to be carrying out the obligations of their positions. Like later seventeenth-century president-governors, Osorio valued concrete action over deliberation, and expected (and received) metropolitan approval for using his own judgment to minimize delays instead of confirming every decision with peninsular authorities.[19] His sense of the urgency of his orders was seemingly validated by news of a Dutch ship in La Yaguana in January 1605 bearing a proclamation from general Paulus van Caerden, offering aid against the Spanish king's "customary tyranny" in destroying these outlying settlements. The Council of the Indies was predictably concerned about residents' ties to Dutch heretics.[20]

By contrast, the two oidores emphasized their responsibility to prevent the military president-governor from abusing his power. Osorio alleged Manso de Contreras and Mejía de Villalobos fomented local resistance mainly to benefit themselves, but the tribunal's magistrates regularly argued for seeking clarification from Spain in cases of disagreement. As was also typical, the letrados were not united in their opposition. Oidor Núñez de Toledo backed Osorio's decision to proceed, and fiscal Arévalo Sedeño received the president-governor's praise for zealously prosecuting the armed rebels in the valley of Guaba.[21] The troops under Osorio's command gave him a decided advantage over the letrados in taking action, especially after 150 more soldiers arrived from Puerto Rico, and the Crown ultimately rewarded him for these forced depopulations, though his request for a seat on the Council of War went unanswered.[22] However, despite his bitter complaint that "a bad judge does more damage with the power he has than many enemies," the two oidores' challenges to his authority were rooted in the intentionally overlapping jurisdictional boundaries of the audiencia and its president that encouraged reliance on the metropole for arbitration.[23] They also suggest that letrados could help focus blame for unpopular Crown decisions on the president-governor and away from the audiencia as a body, while strengthening their own ties to local allies.

The particularly acute rivalry between Osorio and Manso de Contreras during these years also demonstrates how oidores could circumvent the president's more expansive powers. According to Osorio, Manso had initially hoped to be entrusted with the depopulations and was upset at losing control of the process. For the president-governor, the light sentences Manso gave while investigating contraband trade in Azua in 1604 and his hanging of "two poor sailors" to prevent them from implicating elites showed that the oidor was intent on protecting wealthy locals, including his own relatives.[24] However, Osorio's absence from the city during the depopulation campaigns left senior magistrate Mejía de Villalobos as acting president, which worked to Manso's advantage. After an outbound ship was robbed by French vessels near the island of Saona in June 1605, the oidor volunteered to lead a naval patrol, which captured one French ship and its Portuguese prize. Personal involvement in military action was unusual for a letrado, and Manso stressed how exceptional his service to the king was, boasting that this was the best victory city residents could remember from the past fifty years and petitioning the acuerdo for 2,000 ducados from the spoils.[25] Osorio confirmed the outlines of Manso's story when he returned to Santo Domingo in October 1605 but also maintained the oidor was encouraging public criticism of the depopulations. After hearing from the bishop of Santiago de Cuba that "Flemish" merchants were trading in eastern Cuba, where some families from La Yaguana had resettled with foreign help, Osorio saw a chance to get rid of the troublesome magistrate. That same month the audiencia commissioned Manso to go punish those involved.[26]

A year later, Osorio complained that the oidor had waited months before leaving, stopped in Cartagena on personal business, and then wasted more time in Havana before finally traveling east to Bayamo to begin his investigation. For his part, Manso de Contreras claimed that he was forced to purchase his own ship for lack of transportation, and he noted his encounters with pirates and valuable leadership in Cartagena after the death of its governor.[27] While in Cuba, Manso scored a major coup by obtaining some letters that Osorio had sent to Spain; the president had presumed they were lost when the ship carrying them was captured, but they ended up reaching the oidor's network of relatives and allies in eastern Cuba through back channels of contraband trade. Osorio was humiliated and infuriated, not least because the letters gave Manso ample grounds for claiming that he was motivated by personal hatred, and even asked the Council of the Indies to promote the oidor elsewhere so they would not have to work together once Manso returned. Osorio also sent notification to Cuba of formal charges pending against the oidor, but Manso declined to respond on the grounds that Osorio had not shown a royal commission authorizing these accusations. Osorio did get Mejía de Villalobos to testify against Manso, suggesting the oidores' alliance was not unbreakable, but while Manso remained outside Hispaniola there was little the president could do to him.[28]

When Manso de Contreras eventually returned to Santo Domingo in 1608, Osorio first forbade him to enter the city and then tried to forcibly ship him to Margarita using royal orders for Manso to live with his wife or bring her to Hispaniola. Manso got the nuns of Regina Angelorum and other local allies to back his claims that Osorio was persecuting him while he feigned illness to stay home, then took refuge in the Mercedarian convent, and finally fled to the countryside to await Osorio's replacement, Diego Gómez de Sandoval. After the new president-governor arrived in August 1608, tensions faded quickly, largely because Gómez de Sandoval decided that Osorio was only empowered to investigate problems among the oidores and notify them of accusations, meaning that Manso just needed to respond to Osorio's charges. The oidor not only returned to the city but even served as Gómez de Sandoval's letrado advisor the following year before being promoted to oidor in Panama (where he was again embroiled in factionalism).[29]

While these events were transpiring, the audiencia's fiscales pursued their own goals. Arévalo Sedeño, whom Osorio saw mainly as an ally, portrayed himself to the Crown as an energetic reformer of various abuses within the tribunal. After his arrival in August 1603, his reports to the Council of the Indies covered such issues as procedural failures in audiencia and acuerdo sessions, status conflicts over seating order in the cathedral for audiencia members' female relatives, and the city's inadequate defenses. Most seriously, he denounced Mejía de Villalobos and Manso de Contreras for receiving gifts from locals and participating in a trade ring that moved pearls and Chinese silk around the Caribbean, thanks to contacts in Puerto Rico and Margarita and to a former oidor of Santo Domingo promoted to Mexico, Juan de Quesada Figueroa. These efforts paid off in 1605 when Arévalo Sedeño was made oidor of Guadalajara, although Osorio required him to remain at his post until his successor arrived, a show of confidence the fiscal did not appreciate. The next fiscal, Ruy Gómez, who was in Santo Domingo by October 1606, sent similar reports about problems like unlicensed ship arrivals and magistrates' disagreements over judicial decisions.[30] Despite their internal divisions, the letrado ministers were able to cooperate on a few matters, as in 1606 when they all signed a request to raise the oidores' salaries to match other audiencias. Osorio even sent a separate letter of support, although it was denied, as was a similar plea two years later.[31]

At the end of Osorio's time in office, both he and the Council of the Indies evaluated the depopulations as a success. Osorio maintained that an increase in licensed shipping had made goods cheap and plentiful in Santo Domingo and that residents not mixed up in foreign trade felt the city was better off than it had been for thirty years. Spain's peace treaty with England in 1604 and the suspension of hostilities with the Dutch in 1609 also reduced naval attacks in the region. The council considered establishing an Inquisition tribunal on Hispaniola to look after the islanders' moral health, though the plan was not carried out.[32] They did, however, order the audiencia in 1608 to prosecute all "foreigners of the islands of Holland and Zeeland, French, Germans, and English, and the other northerners transported from the Canaries to this region" as well as any Portuguese or Italians in their company. A year later, Gómez de Sandoval reported that his patrols of the depopulated zones had caught some French sailors, though he disagreed with the magistrates about his right to punish them.[33] Also around 1608, Santo Domingo began to receive a yearly sum of money, usually referred to as a *situado* or *situación*, from the treasury of Mexico to pay the soldiers and royal officials on the island, as part of a more active approach to imperial defense. Within a decade this general optimism about the depopulations had vanished, and it was evident that Spanish traffic to the island had decreased.[34]

Gómez de Sandoval's appointment was an unusual one, not least because he had previously been president of the House of Trade (*Casa de la Contratación*) in Seville. The Duke of Lerma, a relative of his, effectively gave him the post by decree, which was a considerable step down in status. Even so, Gómez de Sandoval had military qualifications, and during his fifteen years in office behaved very much like president-governors before and after him.[35] At least in the short term, he reduced tensions in the audiencia simply by taking office, and the court's ministers expressed their approval of their new president in mid-1608. Gómez de Sandoval speedily finished up Osorio's residencia, aided by instructions to forward all accusations related to the depopulations directly to the Council of the Indies, and though he offered an outlet for local criticism of Osorio he declared his predecessor to be a good official. Gómez de Sandoval soon had his own problems, including a meat shortage due to the loss of cattle in the banda del norte, construction delays for Santo Domingo's fortifications, and opposition to his imposition of guard duty on residents, expressed in publicly posted, anonymous verses mocking the new president.[36]

Gómez de Sandoval followed Osorio's lead in sending land and sea patrols to ensure the depopulated zones remained off-limits, although he granted occasional permission to small groups with military escorts to hunt feral cattle and take hides for export. Oidor Mejía de Villalobos claimed, however, that these licenses were merely cover for continued foreign trade.[37] The president-governor's authority over these areas led to a new conflict in 1610 with fiscal Jerónimo de Herrera, who criticized Gómez de Sandoval's summary executions of trespassers. The president noted that, as under Osorio, the condemned were always allowed to confess before being hanged, but Herrera argued that the accused should have the chance to respond to charges, even for crimes deserving death. Gómez de Sandoval told the Crown that the audiencia had turned against him when Herrera allied with Mejía de Villalobos and Narváez y Valdelomar and claimed that the oidores nearly always admitted the fiscal's petitions, harming litigants and the prestige of his office.[38]

By May 1612, the Council of the Indies was discussing additional problems between Gómez de Sandoval and Mejía de Villalobos. The president-governor said Villalobos had a serious drinking problem, which had not been corrected by Osorio's earlier visita of the oidor, and the public scandal it was causing had driven him to gather new testimony and notify the Crown. The oidor, by contrast, reported that Gómez de Sandoval was persecuting him in league with some litigants unhappy with his verdicts. Since he had already endured one visita, Mejía de Villalobos asked to be moved elsewhere or allowed to return to Spain after nine years in Santo Domingo. The councilors appreciated Gómez de Sandoval's zeal but reprimanded him for his year-and-a-half-long investigation, conducted without royal orders, that damaged Mejía de Villalobos's reputation. Just the same, the repeated accusations of alcoholism led them to authorize a secret inquiry by the outgoing bishop-elect of Venezuela and to give Villalobos permission to travel to Spain if necessary. The bishop did not find clear proof, and Mejía de Villalobos was promoted to Panama in 1614, in part to prevent him from retaliating against local enemies, whose involvement in these proceedings helped force his removal from Santo Domingo.[39]

In addition to these internal tensions, the entire audiencia was at odds with Archbishop Cristóbal Rodríguez around 1609. Rodríguez claimed the court's members were encouraging immoral behavior and defiance of his authority, but his heavy-handed use of his office to reinforce his prestige and defend his jurisdiction—from changing seating arrangements in the cathedral to excommunicating the oidores—drove the audiencia to accuse him of abuse.[40] This would not be the last time the tribunal fought with an archbishop, but their troubles with Rodríguez ended when he was made bishop of Arequipa in 1611, and Santo Domingo was left without a resident prelate for many years afterward. The next nominee lingered in the city of Mexico for years, citing his poor health, then disappeared in 1616 after departing for Santo Domingo. In December 1617, the king selected the bishop of Puerto Rico, Pedro de Solier, though he did not arrive until 1619, and then died in April 1620.[41]

Despite the Dutch armistice, Spain had little peace in the Caribbean during the 1610s, and the rise in Spanish shipping that Osorio described in 1608 did not last.[42] The depopulations of northern and western Hispaniola failed to stop foreign ships from coming to the region, and Gómez de Sandoval reported that enemies, mostly English and French, were capturing Spanish vessels and trading in the eastern Caribbean. Despite several victories by the naval expeditions he sent out over the next few years, many led by his son, Gómez de Sandoval wrote in March 1615 that these enemies had been chasing ships entering and leaving Santo Domingo's port for a month. He also stressed the need for a permanent regional defense fleet, though metropolitan plans to reestablish the *Armada de Barlovento* (Windward Squadron) never really took effect in this period, and Spanish and Portuguese shipping remained vulnerable to foreign attacks in following decades.[43]

One of the major themes in the audiencia's correspondence during Gómez de Sandoval's time was his feud with fiscal Herrera. After Herrera's initial interference with the president's military and political authority, Gómez de Sandoval said the fiscal was sowing discord and misusing his office for personal ends. When Archbishop Rodríguez rejected one of Herrera's sons (whom Gómez de Sandoval had recommended) for the chaplaincy of the hospital of San Nicolás in 1610, the fiscal appealed the decision to the audiencia and requested an audit of the hospital's accounts, which the president saw as an unwarranted intrusion into ecclesiastical affairs. Gómez de Sandoval also sent testimony from audiencia sessions to illustrate Herrera's disruptive behavior. In one instance, the fiscal loudly scolded one of the attorneys; when Gómez de Sandoval told him to lower his voice, he retorted that he normally spoke that way and suggested the president just wanted him not to speak. In a separate letter, Gómez de Sandoval even asked the king to name a new president-governor so he could be free of Herrera's attempts to dominate the court.[44]

Herrera maintained that he was merely performing the duties of his office, particularly in looking after the interests of the treasury, and that Gómez de Sandoval was upset at being prevented from freely dispensing royal funds to allies, for example in selecting someone to transport the annual situado. The fiscal also claimed Gómez de Sandoval saw any opposition in terms of a challenge to his honor. Fear of the president made Herrera avoid some audiencia sessions, and he even said he had heard a rumor from "one of the most principal people of this island" that Gómez de Sandoval had threatened to kill him.[45]

Both were chastised for their behavior—separate royal letters in 1611 ordered Gómez de Sandoval to release the fiscal from prison and Herrera to treat the president with fitting respect—but their quarrels and complaints continued. Herrera did take advantage of the fiscal's adversarial role to provoke the president and his other colleagues, but Gómez de Sandoval was also deeply sensitive to any perceived disrespect. In 1613, instead of reporting about expenses involving royal slaves, oidor Narváez de Valdelomar noted, "I have let it be . . . to avoid grievances with his lordship [the president], since I know we will have them if I report the truth." Finally, in mid-1617, after Herrera accused him of giving his own dependents positions in the presidio, Gómez de Sandoval reached a breaking point. Frustrated by his inability to get Herrera, who had been promoted to oidor, to stop challenging his authority, the president-governor forcibly embarked him and one of his sons on a ship to Spain.[46]

Gómez de Sandoval's relief was short-lived. Once in Spain, Herrera made a formal complaint to the Council of the Indies. In it, he emphasized the relentless persecutions he and his sons had faced from the president, which included the discomfort and risk to their lives in the ocean crossing (though Gómez de Sandoval later countered that Herrera was simply unwilling to pay for a better cabin). The council fined Gómez de Sandoval 1,500 ducados for shipping off Herrera without royal authorization but also commissioned Juan de Ibarra y Gueztara, outgoing alcalde del crimen of Mexico, to carry out a visita of both men and sort out who was at fault. Once he learned of these decisions, Gómez de Sandoval sent his wife, doña Mariana de Palacios y Toledo, to present his version of events, but by then Herrera had the upper hand.[47]

Herrera was back on Hispaniola by late 1618 and was no more reserved than before. He aggressively used the royal orders inhibiting both him and the president from involvement in suits of those who testified in the visita; these were intended to stop them from retaliating against witnesses, but they limited Gómez de Sandoval more. In concert with oidor Hernando Ibáñez de Albendea, Herrera could nullify the votes of the other two magistrates in decisions about these orders, preventing Gómez de Sandoval from disciplining certain military officers like *sargento mayor* (sergeant major) Gabriel de Rojas, a witness for Herrera. While Gómez de Sandoval was unable to suspend Herrera from acting as oidor during the visita, the magistrate reportedly screamed at his colleagues and stormed out of the acuerdo when he was recused from specific decisions. In one session, Herrera touched oidor Martínez Tenorio's beard and yelled not to preach at him, since he was seventy and had held far more important posts, then threatened to call for a general visita. Outside of the audiencia, Gómez de Sandoval claimed Herrera regularly failed to remove his hat when they met in public, and once during Corpus Christi, while riding in the president's carriage with the fiscal, alguacil mayor, and other oidores, had exploded because he felt Gómez de Sandoval had made him wait.[48] Ibarra carried out the visita rather cursorily and by May 1619 handed over his investigation to incoming fiscal Diego Gil de la Sierpe, who completed it the following year. The initial copies of these proceedings were lost at sea near Lisbon, delaying matters further, and only Herrera's 1620 promotion to oidor of Panama (where he clashed with another president-governor) ended his fight with Gómez de Sandoval. Neither man received serious punishment.[49]

This running battle offers a useful sense of adversarial relations between president-governors and jurists. Herrera was able to obstruct Gómez de Sandoval's military authority as long as he could base his challenges on royal orders. Gómez de Sandoval warned the entire audiencia he would hold them responsible for weakening the island's defenses against a potential Dutch invasion, but he could not convince enough oidores to bypass the recusations against him.[50] Although his scope for action was much broader than Herrera's as either fiscal or oidor, Gómez de Sandoval was unable to find a legal way to restrain this troublesome letrado, and the Crown disapproved of the unsanctioned measures he took with both Herrera and Mejía de Villalobos. His successors were generally more effective at taking forceful action against the other ministers—with or without cover provided by one of the oidores acting as legal advisor—instead of sending them to Spain, which ultimately worked to Herrera's benefit. Permanent city residents, including the audiencia's support staff, likely played a role in advising these presidents, although the court's letrados were far from powerless.

While the documents produced by the conflict between Herrera and Gómez de Sandoval seem to show that the audiencia was in a perpetual state of crisis, it was actually functioning largely as intended. The records Gómez de Sandoval sent as proof of Herrera's abuse of office demonstrate that the tribunal was divided by a justifiable dispute over the king's intent and that they sought guidance from Spain when they could not resolve these disagreements in the acuerdo. Herrera needed support from at least one more colleague to keep the audiencia deadlocked, even if Gómez de Sandoval saw their alliance as unjust.[51]

Other procedural conflicts were settled with less drama. In 1616 Gómez de Sandoval and oidor Rodrigo de Valcárcel had a jurisdictional dispute after Valcárcel imprisoned Diego Méndez, a soldier and treasury official, over a criminal complaint by a local woman, Beatriz Calderón. On learning of this, Gómez de Sandoval called the oidor to his house at ten o'clock at night to scold him for arresting one of his men without his permission. Valcárcel complained and the acuerdo discussed the matter, and they agreed to advise the king (Valcárcel did not vote but signed the letter). The Council of the Indies confirmed that the president had the right to summon oidores but only for very important cases and "at a more decent hour," and they admonished all the tribunal's members to treat one another courteously and to send full documentation of disputed cases.[52] This exchange reflects the continuing evolution of royal law overseas, where procedures were determined by local interpretation and application, and later reconsidered in Spain. In this case, the dispute between Valcárcel and Gómez de Sandoval led to new orders for all overseas audiencias, even though these did not prevent further jurisdictional conflicts over similar issues.[53]

The death of Felipe III in March 1621 and the expiration of the Dutch truce a month later inaugurated a new period of European hostilities, while Dutch fleets also crossed the Atlantic to assault Spanish and Portuguese ships and ports. After the Dutch captured Bahia in Brazil in 1624, the Spanish Crown devoted substantial naval resources to retake it. The numbers of English and French in the region also began to increase markedly as they established outposts in the Lesser Antilles starting in the 1620s, permanently altering the political balance of the Caribbean.[54] Threats to Spanish vessels and settlements intensified, further depressing licensed trade to Hispaniola. Gómez de Sandoval received news of a possible Dutch invasion as early as 1615 and said in 1623 that over a hundred enemy ships were active near the island following a Dutch defeat at Cumaná. These included twenty-five or more in the depopulated port of Bayahá, which he warned they might seize and fortify, reflecting the continuing effects of an earlier policy decision the audiencia had helped carry out despite the resistance of some of its members.[55]

The next three president-governors—Diego de Acuña, Gabriel de Chaves Osorio, and Juan Bitrián de Biamonte—had to manage these continuing hostilities in the region, but were also determined to impose their will on the court. After Gómez de Sandoval's death in 1623, senior oidor Martínez Tenorio took over as interim president-governor, although unlike most others in this position, he made little use of his temporary powers, aside from informing Madrid about the city's weak defenses. New president Diego de Acuña arrived the following year and was forced to confront these issues when another Dutch fleet attacked Puerto Rico in September 1625 as part of a plan to seize territorial outposts around the Atlantic. The Dutch overran San Juan, leaving that island's governor Juan de Haro barricaded inside its fortress with some troops and other residents. In response to Haro's pleas for aid, Acuña sent food and supplies but claimed he could not spare men or munitions, since the presidio had only seventy poorly provisioned soldiers.[56]

The Dutch proved unable to hold the city but left San Juan in ruins in late 1625, and several ships headed to the waters around Santo Domingo just as Acuña had feared. After months of preying on outbound shipping, they departed southward without attempting a land assault. In May 1626, the arrival of a Portuguese vessel in distress reminded Santo Domingo's residents that they were involved in a global conflict, since it had sustained damage in a fight with a Dutch ship returning from Ternate (in the Maluku Islands) while salvaging a wreck near the island of Saint Helena in the South Atlantic. These events contributed to a sense of panic in the correspondence of royal ministers on Hispaniola as the president, audiencia members, and archbishop pleaded for more men and supplies to protect the island. However, the 1628 capture of much of Spain's silver fleet in Matanzas Bay in Cuba by a large squadron under Admiral Piet Hein only increased the strain on imperial resources.[57]

As president, Acuña dealt with discord in the audiencia even more directly than Gómez de Sandoval. In spring 1625, he threatened Gil de la Sierpe (now an oidor) with bodily harm to force him to surrender written testimony about a status dispute with Juan Parra de Meneses, a more junior oidor who was also Acuña's legal assistant (*asesor*). Gil de la Sierpe claimed the president had previously torn up another copy of this testimony in his face. A year later, Acuña reportedly punched another oidor, Alonso de Cereceda—in addition to touching his beard, arguably a worse insult—after Cereceda complained aloud that doña Ana de Acuña, the president's wife, was improperly involved in audiencia business. Such physical confrontations were rare, but Acuña's actions demonstrate a difference in behavioral expectations for letrado and military officials. The portrait of Acuña these reports offer is of a military commander unwilling to tolerate legal shenanigans or disrespect from bureaucrats; they also strongly suggest the president and his wife were influencing litigation in favor of their allies. Gil de la Sierpe said he was afraid to be alone with Acuña in the acuerdo and asked to be removed from this "living purgatory," where after forty years' service he was unable to protect the cause of royal justice. Cereceda wrote that due to Acuña's mistreatment, he had sent votes via notaries instead of attending audiencia and acuerdo sessions, for which Acuña imprisoned him.[58]

Months later, there was a notable shift in tone. In June 1626, Acuña, Cereceda, fiscal Damián Gentil de Párraga, and "the audiencia" (that is, every letrado minister but Cereceda) all sent letters to Spain claiming that recent problems were only a misunderstanding, and everyone was now cooperating. These rather suspicious expressions of harmony also stressed the importance of Dutch military threats. Cereceda even praised Acuña's handling of the city's defense, noting that for eight months residents had been in arms "day and night for fear of the Dutch enemy, who since leaving Puerto Rico does not depart from these coasts." By 1630, Cereceda was claiming that Acuña had coerced him into writing this letter, though he was barred from making a formal charge in Acuña's residencia.[59] However, while Acuña was surely behind these expressions of solidarity, it is also likely that the remaining oidores and fiscal clearly perceived the risk that inviting a visita investigation might have for their careers and tried to allay metropolitan authorities' concerns. Acuña, who was promoted to president of the Audiencia of Guatemala in 1626, does not seem to have suffered serious consequences from the two oidores' complaints, although he was among those named in the visita general of the Dominican audiencia in 1630.[60]

Although this visita was the defining feature of the administration of Acuña's successor, Gabriel de Chaves Osorio, defensive challenges continued to mount during these years. Before Chaves Osorio's arrival, Acuña and the audiencia reported on foreign subjects in Saint Christopher (Saint Kitts), Martinique, the Îles des Saintes, and Saona, and Acuña feared they might join with nearby Caribs to assault Puerto Rico again. Non-Spanish vessels frequented Caribbean waters, and in 1631 the Dutch established a fortified settlement on Saint Martin.[61] The audiencia's ministers claimed that Hispaniola's residents felt isolated and exposed, and in 1629 they pleaded with the Crown to send eight or ten ships to relieve their "extreme necessity," since there were never enough registered ships or emergency arrivals (*arribadas*) to export local produce or bring in needed goods.[62]

The grim portrait painted by correspondence from Santo Domingo makes Spain's loss of power in the Caribbean seem inevitable, but it also obscures the Crown's aggressive response to foreign encroachment. Spanish forces chased the English and French from Saint Christopher and Nevis in 1629, while another armada ejected the Dutch from Saint Martin in 1633, leaving behind a garrison to hold it. Certainly, these successes were not permanent, and many displaced settlers went elsewhere: English and French subjects came to western Hispaniola and nearby Tortuga, while the Dutch claimed Curaçao in 1634. Nonetheless, they represent an active approach to regional defense, in which the president-governor of Hispaniola played a key part.[63] Chaves Osorio complained about limited supplies but followed orders to keep Saint Martin provisioned. In all, he and his successors sent that garrison at least nineteen different aid shipments up until 1646 in conjunction with other shipments from Puerto Rico's governors, although several were captured by enemies.[64] The Council of the Indies was also receptive to new ideas for strengthening Hispaniola, especially when no Crown expenditures were needed. Among them was a 1632 proposal by Luís Garavito de Aguilar, Santo Domingo's procurador general, to build two ships for a local defense fleet, which were to be partially funded by minting new copper coinage. While the project collapsed after Garavito failed to raise the promised 40,000 ducados in Spain, this agreement reflects an ongoing metropolitan interest in finding solutions for Caribbean problems.[65]

At the same time, the Count-Duke of Olivares's reformist agenda was affecting the entire overseas audiencia system. Although he scaled back even more ambitious plans for reviewing each tribunal, in the later 1620s and 1630s the Council of the Indies ordered visitas generales for Quito, Lima, Santa Fe de Bogotá, Charcas, and Mexico, along with Santo Domingo. Contemporary commentators and some modern scholars have understandably characterized these visitas as a policy failure and waste of resources. Intemperate *visitadores* (investigating judges) made those in Quito and

Santo Domingo especially disruptive, but punishments and fines from all these investigations did not outweigh their cost to the royal treasury, and they definitely did not deter future abuses. Yet these visitas did reinforce the connection between the metropole and each audiencia's district, by providing tangible evidence that the Council of the Indies paid attention to the reports it received and that the king would call his ministers to account for their behavior. All involved knew that these visitas were played out before the eyes of permanent residents, which frequently turned them into a contest over who could best claim to represent royal authority.[66]

Despite the audiencia's transparent attempt to conceal them in 1626, the conflicts of Acuña's time—along with news that oidores were using royal orders from 1550 to engage in trade—helped motivate the visita general for Santo Domingo. In May 1630, the king ordered Alonso Hurtado (previously named for minor posts of *alcalde mayor* and corregidor in Spain) to carry out a detailed investigation into all the city's audiencia and treasury officials. While it was largely a disaster, on par with Juan de Mañozca's tumultuous visita general of Quito a few years earlier, this visita did lay bare serious problems within the audiencia's ranks.[67]

Hurtado's initial interviews with the oidores following his arrival in October 1630 provided seemingly strong evidence of factionalism, abuses, and confusion over procedure. Cereceda claimed, for example, that Parra de Meneses's wife had gotten her husband to vote in favor of certain litigants and had asked Cereceda and oidor Miguel de Verastegui y Otalora to do likewise. Gil de la Sierpe said Parra de Meneses fell asleep during audiencia sessions and was "incapable of his office" due to his poor understanding of law; he also noted that Cereceda had not attended meetings for over five months and that Chaves Osorio was not allowing local attorneys to act as auxiliary judges when the oidores' votes were tied. Otalora said little about judicial problems but complained at length about Cereceda, who behaved like "some incarnate demon or incubus." He described how Cereceda stirred up trouble in the audiencia and city, including spreading rumors and inserting himself into ecclesiastical affairs, in line with similar complaints from Chaves Osorio. Otalora freely admitted to being close friends with the president and to living and dining with him in the casas reales but argued their relationship allowed both to better serve the king. Parra de Meneses's responses were briefer, and he felt his colleagues performed their duties satisfactorily, although Cereceda instigated "noises and scandals."[68] Retired oidor Martínez Tenorio, who was mostly bedridden, had little to add, while fiscal Francisco de Prada was not questioned, since he was in Havana.[69]

Although Hurtado was provisionally named oidor of Panama to incentivize him and give him suitable status, his insistence on the deference he was due as visitador led to a series of escalating clashes with Chaves Osorio that the president-governor ultimately won. According to Chaves Osorio's later complaints, when Hurtado's ship entered the port he rejected the president-governor's offers of hospitality and refused to disembark because he did not receive what he considered a fitting escort.[70] Hurtado next asked and then ordered Chaves Osorio to make his deposition at Hurtado's lodgings instead of sending a notary to the casas reales, as a show of authority. Their ensuing shouting match marked the start of open hostilities. Toward the end of 1630, Hurtado suspended the president and ordered him to leave Santo Domingo, claiming he was blocking the investigation. Chaves Osorio refused to comply, saying it would weaken the city's defenses, and petitioned the Council of the Indies to have Hurtado recused and another judge, such as the archbishop, named to finish the visita.[71]

In the months that followed, Chaves Osorio and his supporters worked to destroy Hurtado's public reputation. The arrival of the annual Tierra Firme fleet—which at that time still visited Santo Domingo semiregularly—under general Alonso de Múxica in January 1631 provided the occasion for raucous public demonstrations (*cantaletas*), in which a crowd of soldiers and sailors ridiculed the visitador and attacked his masculinity. Hurtado was furious, but Chaves Osorio again cited military necessity to block him from prosecuting those behind the cantaletas. In June, Hurtado awoke to find the windows and doors of his house covered with human and dog excrement, with a chunk of it used to affix a slanderous verse, and his predictable outrage was his undoing. Hurtado blamed the deed on Chaves Osorio's coachman Marcos, sergeant Diego Sánchez, and *regidor* (city councilman) Rodrigo Pimentel, a neighbor of Hurtado and friend of the president. However, when Hurtado asked the municipal cabildo to lend him militia soldiers to arrest the perpetrators, Chaves Osorio had reason to accuse him of fomenting rebellion and placed him under house arrest.[72] Chapter 7 includes further details on this public contest, but it was perfectly clear to locals that the visitador had failed miserably at wielding authority over the president. The episode also demonstrates how Hurtado's inability to gain public support prevented him from acting in the king's name.

Meanwhile, across the Atlantic, the Council of the Indies responded to oidor Otalora's reports about Hurtado's erratic behavior by sending out Fernando de Salazar as accompanying judge (*juez acompañado*) for the visita, though they required Otalora to provide 1,000 ducados security in support of his claims. After arriving in late July 1631, Salazar found that Hurtado had been freed at the municipal and ecclesiastical cabildos' request but had suspended the visita. Even before that, oidor Parra de Meneses had been acting as Hurtado's notary, since the original notary returned to Spain over Hurtado's mistreatment, and no local notary would take testimony against the president, especially for an ineffective visitador. Salazar tried to restart proceedings, but Hurtado refused to cooperate and accused him of siding with Chaves Osorio, so Salazar confined himself to investigating the cantaletas against Hurtado and documenting the current situation. Salazar did witness one last bit of theatrics before returning to Spain, when Hurtado fell ill and, thinking he was about to die, called Chaves Osorio to his sickbed, where the two men tearfully embraced and forgave each other. Hurtado recovered and their mutual animosity resumed, but Salazar later said Hurtado had briefly admitted to gathering false testimony against the president.[73]

Salazar returned first and reported to the Council of the Indies, while Hurtado did not leave until November 1632, his investigation of Chaves Osorio still incomplete. Hurtado was not promoted to Panama, though he later became fiscal of the House of Trade. Only in 1635 did the council select Diego de la Rasa, outgoing fiscal of the Audiencia of Manila, to finish visita-related matters, including looking into the disputes between Hurtado and Chaves Osorio. De la Rasa arrived in mid-December of that year, and his work in Santo Domingo (which was simplified by Chaves Osorio's death a year earlier) allowed for the conclusion of the visita process by 1644.[74]

Well before then, the council reviewed Hurtado's completed investigations of the other audiencia personnel and treasury officials and pronounced final sentences during 1634 and 1635. Cereceda and Parra de Meneses received substantial punishments: a year's suspension and a 1,000-ducado fine for the former, and a three-year suspension and 500-ducado fine for the latter, though Parra came to Madrid and got his suspension lifted. Gil de la Sierpe also left for Spain after his provisional suspension but died midjourney in

Cartagena, so the council did not sentence most of his charges; his widow later pursued claims against Hurtado. Otalora did reach Spain, where despite their fiscal's opposition the council absolved him of the cantaletas against Hurtado, possibly thanks to his influential family. They penalized him 300 ducados for other charges, but they also effectively promoted him by moving him to what would have been Hurtado's position in Panama. However, Otalora died shortly after returning to Santo Domingo.[75]

These sentences suggest that the visita did—eventually—reinforce the Spanish Crown's control over distant overseas ministers, but the chaotic and drawn-out process illustrates the limitations of this control. As president-governor, Chaves Osorio had considerable practical autonomy, and support from the military and local elites allowed him to frustrate Hurtado at every turn. By contrast, the visitador's authority was founded on written orders and symbolic actions, and his behavior further weakened his ability to represent the monarch back in Spain. Hurtado's emotional reaction to public humiliation was exactly what Chaves Osorio and his allies intended, since it further disadvantaged the visitador in this unequal contest. Just the same, Hurtado's failure did not harm the more abstract authority of the king, whom Chaves Osorio also claimed to represent. Fernando de Salazar had a clearer sense of the constraints within which he operated and managed to oblige the president to leave the city once they agreed an enemy attack was not imminent. Chaves Osorio did succeed in delaying any real punishment until after his death in 1634, although his estate was tied up in litigation for a decade; de la Rasa reduced the charges against him but still levied penalties of nearly 50,000 ducados, largely for complicity in illicit sales of slaves and merchandise.[76] While Santo Domingo's visita general produced few immediate benefits at the cost of substantial turmoil, the experience was similar to that of other audiencias. Even so, the Council of the Indies continued to use both specific and general visitas as mechanisms for reinforcing royal oversight, if not on the system-wide scale of the 1620s and 1630s.[77]

When Chaves Osorio died, Alonso de Cereceda took over as interim president for roughly a year and a half. For a short time he was the only superior audiencia member, due to Otalora's death and the departure of fiscal Francisco de Prada to Spain to lobby for promotion. Cereceda used his new powers as vigorously as any permanent president-governor, and new letrado ministers complained he was threatening them and encouraging disobedience to the tribunal's orders by restricting its jurisdiction over governmental decisions.[78] One of Cereceda's first actions was to launch a previously planned military assault on the island of Tortuga to the northwest in early 1635, which successfully dislodged the English and French who had begun to fortify it. The campaign relied on news from an Irish informant who had fled Tortuga and then participated in the attack, Juan Morfo Geraldino (John Murphy Fitzgerald). Although Cereceda took much of the credit, he made recommendations for Morfo, the commanding officer Ruy Fernández de Fuenmayor, and several others, and sent a detailed report about other foreign settlements throughout the Caribbean.[79] Cereceda's use of his temporary position seemed to pay off when he was promoted to oidor of Mexico in January 1636, suggesting he had avoided the suspension in his visita sentence.[80]

However, the arrival of Juan Bitrián de Biamonte y Navarra in mid-1636 triggered the residencia of Cereceda's time as interim president-governor, which revealed deep grievances against the oidor. By 1638, Cereceda's fortunes had changed. The Council of the Indies stripped him of his promotion and sentenced him to five years' suspension and 4,600 ducados in fines, and then he was robbed by pirates while returning to Spain and imprisoned for debt after arriving. Although a few years later the council rehabilitated him and made him fiscal of Lima (and gave him more time to pay his fines), the relentless bureaucratic review process transformed Cereceda from a temporarily powerful local official into a supplicant for royal clemency. His denunciation of his fate, in which he declared there was no memory of another oidor being punished like he had, reflected the very real impact of metropolitan oversight on his career.[81]

The nine-year administration of president-governor Bitrián de Biamonte, previously governor of Havana, saw the continuing growth and consolidation of non-Spanish settlement in the region.[82] Spain's severe political and military setbacks in Europe during the late 1630s, culminating in the Catalan and Portuguese revolts of 1640, were not accompanied by major losses in the Caribbean. Yet except for their 1641 eviction of the English from Providence Island, Spanish forces were largely unable to recapture territory in the region.[83] As governor and captain-general, Bitrián continued to aid the Spanish garrison on Saint Martin and to order land and sea patrols of northern and western Hispaniola to capture and execute foreign interlopers.

Residents and royal officials expressed their fear of enemy attacks, and the audiencia's 1643 recommendation to reoccupy Bayahá and Puerto de Plata was followed the next year by news of "pirates" who sacked the town of Azua and carried off about ten women.[84]

Santo Domingo had long been home to a multinational population, despite royal restrictions on non-Spanish migration overseas, but at this time the Crown was especially concerned about the Portuguese and the Irish.[85] In January 1641, the Council of the Indies notified the audiencia and Bitrián de Biamonte of Portugal's recent rebellion against Spanish rule and ordered them to find out whether the Portuguese on Hispaniola were plotting anything; they were also to expel all those who were not long-term residents or could not give proof of nationality. The resulting inquiries produced only a few individuals they felt should be deported to Spain: around twenty unmarried sailors, a priest who had approved of the "treason of the Duke of Braganza" while in New Spain, and a youth who was whipped for celebrating Portugal's independence. In general, though, the tribunal's members maintained that Portuguese residents of Santo Domingo were well-established and peaceful. The council approved of their actions but cautioned them to remain watchful.[86] Shortly afterward, Bitrián informed the king about some 240 Catholic Irish who had fled Barbados and other English islands for Hispaniola in 1642, seeking protection from Puritan persecution. While he was initially willing to allow them to stay, both for the intelligence they had on French and English settlements in the Caribbean and to bolster the island's population, the city's cabildo was less enthusiastic. News of an Irish group living one hundred leagues away from Santo Domingo changed Bitrián's attitude, however, and metropolitan authorities eventually decided all the Irish should be removed, although a few individuals like Juan Morfo remained.[87] Even so, Bitrián saw Irish Catholics as categorically different from other non-Spaniards—mainly Dutch, French, and English—who were caught on Hispaniola and sometimes sent as prisoners to the House of Trade.[88]

The islanders' ongoing search for a viable export product continued without much success in these years, and maritime attacks on commercial vessels further limited access to external markets. Sugar shipments fell sharply early in the century, and limited demand for medicinal crops like cañafístula or sarsaparilla meant they never brought much profit. Ginger and tobacco exports, previously significant, were declining by the 1640s, while experiments with replacements like indigo were unsuccessful. Sporadic communication with Spain made interregional trade more attractive, and the later 1640s saw increasing cultivation of cacao, much of which went to New Spain.[89] However, delays in the yearly situado—funds for 1636 and 1637 did not arrive until 1639, forcing soldiers and royal officials to live on credit—deepened the strain on an overburdened royal treasury, and shifting these payments from Mexico to Cartagena brought little change.[90] This poor economic climate fueled the rise of Rodrigo Pimentel, the regidor implicated in visitador Hurtado's humiliation, whose wealth allowed him to make loans when the situado failed. Pimentel exerted unrivaled influence over Santo Domingo and its audiencia from the 1630s up to his death in 1683, although his general relationship to royal administration was much like that of other local elites.[91]

The audiencia was divided by further infighting under Bitrián de Biamonte, and some of the letrados claimed he undermined its independence as a judicial body and advisory council. In 1639 oidor Pedro Álvarez de Mendoza protested that Bitrián had forced the city's regidores to pen complaints against his "cruel" investigations, in addition to usurping cases under the tribunal's jurisdiction.[92] The pugnacious fiscal Francisco Alarcón Coronado, who served from 1637 to 1654, claimed that the president-governor took away his seat in the court's chambers after he questioned the payment to Bitrián's nephew for fetching the situado. Bitrián then fined him when he petitioned the audiencia about this and other matters.[93] In 1642 oidor Pedro Luis de Salazar, Bitrián's staunchest opponent, sent the Council of the Indies a list of seventy-four accusations to include in the president's residencia. According to Salazar, Bitrián boasted about spending 30,000 ducados to dodge previous residencia charges in Havana (with help from an English merchant in Seville, Richard Sweet). Moreover, the "crazy" president-governor made poor military decisions, dispensed royal funds to his favorites, gave his allies legal immunity, controlled trade and permitted contraband, extorted money and jewelry from residents, and barred the court's notaries from reading petitions before the audiencia without his approval. Much of what Salazar described was meant to shock metropolitan authorities, such as Bitrián's alleged comment that "the king doesn't know what is ordered, nor the council what it provides."[94] By contrast, two other oidores, Juan Melgarejo Ponce de León and Juan de Retuerta, served as Bitrián's legal assistants. For his part, Bitrián maintained that letrado ministers' "partiality" toward litigants harmed the audiencia's public reputation, and he criticized several of them for openly eating together with the archbishop and Pimentel while the latter was involved in suits before the court.[95]

Other challenges for the tribunal had little to do with the president-governor. In late 1640 the oidores reported that they had left a recent suit from Venezuela undecided because Salazar was in Havana, Álvarez de Mendoza was blind and ill, Alarcón Coronado and Retuerta were ineligible, and Melgarejo could not agree on a verdict with the only two local letrados who could act as auxiliary judges.[96] They also encountered resistance to their regional authority: in mid-1642, despite having Bitrián's support, Melgarejo was unable to assume the temporary governorship of Puerto Rico because the recently deceased governor's illegally chosen replacement ejected him from San Juan.[97]

Relations with the church were relatively untroubled during these years, largely because there was no archbishop in Santo Domingo for most of the 1640s. Archbishop Facundo de Torres had actually cooperated with the audiencia in 1639 when Melgarejo forcibly entered the convent of Regina Angelorum in pursuit of a female murder suspect, to the anger of the local Dominican monks.[98] After Torres died in 1640, his successor Diego de Guevara y Estrada also died following his departure from Mexico a few years later. The next two nominees declined the post, though the third, Francisco Pío Guadalupe de Téllez, finally accepted and left for Hispaniola in 1650, where he remained until his death a decade later.[99]

The three president-governors who followed Bitrián de Biamonte over the next ten years—Nicolás de Velasco Altamirano, Luis Fernández de Córdoba, and Andrés Pérez Franco—were all seasoned military commanders primarily chosen to safeguard Santo Domingo in the face of foreign encroachment in the Caribbean, though none survived more than a few years in office. Velasco's arrival in mid-1645 heralded the start of Bitrián's residencia and the new president's initiation into audiencia politics. Fiscal Alarcón Coronado tried unsuccessfully to stop Velasco from naming oidor Melgarejo, a known ally of Bitrián, as his legal assistant and was barred from presenting complaints in the residencia. During the proceedings, Alarcón, along with oidores Salazar and Francisco Pantoja de Ayala, wrote about Bitrián's dishonesty in arranging letters and testimony in his favor to disguise popular resentment against him and escape the consequences of his misbehavior. They maintained that the ex-president intimidated other local residents into silence and used Melgarejo to get Velasco to disregard hundreds of charges from the fiscal.[100] As they feared, Velasco pronounced a light sentence against Bitrián in March 1646, declaring him a zealous royal servant who had ably defended the city and island. Yet they carefully avoided blaming Velasco for this outcome in their correspondence, suggesting a concerted effort to establish a good relationship with the incoming president. Bitrián reported on Hispaniola before the Council of the Indies in Madrid the following year and later became president-governor of Panama. While Velasco and Melgarejo were eventually ordered to justify their actions, Bitrián's residencia shows that targeting the fiscal was an effective way to handcuff the letrado ministers.[101]

Velasco did have more success than Bitrián at cooperating with the other audiencia members, although he was preoccupied with defense during his brief time on the island. Local initiative helped supplement limited imperial resources, as with the launch of an eighteen-gun galleon financed by residents of Santo Domingo in early 1645, even if this did not really prevent enemy vessels from cruising Caribbean waters.[102] To offset ongoing English settlement efforts, Velasco was ordered to attract Catholic Irish in the "rebel islands" of the Lesser Antilles to serve the Spanish Crown, at the same time he was to stop unauthorized settlement in Spain's territory.[103] In June 1647, the Crown sent him intelligence from the Spanish ambassador in England about plans to seize control of Hispaniola, a precursor of Oliver Cromwell's 1655 "Western Design." However, European political reorientation at the end of the Thirty Years' War was reflected in a slight reduction in hostilities in the Caribbean, and in the summer of 1648 the king informed Velasco of the recent peace with the Dutch while warning him to remain on guard.[104]

Following Velasco's death later that year, senior oidor Juan Melgarejo Ponce de León became interim president until 1650. As with other temporary presidents over the next two decades, Melgarejo embraced his expanded authority while he held it, especially to redress what he saw as serious threats to the tribunal's authority. According to the audiencia, both Bitrián and Velasco had required the relator and notaries to get their approval before reading petitions to the court, including those from the fiscal, allowing the president to choose which issues were heard.[105] Both men also made the books of royal orders inaccessible to letrado ministers by keeping them in their living quarters, so that letters from the king had not been announced or acted upon; moreover, they had withheld jurists' pay and moved the court to a cramped and noisy room after taking over its usual chambers in the casas reales. All this was done to subjugate the tribunal to the president-governor, the letrados claimed, and they asked for specific royal orders to prevent these abuses from being repeated in the future.[106]

As governor, Melgarejo also sent military expeditions against maroon communities in the mountainous interior of the island and French interlopers around Jaragua on the south-central coast. He claimed both as qualified victories (the first captured or killed around thirty "fugitive rebel blacks" but could not find other groups, while the second killed thirty-four Frenchmen and retreated when more arrived) but urged the king to send more soldiers.[107] In February 1650, Melgarejo also had to deal with alarming news from Mexico that the Portuguese in Buenos Aires had massacred Spanish residents, which had led the viceroy and audiencia of Mexico to disarm Portuguese inhabitants and move them thirty leagues from mines and the coast. Although this uprising never actually happened, the Dominican audiencia took the report seriously at the time, and Melgarejo put troops on alert and suspended nearly fifty Portuguese presidio soldiers, still serving ten years after Portugal had broken away from Spanish rule. In the ensuing debate in the acuerdo, Melgarejo and oidor Pantoja wanted to follow Mexico's example but were opposed by Alarcón Coronado and oidor Fernando de Cepeda, who argued that the Portuguese on Hispaniola had caused no problems and deserved no mistreatment. Since their votes were tied, Melgarejo remitted the decision to Spain, although he also ordered a review of all resident foreigners in the city in early March.[108]

While Melgarejo collaborated closely with the audiencia during his time as president-governor, his interim status and efforts at reform likely encouraged challenges to his authority. During 1649 and 1650, Melgarejo informed the Council of the Indies about disrespect from Alarcón Coronado and said oidor Cepeda wanted to share the duties of interim president by turns each month. The municipal cabildo of Santo Domingo wrote in support of Melgarejo, however, and these two ministers were later reprimanded.[109] He also had continuing problems related to a 1648 incident, when a Spanish woman and an enslaved African man about to be executed were forcibly taken away from the audiencia's officers by a mob and given sanctuary in the hospital of San Nicolás (see chapter 7).[110] Melgarejo's efforts to extract them angered both regular and secular clergy, which may explain why he ended up relying heavily on Rodrigo Pimentel's assistance, since naming the wealthy regidor his *teniente* (deputy or assistant) gained him the support of the city's cabildo and local militia companies.[111]

The next president-governor, Luis Fernández de Córdoba, who took over in the summer of 1650, was less tolerant of opposition and flatly rejected the fiscal's request to allow appeals to his decisions about assigning specific duties to the letrado ministers to preserve the "supreme authority" of his office.[112] Fernández de Córdoba also sharply criticized oidores Cepeda and Salazar for judicial abuses and for the headaches they caused him. Cepeda, for example, who Fernández de Córdoba fined 100 pesos for his poor work and defiance, tried to hide in the Mercedarian convent to escape a commission on Margarita and Cumaná, though he eventually departed.[113] In early 1651 Fernández de Córdoba requested that senior oidor Salazar be barred from becoming interim president in the event of his death because he felt the magistrate was completely unsuited to govern. Indeed, in March, after less than a year on Hispaniola, Fernández de Córdoba succumbed to an epidemic; however, Salazar only outlived him by three days as temporary president-governor, and the position passed to oidor Pantoja de Ayala.[114]

The audiencia, now reduced to two oidores and a fiscal, seems to have enjoyed relative peace for roughly a year. Local elite Bernardo de Figueroa y Castilla's letter claiming that Pantoja was largely a figurehead controlled by Rodrigo Pimentel hints at how this peace was achieved and reflects how wealthy residents made the tribunal part of their own factional struggles.[115] When president-governor Andrés Pérez Franco assumed his post in the spring of 1652, the balance of power in the audiencia and city once more changed dramatically. An old career soldier, Pérez Franco had little patience for criticism from jurists and used his military authority to dominate the letrado ministers. Within a half year, oidores Pantoja and Juan Francisco de Montemayor y Córdoba de Cuenca reported that the president was running roughshod over their privileges, freely revoking the tribunal's provisions and repealing its sentences, and justifying his actions by declaring a state of war. Pérez Franco persecuted the letrados and encouraged public disrespect against them; on hearing that Pantoja had been promoted to Guatemala, the president suspended his salary and tried to forcibly ship him there before his papers had arrived, then seized his property when he took refuge in a convent, leaving Montemayor as the only voting oidor.[116] Pérez Franco's poor health and lack of interest in the fine points of law led him to proclaim shortly before his death that that the city's *alcaldes ordinarios* (judicial officers), not the senior oidor, were to govern in his stead. Despite one of the cabildo members' abortive attempts to use these orders a week later, this patently illegal provision was not carried out, and as the only resident magistrate Montemayor took over as acting president-governor in August 1653.[117]

Across the Atlantic, the Council of the Indies was unaware of Pérez Franco's death and recommended accepting his request for retirement in view of his failing vision, faulty memory, and various illnesses, plus the turmoil he had caused in Santo Domingo and the military importance of his position.[118] The council members also felt this was an ideal moment to consult with the king about "the utility and necessity there is of making a new selection [*nueva planta*] of a president and the other ministers of that audiencia, and with such a favorable circumstance now as the proposition that the president makes of leaving his post, and only one oidor remaining in that audiencia since another two have died."[119] They went on to name a new president, four oidores, and a fiscal for Santo Domingo during 1653 and 1654. If this strategy did not prevent new conflicts among the audiencia's members a few years later, it was certainly less expensive and disruptive than another visita general.[120]

Nevertheless, their discussion reveals a fundamental assumption that the audiencia as an institution was sound and that troubles within the Dominican tribunal were largely the fault of individual ministers. They were not entirely mistaken, as men like Pérez Franco, Francisco Manso de Contreras, Alonso de Cereceda, and Jerónimo de Herrera generated considerable strife during their time on the island and tended to persist in such behavior when promoted elsewhere. Yet struggles over jurisdiction and precedence were endemic to Habsburg bureaucracy and the society it was embedded in throughout Spain's vast empire, above and below the level of the audiencia.[121] Even during periods of discord, the Dominican audiencia continued to operate as a royal court of justice, but tensions between president-governors and letrados were a persistent source of complaints to the council. Metropolitan desires for strong military leadership to defend the island from the mid-1620s onward were only intensified by news of English invasion plans and ensured that these internal conflicts continued into the later seventeenth century.

3

Audiencias and President-Governors, 1653–1700

Following the death of Andrés Pérez Franco, the residents of Spanish Hispaniola survived an English invasion attempt in 1655 only to experience continuing royal neglect, foreign encroachment, and population decline, alongside natural disasters and epidemics, in the later seventeenth century. While the assault was in many ways a defining moment for the city of Santo Domingo that drove home its military importance to the Crown, its immediate practical impact on the audiencia was limited, aside from president-governor Félix de Zúñiga's restriction of its authority in the later 1650s. In the decades that followed, the tribunal did face new financial difficulties that deepened its reliance on local elites as well as a frequent lack of personnel and tenuous communications with the metropole; toward the end of the century, defense concerns led to a significant loss of privilege for the magistrates with the creation of a military assistant who would serve as temporary governor instead of the senior oidor. Just the same, even while the Spanish Crown struggled to control an increasingly multinational Caribbean, the audiencia played a key role in maintaining connections between Madrid and Hispaniola and facilitating metropolitan efforts at revitalizing the island.

Oidor Juan Francisco de Montemayor remained interim president-governor from mid-1653 to the spring of 1655. One of the more distinguished jurists to serve on the Dominican audiencia, Montemayor seized this opportunity to demonstrate his worth to the king.[1] Together with Jerónimo de Alzate, a fiscal of Guadalajara temporarily "deposited" as oidor in Santo Domingo during a visita, he tried to repair the damage Pérez Franco had done to the cause of royal justice. According to them, the former president had not only required petitions to the audiencia to have his approval but also usurped the jurisdiction of the city's alcaldes ordinarios by personally judging civil and criminal suits. In response to the open contempt Pérez Franco had induced presidio soldiers and cabildo members to show audiencia magistrates, Montemayor and Alzate stressed that as the oldest tribunal in the Indies they deserved the same respect as other audiencias.[2] Montemayor also seems to have sought help from Rodrigo Pimentel—whom Pérez Franco had tried to exile to Spain, though his death shortly afterward allowed Pimentel to return from Puerto Rico—as a powerful local ally who could bolster the court's public reputation. Montemayor and oidor Francisco Pantoja de Ayala later received orders to end their friendship with Pimentel, which Montemayor obeyed, but his oblique reference to the exaggerations of "ill-intentioned people" again suggests that local elites' power struggles were regularly played out through the audiencia.[3]

As interim president, Montemayor's most noteworthy achievement was the decision to attack Tortuga in January 1654, which he added to previous claims about his military service. Its fort surrendered to Spanish forces after an eight-day siege, and several hundred English and French inhabitants were ejected, while about fifty English subjects swore obedience to the Spanish king. To prevent reoccupation, the Spanish also left a garrison of some 140 men under Juan Morfo (though Montemayor mistrusted Morfo and soon recalled him). Montemayor presented himself to the Crown as a bold yet judicious governor, gathering intelligence and convening juntas of finance and war before ordering the assault, without neglecting city defenses while these troops were away.[4] The capture of Tortuga earned Montemayor praise from seventeenth-century writers and later historians alike; in particular, Manuel Arturo Peña Batlle, who wryly dubs the oidor "Don Quixote Montemayor," sees him resolutely laboring to defend Hispaniola despite metropolitan disinterest or resistance, following Montemayor's own claims. Yet he had no lack of local critics, among them Santo Domingo's archbishop, who faulted him for being young, inexperienced in war, and Aragonese.[5]

Spanish Hispaniola faced its most serious military threat of the century the following April, when an English fleet of fifty-six ships, carrying over seven thousand men, laid siege to Santo Domingo in an effort to capture the entire island.[6] This invasion marked the next three president-governors sent to the city: Bernardino de Meneses, who led the defense; Félix de Zúñiga, who was meant to strengthen its future military readiness; and Juan de Balboa Mogrovejo, who was sent to fix the problems Zúñiga caused. The

Spanish had known about Cromwell's "Western Design" for some time, and both resident officials and peninsular authorities were justifiably worried about Santo Domingo's ability to withstand a large-scale assault. Montemayor reported in late 1654 on improvements to its fortifications, which he claimed were good even though the approach from the Haina River (where the English later landed) was still open; he also stressed the need for missed situado payments. Peninsular authorities, facing a general scarcity of resources and news of another invasion attempt against Tobago, scrambled to send troops, munitions, and a suitable commander to the island.[7] On April 8, Bernardino de Meneses Bracamonte y Zapata, Count of Peñalba, arrived at Santo Domingo with two hundred soldiers, plus four recently named oidores and a fiscal, less than two weeks ahead of the English armada. Meneses found the city poorly prepared for the coming assault, with only 170 of the 300 presidio soldiers able to bear arms and the city walls still unfinished, but hastened to make ready in the time available.[8]

For residents of Santo Domingo, their successful defense against the 1655 invasion was nothing short of miraculous. Indeed, in both Hispaniola and Spain it was attributed to God's favor (while some among the English saw their defeat as divine punishment).[9] Over twenty-two days, the heavily outnumbered locals, including "black and *mulato* slaves," repulsed two separate attempts by the English forces, and one account maintained that only thirty-two Spanish troops were killed or wounded. Meneses reserved special praise for the island's *lanceros*, mixed-race militia companies from the interior who harried the English along the road from the mouth of the Haina. Audiencia ministers also assisted; during and after the siege they only held sessions two days a week due to their involvement in defense preparations.[10] Although their participation—institutionally or individually—was not decisive, the presence of the audiencia in Santo Domingo reflected a history of greater metropolitan concern for the city that made it a more difficult target than Santiago de la Vega in Jamaica.[11] The capture of Jamaica gave the English an important central Caribbean base, but their defeat on Hispaniola meant that Spain's administrative structure in the region and the audiencia's relationship with its district remained largely unchanged through the end of the century.

The Spanish garrison on Tortuga was not recalled until the fall of 1655, well after the English siege.[12] Contemporary and modern critics have charged that Meneses dismantled Tortuga to prevent Montemayor's achievement from overshadowing his own, or because shortsightedness or the malign influence of others prevented him from understanding that this would ensure foreign domination of northwestern Hispaniola.[13] Montemayor claimed Meneses only grudgingly followed orders to consult with him about Tortuga and disregarded his arguments for keeping it. Certainly, the dispute over Tortuga was part of a larger struggle between the two: Montemayor felt Meneses had stolen the credit he deserved, while Meneses was unimpressed by a jurist who, as interim president, used to visit the fort in the mornings for "an hour or half-hour with his boots and spurs," and was still styling himself governor and captain-general a year later.[14]

Yet in the broader imperial context the decision to demolish the fortifications on Tortuga and withdraw its garrison is understandable. Tortuga had been discussed at length in Spain, and Meneses was instructed to plan for abandoning it. He was to confer with Montemayor and was able to decide to hold Tortuga, but metropolitan assumptions were that doing so meant risking all of Hispaniola, as shown in the king's orders: "It is true that maintaining a presidio on Tortuga is not enough so that with it the island of Hispaniola and its presidio of Santo Domingo be defended, and that instead it would be to add care to care and obligation to obligation, when there are so many places that call at the same time for the need of assistance and presidios across the expanse of my monarchy."[15] Meneses's uncle Pedro Zapata, governor of Cartagena, went further in faulting Montemayor for attacking Tortuga at all, arguing that unless the Spanish could be certain of chasing all foreigners from the Caribbean, it would be better to have everyone "live on the alert and keep what they have and not provoke the enemy."[16] Later commentators highlighted Tortuga's role in enabling French occupation of Hispaniola and fostering piracy, but at the time peninsular authorities believed Montemayor's plans to hold it were overly optimistic, especially when they anticipated further attempts against Santo Domingo. Even so, the Council of the Indies appreciated his actions as interim president and promoted him directly to oidor of Mexico.[17]

The years following the defeat of the English invasion were difficult ones for the city and island. In response to Meneses's reports, a grateful Felipe IV and his advisors issued rewards for those who had helped with the defense, including the audiencia ministers, and decreed an annual holiday to celebrate the victory. This news was received with some cynicism on Hispaniola;

those who were given *encomienda* grants in Venezuela appreciated the recognition but did not expect to receive them, while few believed the 500 pesos for the poor would materialize.[18] Meneses himself was deeply disappointed with his promotion to the presidency of Charcas, a higher-status position with better pay, since it signaled a lack of confidence in his military leadership. As he was already 20,000 ducados in debt, the travel expenses for this post were also a serious problem, but his pleas for a less distant position or permission to remain in Santo Domingo—which continued as he traveled to Cartagena—were not granted. He felt Montemayor was behind his removal, and he claimed that this "Aragonese *hidalgo*" had wanted the English invasion to succeed to make him look bad. Moreover, he had sent conflicting reports about the city's defense and conspired with Puerto Rico's governor to ensure his own letters arrived in Spain first. To Meneses, Montemayor was lazy, immoral, and insufferably arrogant about his service record and the favor he enjoyed in Madrid. When Meneses took Montemayor's residencia as interim president-governor, he levied substantial fines and forbade him to leave for Mexico before paying.[19]

After the 1655 English attack, the Council of the Indies did indeed want a veteran commander to replace Meneses, suggesting they had selected him because he was available in an emergency rather than for his military talents or experience. Their search was complicated by the position's unpopularity, however, and the first nominee declined while the second asked for too many concessions. The man they eventually sent, Félix de Zúñiga y Avellaneda, "Count of the Holy Empire," had fought in Europe under the Austrian Habsburgs. Shortly after arriving in 1656, Zúñiga remarked that he was only on the island "as long as my exile should last"; it is unclear whether he was forced out of a previous post, but the council would regret choosing him.[20] Meneses recognized Zúñiga as a "great soldier of Germany and Flanders and the frontiers of Portugal," but did not enjoy hearing his successor's criticism of the city's fortifications—which Meneses argued were suited to warfare in the Indies and Hispaniola's economic limitations—or of Meneses's decision to abandon Tortuga. Zúñiga quickly ordered the demolition of the recently constructed fort across the Ozama River, calling its designer a "traitor," since enemies might use it to besiege the city, and blamed Meneses for a wasteful and useless project. Meneses sailed for Cartagena soon afterward, his passage paid by local supporters, but died there about a year later.[21]

Zúñiga was even more authoritarian than Pérez Franco with the letrados, and within months oidor Gaspar Vélez Mantilla and fiscal Bernardo Trigo de Figueroa began to write Spain about his harsh treatment and open mockery of them. Vélez Mantilla further maintained that, despite his experience, Zúñiga had not inspected the walls or roads or done anything to improve local defenses and added, "I have never seen such a strange gentleman in my life."[22] By contrast, Zúñiga said the oidores had ignored pending suits and insinuated themselves into the island's political and military government, though he intended to confine them to their proper role, "which is only a court of justice." Zúñiga initially seemed to sympathize with Montemayor, who had been unable to leave for Mexico, but later put him under house arrest over claims brought by Dutch ship owners. Meneses also wrote from Cartagena to inform the Council of the Indies that Zúñiga had imprisoned and persecuted Montemayor and oidor Alzate.[23]

Zúñiga soon came to rely heavily on Rodrigo Pimentel. Together, they dominated local government and maintained a lucrative trade with foreign ships, facilitated by staffing the treasury with Pimentel's friends and relatives. Over the next two years, peninsular authorities received numerous reports about Zúñiga's despotism from Trigo, Vélez Mantilla, Montemayor, oidor Andrés Martínez de Amileta, and various military and ecclesiastical figures, despite the efforts of the president and his allies to stop their letters leaving the island.[24] In August 1658, the Council of the Indies met to consider the accusations against Zúñiga, which included interfering with audiencia decisions and swearing at, threatening, imprisoning, and exiling the letrado ministers, along with illicit commerce. The council members were likewise alarmed at the power Pimentel had gained under Zúñiga, emphasized by an anonymous protest message painted on the casas reales reading "there is no more law nor more king than don Rodrigo Pimentel."[25]

However, the complaints against Zúñiga also show that the audiencia was internally divided and that allegiances shifted. Trigo de Figueroa and Vélez Mantilla consistently criticized Zúñiga, but Martínez de Amileta had tried to curry favor with him early on before becoming an opponent. Oidores Diego López de la Puerta and Andrés Caballero served as the president's legal assistants, which alienated them from their colleagues; when López de la Puerta became too independent, Caballero apparently allied with Zúñiga and Pimentel and was later accused of complicity in their crimes. Former oidor

Montemayor, still waiting to leave for Mexico, at first supported the president and Pimentel but was later banished from the city when he angered them.[26]

The council members agreed that the long list of accusations warranted removing Zúñiga from the island and belatedly recognized that his nature "is not and never has been suited to govern audiencias or matters of justice, government, or patronage."[27] However, they took pains to avoid injuring his reputation and ordered him back to Spain on the pretext that he was wanted for the king's service, giving them time to investigate the charges against him. In October 1658, they chose Juan de Balboa Mogrovejo, governor of Gibraltar, to replace Zúñiga, restore royal oversight, and safeguard the island. At the same time, they commissioned Sancho de Ubilla—initially named fiscal of Santo Domingo but upgraded to oidor and then made oidor of another (unspecified) audiencia to enhance his authority—to carry out visitas of Zúñiga, Rodrigo Pimentel, oidores Caballero and Martínez de Amileta, and others. Although such investigations had been recommended for Santo Domingo at least five years earlier, the need was now pressing.[28]

While Zúñiga was likely the most disruptive president-governor of the century, his administration essentially continued earlier patterns. His unyielding opposition to the tribunal's judicial independence or its advisory role in governance was that of a military commander who tolerated no challenges, especially from jurists. His predecessor Meneses had even recommended (with the letrados' agreement) moving the audiencia to somewhere like Caracas to allow Hispaniola's governors to focus on defense and avoid recurring military-letrado conflicts. Through the turmoil of these years, the audiencia continued to carry out much of its usual business, subject to unusually strong influence from Pimentel, and Zúñiga consulted the acuerdo about matters like coinage. Zúñiga may have been a tyrant, but his clashes with the audiencia or reliance on local elites were not fundamentally different from those of other seventeenth-century military presidents.[29]

Balboa and Ubilla reached Santo Domingo on the same ship in August 1659 and agreed to announce that Zúñiga was needed in Spain rather than imprisoning him and sending him back in disgrace, even if it was common knowledge he was being recalled for abuse.[30] They soon found out, however, that opposition to Pimentel's control of the city under Zúñiga was not nearly as universal as it had seemed in critics' letters. Pimentel's fall from power also ended the flow of illicit commerce to the port, meaning residents lost access to both imports and buyers for their produce, increasing popular resentment of Ubilla and Balboa.

Ubilla, who had Balboa's full support in legal decisions and reports to Spain, immediately began proceedings against those accused of colluding with Zúñiga and Pimentel. Notary Francisco Facundo de Carvajal, for example, was jailed and his property seized. Ubilla imprisoned Pimentel himself for about ten months before embarking him for Spain. According to Balboa, Pimentel continued to command his supporters up to his departure and even sent some to Venezuela to protect them from Ubilla and preserve his regional connections.[31]

Balboa and Ubilla expected local gratitude for their plans to end abuses, but they ended up deeply disenchanted with the inhabitants of Santo Domingo and most of the audiencia's ministers. Three months after arriving, Balboa looked back on the "applause" that had greeted him as temporary enthusiasm for a new administration and declared that locals' economic distress was largely voluntary, the product of "greed in some and laziness in the rest (and this is immense)."[32] In early 1660 Ubilla claimed ex-fiscal Trigo de Figueroa was angry over Ubilla's lenient residencia sentence and wanted revenge. Their sense of the hostility they faced was captured in Ubilla's report that Balboa had fallen gravely ill and was only recently able to rise from bed; Balboa himself believed he was poisoned because of his efforts to clean up the island.[33]

The following year, as Ubilla was carrying out visitas of Martínez de Amileta and Caballero, letters to Spain testified to the animosity that continued to divide the tribunal. Over three months, Martínez de Amileta wrote at least five times to complain about the injustices Balboa and Ubilla had inflicted on him, including four months' exile to Higüey, forty leagues from Santo Domingo. According to him, their needless delay of his promotion to Panama was punishment for his and his allies' reports about their misdeeds. Caballero claimed he and his son (a former port guard also under investigation) had been similarly attacked by the president and visitador, who were intent on ruining him due to the slander of Martínez de Amileta and Trigo de Figueroa. Fiscal Jacinto de Vargas Campuzano and oidor Vélez Mantilla also said Martínez de Amileta had falsely denounced several colleagues, while procurador Juan de Rosados maintained that Vélez Mantilla was simply harassing Pimentel's associates and oidor López de la Puerta was too friendly with Balboa to stop it.[34]

Meanwhile, Balboa sent a long letter of his own denouncing the falsehoods of Martínez de Amileta, Pimentel, and their allies, in which he asserted that the oidor had previously lied about Meneses and Zúñiga, sometimes using an assumed name. He railed against the power of a letrado like Martínez de Amileta to question his actions and accuse him of dishonesty or immorality, despite his extensive military services, his exemplary life, and his efforts to break merchants' control over the prices of basic necessities. Furthermore, he claimed "among the things that have provoked [him] to laughter" was the willingness of Hispaniola's gossip-loving residents to believe anyone who challenged military decisions made by experts like himself and his predecessors.[35] Yet the defensive tone of his unsolicited explanations for complaints against him may have validated metropolitan authorities' concerns about his leadership.

During these years, Hispaniola felt the impact of the growing foreign presence in the Caribbean. The English finished off local resistance on Jamaica and defeated Spanish attempts at recapture, becoming unwelcome but permanent neighbors.[36] In 1660, a year after the end of the Franco-Spanish War, a mostly French force sacked Santiago de los Caballeros, reportedly killing some 160 men. This reflected poorly on Balboa's military competence, since—as his detractors emphasized—he had disbanded the troops protecting the island's interior.[37] Meanwhile, European campaigns consumed men and money as war with Portugal continued beyond 1659, limiting what Spain could spend on Caribbean defense.[38] Although the Dutch were now allies, they exploited opportunities for trade in Spanish ports.[39] Nicolas Jansen, a Dutch shipowner, complained that after assisting with the 1654 Tortuga assault, he had been imprisoned, his slaves confiscated, and his two ships sunk to block Santo Domingo's harbor in 1655. Ubilla investigated after the States General pressured the Spanish Crown, and Jansen received special trade privileges to recoup his losses.[40] Royal officials on Hispaniola needed to pay close attention to such diplomatic considerations in the later part of the century.

The four president-governors who followed Balboa—Pedro de Carvajal y Cobos, Ignacio Zayas Bazán, Francisco de Segura Sandoval, and Andrés de Robles—all served for significantly longer than the previous six appointees, starting with Nicolás de Velasco in 1645, and managed to establish greater stability within the audiencia. Balboa was made governor of Chile in early 1661, after less than two years in office, and in April Carvajal y Cobos was named to replace him. This transition coincided with the return of Rodrigo Pimentel, who turned the Crown's need for money to his advantage. As visitador, Ubilla was able to recommend granting guilty individuals a chance to purchase letters of *indulto* indemnifying them for past offenses; however, neither he nor Balboa anticipated that Pimentel would be able to buy such an indulto after they shipped him to Spain, though Pimentel boasted of that very possibility. Pimentel arrived in Seville a prisoner but used his wealth and formidable negotiating skills to gain permission to plead his case in Madrid, and in July 1661 he was granted an indulto for serving the king with 7,000 pesos in cash. Before Carvajal sailed for Santo Domingo in the company of Archbishop-elect Francisco de la Cueva Maldonado, Pimentel met both men and reportedly gained their confidence in preparation for his own voyage home shortly afterward. Balboa's brother later claimed Pimentel had converted them into "instruments of his vengeance."[41]

Carvajal was meant to take Balboa's residencia after his arrival in August 1661, but the Council of the Indies subsequently decided that he would be too busy with defense and gave Ubilla the task. Even so, reports about Balboa's misconduct led them to order him to remain on Hispaniola or come to Spain during his residencia instead of going directly to Chile, another vital military position even further from royal oversight. Carvajal also sent the council his preliminary findings, which contained strong indications that both Balboa and Ubilla had committed abuses. Ubilla finished Balboa's residencia by December 1661, sentencing him to a few thousand pesos in fines and restitutions for mostly minor offenses and declaring him worthy of his promotion. When the council members in Madrid compared Ubilla's list of thirty charges with the seventy-one more serious accusations Carvajal had made, they agreed further review was needed.[42]

The political climate on Hispaniola also turned against Balboa and Ubilla. In May 1662, López de la Puerta and Vargas Campuzano (recently made oidor) wrote as the audiencia to praise the new president and archbishop for relieving the city from Balboa's "bad government." The city's cabildo told the king that Balboa's main goal had been to enrich himself and that he had prevented them from reporting the "miserable state" of Santo Domingo, while his accomplice Ubilla omitted these complaints from his residencia.

Archbishop de la Cueva went further a year later, stating that Balboa effectively controlled Ubilla, and that "two demons" could not have done more harm than they had with their falsehoods. He also claimed they spread rumors that Pimentel had bribed Carvajal, although he insisted the new president had behaved with the impartiality of "an angel."[43]

Ubilla finished most of his commissions before his death in Santo Domingo in 1665, but due to these accusations against him the Council of the Indies sought more information before passing final sentences. In 1666 the council sent their own relator, Rodrigo Navarro de Mendoza, to complete Balboa's residencia and tie up loose ends from Ubilla's commissions. He eventually declared Ubilla a model judge who had been maligned by Pimentel's allies. Balboa's residencia process lasted nine years; the council's first nominee to retake his residencia was captured and imprisoned in Algiers, and the second died before departing, and only in 1669 did the council review Navarro's findings and sentence Balboa, fining him 3,400 pesos. His promotion to Chile had long since evaporated, and although he later became president of the Audiencia of the Canary Islands, he struggled to recover his outstanding salary and pay his penalties and debts.[44] Balboa blamed Pimentel and his supporters for his misfortunes, beginning with his removal of Zúñiga a decade earlier. Yet he never secured effective local support to counterbalance the opposition he faced from influential elites and royal ministers, and his own actions left him open to accusations similar to those leveled against Zúñiga.

Rodrigo Pimentel, who was briefly exiled from the city after his arrival, quickly regained much of his former power, although his role was never again as public as it had been during Zúñiga's administration. He took minor clerical orders while in Spain and later became a chaplain in Santo Domingo, limiting the jurisdiction secular judges had over him. Pimentel also made aggressive use of the judicial system in other ways—for example, in lodging complaints against his enemies with visitador Navarro to discourage opposition or in suing to force Balboa to return 3,000 pesos previously taken from him. The superficially polite but increasingly confrontational tone of three letters Pimentel wrote Balboa between 1659 and 1661, from the city's presidio, Cádiz, and Madrid, suggests a man secure in his ability to navigate, manipulate, or bypass the legal process to achieve his aims.[45] Although Navarro substantiated many of Ubilla's charges against Pimentel, most were nullified by the indulto, and his punishment was little more than the inconvenience of provisional fines, which were overturned on appeal. Navarro did, however, deny Pimentel copies of letters written by his opponents to prevent further public discord. Generally, Pimentel remained on good terms with Carvajal and later president-governors, while his gifts to the church improved his public reputation. Most importantly, the loans he made to the royal treasury on the account of the situado guaranteed his continued involvement in the administration of the city and island.[46]

Carvajal served out his full eight-year term, during which the audiencia was somewhat quieter. From Madrid's perspective, it often seemed that the key to ending bitter factionalism was the right combination of ministers, and Martínez de Amileta's promotion to Panama certainly removed a major antagonist.[47] In 1667 visitador Navarro revealed another reason for relative peace in Santo Domingo when he reported that Carvajal and Archbishop de la Cueva were suppressing litigation by barring soldiers and clergy from testifying without their permission. Navarro felt Carvajal was generally an excellent governor, even after looking into Balboa's complaints, but expressed concern about the archbishop's influence, since the prelate was also a vocal defender of Pimentel.[48] The Council of the Indies eventually had Carvajal and de la Cueva reprimanded for impeding the administration of justice. Broadly speaking, public clashes within the audiencia's ranks were less frequent from then until the end of the century, in part because metropolitan authorities were less receptive to letrados' challenges to the president-governor's authority, although more frequent promotions also helped prevent protracted feuds like that of Gómez de Sandoval and Herrera decades earlier.

Local and regional defense occupied much of Carvajal's attention, as international conflict in the Caribbean continued despite a few years of nominal peace in Europe around 1660. Although the French Crown pursued more formal oversight of Tortuga and western Hispaniola, the French inhabitants' relationship with their Spanish neighbors remained mostly antagonistic.[49] Two years after the French attack on Santiago de los Caballeros, Carvajal sent an expedition, led by Juan Morfo, to the western coast in 1662, which killed a captain and took a few prisoners. Carvajal also received news in 1661 of the marriage agreement between the recently restored Charles II of England and Catherine of Braganza, "daughter of the rebel [João IV] of Portugal," with a warning to exercise caution with English ships, giving neither pretext for hostilities nor permission to trade.[50] However, English attacks on Spanish shipping and settlements continued, and Carvajal and the audiencia reported a new assault on Santiago de Cuba in October 1662. The English destroyed part of the town and left a letter from Jamaica's governor defending their use of force over the right to free trade that "God and Nature have permitted and given to all societies of men."[51]

The death of Felipe IV in September 1665 and regency of Mariana of Austria brought little change in the chaotic political situation in the Caribbean, and with limited material support from Spain, Carvajal and other governors in the district attempted to coordinate regional defense. Fighting between England and France also impacted Spanish Hispaniola, as in 1666 when a group of Irish families expelled from Saint Christopher by the French arrived from Puerto Rico and were sent to Spain.[52] Given the uncertainty of these years, Carvajal requested further instructions regarding the English, and in 1669 the Crown ordered him to announce that the current peace with England did not apply in the Indies, so the Spanish could freely retaliate against aggressions.[53] Metropolitan authorities hoped such limited hostilities might enable the recovery of lost territory in the Caribbean by local commanders acting on their own initiative, although this gamble nearly always worked out to Spain's detriment.

Meanwhile, Atlantic and regional shipping to Hispaniola grew increasingly unreliable, and unofficial or emergency arrivals to the port became an even more important lifeline for residents. The annual situado payment often failed to arrive, and a 1664 junta of the audiencia and treasury officials reported that they had only received one situado in three years, which did not include funds for missed years or fortifications. They stressed their efforts to avoid taking forced loans from residents, who either had little to give or had already loaned considerable sums to the royal treasury.[54] Hispaniola was also hit by natural disasters, particularly in 1666 when a major storm followed an epidemic that killed much of the enslaved population, causing additional deaths and destroying buildings and crops, even as a cacao blight wiped out one of the few viable exports. For these reasons, the audiencia's ministers suspended orders to collect a monetary donation (*donativo general*) from inhabitants, although they and the treasury officials contributed what they could.[55] New hurricanes followed in 1668 and 1672, plus an earthquake in 1673, and economic output and external trade sank to new lows. Despite numerous appeals for royal aid to rebuild export production, Spanish

Hispaniola relied heavily on livestock raising and subsistence farming for the rest of the century.[56]

Independently of the audiencia, Carvajal tried to compensate for a drop in imports of enslaved Africans by overseeing the conquest of several maroon settlements (generally called *manieles*) in the Sierra del Maniel between 1665 and 1667. His reports took credit for killing or removing up to 460 former captives in these mountain refuges and destroying communities that had existed for a century or more at no cost to the treasury.[57] Yet the royal approval this earned Carvajal did not shield him from being reprimanded along with the rest of the audiencia for the acuerdo's 1667 decision to blockade the convent of Santa Clara to force the nuns to surrender a woman accused of scandalous behavior. The queen regent was unconvinced by their claims that they were defending the Crown's privileges, and she declared their actions "unworthy of ministers [she had] named to administer justice and give an example to the rest," fining Carvajal, oidores Vélez Mantilla and Pedro de Carvajal y Vargas, and fiscal Juan Pizarro Cajal y Monrroy 1,000 pesos each.[58]

Carvajal's relations with the audiencia were reasonably cooperative to the end of his time in office, and he was replaced by Ignacio Zayas Bazán without incident in 1671. In Zayas's nomination, metropolitan authorities emphasized Hispaniola's strategic importance, since "in addition to being invaded by corsairs, the French have a foothold on the northern part of the island, which should be cause for great concern." By summer 1672, Carvajal was in Madrid providing up-to-date information on Santo Domingo's defenses.[59] Around this period, the volume of correspondence coming from the president-governor began to increase markedly in comparison to that from letrado ministers or the entire tribunal; even so, the lack of extant letters from any audiencia members for all of 1670 and much of 1671 suggests particularly unsafe seas during these years.

Changes in the oidores' ranks during the 1670s reflect the difficulty of managing overseas administration from Madrid. In 1672 the Council of the Indies restored oidor Andrés Caballero to the audiencia with full seniority after nearly a decade of effective suspension from office, though he died roughly a year later.[60] Two years later, oidor Agustín Félix Maldonado de Salazar derailed metropolitan arrangements when he declined a promotion to fiscal of Guadalajara due to poor health. Since Jerónimo Chacón Abarca had already been sent to replace him, the Cámara had to rearrange the tribunal's roster to move Maldonado to either Caballero's now-vacant position or the place of a recent nominee for oidor who was made fiscal of Panama before departing. In 1676 Maldonado was again promoted, this time to oidor of Guadalajara, although his replacement, Juan Palacios de la Bastida, asked to take possession even if Maldonado declined again. Maldonado did move to Guadalajara, but in this instance the Cámara's members sought to avoid creating a temporary, supernumerary position with a new salary. Despite its low status, the Dominican tribunal was fully part of the complex system of overseas bureaucratic patronage.[61]

The 1670 Treaty of Madrid with England meant the president-governor and audiencia had to communicate cautiously with English officials in the region. After notifying Jamaica of this peace in mid-1671, Zayas Bazán reported that its governor and most of the inhabitants of Port Royal had welcomed the news; however, "the general [Henry Morgan] and leaders of the pirates"—just back from Panama and plotting new attacks—"threw down their canes and swords, howling like beasts." Meanwhile, Thomas Lynch, the incoming governor of Jamaica, wrote Zayas to affirm cordial relations and offer reinforcements of men or munitions, especially against the French. Zayas's reply (translated into Latin by oidor Maldonado) expressed his hopes that Lynch would work to restrain the "piracies, robberies, and damages" outlawed by the treaty.[62]

This peace also offered tempting opportunities for illicit trade. In January 1672, Zayas Bazán reported that two English vessels had come to Santo Domingo requesting supplies, then complained when a junta he led granted them provisions but denied them entry to the port. The exasperated president argued that the treaty's provision for aiding vessels in distress made trade inevitable and gave the English a pretext for claiming he was violating its terms. He was later reprimanded and fined, along with the audiencia ministers and treasury officials, for a similar case involving a Portuguese captain who arrived in mid-1671 and was permitted to sell his battered vessel and its cargo. Zayas Bazán melodramatically proclaimed he "would have retired to a convent" out of shame were he not married, while the oidores simply asked for their fines to be excused due to poverty.[63] In general, though, the Council of the Indies' insistence on strict observance of orders barring foreign trade was not easy to reconcile with the nature of emergency arrivals, Santo Domingo's lack of shipping, or local hunger for trade of any kind.

Apart from a heated clash between the audiencia and Archbishop Juan de Escalante Turcios y Mendoza in 1675 and 1676, Zayas Bazán's administration was not marked by serious personal conflicts. When he died in mid-1677, oidor Maldonado became interim president-governor, though days later, after hearing of his promotion to Guadalajara, he ceded the position to Juan Padilla Guardiola y Guzmán, to the city cabildo's relief.[64] Padilla, who served over a year, industriously used his new military and political powers to add to his service record and improve his prospects for advancement. Padilla followed up on information provided by Zayas Bazán by sending the council an intercepted French plan to seize Hispaniola and Florida with possible naval support from the Count d'Estrées, who had recently captured Tobago from the Dutch. In view of this threat, Padilla rebuilt and extended local fortifications and ordered attacks on the French near Guaba during 1677 and 1678. According to him, some sixty men chased off two hundred French cattle hunters in the first attack, killing twenty and burning three thousand hides. The second group of Spanish was surprised by eight hundred French troops a day before they finished assembling, but the roughly 270 men already there drove them off; as a result, Padilla claimed, the French governor overestimated Spanish defensive strength.[65] Fresh rumors about the imminent arrival of d'Estrées's armada made Padilla recall these forces before they could destroy French settlements, but his reports—which he was also ordered to send to the viceroy in Mexico—were used to formulate Spain's response to the organization of French Saint-Domingue.[66]

As the French population multiplied, enslaved Africans took advantage of the two nations' conflict by fleeing to the Spanish side for shelter, which Padilla felt was worth encouraging to undermine the enemy. Previously, these refugees were hired out to Spanish inhabitants as wage laborers, though their wages were rarely paid. In October 1677, Padilla wrote that he had set apart some unused land to be settled by about fifty former captives so that others would want to escape from the French and bolster Spanish defenses. This later became the town of San Lorenzo de los Negros de Mina. The Crown approved, and two years later fiscal Juan Garcés de los Fayos reported that this policy was having the desired effect. Such initiatives as acting president-governor eventually helped earn Padilla promotions to Guadalajara and Mexico.[67]

During these years, letters from the Dominican tribunal's ministers also emphasized the island's poverty and their limited authority outside of Hispaniola. In September 1677, Garcés de los Fayos said their relator, procurator for the poor, doorman, and other auxiliary officials were all threatening to quit over nonpayment of their salaries, partly because the audiencia was unable to collect fines in Venezuela. A month later, he and Padilla again claimed that Caracas and Cumaná were disregarding their orders on the pretext that the tribunal was not to authorize district investigations for "minor reasons" (*leves causas*); they suggested moving the audiencia to Caracas or sending an oidor there for an annual visita. In mid-1678 Padilla said no funds had entered the treasury for eleven months, forcing him to borrow 11,000 pesos (to be paid in New Spain).[68] At the municipal cabildo's request, the audiencia wrote to confirm the islanders' abject poverty and ask for ships to buy their produce, though they did not go as far as Archbishop Domingo Fernández Navarrete, who suggested open foreign trade. The audiencia generally sympathized with residents' complaints of economic isolation, while Navarrete characterized their poverty as largely "voluntary," arguing that many "wanted to live their whole lives in idleness," and consumed "silks, lace, and foreign goods" yet claimed they had nothing to eat. In response, the council ordered the audiencia to seek a "remedy for the laziness and luxury of the principal subjects."[69]

The next president-governor, Francisco de Segura Sandoval y Castilla, relieved Padilla in autumn 1678. The following spring, he wrote that new orders for the oidores to attend musters and help ensure troop numbers remained full were making them interfere with his government, though this did not seem to provoke new jurisdictional or personal clashes. Instead, the Council of the Indies rescinded these orders after receiving his letter, and Segura later praised the cooperation of Garcés de los Fayos, now an oidor.[70] The tribunal's main problem during Segura's presidency was a shortage of letrados, whether resident ministers or locals who could practice law or serve as temporary judges. Oidores Chacón Abarca and Padilla received promotions in 1678 and 1680, and new nominees for their positions either declined or were moved elsewhere before leaving. In 1681, despite his unusual request to "change estates" and be given an ecclesiastical post, oidor Francisco de Cárdenas was made oidor of Panama, leaving the audiencia with only Garcés de los Fayos and relator Gregorio Semillán Campuzano for several months, since Cárdenas was already in Puerto Rico for a commission. As the only available lawyers in the city were two priests, who could not participate in criminal cases, the Dominican tribunal's ability to dispense royal justice was sharply limited.[71]

One mechanism the Council of the Indies had for managing vacancies was temporarily relocating ministers, especially those under investigation, from other audiencias. Oidor Thomás Pizarro Cortés was sent to Santo Domingo from Guadalajara "in deposit" in March 1680; while illness prevented him from arriving until July 1683, he served on the Dominican tribunal until late 1686, carrying out several district commissions during that time. Another Guatemalan oidor, Benito de Novoa Salgado, did not go to Hispaniola as instructed in 1678 because he was cleared of charges before leaving. Chacón Abarca, sent to Guatemala to fill his place, was allowed to remain as a supernumerary oidor until a permanent position opened up.[72] These relocations were used infrequently and were not particularly effective for resolving staffing problems, as Pizarro Cortés became the court's sole magistrate in March 1685; however, they did reinforce Santo Domingo's connection to the other tribunals and allow the Crown to employ otherwise inactive ministers. A general increase in interim and supernumerary appointments during these years also offered a few Dominican ministers like Chacón Abarca a provisional spot in another audiencia.[73]

Like his predecessors, Segura wrote about local poverty, which moved him to suspend another forced donation in 1678 until at least the arrival of another situado, because residents "did not even have enough to dress themselves, and the principal people leave to live in the countryside for not being able to appear in the city."[74] In 1683, even as Segura requested aid directly from the viceroy of New Spain, the Crown ordered Hispaniola and Puerto Rico's situados moved from Panama back to Mexico, though they were still paid sporadically. Metropolitan advisors did not sound overly concerned about limited shipping between Santo Domingo and Spain; a 1680 royal letter noted that one vessel had recently received a license to go to Hispaniola and that others could freely request them. Yet resident officials remained responsible for strictly enforcing commercial restrictions, and in spring 1679 Segura reported that he had carried out instructions to fine the treasury officials for negligence in ship inspections while confirming other orders to assist Portuguese vessels in distress without permitting them to trade.[75]

Ongoing war with France finally ended in the fall of 1678 with the Treaty of Nijmegen, which was not announced in Santo Domingo until April 1680.

The fragility of this peace was readily apparent when the long-feared armada of the Count d'Estrées, reduced to nine warships, came to the port that July. Segura deflected the French vice-admiral's requests for low-status prisoners or permission to take on water in the Haina River, which he saw as a transparent attempt at reconnaissance. Likewise, whether in his exchanges with d'Estrées or in his letter about the treaty to the governor of Saint-Domingue Jacques Neveu de Pouancey, Segura carefully failed to acknowledge any French settlements other than Tortuga (of limited importance by then) to maintain Spain's legal claims; however, he informed the king that "in reality" there were seventeen on the main island.[76] The French governor played his own game, and his response stressed both his desire for peace and the impossibility of giving away land the French had held "by right of conquest" for over thirty-four years. He invited Segura to agree on a boundary largely to strengthen French claims to this territory. Frank Peña Pérez argues that Nijmegen marked de facto recognition of the French presence, which was later formalized, but the two governors did not alter these positions in later correspondence.[77]

Segura's fall from grace was set up by a Dutch captain who turned out to be a pirate. Nikolaas van Hoorn arrived at Santo Domingo with an English ship in late 1682 to request water and provisions, but the treasury officials caught him trying to sell African captives and opened proceedings against him. Despite the evidence, Segura—advised by an aged Rodrigo Pimentel—allowed Van Hoorn to leave port in January 1683 after surrendering twenty-four slaves, valued at a substantial 6,000 pesos, as security. Van Hoorn reportedly sailed off cursing the Spanish and promising to burn Santiago de Cuba in retaliation, which Segura regarded as an idle threat but still relayed to the governor in Havana. In May 1683, Van Hoorn and another pirate, Laurens de Graaf, captured and sacked Veracruz for five days, leaving with up to 3 million pesos' worth of silver, gold, indigo, cochineal, and other valuables plus some 1,500 prisoners, according to initial reports. Blame fell squarely on Segura, and the Council of the Indies suspended him immediately and sent Simón Ibáñez, an oidor-elect of Santa Fe promised a place in Mexico as incentive, to investigate and punish him.[78]

Segura's nominally interim replacement Andrés de Robles—who received the full salary and served for six years—arrived in June 1684, around the same time as Ibáñez. Within months, the investigation revealed Segura had known of Van Hoorn's piratical activities and colluded with Pimentel and his allies to profit from illicit trade. Ibáñez sentenced the former president to death and loss of goods, although the execution was never actually carried out. Segura wrote that Ibáñez was prejudiced against him and proceeded too hastily, and the king ordered him to be freed from prison, placed somewhere "decent," and paid his outstanding salary in 1685 while his case was under review.[79] Ibáñez also condemned the treasury officials to two years' suspension, though they protested that the peace with England prevented them from inspecting Van Hoorn's ship. Gregorio Semillán Campuzano, the audiencia's relator and *promotor fiscal* (treasury prosecutor) for Ibáñez's investigation, said local supporters of Segura and the treasury officials were furious with him because of these sentences, suggesting there was a standing arrangement to overlook irregular trade.[80]

At this time, the Council of the Indies was also searching for ways to populate Spanish Hispaniola as the numbers of French continued to grow.[81] They had considered proposals to resettle Canary Islanders since at least 1663 and by late 1683 were making concrete arrangements to transport one hundred Isleño families (despite complaints from Seville's Consulado, a powerful merchants' association, about the incentives the council offered). In October 1684, captain Ignacio Pérez Caro at last arrived at Santa Cruz de Tenerife, where 534 individuals "embarked gladly" for the voyage to Santo Domingo. The following March, president-governor Robles reported that Pérez Caro had delivered them safely and departed, although some migrants later described this resettlement as a traumatic experience. Plans for an annual transport never materialized, but this marked the early phase of a long-term movement of Isleños to Hispaniola, which would help drive a moderate population increase toward the end of the century.[82] Pérez Caro assisted Robles while he was there and made a later trip to the island with supplies and a vessel to be rebuilt into patrol ships, but his 1684 voyage was his introduction to the city he would return to as president-governor six years later.[83]

Robles faced piracy and contraband trade during his time in office, as he had previously done while governing Buenos Aires. He received numerous intelligence reports from Spain and other parts of the Caribbean about regional threats; for example, in April 1685 a royal letter warned that eighteen ships, some with French patents and others on their own account, had departed Vlissingen the previous summer to "go pirate" in the Indies, while other vessels from England, Brittany, Rotterdam, and Amsterdam came seeking trade or plunder. Although Robles initially boasted that foreign traders "will have very poor success in this island as long as I govern it," his attitude was somewhat more complex two years later.[84] In 1687 he wrote that local inhabitants were lacking in "love and zeal" but their trade with English and Dutch merchants—practiced "even more openly in the other islands and mainland"—was mainly the result of a lack of clothing, as it had been nearly three years since an officially registered ship had arrived. He did not condone illicit trade but asked for Spanish ships to bring "enough clothing for a year" to stop foreigners from carrying off the island's limited wealth. The Council of the Indies did consider ordering annual voyages to Hispaniola but dropped the matter on finding that a new ship had obtained a license to go there.[85] To the great relief of both Santo Domingo and Madrid, a substantial situado payment of 122,000 pesos arrived from Mexico soon afterward, plus another 80,000-peso payment the following year. Yet after a few years of reduced or missed situados, the treasury was again empty.[86]

Late in the century, the Crown continued to try to address Santo Domingo's military and economic problems within the limits of available resources. In March 1686 the council's president, the Marquis of los Vélez, requested and received Carlos II's approval for a special junta to review and discuss proposals concerning Hispaniola. This junta, which met at his lodgings, included three members of the Council of the Indies best informed about the island, three members of the Council of War, and the secretary of New Spain. Their high status indicates that the metropolitan bureaucracy was genuinely willing to entertain extraordinary measures to confront the French and preserve and restore Hispaniola. Even so, their interest in ideas like Manuel de Fonseca's plan for a commercial association in the Spanish Netherlands to trade with and repopulate Hispaniola and Puerto Rico was neutralized by wrangling over logistics and vehement opposition from the Consulado. With the outbreak of war with France in 1689, responsibility for defending the island largely reverted to the president-governor.[87]

Lack of personnel continued to trouble the audiencia under Robles, who asked shortly after arriving that ministers who had been promoted elsewhere be required to attend audiencia sessions until their departure. At that time, three former oidores were still drawing salaries while waiting for transportation, leaving only oidor Pizarro Cortés and the frequently ill fiscal Joseph de Salazar to carry out business, which Robles said greatly delayed the judicial process. His request was granted, allowing the audiencia to benefit from Hispaniola's poor maritime communications, as outgoing ministers were often delayed months or years.[88] Robles himself complained of health problems in 1685 and asked for permission to leave his post but was instead given the rank of general of artillery as an incentive to stay. When Pizarro Cortés left for commissions in Cuba in late 1686, oidor Fernando de la Riva Agüero became the only resident magistrate, as the other recently named letrados had either not yet left Spain or were occupied with district investigations. Even when new appointees arrived in 1687, two oidores temporarily refused to take possession over a seniority dispute.[89]

Jurisdictional and personal conflict among audiencia members still happened under Robles but was less dramatic than earlier in the century. Rodrigo Pimentel's death in 1683 removed an important source of discord, though local elites continued to be intimately involved in the tribunal's affairs.[90] The 1680 *Recopilación de Indias*—copies of which reached Hispaniola in early 1683—also helped forestall some procedural disputes, and the audiencia regularly referred to it from then on. Robles himself sometimes butted heads with the letrados, although he was the one reprimanded after blaming oidor Pizarro Cortés for failing to cooperate in a decision about unregistered goods in a ship from Cartagena.[91] In 1687, instead of following instructions to ship oidor Fernando de Araujo y Rivera to Spain for taking his mistress to Margarita, Robles put her in a convent and allowed Araujo to stay due to a lack of judges; he was again rebuked for disobeying orders. Araujo may still have resented Robles, who later asked that Araujo be accompanied by another oidor for his 1690 residencia. While this oidor, Diego Antonio de Oviedo y Baños, was generally more lenient, both held Robles responsible for foreign trade and shoddy work on the crumbling city walls and fined him some 30,000 pesos. Ultimately, the Council of the Indies overturned many of their condemnations for lack of proof or in view of the logistical challenges Robles faced.[92]

The last two president-governors of the century, Ignacio Pérez Caro and Severino de Manzaneda, represented an experiment with selling this post followed by its decisive remilitarization. Pérez Caro, the captain who had brought Canary Islanders to Hispaniola in 1684, was the only superior minister of the Dominican audiencia to openly purchase his office during the seventeenth century. He did so primarily to extract some benefit from his previous services to the Crown, which had left him with little more than the title of admiral and increasingly worthless claims to compensation. In late 1689 Pérez Caro agreed to pay the Crown 32,120 pesos *escudos*—12,000 in cash and the rest in canceled debts—and was granted the position of president.[93] However, his lack of a military background plus the way he acquired the office made him vulnerable to accusations of self-interest, even though his behavior was not substantially different from that of earlier president-governors.

Pérez Caro joined an audiencia that was still shorthanded. In 1691 they reported on their difficulties sentencing criminal suits involving bodily injury, which required three judges, but the only temporary magistrates available were clergy members, who were barred from these cases. The Council of the Indies responded that two unanimous votes would be sufficient (though more were preferable whenever possible), and that judges with less formal qualifications could make decisions for minor offenses. The oidores also complained that their inability to pay bailiffs to carry their staff of office (*vara*) meant they were reduced to patrolling the streets without proper support; indeed, Oviedo's personal servants had broken up a recent sword fight in the street. The council's reply—"customary practice is to be kept"—signaled their aversion to new expenses.[94]

Since Santo Domingo only had two permanent oidores, both constantly ill, Pérez Caro took some liberties with his 1692 orders to retire supernumerary oidores and give them half pay, and he kept Oviedo on at full salary to avoid "grave detriment to the administration of justice." For the same reasons, he permitted another supernumerary appointee, oidor Sebastián de Cereceda y Girón, to collect his entire salary after arriving in 1695. The council approved of Oviedo's continuation and moved him to a numerary position, but in Cereceda y Girón's case, Pérez Caro was told to restore half of his pay to the treasury. By that time they had already decided to remove Pérez Caro from office, yet these exchanges illustrate how metropolitan efforts to restrict the sale of judicial offices were tempered by conditions overseas.[95]

Despite his lack of experience, Pérez Caro assumed the military responsibilities of his office on arriving in mid-1690, when war with France was ongoing. This included following up on Robles's work to reconstitute the two troops that patrolled the island's interior, improving the city's fortifications, and reviewing the presidio soldiers. A month later, some nine hundred French troops marched on Santiago de los Caballeros—previously a connection point for contraband trade—and offered the residents a choice between pledging allegiance to France or being put to the sword. After minor engagements with Spanish forces, they burned down part of the city and retreated before Pérez Caro could dispatch reinforcements. Santiago's cabildo wrote Pérez Caro and asked to move elsewhere for safety, though the president-governor sent additional soldiers and later visited in person to survey the defenses and encourage residents to remain.[96]

The Spanish counterattacked in early 1691 with naval support from the Armada de Barlovento following months of planning and some frontier skirmishes. As commander, Pérez Caro chose ex-president Segura Sandoval, who sent three hundred lanceros to reinforce the armada, then led nine hundred troops overland. They met the French on January 21 at el Limonar del Guárico (Limonade to the French) and decisively defeated them, killing the governor Pierre-Paul Tarin de Cussy and several hundred of his men. Next, the armada's forces helped secure the region, as most of the French inhabitants fled toward Port-de-Paix. Spain's victory was celebrated on and off the island; Pérez Caro described it as Hispaniola's "most glorious" day in thirty-five years, while Mexican intellectual Carlos de Sigüenza y Góngora published a detailed account of it later that year.[97]

Segura received credit, and his daughter was later able to obtain Crown aid, although he died before another attempt the following spring (apparently still formally a prisoner). Local soldiers, however, were upset that the armada got most of the plunder from the 1691 attack, and many deserted for fear that the commander of the 1692 expedition, Pedro Morel de Santa Cruz, intended to keep any spoils for himself. An unsigned letter to the Council of the Indies' president, presumed to be from oidor Araujo, accused Morel of cowardice and claimed that Pérez Caro wanted military help from the English on Jamaica and the Dutch on Curaçao as a cover for foreign trade. Araujo, along with treasurer Juan Mariño de Crestelo, did sign other letters from April 1691 onward criticizing these campaigns and accusing Pérez Caro of misusing royal funds, allowing contraband, and—most seriously—returning ninety English "pirates" to the Jamaican governor. By early 1692, the council was questioning Pérez Caro's suitability as governor of the island their fiscal called "the only rampart of the Indies."[98]

Pérez Caro did not help his case by writing the Mexican viceroy in 1692, asking for money and troops and outlining his plans for fighting the French. Since the Armada de Barlovento only had small ships, Pérez Caro proposed asking Jamaica's governor, who was also facing French depredations, for naval support to help eradicate the French from Hispaniola. Viceroy Galve told Pérez Caro in no uncertain terms to avoid "dangerous" correspondence with foreign governors unless absolutely necessary, but he did send 70,000 pesos (less than Pérez Caro wanted but "more than what was possible in the present state of the royal treasury") to maintain pressure on the French. Galve also forwarded Pérez Caro's letter and his response to Spain.[99]

Before this point, the viceroy of New Spain had no real oversight of Hispaniola, even though metropolitan authorities had begun encouraging regional coordination. In 1691 Galve himself found it "impractical" to send a treasury official to Santo Domingo to review troops and did not appear to want new responsibilities in the Caribbean.[100] Nonetheless, Pérez Caro's ill-considered suggestions, while framed as military pragmatism, led to a loss of authority for both president-governor and audiencia. In early 1693 the Council of the Indies reinforced Galve's warning and notified Pérez Caro they had named a *cabo subalterno* (assistant or "subordinate" commander) for his office, so he would not have to leave the city undefended by leading campaigns in person. This new official would outrank all other resident commanders, preventing competition with local officers and would also take over as interim president, governor, and captain-general instead of the senior oidor. Plans for a joint English operation against Saint-Domingue were actually in motion by then, but the decision to work with foreign allies had to come from the metropole, not overseas officials acting on their own initiative.[101]

The first cabo subalterno, Gil Correoso Catalán, was a career military man who had previously governed Santiago de Cuba. Predictably, audiencia ministers protested that this new position infringed on their privileges. Pérez Caro, while promising to cooperate with Correoso, also complained about the viceroy's power to name an interim replacement for the cabo subalterno. He argued that presidents of praetorian audiencias had always filled such vacancies without a viceroy's interference, just as the audiencia had the right to fill his position in case of his death. Pérez Caro perceived—correctly—that his reputation was at stake, since he was the reason for the loss of these customary privileges, even though he claimed credit for giving the Spanish more victories in three years than Hispaniola, or "all of America," had seen in thirty years.[102] However, active war increased metropolitan advisors' estimation of the island's strategic importance, and the Council of the Indies ignored Pérez Caro's praise for the accomplishments of previous interim president-governors since they had decided that structural changes were required to ensure military commanders always oversaw Hispaniola's defense.[103]

Meanwhile, Correoso sought to maximize his position's prestige even before departing—ostensibly to ensure obedience from soldiers and military officials—and was granted the title of "teniente de maestro de campo general." After arriving in early 1694, he alienated the magistrates by demanding the place immediately after the president in public functions to display his symbolic superiority to them, the cabildo, and all other local authorities. Eventually, the council decided that he should appear behind the senior oidor unless acting as governor, though negotiations about other privileges continued.[104]

News of a planned Anglo-Spanish operation caught Dominican officials by surprise in April 1695, after over a year without letters from the Crown.[105] The English squadron arrived at Santo Domingo later that month, followed by the Armada de Barlovento. A junta of Pérez Caro, the letrado audiencia ministers, and Spanish naval officers set guidelines for working with the English, and then starting in late July, the combined forces captured Guárico (Cap-François to the French, modern Cap-Haïtien) and Port-de-Paix. Throughout this campaign, the Spanish were warned to watch for English treachery, especially in claiming territory taken from the French. Relations between the allies nearly turned violent after naval forces under Admiral Robert Wilmot seized the opportunity to loot Port-de-Paix. Certainly, there was no great love between the two sides; Archbishop Fernando de Carvajal y Rivera recounted with relish the claim of Laurens de Graaf's wife that, had the Spanish not been there, the French women alone could have beaten the English to death. After the sack of Port-de-Paix, however, it was clear that this alliance could not last, and the English forces departed.

The joint offensive did cause significant though not irreparable damage to Saint-Domingue, but in the long run France had greater resources than Spain for sustained warfare.[106]

The operation further strained relations between Correoso and Pérez Caro, who complained to Viceroy Galve and the king that Correoso forced him to "beg news" from others instead of sending reports and ended the campaign with no consultation. When an unspecified "accident" left him briefly unconscious, Pérez Caro became more concerned about Correoso's possible succession and tried to convince metropolitan authorities that the cabo subalterno was too old to serve as temporary president-governor.[107] For his part, Correoso did not consider Pérez Caro a valid military superior.

The situation changed drastically in 1696, when Correoso was ordered to arrest Pérez Caro until he could be investigated. Severino de Manzaneda y Salinas, the interim governor of Cuba named as his replacement, did not receive the news until later (possibly thanks to Pérez Caro's allies) and did not actually reach Santo Domingo until mid-1698. Until then, Correoso was acting governor, captain-general, and president, occasionally alternating with his second-in-command Gaspar de Arredondo, a former governor of Puerto Rico, when he was out of the city.[108] Communications between Madrid and Hispaniola were particularly difficult in these years; the orders for Pérez Caro's removal came nearly four years after the initial concerns of the Council of the Indies, which was not sure whether Correoso was still alive in 1696.[109]

Open factional conflicts again affected the audiencia during the 1690s, even though it rarely had more than two resident letrado ministers. The complaints of oidor Araujo, treasurer Mariño, and sargento mayor Joseph de Piña were the basis for Pérez Caro's arrest, while Pérez Caro claimed Araujo, a countryman of Mariño, was negligent, hostile, and untrustworthy, and Piña was completely incompetent.[110] Sending new magistrates proved challenging, however. When Cereceda y Girón, who had been granted a future place on the audiencia, was appointed oidor in 1695, all its positions were technically filled. The king had recently halted concessions of future places, but Santo Domingo's fiscal was in Spain, two oidores were in Caracas and Cuba, and there were no local letrados even to act as relator, greatly delaying judicial matters. Metropolitan efforts to get a lawyer to move there failed, so the Cámara agreed that Cereceda y Girón could serve as supernumerary oidor with half salary until a permanent place opened up, since he was qualified. Cereceda y Girón arrived that September, and within a month he and fiscal Pedro Marín y Muñoz were the only resident letrado ministers.[111]

At the same time, military expenses made salaries more tenuous than usual.[112] In 1694 the Crown told Pérez Caro to collect another donation for European wars, but in consultation with the audiencia and the archbishop he decided that local residents had already helped fight the French and instead offered 4,000 pesos from the recent campaign against Saint-Domingue, discounted from situado payments. Pérez Caro also said he would follow instructions for all royal officials to give a third of their salaries to the Crown but noted that his fellow ministers would be disappointed and that his salary could not cover his daughter's vows to enter a convent in Seville.[113] In May 1698, Correoso reported there had been no situados for three years, and though he had been trying to keep up monthly infantry payments using loans from residents, they were now nearly bankrupt and desertions were rising. He also complained that, a year earlier, oidores Cereceda y Girón and Diego Bartolomé Bravo de Añaya had gotten a friend in the treasury to pay them before the soldiers, despite his suspension of their salaries. Correoso's own request for full pay for his twenty-three months as interim president-governor was rejected by the audiencia and not reviewed in Spain before his death, suggesting the Crown did not see him as the equal of Robles or Manzaneda (both nominally interim appointees), or previous officeholders.[114]

The extraordinary disappearance of Archbishop Carvajal y Rivera in 1698 reinforces a sense of desperation in royal ministers' letters. For nearly a decade, the prelate sent increasingly emphatic reports about the island's grim moral and economic condition, even railing against the Council of the Indies, the House of Trade, and the Consulado—"that evil triumvirate of Seville, son and heir of that ancient one composed of Caiphas, Herod, and Pilate"—for trade restrictions.[115] After being denied permission to return to Spain, he retreated to the countryside, then crossed the Atlantic to France in a small ship and traveled to Madrid, all the while writing about Hispaniola, which remained without a resident archbishop for several years.[116]

Manzaneda took over as president-governor in mid-1698, making him responsible for the delicate task of observing the 1697 Treaty of Ryswick with France, which ended the war but left territorial boundaries in the Caribbean deliberately ambiguous. Although James Pritchard asserts that the treaty "finally acknowledged French sovereignty over the western portion of Hispaniola," the Spanish were still insisting that France's occupation of this territory was illegitimate years later.[117] Manzaneda was expected to prevent the French from expanding further and push them back if possible without provoking hostilities or revealing his orders to this effect. Certainly, despite this diplomatic game, the French retained effective possession of Saint-Domingue. Yet from the perspective of Madrid and Santo Domingo, these technicalities mattered, and at the turn of the century the Spanish harbored at least faint hopes of recapturing the entire island.[118]

At the same time, Manzaneda investigated Pérez Caro—eventually levying major penalties, though his sentences were overturned in 1704 and Pérez Caro was restored to office—and fought with oidor Cereceda y Girón, who had become the audiencia's sole magistrate months after Manzaneda's arrival. Their relationship rapidly degenerated as they reprised a familiar kind of military-letrado conflict.[119] Cereceda y Girón claimed, writing personally and as the audiencia, that Manzaneda was needlessly antagonistic and publicly undermined the tribunal's reputation; in addition to overstepping his jurisdiction while blocking the audiencia from reviewing his decisions, the president also harassed the court's relator (and one of its only lawyers) Francisco de la Sota Palacios until he took refuge in the Mercedarian convent. According to the president, however, Cereceda y Girón was in league with local merchants (many of them Pérez Caro's allies) and slandered Manzaneda to obscure his own involvement in illicit trade. He also explained that Sota Palacios was a deserter from Puerto Rico and Cereceda y Girón's dependent, who was appointed lawyer and temporary relator without proof of his studies.[120] The Council of the Indies approved of how Manzaneda had handled foreign trade, relations with the French, and Cereceda y Girón's habitual tardiness but also severely chastised both men, warning them to cooperate and avoid making innovations contrary to royal law.[121] It is not clear this had much effect.

Their dispute does reflect the audiencia's return to a seminormal routine after the Nine Years' War. Manzaneda and Cereceda y Girón continued to attend to the tribunal's business, and letters they signed together as the audiencia show they maintained some pretense at collaboration even though their mutual hatred continued.[122] Parallels with the disagreements between oidor Pedro Sanz Morquecho and president-governor Diego de Osorio a hundred years earlier are more than coincidence and underscore how such tensions were inherent to the composition of the Dominican tribunal.

In general, although Hispaniola and the Caribbean experienced dramatic changes during the seventeenth century, the Audiencia of Santo Domingo was marked by substantial continuity, despite its connections to major events and developments in this time: the depopulations of 1605–6, the 1655 English invasion, the rise of French Saint-Domingue, or the collapse of export production later in the century. A conjunction of factors in the 1690s—including metropolitan interest in reform, Pérez Caro's purchase of office, and war with the French—led to one significant structural change, the creation of the cabo subalterno, so that oidores no longer acted as temporary governors. This lasting militarization of the president-governor's position, driven by concerns over the vulnerability of Santo Domingo, foreshadowed a broader rejection of the sale of overseas governorships in the first part of the eighteenth century. Even so, the loss of these privileges still did not allow Dominican president-governors to dominate the audiencia, and military-letrado friction continued into the eighteenth century.[123]

Madrid's difficulties in managing the Dominican audiencia's personnel seem to have increased in the 1680s as the numbers of office-seekers rose and audiencia positions became available for purchase, particularly in higher-status tribunals.[124] Yet this difference was largely one of degree; the Council of the Indies had faced complications from unexpected deaths, district commissions, reports of abuses, or slow and unreliable communication long before this point. While there was no new visita general during the period covered in this chapter, Ubilla's commissions or the protracted investigations of Balboa Mogrovejo and Pérez Caro represented similar problems in overseeing the conduct of the tribunal's ministers. Broadly speaking, the challenges of metropolitan oversight for the audiencia remained relatively consistent from 1600 to 1700.

The audiencia's correspondence seems to support a well-worn narrative of crisis and decline for Spanish Hispaniola, especially in the later seventeenth century, but from a broader imperial perspective the island's problems appear less exceptional.[125] Issues like poor communication and local poverty affected many parts of the Spanish Caribbean, like Margarita or Florida, while enemy attacks and contraband trade also marked the even more remote Philippine and Chilean audiencias.[126] Despite more reliable pay and better living conditions, officials in wealthier districts like Charcas, Quito, Peru, or New Spain still complained about overburdened treasuries and pursued various methods of self-enrichment.[127] Likewise, although letters from the Dominican audiencia tend to emphasize international conflict, the history of the seventeenth-century Spanish Caribbean was more than just a failure to halt foreign encroachment. The increasing presence of non-Spaniards on and around Hispaniola created informal and enduring commercial connections that Spanish residents came to rely on. However, if local claims of poverty and isolation were not unique, they were still grounded in the experiences of the seventeenth century, and the Dominican tribunal played a crucial role in conveying these narratives to the metropole and supporting genuine (though rarely successful) efforts to revitalize Hispaniola.[128]

The overview of the Audiencia of Santo Domingo in this and the preceding chapter also usefully illustrates the general messiness of the overseas audiencia system in operation, as opposed to the portrait offered by royal laws. Shortages of resident ministers were common, and personal clashes among the tribunal's officials were characteristic of Habsburg bureaucracy at all levels. These may have exasperated metropolitan authorities but strengthened audiencia members' dependence on the figure of the king.[129] The constantly changing body of officials who staffed a shorthanded and divided tribunal in Santo Domingo, who struggled over precedence and jurisdiction, and who were often motivated by self-interest, represented the face of royal justice in the Caribbean. For all their shortcomings, the monarch and Council of the Indies felt they met the needs of the district well enough to preserve the same basic framework across the entire century. The next two chapters will focus on how the audiencia cooperated and conflicted with other authorities in the city and in the wider region during this time.

4

Local Institutions

Within Santo Domingo, the audiencia regularly interacted with several other secular and ecclesiastical authorities and institutions that constituted the machinery of overseas administration. These included the audiencia's own president in his capacity as governor and captain-general, the treasury officials, the municipal cabildo, and religious figures and bodies from the archbishop and canons of the city's cathedral to convents and hospitals. However, the divisions between their powers and rights were in practice often ambiguous, leading to occasional disputes. For example, the archbishop was responsible for correcting spiritual transgressions but was supposed to ask the alcaldes ordinarios of the city cabildo or the audiencia to apprehend suspects and make corporal punishments for related crimes. Yet some archbishops rejected this assistance, seeing it as an intrusion into their jurisdiction. Although the audiencia's letrado ministers might feel they were the city's most important royal representatives, the Council of the Indies periodically reminded them of the practical limits of their authority and their duty to cooperate with other institutions.

None of these administrative entities can be separated from its social context; collectively or individually, they do not represent a state that was distinct from local society, as is discussed at greater length in chapter seven.[1] Neither were they always separate from each other; sometime before 1633, Manuel González de Melo served as temporary royal treasurer, the audiencia's registrar, and the city cabildo's *fiel ejecutor* (who handled financial business).[2] Just the same, institutional boundaries mattered, and metropolitan authorities as well as other local officials and city residents regarded the audiencia as a corporate entity, even as they recognized or exploited divisions among its personnel. Jurisdictional and ceremonial contests among institutions offer clues about the nature of royal administration and its relationship to a society it both supervised and belonged to. Their status was continually reestablished in the public arena of Santo Domingo and, like jurisdiction, could be lost permanently if challenges were not contested. The audiencia had to actively defend both against other local authorities to preserve what its ministers saw as their rightful role.

The greatest challenges that the letrado members of the audiencia faced during the seventeenth century came from their own presidents. Starting with Lope de Vega Portocarrero in 1587, the capa y espada president-governors in Santo Domingo had military authority over all soldiers and militia troops on the island and responsibility for local and regional defense. While they did not vote in judicial cases before the audiencia, these presidents, governors, and captains-general had numerous options for restricting the tribunal's authority.[3] Hispaniola remained a crucial military outpost throughout this time, and metropolitan authorities gave great weight to claims of military necessity.

The combination of different, complementary powers in a single figure was common throughout Spain's domains; the viceroys in Mexico and Lima, whom Solórzano Pereira called "governors of greater capacity," were but one example. In Santo Domingo, the president-governor was to supervise the audiencia without impeding the magistrates' judicial duties and to consult with them in the acuerdo about major decisions. For their part, the letrados were not to interfere with military matters beyond offering advice.[4] In this way, the audiencia had a share in the president's political authority and could even review some of the decisions he made as governor, though for other matters his decisions were final, subject only to Madrid's approval. However, many seventeenth-century president-governors made a concerted effort to extend their political and military jurisdiction and to prevent any appeals. As military officers, most were accustomed to having the power to command inferiors and envisioned their relationship with the audiencia very differently from their letrado colleagues.

For such reasons, recurring disputes between president-governors and the rest of the tribunal in Santo Domingo were rooted in the structure of imperial administration. Peninsular authorities disapproved of open conflicts, but given their repeated rejection of requests to move the audiencia elsewhere they did not feel it was a serious enough issue to warrant separating the governor from the tribunal. Indeed, the audiencia remained on Hispaniola partly due to defense concerns, since the title of president helped bolster the prestige of a vital but undesirable military posting. If the tribunal did not really hold these men in check, it did make them more accountable to Madrid for their actions. Certainly, jurisdictional disputes and personal squabbles were common throughout Spain's imperial bureaucracy, and subordinate audiencias also fought with their letrado presidents.[5] Just the same, much of the friction between the president and the magistrates in Santo Domingo stemmed from this distinction between military men and letrados.

By the seventeenth century, royal legislation about this relationship was relatively clear. Although the president-governor was not to participate in judicial suits, as governor and captain-general he could issue proclamations or settle disputes related to matters of government (*gobierno*) or war (*guerra*) with the help of a trained jurist acting as legal assistant. Appeals to his governmental decisions went to the audiencia, but his military sentences could only be reviewed by the Junta de Guerra (War Committee) of the Council of the Indies. In cases of doubt, the president had discretionary power to reserve certain suits for himself by declaring which category they belonged to—justice, government, or war—and whether or not the audiencia could get involved. If they did not agree with him, the oidores could inform the Crown, but had to follow his instructions until a response arrived.[6] Yet since many presidents felt that letting the audiencia review any of their decisions or challenge their control over the situado lessened their authority and prestige, they aggressively claimed jurisdiction to forestall appeals, while the magistrates often sought to preserve and expand their oversight of the president-governor.[7]

Diego Gómez de Sandoval's administration provides a useful illustration of this dynamic and of some genuine uncertainty about royal policy. In summer 1609, he adjudicated a dispute among some captains and ship owners over who could load cargo first and then denied appeal to the audiencia by declaring this a governmental matter. The Council of the Indies, after comparing his report with the audiencia's, ordered Gómez de Sandoval in May 1610 to explain his actions, since the Audiencias of Mexico and Lima did receive appeals from the viceroys' governmental decisions.[8] Gómez de Sandoval did not provide details about the suit in question but claimed that in 1590 the king had granted president-governor Vega Portocarrero sole authority over governmental matters due to quarrels about filling interim district positions. According to him, these orders had been repeated for all subsequent presidents, and so the audiencia had not reviewed any of these kinds of decisions; appeals from governmental sentences of the city's alcaldes ordinarios also went to him rather than the audiencia. He also noted that, while many litigants came directly to him to settle judicial disputes, "most or all of the time I have remitted the cases to the audiencia." Finally, he argued, "the aversion [the oidores] have to the will of their head" was such that they would overturn his decisions out of defiance if given the chance, and so allowing appeals would only sow discord.[9]

The Crown's response in September 1611 was uncharacteristically clear: the initial dispute over cargo was a judicial matter and should have gone before the audiencia, as should all similar cases in the future, and in general the king's will was that the tribunal would determine appeals from the president's decisions in governmental cases. Such transatlantic exchanges show that even if Spain had a reasonably stable framework for overseas administration by this point, it continued to be subject to constant adjustments and clarifications, a process also reflected in the 1680 *Recopilación de Indias*.[10] Gómez de Sandoval understood that the shift to a military president-governor in Santo Domingo was a recent innovation but had conflated the powers of his offices. While he retained the sole right to make interim appointments in the audiencia's district (something he complained fiscal Jerónimo de Herrera was interfering with in 1612), his other governmental decisions could be appealed to the audiencia.[11] In this instance, both sides seemed to understand that the president's executive authority—which did give him considerable power to set procedure in the short term—was contingent on metropolitan approval. The letrados opposed Gómez de Sandoval's initial declaration in the acuerdo that the case was governmental and not open to appeal, but they recognized his right to make such declarations and to provisionally override their objections and then exercised their own right to inform the Crown to seek a remedy.

Other uncertainties remained. Around the same time, Gómez de Sandoval also received royal instructions from 1610 confirming that, as captain-general, he was to decide all suits involving the island's military officers and salaried soldiers and that in times of active warfare this authority extended to militia soldiers, including many local elites. These orders expressly forbade the audiencia from interfering with these appeals. Gómez de Sandoval even prematurely thanked the Council of the Indies' secretary for New Spain for what he thought was royal confirmation of his exclusive jurisdiction over matters of war, which he presumed (wrongly, as he soon learned) also applied to governmental cases, and asked the secretary to help maintain the audiencia's subordination and preserve "peace between the head and the members."[12] Gómez de Sandoval's 1616 dispute with oidor Rodrigo de Valcárcel over the imprisonment of a soldier who also worked in the treasury shows he continued to defend his jurisdiction, and his general opinion remained that giving the audiencia too much independence would leave "his hands tied."[13]

Later president-governors shared his concerns about the tribunal's potential to undermine their authority and found other, usually extralegal ways to reduce its reach. In the 1640s, Bitrián and Nicolás de Velasco were accused of ordering notaries and the relator to get their approval before presenting any petitions to the audiencia, even those from the fiscal, ostensibly to stop "indecent" litigation. Oidor Salazar observed that petitions had to be signed by a lawyer, which already limited frivolous suits, and claimed both presidents were simply delaying judicial proceedings, sometimes indefinitely, by holding up petitions. Furthermore, the letrados claimed, Bitrián and Velasco prevented them from consulting the books that recorded royal orders for the audiencia, leaving them ignorant of the king's will. Bitrián also deprived fiscal Francisco de Alarcón Coronado of his separate seat in the audiencia, contrary to royal laws, reducing his ceremonial standing.[14] Andrés Pérez Franco sidestepped jurisdictional debates by repeatedly declaring military emergencies to gain wartime powers. Félix de Zúñiga was probably the most direct in threatening or imprisoning the letrados to bend them to his will between 1656 and 1659, before the Council of the Indies sent Juan de Balboa Mogrovejo to remove him. However, Luis Fernández de Córdoba expressed the feelings of many president-governors when he wrote, in response to challenges from Alarcón Coronado, that if the audiencia could hear appeals from his orders, it would be as if "the subjects were to become superiors, and those who should obey were to give laws to those whose office was to govern them."[15]

Contemporary attitudes about the categorical differences between military officers and bureaucrats are fundamental to understanding these perennial conflicts. Both kinds of men laid claim to honor in the sense of public reputation, as did contemporaries on both sides of the Atlantic at all social levels, but the president-governors—two with the title of "Count"—usually stressed their lineage and willingness to risk their lives for the king. While letrados sometimes used similar language, their reputation was understood in the city as coming primarily from the office granted by the king rather than their own person or family. Practically speaking, in the eyes of elites, soldiers, and president-governors, the letrados were less honorable, a view fed by the increased militarization of the island's society in the later seventeenth century.[16] Francisco Segura Sandoval, protesting 1678 orders for oidores to help supervise troops, asked that military matters be left to men like him "who know how to spill their blood for [his] majesty." Zúñiga was reportedly much more blunt in 1658 when he stressed that his "blood and employment in the sight of an emperor are not like those of some born in a dung heap," meaning oidor Andrés Martínez de Amileta.[17] In his feud with fiscal Herrera, Gómez de Sandoval claimed, "[Since] men of my quality are obligated to serve his majesty with life and property, I do not think it is right to have my honor at risk, finding myself alongside a man so defiant and arrogant that he should oblige me with his words so that, forgetting the obligations of a minister, I should fulfill those of my parents."[18] Physical violence between audiencia members was uncommon, but concern over public disrespect in the mid-1620s drove Diego de Acuña to threaten to knock out oidor Diego Gil de la Sierpe's teeth and to assault oidor Alonso de Cereceda, even pulling his beard "for greater injury."[19]

Unlike president-governors, oidores and fiscales had few options for enforcing their claims to honor, which was readily apparent to city residents. Cereceda suggested that he would have responded to Acuña's attacks in kind were he not an oidor, but even this oblique allusion to a fistfight over honor was unusual for letrados. More typical was Gil de la Sierpe's 1619 claim that fiscal Herrera's insults jeopardized "his honor and reputation" or his 1625 complaint about Acuña's bullying, in which he described himself as "an ant" whose office allowed him to represent the very person of the king thanks to the "justice and liberality of [his] majesty."[20] In 1677 fiscal Juan Garcés de los Fayos wrote about Archbishop Juan de Escalante Turcios y Mendoza's accusations of bigamy, which sullied "the honor of the pure and clean blood that by the mercy of God [he] inherited from [his] parents" and, by extension, publicly disrespected the royal seal. Likewise, after a visita led to his removal from office in 1601, oidor Simón de Meneses claimed he was left without "reputation or honor" after years of diligent service to the king.[21]

Given the multiple ways that seventeenth-century audiencia ministers used the terms *honrra* and *honor*, it is not particularly useful to insist on an overly precise definition of honor, but in the sense of publicly acknowledged status it was a central concern for military presidents. Letrados were keenly aware that president-governors' claims to social preeminence were bolstered by the presidio soldiers they commanded, as oidores Juan Francisco Montemayor and Jerónimo de Alzate pointed out in 1654.[22] Belittling oidores and fiscales allowed president-governors to remind them and residents that soldiers were more important than bureaucrats. Both Zúñiga and Balboa reportedly mocked the magistrates and their robes of office, while Pérez Franco encouraged elites not to attend oidor Diego de Orozco's burial in 1653. Oidor Pedro Luis de Salazar claimed that Juan Bitrián de Biamonte derisively addressed them as "the licenciados," "those men," or "brother acolytes" and once even shouted at them, "I swear to God that you can't even urinate without my permission—here there is nothing more than me."[23]

Visible marks of distinction also reinforced the special status of military presidents, whose higher salaries were partly to permit them to live with fitting decorum. Unlike magistrates, they usually had a carriage to move around the city, though they let audiencia members and others ride with them.[24] Their clothing and symbols of office also differed; both Ignacio Zayas Bazán and Segura Sandoval had to be told to stop carrying their staff of command (*bastón*) during audiencia and acuerdo sessions and to dress in black with a starched collar (*golilla*) rather than in military garb, no matter what their predecessors had done. Segura, unhappy about these orders, argued without success that changing clothes in the Dominican heat was unhealthful and would prevent him from attending to matters of war quickly.[25]

In 1609 Dominican president-governors received special permission to select an oidor as their legal assistant, which also helped create or widen divisions among letrado ministers.[26] While this provision was meant to offset a shortage of qualified lawyers in the city, the president's choice of legal assistant came to be seen as a special honor and sign of allegiance. Velasco's choice of Juan Melgarejo Ponce de León as assistant in Bitrián's residencia in 1645 upset the other letrados, since Melgarejo had previously been Bitrián's assistant and would presumably help hide his crimes. Zúñiga switched from Diego López de la Puerta to Andrés Caballero when the former showed an inclination to question his orders. By contrast, oidor Thomás Pizarro Cortés was the only legal assistant available to Andrés de Robles in a 1685 case about an emergency ship arrival but, to Robles's frustration, refused to support his sentence because it would subordinate the opinion of "a lettered man to that of a layman." Since presidents of other audiencias could not use oidores in this role, letrados in Santo Domingo sometimes contested the president's ability to co-opt one of their number, though Salazar's belief that Bitrián and Fernández de Córdoba were breaking royal law by doing so was easily disproven. Later in the century, fiscal Joseph de Salazar complained that Segura Sandoval also wanted the fiscal's help with cases outside the audiencia's jurisdiction.[27]

The idea that the senior oidor would hold their powers due to their absence or death did not sit well with many president-governors. In 1644, due to recent skirmishes with enemy ships and an assault on Azua, Bitrián asked the king to order that a soldier would take over his military duties, as in Chile and Panama. Fernández de Córdoba was more worried about the personal shortcomings of oidor Salazar in 1651, arguing he was irresponsible, disliked by locals, and "totally ignorant in matters of war."[28] Pérez Franco's attempt, days before death, to have alcaldes ordinarios and military officers assume the political and military government of the island might have been temporarily effective, had most of the city's cabildo not cooperated with the audiencia to recognize oidor Montemayor's succession. Even interim letrado presidents—who were theoretically supposed to govern jointly with the audiencia but in Santo Domingo usually just assumed the governorship—might distance themselves from the tribunal. Oidor Cereceda, for example, was accused of denying appeals from his decisions to the court and demanding that his letrado colleagues present petitions at his lodgings after becoming acting president in 1634. Despite notable achievements by some interim letrado presidents, by the 1690s metropolitan authorities came to believe that jurists should never command a strategic military outpost, and so the cabo subalterno position was created.[29]

Throughout the seventeenth century, oidores and fiscales resisted president-governors' attempts to limit the audiencia while seeking to expand their own jurisdiction. The long-running quarrel between fiscal Herrera and Gómez de

Sandoval started around 1610, when Herrera brought suit in the audiencia over summary executions of individuals caught in the depopulated areas. In this case, Gómez de Sandoval had royal orders barring the tribunal from interfering in his commissions, and he had hanged the leader of an uprising in Guaba outside the city precisely to avoid delays from the audiencia. However, Herrera continued to challenge Gómez de Sandoval's authority on multiple fronts. In 1619, after Herrera returned from his temporary exile to Spain carrying royal orders blocking the president from punishing sargento mayor Gabriel de Rojas, Gómez de Sandoval rather theatrically offered to resign as captain-general rather than endure defiance from his officers. (The oidores were not convinced this actually put the island at risk.)[30] Later presidents like Fernández de Córdoba and Zúñiga maintained that the letrados interfered more freely in governmental and military affairs under oidores serving as temporary presidents. In 1652 and 1654, in view of Pérez Franco's repeated abuses of emergency powers, the magistrates requested that his ability to make such declarations be suspended or sharply restricted. However, the Council of the Indies felt it was important to safeguard "the preeminences that legitimately belong" to all fighting men on the island, and they confirmed the original orders from 1610, with some caveats: the president-governor should not use this privilege on a whim or in suits over inheritance, commercial debts, or crimes committed by individuals before becoming soldiers.[31]

Metropolitan authorities sometimes blurred the boundaries between presidents and letrados, especially in 1678 when the oidores were also instructed to attend musters and drills and help verify troop numbers and salary payments. Although this was a logical enough use of resources from Madrid's perspective, Segura argued that it contradicted orders giving him exclusive authority over such matters; moreover, when they tried to "attend to things they do not understand," the oidores did little but harass and dispirit the soldiers.[32] Segura saw the magistrates' involvement as a loss of power for him and convinced the council to withdraw these orders.

Some audiencia ministers were particularly adept at making life difficult for presidents, who were generally accustomed to having soldiers obey them. The clearest example is fiscal and oidor Herrera, a tireless antagonist of Gómez de Sandoval, though late in the century Severino de Manzaneda made similar complaints against oidor Sebastián de Cereceda y Girón. In

1630 Gabriel de Chaves Osorio described his problems with oidor Cereceda, who had not attended audiencia or acuerdo sessions for three months for fear that soldiers would kill him, though he left his house freely at all other times of day and night. The exasperated president wrote, "If not for the decorum and veneration due to the robed judges, as persons to whom your majesty has entrusted your conscience and the property, lives, and honor of your vassals," he would have locked him up instead of just fining him. In 1634 Chaves Osorio again reported that Cereceda had refused to come to the acuerdo for over a year, claiming the president was his mortal enemy, yet he did attend audiencia sessions on Tuesdays and Fridays, when the two were regularly alone together and even rode in the president's carriage. Chaves Osorio found it hard to believe he should only want to kill Cereceda on Mondays and Thursdays and offered to pay with his head if his claims were proven false.[33] Although Cereceda's behavior was atypical, it hints at how trying it could be to manage unruly letrados.

All the same, most of the time presidents collaborated with the rest of the audiencia well enough to maintain the appearance of a functioning appellate court. Conflicts with other authorities, such as the city's archbishop or regional governors, might also draw them closer together. Even presidents like Bitrián, who fought the letrados over several issues, regularly remitted judicial cases to them and consulted with them in the acuerdo about governmental decisions. Individual jurists also made personal connections with presidents; Cereceda's fellow oidor Miguel de Otalora was friends with Chaves Osorio from the time they left Madrid together. By the early 1660s, after a couple of decades of short-term president-governors alternating with interim senior oidores, disputes over the boundaries of justice and government became less common, suggesting the tribunal's relationship to its head eventually became more stable.[34]

Nonetheless, some opposition between the audiencia and its president was inherent to their overlapping jurisdictional spheres and to contrasting military and letrado perspectives on royal administration. All the tribunal's members understood that the court's power, and the president-governor's, depended on public recognition and could be permanently affected by even minor changes in protocol. The population of Santo Domingo saw president-governors as more important than letrado ministers; even so, compared to Chile, where the audiencia was distant, or Mexico, where the viceroy had much greater status, the men who governed Spanish Hispaniola were habitually concerned about the letrados exceeding their proper limits.[35] Oidores and fiscales, by contrast, claimed the presidents impinged on the court's judicial and administrative functions. In 1656 Zúñiga was taken aback by the oidores' strong reaction to his orders for presidio soldiers to begin accompanying them on walking patrols of the city (*rondas*). The magistrates declared that they would give up their positions before agreeing to this change, reading it as subordination to the military. The Crown ultimately upheld their objections and reinforced the privilege of carrying out these duties unaided by the president-governor.[36] In Santo Domingo, the combination of a military supervisor and a superior judicial institution remained a source of friction throughout the seventeenth century, but the Council of the Indies never felt the potential for good governance through cooperation was outweighed by the problems this created.

The officials of the royal treasury (*real hacienda*) of Santo Domingo generally had a much less combative relationship with the audiencia, though they protected their own jurisdictional boundaries and occasionally criticized the tribunal's ministers. Since they managed the king's finances—kept in the *cajas reales*, used literally and figuratively to refer to royal strongboxes and accounts—they worked especially closely with the audiencia's fiscal, and the president in his role as governor; however, the oidores were sometimes given various kinds of financial oversight. The treasury officials also paid the salaries of royal ministers and soldiers, which depended heavily on the irregular arrival of the situado, supplemented by loans from local elites.[37]

In larger urban centers like Mexico, three superior officials oversaw the treasury: a *factor*, *tesorero* (treasurer), and *contador* (comptroller), who jointly judged financial suits, though the Crown suppressed Santo Domingo's factor in 1604 to save money. The Dominican contador and tesorero worked in the casas reales, the same building where the president lived and the audiencia met. Their support staff consisted of notaries, port guards, and a chief clerk (*oficial mayor*) who did much of the actual bookkeeping.[38] Some treasury officials came from Spain, while others were from local families; they were below audiencia ministers in status, but their yearly salaries of 800 ducados (half that of oidores and fiscales)—and far more importantly, their control of the royal coffers—meant they enjoyed moderate prestige, and several served for decades.[39]

Audiencia members regularly interacted with treasury officials to help ensure they collected and recorded income, spent funds with proper authorization, and remitted certain duties, like those on slave sales, to Spain. The president-governor had the power to order them to release money (subject to later punishment if the Crown disapproved), while the audiencia had to convoke a junta with the president and treasury officials to justify extraordinary expenditures. The contador and tesorero also participated in other juntas about situados, military expenses, and other financial matters and made recommendations about using limited royal funds.[40] Their correspondence offered the Crown yet another perspective on the island's administration, although much of it simply relayed news—like the arrival or death of royal ministers and the collection of duties and fines—or confirmed royal orders to make payments. Occasionally, however, they gave opinions and alternate viewpoints, as with their reports that fines levied by visitador Rodrigo Navarro were largely uncollectable, that the president and oidores were receiving gratuities (*propinas*) beyond their salaries in the late 1670s, and that oidor Cereceda y Girón and fiscal Marín y Muñoz tried to avoid paying certain duties by claiming to be residents of Hispaniola.[41]

In the port city of Santo Domingo, another key duty of the treasury officials was supervising maritime traffic, usually in conjunction with audiencia members. Typically, the president-governor decided whether to allow entry for ships that arrived, after which the contador and tesorero, the audiencia's fiscal, and one or more port guards inspected the vessel and its documents to verify that the cargo and crew matched its official manifest (*registro*). If they discovered unregistered or prohibited merchandise (including African captives) or if the ship had made an emergency arrival, the fiscal normally requested that the ship and its contents be forfeited to the royal treasury. In that case, the treasury officials inventoried the cargo, questioned the crew, and issued a verdict, which could be appealed to the audiencia. President-governors might get involved, as in 1638 when three men arrived aboard a battered French vessel and gave Bitrián information on French settlements in the region. Oidor Pedro Álvarez de Mendoza's attempts to carry out a special investigation into contraband slaving around this time met with both assistance and obstruction from the treasury officials and the audiencia;

however, the case suggests that the contador and tesorero were generally willing to collaborate as long as doing so did not violate royal orders or compromise their own authority.[42]

Only a handful of times during the seventeenth century did the treasury officials make serious complaints about audiencia members, though most were related to president-governors' abuse of office. For example, they protested interim president Cereceda's reversal of their sentences against slave merchants and seizure of the treasury keys in 1636, described Bitrián's mishandling of royal funds in 1646, and reported that Pérez Franco was enlisting Portuguese soldiers in 1652. They also sometimes allied with the president against the audiencia's magistrates, according to oidor Melgarejo's 1649 claims that the treasury officials and president Velasco had challenged his commission to investigate emergency ship arrivals.[43]

The audiencia remained alert to the possibility of the treasury officials overstepping their jurisdiction and in 1609 reported that the contador and tesorero were improperly judging personal disputes. The acuerdo proclaimed they could only collect duties and bring suits about illicit cargo before the city's alcaldes ordinarios and ordered them not to hear claims unless directly related to royal accounts. In response, both the treasury officials and the municipal cabildo submitted petitions defending their own privileges. Ultimately, the audiencia allowed pending cases to proceed but told the Crown that giving treasury officials wider jurisdiction would disrupt the island's tenuous commerce.[44] In 1625, after tesorero Diego Velarde de Aguilar complained about their interference, the tribunal was ordered to abstain from several cases. The tribunal's members took this as a significant challenge and asked the king to "look after and conserve the authority of this [his] royal audiencia, both for this and for the consequence that will result in dishonor of it." Yet in the same letter they described how the audiencia had disagreed on a verdict for a shipment of flour and hides from Caracas that Velarde and fiscal Damián Gentil de Párraga had denounced to them, and so in Spain the treasury did not appear to be the source of the problem. In 1671 the Council of the Indies again upheld the treasury's separate privileges, rejecting the audiencia's objections to allowing the treasury officials to audit the accounts of their predecessors.[45]

Kenneth Andrien has characterized the sale of Peruvian treasury positions starting in the 1630s as a turning point for overseas administration, in which Crown oversight was weakened as local elites gained greater control of royal finances. In Santo Domingo, several treasury officials did purchase their posts for substantial sums, but although some contemporaries argued that such sales let in unsuitable candidates, it is difficult to prove that these later officeholders were more self-seeking than earlier ones.[46] Treasury positions remained desirable despite the island's impoverishment, and some officials amassed considerable wealth. In 1649 contador Lucas de Soria Pardo paid nearly 1,200 ducados so his son Diego de Soria Pardo could become tesorero, while Rodrigo Pimentel strengthened his control of trade by installing his brother-in-law as contador under Zúñiga.[47] Those who administered Crown funds could be valuable friends; tesorero Juan Mariño de Crestelo allied with oidor Fernando de Araujo against Ignacio Pérez Caro, and contador Juan de Soria Pardo paid magistrates against Gil Correoso's orders.

Santo Domingo's treasury was audited very irregularly during the seventeenth century. In 1626 the Council of the Indies noted they had not seen Hispaniola's accounts for nine years. While the tribunal of accounts in Havana nominally supervised Dominican finances from midcentury onward, president-governors and oidores usually carried out treasury reviews, and occasionally fined and suspended these officials for shortfalls.[48] Late in the century the contador and tesorero were charged with allowing 1,000 pesos to be stolen from their offices, while in 1679 their own reports earned them fines and a formal reprimand from the Crown for not inspecting ships in person. Investigations of the treasury officials often revealed president-governors' involvement in misappropriating royal funds.[49]

When treasury officials appeared with the audiencia, protocol dictated that their lower place in the administrative hierarchy be advertised. In 1609, after the president, two oidores, and the treasury officials sat together in chairs during an audit, the audiencia requested that the contador and tesorero be provided benches instead, to emphasize this distinction. However, a year later Gómez de Sandoval made a special bench for them in the city's cathedral, near the fiscal's seat, since he felt that "after the audiencia they and their wives should be differentiated from the other people."[50] In general, audiencia members conceived of the treasury as beneath them in prestige and jurisdiction but still a key piece of royal administration. Its officials usually cooperated with the audiencia and especially its presidents and fiscales, but when necessary they communicated with Spain to defend against undue interference from the tribunal.

Santo Domingo's municipal cabildo, by contrast, was definitely willing to confront the audiencia, particularly when they felt their customary privileges were threatened. Both as a group of men from wealthy and powerful families and as the official voice of the city, the cabildo's members did not automatically defer to the tribunal's ministers, some of whom were their debtors, but rather used the audiencia to pursue their own agendas.[51] The president-governor theoretically oversaw the cabildo, especially to monitor the elections of alcaldes ordinarios and the sale of regidor positions. However, these local elites—or factions of them—regularly allied with him for mutual benefit, most notably in the 1650s when Rodrigo Pimentel and Zúñiga dominated the city. Regidores also befriended or co-opted letrado ministers for their own purposes. At the same time, cabildo members worked with the audiencia to advocate for Santo Domingo throughout the century.

Although audiencia ministers generally saw Santo Domingo's cabildo as a lesser local institution, it had considerable autonomy and exerted influence across the Atlantic. The regidores frequently wrote the king about a variety of issues, whether to push for tax relief or report oidores' misbehavior, and in response the Crown often directed the audiencia, treasury officials, and archbishop to provide further details. The municipal cabildo also sent representatives to Spain to defend their interests in person, despite royal efforts to curtail this practice in 1621.[52] These strategies could permit the cabildo to counterbalance the authority of the audiencia and its president.

Regidores actively resisted some changes in Crown policy, for instance when president-governor Diego Osorio implemented royal orders to begin selling the office of *alférez mayor* early in the century. Shortly afterward, following cabildo members' even more vociferous opposition to the depopulations, Antonio Osorio sought to rein in their excessive independence. He claimed regidores showed little respect for the audiencia, and it was a "general practice among them to say that they remove and install presidents and oidores." While the Dominican cabildo's meetings were previously unsupervised, in contrast to Mexico or Lima, he observed that their decisions on matters like collecting the *alcabala* (a sales tax), distributing meat, or imposing *sisas* (additional taxes on food) affected the entire island. Osorio ordered the cabildo not to meet without informing him first so that he could observe in person if he were available, though since he was usually busy, he admitted this was mainly a ploy to keep them uncertain. He also auctioned regidor positions for 750 and 1,500 ducados, in contrast to the 300 or 350 ducados previously paid, and he put the fiel ejecutor's office up for sale. The Council of the Indies approved most of these actions, apart from selling the fiel ejecutor post, which its own fiscal argued would deny regidores a coveted privilege.[53]

After Osorio, Gómez de Sandoval watched the city's cabildo more closely, and said in 1610 that he or an oidor in his place supervised its yearly elections. When asked about a general proposal to reduce the number of alcaldes ordinarios throughout the district and limit their jurisdiction, he recommended against making major changes. Since their decisions could be appealed to the audiencia, he reasoned, the alcaldes ordinarios allowed the king's subjects to "reach justice with convenience" and represented an important social distinction for local elites, but these new restrictions would demoralize them without improving the judicial process.[54] His lack of concern over appeals also indicates that there was little judicial competition between Santo Domingo's alcaldes ordinarios and the audiencia.

Sharp factional infighting marked the municipal cabildo at certain times in the century, prompting the intervention of the president or oidores. In 1641, following unusually contentious elections, Bitrián asked the king to require the cabildo to choose one local (*criollo de la tierra*) and one "Spanish" alcalde ordinario—that is, one from an old family and one from a newer family—to prevent further altercations. Most cabildo meetings, however, were conducted in the absence of the president-governor or his representative, unless there was a special need for observation.[55]

The majority of the conflicts between the audiencia and cabildo during the seventeenth century were over precedence rather than jurisdiction, with rare exceptions like a 1607 dispute over whether alcaldes ordinarios had authority over the audiencia's support personnel. Nearly any change the audiencia made that affected cabildo protocol earned a protest to the king, followed by royal instructions to explain what had been done and why. In 1602 Antonio Osorio received orders to revoke oidor Sanz Morquecho's decision to end the cabildo's customary privilege of attending militia musters with the president as a body, not as individuals.[56] Five years later, the audiencia complained that the cabildo, by walking ahead of them in religious processions, was upending the established order of royal authorities. According to the tribunal, in the past the president-governor and audiencia had been directly behind the archbishop's party, but the cabildo petitioned for this place and then simply stopped attending processions when they were denied. The audiencia next ordered them to show up "in the form of the cabildo" or be fined fifty ducados each and notified the Crown. The cabildo members countered by presenting the acuerdo with royal orders from 1583 and 1600, plus a new declaration, in favor of the marching order they wanted. While the audiencia complained that the distance between them and the archbishop hurt the image of royal justice, they had misunderstood the king's intentions: walking at the end was meant to emphasize their importance, which was more obvious in larger processions in major cities like Mexico. Once that was clarified, the regidores openly boasted about their symbolic victory.[57]

Cabildo members could also frustrate letrado audiencia ministers' claims to social precedence, which rested on their offices and their education and bureaucratic services. Like president-governors, most local elites valued military service and lineage as more meaningful markers of status, and—though they recognized that the audiencia's presence raised the city's standing—they could remind magistrates that their reputation depended on public acknowledgment.[58] This was especially evident in the 1650s under presidents Pérez Franco and Zúñiga, both deeply hostile to bureaucrats. The audiencia complained when, at Pérez Franco's urging, the alcaldes ordinarios and all but a few regidores failed to attend oidor Orozco's burial in 1653, and they complained again the following year when no cabildo members met the audiencia or helped carry fiscal Alarcón Coronado's body for his funeral. The Council of the Indies agreed that such open displays of disrespect were unacceptable and ordered the cabildo to attend public events when the audiencia requested it.[59] Just the same, Santo Domingo's residents understood that without the president-governor's support, the magistrates had limited control over the regidores. With it, however, the audiencia could make changes affecting them, as in the mid-1680s when the entire tribunal sided with the archbishop to stop the regidores from wearing swords while taking communion.[60]

Throughout the century, the municipal cabildo expressed their approval or disapproval of audiencia ministers to the Crown. For example, they reported fiscal Pedro de Arévalo Sedeño's insults against city residents in 1605, complained about Bitrián's and Balboa's abuses in 1638 and 1662, and praised Zayas Bazán and recommended promoting him in 1672 and 1674. As wealthy elites, the regidores were aware of and frequently involved in the court's internal politics and believed the king needed their perspective, as in 1684 when they wrote about outgoing oidores and fiscales who failed to leave powers of attorney for their residencia processes. In 1650, after president Velasco's death, they let Madrid know that fiscal Alarcón Coronado and oidor Cepeda were causing problems for interim president Melgarejo, unlike oidor Francisco Pantoja de Ayala. A year later they thanked the king for sending president Fernández de Córdoba but criticized Cepeda, Alarcón Coronado, and oidor Salazar, and then within months wrote approvingly of Pantoja as temporary president and asked that the more senior Cepeda not be allowed to return from commissions in Margarita to succeed him.[61]

These letters did not always represent the unanimous feelings of all the cabildo's members—or most of the city's inhabitants—but do reflect political divisions and alliances in Santo Domingo. In some cases, the cabildo might be dragged into disputes between audiencia members, as in the late 1630s when, according to oidor Álvarez de Mendoza, president Bitrián threatened the regidores with fines to coerce them into writing against him.[62] At other times, the cabildo found creative ways to resist perceived assaults on their interests or privileges. Over the course of 1699 and 1700, when president Manzaneda accused the cabildo of involvement in illicit commerce, both the cabildo and oidor Cereceda y Girón (as the audiencia) complained about his interference with the elections and authority of the alcaldes ordinarios. Cereceda y Girón also showed support by confirming (again as the audiencia) the "immemorial" custom of having an alcalde ordinario sit beside the president-governor in his carriage during some public festivities.[63]

For most of the century, however, the cabildo and audiencia maintained a productive working relationship—for example, in the tribunal's recommendations of regidores' requests to levy additional taxes—largely because neither could afford to seriously alienate the other. Although the cabildo was more immediately concerned with conveying the problems of the city and island to the Crown, audiencia ministers stressed similar themes in their letters, confirmed the cabildo's pleas for aid, and sent reports and proposals for the benefit of their temporary home. Both institutions' members understood that their requests were more effective when they agreed, and so the cabildo seconded the audiencia's pleas for salary raises, while the audiencia wrote recommendations on behalf of individual regidores. The cabildo's opposition to the idea of moving the tribunal to Havana in 1608 revealed their fears about the harm losing it would cause Santo Domingo. Regidores could profit from the audiencia's internal divisions, as in Zúñiga's time when Rodrigo Pimentel practically controlled the court, but presidents and oidores alike periodically defended the need to collaborate with local elites.[64]

Pérez Franco's 1653 attempt to have the alcaldes ordinarios assume his powers as governor after his death offers a final illustration of how these two institutions interacted. The cabildo had previously sided with him against the audiencia, but after he died, most of its members were unwilling to support this radical change. Only alcalde ordinario Baltasar Fernández de Castro—seizing on a moment when his rival Pimentel was off the island—pushed for the cabildo to follow Pérez Franco's illegal orders, arguing that many royal orders were subject to local interpretation. The rest of the cabildo knew this breach of law and precedent might benefit Fernández de Castro temporarily but would cost them all in the long run, and they went out as a group to receive senior oidor Montemayor as interim president when he arrived during their discussion.[65] A few years later Pimentel, with much greater local support and financial resources, openly functioned as Zúñiga's second-in-command, but by the 1660s a kind of balance was reestablished and elites' influence was less overt.

For Santo Domingo's cabildo, the audiencia was more often useful as an ally than an adversary. For their part, the tribunal's ministers usually had little interest in fighting with wealthy locals who could complicate their lives. Aside from occasional incidents when the cabildo clearly demonstrated that it was not subservient to the magistrates, these institutions' shared desire for the material improvement of Spanish Hispaniola brought them together.

By contrast, the Catholic Church on Spanish Hispaniola, and in particular the archbishop of Santo Domingo, represented a different sphere of authority from the secular audiencia, providing a basis for some sharp confrontations with the tribunal and its ministers. Once again, cooperation with ecclesiastical figures and institutions was the norm for most of the century, but infrequent clashes with the church were public spectacles that mixed jurisdictional issues with precedence and the production of custom. Judicially, there were two main mechanisms for interactions between the church and secular institutions: the *auxilio del brazo seglar* (help from the secular arm) or auxilio and the *recurso de fuerza* (recourse of force) or fuerza. The auxilio allowed religious officials to request assistance from lay authorities, usually for something like physically apprehending a suspect, while the fuerza—a cornerstone of Spanish royal patronage over the church to be used only when absolutely necessary—gave the audiencia the power to halt and take over cases pending before ecclesiastical judges or lift spiritual penalties of censure. The audiencia was obligated to lend support when church authorities asked for it and was instructed to use the fuerza in moderation, as it often provoked an outcry from clerics. Since Santo Domingo did not have a permanent Inquisition, the audiencia's jurisdiction over some religious matters created potential confusion and invited accusations of abuse. Even legally justified royal oversight of the church was challenged during this period by several of Santo Domingo's archbishops, who went to extremes to prevent the audiencia from restricting their spiritual and temporal authority.[66]

Religion was fundamental to the audiencia's legitimacy and an integral part of its routine, and its members began each day with a private mass by their own chaplain as an acknowledgment that their judgments were made before God. The president, oidores, and fiscal sat in individual seats in the cathedral, a privilege that proclaimed their special relationship with the church, as did the tribunal's participation in religious processions.[67] However, this link was also a vulnerability, since spiritual condemnations of the court's ministers from the archbishop or other religious figures carried great weight with the city's inhabitants, while the audiencia had only limited practical control over clergy, especially the archbishop himself. Santo Domingo's audiencia and archbishop were both relics of an earlier time when Hispaniola was a key part of Spain's new empire, but by the seventeenth century the archdiocese was no longer a desirable assignment; several nominees declined the post, and the city's archbishops were promoted to bishoprics of places like Yucatán, Arequipa, Cusco, and Bogotá. However, as the highest-ranking ecclesiastical figure in a district that roughly overlapped with the audiencia's—nominally including Puerto Rico, Venezuela, Santiago de Cuba, and (before 1655) Jamaica—the archbishop's stature made him a formidable opponent.[68]

Sometime around 1610, early in Gómez de Sandoval's term, Archbishop Cristóbal Rodríguez criticized the audiencia at length following his inspection tour of the island's parishioners, accusing its ministers of impeding his ecclesiastical authority, ignoring public sins, and generally setting an impious example for locals. Since arriving two years earlier, he said he had hardly seen a lashing, hanging, or other public punishment, but "everyone, whether *mulato*, black, or white, got away with whatever they pleased," incidentally reflecting anxieties about controlling a mixed-race society that sometimes also surfaced in audiencia ministers' letters. He also claimed the oidores meddled in church affairs and prevented ecclesiastical judges from remedying Hispaniola's moral ills, even siding with the guilty to emphasize their own power. According to Rodríguez, after he rejected an unsuitable candidate for chaplain of a local hospital, one of the oidores encouraged the aspirant to appeal to the audiencia. The audiencia also abused the fuerza, ordering its bailiffs to violate ecclesiastical sanctuary to retrieve delinquents, but delayed or withheld the auxilio when asked to imprison individuals for religious offenses. He felt audiencia ministers were driven by jealousy and self-importance, as shown by their order that his own bailiff should only carry a plain staff of office instead of a silver-topped one. Likewise, in a recent procession of the miraculous cross of La Vega, the oidores had not shown up at the cathedral to accompany him and then nearly refused to enter the Dominican convent because the service had started before their arrival. Rodríguez singled out fiscal Herrera as the church's worst enemy due to the joint decision he and Gómez de Sandoval made to remove Herrera's son as chaplain of the hospital of La Concepción. Since then, Herrera had asked the audiencia to require ecclesiastical judges to prove they had not exceeded jurisdictional limits and to suspend the resolutions of a recent archdiocesan synod until the Council of the Indies had approved them.[69]

Much of what Rodríguez complained about was not actually illegal and stemmed from his antipathy to secular control of the church; for example, synods had to receive royal endorsement before their official publication. The audiencia claimed that Rodríguez—who held "some extraordinary and harmful opinions to law and [his] majesty's possession"—was the one overstepping his authority and changing customary practices to increase his own prestige. According to them, he had abused his spiritual powers by excommunicating or threatening to excommunicate all the oidores and the fiscal during their disagreements, as he had done to force an outgoing vessel to load his ginger. Rodríguez and his *provisor* (diocesan judge) directly interfered in nonreligious matters instead of requesting assistance, then complained when the audiencia used the fuerza to correct them. He also made them wait in front of his house during processions and told priests to stop welcoming them during services in the cathedral, even as he moved his own chair closer to the choir and began using the title "most reverend lordship and primate of the Indies" to elevate himself over them.[70] Here, both archbishop and audiencia expected metropolitan authorities to defend their rightful authority.

After another conflict in the late 1620s when Chaves Osorio tried and failed to take the administration of the Gorjón seminary away from Archbishop Oviedo, the tribunal had relatively good relations with the city's prelates.[71] During the 1650s the audiencia again fought with Archbishop Francisco Pío Guadalupe Téllez after he publicly excommunicated oidor Montemayor for investigating a priest's misbehavior and then recused oidor Pantoja from the appeal.[72] Although he later agreed to suspend the censure, Pío Guadalupe showed residents he could effectively nullify the secular tribunal's power over the church. The Council of the Indies pointed out that oidores could not directly prosecute clergy members but did have the right to report on sedition and public disturbances and admonished all parties to proceed with more decorum in the future. This seems to have made little impact on Pío Guadalupe, since in 1656 Montemayor complained the archbishop had once more excommunicated him without explaining why or hearing his defense, and even the council's fiscal recognized that Pío Guadalupe had a history of aggressive opposition to secular oversight.[73]

The audiencia's most acrimonious clashes with an archbishop happened in the mid-1670s. On arriving in 1674, Archbishop Juan de Escalante Turcios allegedly insulted their royal authority by having one of the city's public notaries take his oath of office instead of one of theirs. The audiencia initially assumed he was unaware of normal procedures, but soon Escalante began making changes to services in the cathedral to distance himself from the tribunal, such as sitting under a canopy or using his own paten (a small plate used in communion) during mass rather than sharing theirs. He also boasted that his cousin at the royal court would ensure he could do as he wished. From Escalante's perspective, however, the audiencia was not fulfilling their obligations to the church, as shown by a visita he took of his new congregants that revealed over 112 extramarital relationships, many involving local elites. Although Zayas Bazán granted the auxilio when requested, Escalante said the audiencia sided with the city cabildo to stop him from punishing the guilty, forcing him to resort to excommunicating some cabildo members. In this early round, the audiencia was reprimanded for obstructing the archbishop's jurisdiction and for not observing proper ceremony in the cathedral.[74]

In August 1676, the situation got much worse. After he challenged their use of the fuerza, the audiencia claimed Escalante excommunicated two oidores and three notaries when they ordered him to show documentation justifying the use of ecclesiastical censure in criminal cases. Milder measures were ineffective, since the archbishop refused to respond to written requests and excommunicated those who notified him, and so the acuerdo voted to exile him from the Indies, while suspending execution until the king could be informed. Escalante, enraged, ordered all the city's churches and monasteries to ring their bells without stopping and threatened to halt religious services throughout the island. Peace was eventually restored through the mediation of the cathedral chapter and municipal cabildo, but Santo Domingo's inhabitants were painfully aware of this contest for supremacy. The archbishop then marched through the city with some forty clergy members and his processional cross to the casas reales to berate the audiencia members in person until Zayas Bazán could calm him down and persuade him to leave.[75]

The audiencia's reports emphasized their defense of the king's jurisdiction, which they insisted "recognizes no superior in temporal matters." In addition to making decisions and spiritual punishments in secular cases, Escalante was also denying them the right to review his records, let alone hear appeals. In letters peppered with religious references, they claimed Escalante was treating them like he had previously treated the governor of Campeche; they also insinuated that he ignored the spiritual needs of his flock and even that he had an illegitimate son with an Indian servant. For both sides, the distance from royal supervision turned disagreements into a public competition for dominance—the president and other oidores forced excommunicated senior oidor Agustín Félix Maldonado to accompany them to mass precisely to show locals that Escalante's censure was invalid. However, in the short term, the formidable spiritual weapons at the archbishop's disposal could handcuff the audiencia, and Escalante's strategy of withholding church documents ultimately paid off. In the absence of written evidence against him, the Council of the Indies simply promoted Escalante to Yucatán.[76]

The personalities of individual prelates were clearly an important ingredient in such struggles, but the clergy's general conviction that they needed to be vigilant about secular encroachment meant that otherwise cooperative archbishops automatically resisted the audiencia. Archbishop Francisco de la Cueva Maldonado, a good friend of president Pedro de Carvajal y Cobos, rejected the tribunal's 1665 attempt to receive an appeal to the will of a woman who had given her property to the church and temporarily excommunicated senior oidor Gaspar Vélez Mantilla and recused other magistrates to stop them from pursuing the matter. De la Cueva wrote that his predecessors had faced similar assaults on their privileges, and now audiencia ministers slandered him and obliged him to take drastic measures, even though he had baptized their children and come to their houses for confirmation. In the audiencia's version, the archbishop used spiritual threats to usurp their judicial role, while fiscal Juan Pizarro Cajal added that inhibiting the oidores rendered him unable to defend the king's interests.[77]

On balance, such episodes were infrequent and do not represent day-to-day relations between the audiencia and most archbishops throughout the century. Their report on the 1622–23 provincial council held by Archbishop Pedro de Oviedo and supervised by Gómez de Sandoval, in which the tribunal's members praised participants for their attention to God and king and willingness to travel to Santo Domingo, reflected a more typical attitude toward the church.[78] Audiencia ministers frequently requested material aid for the impoverished archdiocese, as in 1633 when they and the municipal and ecclesiastical cabildos wrote in support of an extra 1,000 ducados per year for Archbishop Facundo de Torres. In 1679 Segura Sandoval lamented that Archbishop Fernández Navarrete was reduced to celebrating mass in the cathedral with a single candle for lack of wax, although the audiencia was not willing to give up their own Lenten sermons in the casas reales.[79]

Even prelates who fought the secular tribunal could be situational allies. In 1611 the audiencia asked that Archbishop Rodríguez be given more time to repay a royal loan, while in 1657 Fernández de Córdoba reported Archbishop Pío Guadalupe was calling the audiencia "very powerful lord" during services, something denied to the king himself while the communion host was uncovered.[80] During long periods when Santo Domingo had no resident archbishop, the secular tribunal usually asked for these vacancies to be filled quickly. Meanwhile, local supervision of the church normally devolved to the canons of the cathedral chapter, who tended to avoid conflict with the audiencia despite their own internal factionalism.[81] For much of the seventeenth century, archbishop and audiencia coexisted without strife, even if the potential for fights over jurisdiction and privileges was always present.

Only occasionally did the audiencia report on other ecclesiastical institutions in the city like monasteries and hospitals.[82] What problems there were often involved the right of sanctuary, since when criminal suspects took refuge in sacred spaces the court faced a difficult choice between provoking widespread outrage or accepting limits on the reach of royal justice. Interim president Melgarejo discovered this in 1639 after ordering soldiers to break down the doors of the convent of Regina Angelorum to retrieve a woman accused of murder. Although he had the backing of Archbishop Torres and a relevant papal bull, plus the assistance of Rodrigo Pimentel and another cabildo member, Melgarejo's actions infuriated local Dominican friars, who criticized Torres for not excommunicating him. The king later commanded Melgarejo to justify his decision, and the ill will it generated may have led to a more serious challenge in 1648, in which two prisoners headed for execution were forcibly taken into the hospital of San Nicolás and belligerent clergy confronted Melgarejo when he tried to extract them. Similarly, the acuerdo's 1667 order to seal off the convent of Santa Clara until the nuns turned over another female suspect was widely unpopular and earned the tribunal's members a royal rebuke.[83]

Although Inquisition cases were sometimes forwarded to Cartagena, the distant Holy Office had little direct impact on the audiencia.[84] The Inquisition did have local agents in the city—among them oidores Juan Martínez Tenorio and Miguel de Otalora—and occasionally affected the audiencia, as in 1648 when oidor Salazar was accused of blasphemy and heresy by the bishop of Puerto Rico during an investigation there; he sailed to Spain to clear his name (and seek promotion) but was reprimanded for leaving without permission and sent back.[85] Inquisition officials briefly visited Santo Domingo in 1610, en route to Cartagena, and lodged with Gómez de Sandoval and Martínez Tenorio. The role of secular authorities in defending the Christian faith was reflected in the attendance of the audiencia, the archbishop, and both municipal and ecclesiastical cabildos when the inquisitors published the Edict of the Faith in the cathedral.[86]

For the most part, the audiencia and its president were meant to report on church affairs and clergy members so that problems could be resolved through the church hierarchy. In 1607 Antonio Osorio informed the Council of the Indies about a Jesuit preaching against the depopulations and saying it was a sin to kill foreigners and that the president had no authority to silence him. The council members notified the priest's superiors to have him recalled to Spain and barred from returning to the Indies.[87] Over the century, the tribunal's members provided information on other church issues; for example, in 1667 fiscal Pizarro Cajal claimed that Archbishop de la Cueva was mistreating one of the canons and exaggerating the need for additional income, while in 1694 Pérez Caro described turmoil in the Mercedarians' conventual elections, along with the protests Archbishop Carvajal y Rivera made when he and oidor Manuel de la Cruz Ahedo tried to mediate.[88]

Despite episodic conflicts and some deliberate meddling in church politics—such as oidor Cereceda's interference with the cathedral chapter in the 1630s—the tribunal's recommendations for material aid for the archbishop or convents best represent their usual relationship with local clergy.[89] As the century progressed, the audiencia's reliance on priests to fill in as lawyers, judges, and fiscales only added to its members' reasons for staying on good terms with the church. Yet their relations with ecclesiastical authorities were qualitatively different from those with secular institutions in the sense that the clergy's spiritual power resonated deeply with local residents and could gravely harm the tribunal's moral standing. Likewise, religious figures were less likely to feel that the secular court's presence in Santo Domingo elevated their importance, in contrast to the municipal cabildo. The audiencia never really reached a state of equilibrium with the church, which remained a potential threat, as illustrated by Pérez Caro's 1694 complaint that Archbishop Carvajal y Rivera committed the "monstrosity" of starting the Corpus Christi mass before the court's members arrived.[90]

Confrontations between the different authorities and institutions in Santo Domingo were rare, but jurisdictional issues and contemporaries' keen awareness of symbols and gestures of privilege and precedence made them a recurring feature of this era. Although they had a duty to cooperate for the good of the city and island, local authorities' relationships could be complicated. In 1653, for example, not long after his first temporary excommunication by Archbishop Pío Guadalupe, oidor Montemayor courteously notified the prelate of president-governor Pérez Franco's death to enlist church support against the alcaldes ordinarios assuming interim control of the governorship. Personal alliances also cut across institutional boundaries, as for Zúñiga and regidor Rodrigo Pimental or Carvajal y Cobos and Archbishop de la Cueva; Pérez Caro also claimed oidor Araujo revealed the acuerdo's secrets to Archbishop Carvajal y Rivera. Disputes with other authorities—including transient ones like visitadores—could sharpen the audiencia's internal divisions or could unify its members, as in 1630 when Chaves Osorio convinced excommunicated oidores Cereceda and Otalora to attend public festivals with him in defiance of Archbishop Oviedo.[91] In letters to the Council of the Indies, the tribunal's ministers frequently emphasized their corporate identity and defense of the jurisdiction and prestige of royal justice. Yet the audiencia regularly collaborated with the municipal cabildo, treasury officials, local church figures, and their own president, and the Spanish Crown relied on the multiple perspectives they provided to stay informed about its overseas territories.[92]

Conflicts between the tribunal and other local authorities, though infrequent, can usefully illuminate audiencia members' understanding of the boundaries of their authority and, more broadly, the intersection between overseas administration and its cultural context. As all knew, customary practice was nearly as important as law, and changes to ceremonial markers of rank and privilege could lead to a real loss of power, particularly given local residents' greater allegiance to the church or to military presidents. While the Council of the Indies upheld the court's right to determine appeals from many of the president-governors' decisions or to exercise limited oversight of ecclesiastical affairs, they expected magistrates to act with discretion and corrected them when they exceeded their authority or caused public scandal. Ultimately, the audiencia's complaints to the metropole about disputes with other authorities in Santo Domingo reinforced all these institutions' reliance on the monarch as the arbiter of their proper relationship.

5

District Supervision

In contrast to its generally cooperative relations with authorities in Santo Domingo, the audiencia was more likely to fight with officials and institutions elsewhere in its district, though their interactions were far less frequent. Oidor Juan Padilla Guardiola summarized the court's perspective in 1675, after Caracas's alcaldes ordinarios had stopped him from taking over as interim governor of Venezuela following the death of Francisco Dávila Orejón. According to him, they organized a public demonstration in which the crowd shouted "death to the oidores, and long live the governing alcaldes," showing that the entire province was living "above the law" and had no respect for the audiencia's orders. The Council of the Indies did not agree, and reminded him that the cabildo of Caracas had held the privilege of governing all of Venezuela during vacancies since 1560. They also reprimanded Padilla, Ignacio Zayas Bazán, and the entire audiencia, for improperly sending a governor and for taking twenty-five infantry soldiers and four artillery pieces away from Santo Domingo for Padilla's voyage.[1] Fiscal Juan Garcés de los Fayos urged the council to reconsider, claiming that Santo Domingo's president-governor had been in "immemorial possession" of the right to name temporary governors for Venezuela—indeed, two former interim governors were still living—and that the governing alcaldes permitted contraband and ignored foreign threats. The council remained unmoved.[2]

Padilla's report sounded a common refrain in the audiencia's seventeenth-century correspondence: that the regional authority of the tribunal and its president was constantly being challenged. Certainly, provincial authorities did regularly reject the audiencia's provisions, but audiencia members' conception of their role in district supervision often did not match Madrid's. Compared to regional governors, the presidents, oidores, and fiscales of Santo Domingo saw themselves as more immediate representatives of the king, with the power and the responsibility to remedy pressing issues in their district, subject to later review by the slower-moving Council of the Indies. Yet the Crown usually treated the audiencia as one of several potential resources for managing the Caribbean, not as an exclusive administrative hub. Metropolitan authorities were also well aware that audiencia members often sought to elevate their prestige at other institutions' expense, and permitting them to freely interfere in district affairs caused more problems than it solved. For such reasons, together with the significant logistical challenges of intraregional communication, the Dominican tribunal was never allowed to establish definitive supremacy over provincial officials, although it retained appellate jurisdiction in the district. However, the potential for intervention created an enduring and unresolvable tension, in which the audiencia perpetually wanted more oversight while regional officials fought for greater autonomy.

The 1680 *Recopilación de Indias* described the Audiencia of Santo Domingo's district as encompassing all the islands of the Caribbean and the South American coast, plus the mainland from Guyana in the east to Río de la Hacha in the west, so that the tribunal shared land and sea borders with the districts of the audiencias of Santa Fe, Panama, Guatemala, and Mexico and with the "provinces of Florida." The official limits of this region remained mostly unchanged throughout the seventeenth century, apart from the transfer of Maracaibo to Santa Fe's district in 1676.[3] Practically speaking, the audiencia's judicial and administrative oversight within these boundaries was very uneven. Oidor Pedro de Carvajal's account of the distribution of stamped paper in 1666 offers a sense of how Santo Domingo communicated, indirectly and unreliably, with its provinces: between January and June, he sent consignments of paper in different ships to Puerto Rico, Maracaibo (for distribution in Venezuela), Cumaná (for distribution to Margarita), and Santiago de Cuba (for distribution to Havana), though not to Río de la Hacha, since no ships were available.[4] Despite recurring transportation problems, the audiencia was used throughout the century to collect and disseminate information and to provide officials for district assignments in addition to receiving judicial appeals. The Crown intended the tribunal to work with rather than against provincial officials, although many audiencia members felt that they needed to take an active role in stopping regional abuses. The outcome of their interventions depended greatly on circumstances.

By 1600, Santo Domingo was neither an effective center for regional communications nor an attractive destination for new migrants, yet the Council of the Indies' consistent refusal to move the audiencia elsewhere was more than mere nostalgia for the previous century. Despite the enthusiasm of its ministers for a variety of relocation proposals, metropolitan authorities generally echoed the arguments of Santo Domingo's elites: that transferring the audiencia to Havana or Caracas would only encourage more people to abandon Hispaniola, to the benefit of Spain's enemies.[5] Throughout the seventeenth century, the audiencia remained nominally supreme within its district and functionally independent of external authorities, especially the viceroys of New Spain. What correspondence there was between the president-governor on Hispaniola and the viceroy was most often related to the yearly situado, and more rarely about military affairs like soldiers sent to bolster the 1654 campaign on Tortuga or the English invasion the following year. Contacts became somewhat more frequent beginning in the 1670s and 1680s, when the Dominican president-governors were ordered to relay news of enemies to Mexico, although instructions to Francisco de Segura Sandoval to route information through Havana suggest some practical awareness of Hispaniola's limited maritime connections. Even after 1693, when Viceroy Galve was given the right to name interim cabos subalternos for Santo Domingo, Mexican viceroys made no move to establish any kind of control over the Dominican tribunal, which offered no real reward in terms of prestige or patronage.[6]

From the Crown's perspective, the audiencia's primary function within its district was as a court of appeal. In addition to civil and criminal cases of first instance originating within five leagues of the city of Santo Domingo, the tribunal was to determine cases of second instance—appeals—from lesser justices like alcaldes ordinarios, governors, or treasury officials throughout the district. They could also receive most appeals from commissioned judges operating in the Caribbean region, many of them Dominican oidores performing special investigations, so that the audiencia was supposed to be superior to nearly all other judicial authorities within its district.[7]

However, both legal and practical limitations helped determine which suits actually came to Santo Domingo. Certain sentences could not be appealed further, like low-value cases decided by alcaldes ordinarios, while others such as residencia verdicts involving the royal treasury could only be appealed directly to the Council of the Indies. Generally, the audiencia tried to keep their appellate jurisdiction as broad as possible, though the Crown did not always confirm their claims. In 1623, in response to the governor of Havana's report about the cost and delay of appeals to Santo Domingo, the council raised the monetary limit for claims determined by local alcaldes ordinarios that could not be appealed from 60,000 to 90,000 maravedís (160 to 240 ducados); they also asked the audiencia to explain why they had fined the governor's letrado assistant 100 ducados for declaring sentences finalized (*pasada en cosa juzgada*) after a year without appeal, following royal law.[8]

Ecclesiastical and military privileges also restricted the tribunal's regional jurisdiction. While it was barred from directly sentencing clergy or deciding religious matters, the audiencia was able to employ the fuerza outside the city when they felt an ecclesiastical judge was incompetent or deliberately trespassing into secular affairs. Actual use of the fuerza within the district seems to have been infrequent, and in 1692 the audiencia ministers were chastised for not pursuing a suit over an ecclesiastical benefice in Caracas because they had heard that both sides had settled their differences.[9]

Jurisdictional conflicts with military authorities were considerably more common. The Council of the Indies' concerns about the tenuous defenses of Caribbean territories meant that they did not want the Dominican court impeding provincial governors' orders or encouraging complaints from soldiers. In late 1608, shortly before issuing similar instructions for Diego Gómez de Sandoval, Felipe III decreed that the judgments of the governors of Puerto Rico affecting soldiers and militia officers—and militia soldiers during wartime—could only be appealed to the Junta de Guerra. This concession was also granted to other regional governors, who cited it throughout the century to defend their military autonomy. While such orders gradually circumscribed the Dominican tribunal's oversight of these governors, the audiencia still found numerous reasons to intervene in extrajudicial affairs around the Caribbean.[10]

Even for lawsuits from the district that could be reviewed by the audiencia, the potential benefits of an appeal were often outweighed by the expense, time, and uncertainty involved. Moreover, provincial governors or alcaldes ordinarios who were supposed to remit cases to the audiencia might still deny appeals outright or make the process extremely difficult for litigants. Toward the end of the century, oidor Fernando de Araujo y Rivera claimed that governors were charging exorbitant fees for licenses to sail to Hispaniola, blocking commerce along with judicial appeals and leaving the audiencia with little to do. When the audiencia did overturn governors' decisions, its authority was not always accepted outside Santo Domingo, and on further appeal the Council of the Indies might not agree that they had jurisdiction or confirm their sentences.[11] In the absence of records of most of the suits determined by the audiencia during this period, it is difficult to estimate the proportion that originated outside Hispaniola. However, scattered references to district appeals—a female litigant from Havana whom oidor Gonzalo Mejía de Villalobos was accused of having a sexual relationship with early in the century, or an appeal from Severino de Manzaneda's decision to execute an enslaved man in Havana that followed the new president-governor to Santo Domingo in the 1690s—suggest they were less common than local cases. (The last case, in which the audiencia overturned the death sentence and instead condemned the accused, Francisco Arara, to loss of his right hand, two hundred lashes, and ten years of public service for killing his owner, offers a glimpse of the range of suits the oidores judged as well as what justice looked like in a slaveholding society.)[12] However, from the Crown's perspective, the audiencia offered what it considered sufficient access to royal justice for the district's inhabitants.

The Dominican tribunal was also involved with regional administration in other ways. Metropolitan authorities commonly treated it as one of several sources of information about the Caribbean in the hopes that its ministers would have useful insights or be able to locate knowledgeable travelers. In 1608, for example, the governor of Cartagena and the audiencia were ordered to evaluate the governor of Cumaná's recommendation to relocate the inhabitants of the neighboring area of Cumanagotos to his city. In 1665 the president and oidores were asked for a detailed report on a copper mine concession in Cocorote in Venezuela; they said that they knew the mine contained poor-quality copper but did not have any recent news for lack of ships. The audiencia was usually not the only respondent, as in 1638 when it, the fiscal, and the treasury officials of Santo Domingo plus the governor and treasury officials of Puerto Rico were all instructed to give opinions on a proposed tobacco tax on Puerto Rico.[13]

The Council of the Indies used all overseas audiencias as a network for disseminating general proclamations, like a 1693 blanket decree about creating schools to teach Indians the Castilian language, which the Dominican tribunal dutifully forwarded to "the governors and other justices of the district and jurisdiction of this audiencia." In many cases, they only needed to pass on instructions to provincial authorities, as Manzaneda and oidor Cereceda y Girón did in 1699 for several orders received in the previous years. Sometimes, however, audiencia ministers might assemble a more detailed report, such as the one they sent about *tazire*, an alcoholic beverage used by Indians within the district, building on information from Cumaná and Puerto Rico.[14]

Like all other overseas authorities, the audiencia was also to forward information to Spain on their own initiative as needed, whether in response to foreign hostilities or for something like the Franciscans' 1640 request to rebuild a convent in Cumaná.[15] Hispaniola's president-governor had a particular obligation to advise the Crown of dangers, financial opportunities, or anything else concerning the good government of the island and district, usually in consultation with the acuerdo. In such ways, the audiencia—alongside the region's cabildos, treasury officials, governors, and church officials—acted as the king's eyes and ears to clarify, corroborate, or correct news from the Caribbean.

The elevated status of the Dominican tribunal and its president-governor often led the Crown to route district investigations or the collection of duties and fines through the audiencia, although its ministers were usually meant to delegate this work to regional agents. In 1672, after the queen regent told them to ensure that penalties for improper ship entries were deducted from the salaries of governors and treasury officials in Puerto Rico, Caracas, and Trinidad, the audiencia collectively decided sending word to local alcaldes ordinarios was the most effective approach.[16] Similarly, in 1643, oidor Juan Melgarejo Ponce de León acknowledged receipt of four *cartas ejecutorias*—letters summarizing the legal process behind a royal decision that was to be immediately executed—with condemnations for residents of Caracas and the interior of Hispaniola, which he was working on collecting. Six years later, as interim president, he reported that he was remitting fines from other executory letters for Caracas, Cumaná, and Santiago de Cuba as he received them from those treasury officials.[17] The Crown did not systematically involve the audiencia in all regional issues but was more likely to when they concerned multiple places or when provincial authorities did not respond quickly enough. Occasionally it was simply a matter of convenience, as in 1697 when the senior oidor was told to collect an outstanding 500-peso fine from president-elect Manzaneda on his arrival for failing to investigate the loss of a galleon as governor of Havana.[18]

The Crown's use of the audiencia to administer the stamped paper duty beginning around 1640 typifies the piecemeal and opportunistic way the court's authority within the district was constructed. The practice, which mandated the use of paper stamped with seals of differing values for official documents, was started by the Count-Duke of Olivares in the later 1630s.[19] In Santo Domingo, an oidor named by the president was responsible for receiving blank paper and stamps valid for a certain number of years and then sending stamped bundles to provincial officials, collecting the fees, and remitting them to Spain. Secondary personnel actually did much of this work; Antonio de Heredia, chief notary of the audiencia, described volunteering as treasurer of this duty several times and overseeing paper shipments to the "nine places" of the district in 1642 or the "ten places" in 1659 (he did not name them). The task was not always done punctually, and in 1693 Ignacio Pérez Caro learned Margarita was out of stamped paper because the oidor in charge of it had not carried out the duty he inherited from a former colleague.[20]

When the *Recopilación* was published in 1680, the Council of the Indies again charged the Dominican tribunal with delivering copies throughout the district and collecting thirty pesos for each set of volumes. In 1683 the audiencia reported giving out twenty-three in Santo Domingo and dividing the remaining twenty-seven among the governors of Venezuela, Puerto Rico, Havana, Cumaná (who was to send sets to Margarita and Trinidad), and Santiago de Cuba (who received them in person, since he happened to be in Santo Domingo); they also noted there were not enough for all the cabildos in the district.[21] In general, using the audiencia for distribution and collection usually involved substantial delay, which was acceptable when metropolitan authorities were less concerned about timeliness than with the eventual results. Handling such matters through the audiencia was also normally less expensive and troublesome than sending out a commissioned agent and allowed the Crown to remind district officials of their place in a larger system of imperial administration, with multiple avenues for oversight.[22]

The audiencia encountered much more resistance when they sent people rather than letters to the provinces, whether on the Crown's instructions or independently. Nevertheless, they did so throughout the century, though their agents' interventions were more likely to succeed with explicit royal backing. Madrid regularly employed the Dominican tribunal's ministers elsewhere in the Caribbean region, and the audiencia was often shorthanded because one of its members—at times all but one—had to leave Hispaniola for district commissions. As early as 1601, oidor Juan Alcázar de Villaseñor's departure for Puerto Rico meant that Pedro Sanz Morquecho was left alone as oidor and interim president. Marcos Núñez de Toledo, who had been promoted to Guatemala, went to Havana (where he later died) to perform a visita of that governor in 1605, and the next year Francisco Manso de Contreras followed his colleague to Havana while Mejía de Villalobos sailed for Puerto Rico. Likewise, in 1681 oidor Juan Garcés de los Fayos became the sole resident magistrate when his colleagues traveled to Cumaná and Puerto Rico, and in 1686 Thomás Pizarro Cortés left behind newly arrived oidor Riva Agüero to carry out royal commissions in Cuba. Metropolitan council members were aware that these district assignments drained Santo Domingo of magistrates, and justified a supernumerary appointment to the audiencia in 1660 due to a pressing need for investigations in Santiago de Cuba, Havana, Puerto Rico, and Caracas.[23]

Santo Domingo's oidores and fiscales were not the only possible candidates for special commissions around the Caribbean, which were also assigned to other provincial officials, clergy members, and ministers of different audiencias. The Council of the Indies tended to pragmatically select individuals traveling to or resident in the region rather than defaulting to the Dominican tribunal. In 1612, for example, the bishop-elect of Venezuela was instructed to verify reports of Mejía de Villalobos's public drunkenness while on Hispaniola for consecration, and six years later Juan de Ibarra y Gueztara was commissioned to investigate Gómez de Sandoval and Jerónimo de Herrera en route to his new post as alcalde del crimen of Mexico. Mateo de Mata Ponce de León, oidor-elect of Santa Fe, was supposed to stop in Caracas in 1675 to take the residencia of former governor Dávila Orejón and follow up on other accusations, though he journeyed onward after learning that Dávila Orejón had died, and the residencia was later done by Cuba's auditor general.[24] The Crown also gave commissions to Santo Domingo's ministers on promotion, as in 1653 when oidor Francisco Pantoja de Ayala had to complete investigations in Havana before moving to Guatemala.[25]

Only rarely did the Council of the Indies send peninsular officials. Their 1666 decision to appoint their own relator, Rodrigo Navarro, to untangle Juan de Balboa Mogrovejo's residencia and finish up Sancho de Ubilla's commissions reflected how important these tasks had become to the Crown (as did Navarro's promotion to oidor of the House of Trade). While in the Caribbean, Navarro was also ordered to audit Venezuela's treasury, forestalling another potential challenge to the audiencia's regional authority.[26]

Just the same, although the tribunal in Santo Domingo could not order visitas or *pesquisas* (another kind of special investigation) of regional governors on its own initiative, the Crown did make regular use of the audiencia as a pool of sufficiently high-status judges who could rein in these governors' tendency to disregard inconvenient royal laws. Such commissions were given to individual ministers, not the audiencia, which was often specifically inhibited in their instructions.[27] Oidor Padilla, for example, was sent to Cumaná, where he remained until 1683, as special investigator and interim governor following his 1680 promotion to Guadalajara. His effectiveness in both Santo Domingo and Cumaná earned him additional commissions, and he soon became oidor of Mexico.[28]

The most common chore given to Santo Domingo's ministers was the residencia of a district governor, when the Council of the Indies felt the incoming replacement should not do it. In 1653 and 1654, after reports of problems on Margarita, the council members wanted an oidor to take ex-governor Fernando de Mendoza Mate de Luna's residencia, though they changed nominees three times before settling on Andrés de Caballero, with fiscal Bernardo Trigo de Figueroa as alternate.[29] Like most investigations, these residencias regularly generated complaints. In 1631 Havana's cabildo claimed that fiscal Francisco de Prada had aggressively interfered in government matters like trade, impounded locals' property to collect fines, and charged excessive salaries in the residencia of governor Lorenzo de Cabrera y Corbera. Oidor Caballero, by contrast, was accused of maintaining improper friendships with governors in Puerto Rico and Margarita and accepting gifts in exchange for favorable residencia sentences.[30]

Organizing commissions from Spain created some complications, and even getting nominees to travel to the Caribbean could be difficult. Thomás de Oña accepted a position as oidor of Santo Domingo in 1673 and was then tasked with investigating foreign ship entries in Río de la Hacha, which oidores Agustín Félix Maldonado and Pedro Carvajal had not done before being promoted. However, Oña was made fiscal of Panama prior to leaving, creating a vacancy in Santo Domingo; although he might still have carried out this commission, the following year he declined the post in Panama in favor of continuing to work for the Council of Castile. Personal connections could also affect district commissions, as when oidor Cruz Ahedo was ordered to investigate the nephew of Puerto Rican governor Gaspar Martínez de Andino around 1689, but president-governor Andrés de Robles, a friend of Martínez, delayed his departure long enough for the nephew to escape to Curaçao.[31]

Judges who carried out peninsular commissions still encountered local resistance, usually led by allies of those they were charged with investigating. In 1686 oidor Pizarro Cortés traveled to Santiago de Cuba to look into allegations of illicit trade against its governor, Gil Correoso Catalán (later cabo subalterno of Santo Domingo). When Pizarro Cortés removed Correoso from office and took over as political governor, Correoso's son Gregorio threatened him with a sword, and the sargento mayor acting as military governor prevented him from completing his commission. Three years later, the Council of the Indies ordered oidor Jerónimo de Córdoba to go punish this disobedience and resume the investigation, although only in 1693 did oidor Oviedo y Baños, named in third place, arrive in Santiago to finish what Pizarro Cortés had started.[32] Such challenges and delays tempered the hopes of regional inhabitants that commissioned judges from the Dominican tribunal would provide relief from the abuses of local authorities.

The Audiencia of Santo Domingo was empowered to send its own orders and issue commissions in response to certain kinds of urgent regional problems, but without the Crown's backing, their involvement was much more likely to be disputed. Even though the acuerdo's provisions carried the royal seal and were worded (and meant to be treated) as coming from the king himself, district officials knew the difference and vigorously and effectively opposed the Dominican tribunal's attempts at supervision.[33] Audiencia ministers frequently complained about provincial disobedience, but metropolitan authorities were acutely conscious that the tribunal's interventions usually generated further conflict. Accordingly, when reports of abuses or fraud could not be addressed locally, the council members preferred to decide how to proceed and whom to send instead of trusting the audiencia, even if it took considerable time. Regional officials were quite familiar with

Felipe II's repeatedly reissued orders instructing audiencias to delegate special investigations in the district to local governors, corregidores, or alcaldes mayores "unless it were in inexcusable cases, and at the cost of those who request them, and without excessive salaries."[34]

When Santo Domingo's acuerdo voted to launch investigations for matters they believed were inexcusable and could not be trusted to local agents, they did so knowing they would eventually require peninsular approval. This did not always happen as the tribunal's members expected, and instead of being thanked for confronting provincial abuses—or scolded for inaction—they could be reprimanded for overstepping jurisdictional boundaries.[35] Moreover, without royal authorization or effective force to compel obedience, the audiencia's delegates often had to rely on persuasion and bluster or take advantage of local factionalism to accomplish their aims.

A few examples can illustrate both the court's perspective and some reasons for limiting its autonomy. When Manso de Contreras went to eastern Cuba in 1605 in pursuit of residents of La Yaguana who had fled the depopulations, he carried authorization from Antonio Osorio and the rest of the acuerdo. Letters from Cuba, especially an alarming report from the bishop of Santiago, had convinced them to take immediate action against ongoing foreign trade there. However, Manso first wrote Spain to request money for expenses, including the ship he bought for the journey, and then made a long stop in Cartagena, where (he said) he helped resolve "some seditions" among local officials. He sailed for Havana in June 1606 and allied himself to governor Pedro de Valdés; although it was outside his commission, Manso remained there several more months to gather evidence on resident elites he claimed were underwriting Cuba's illicit commerce. After Manso finally reached eastern Cuba, he charged over four hundred different individuals with involvement in contraband trade, and accused authorities like Pedro Romero Tamariz, an alcalde ordinario of Santiago, of protecting it and trying to bribe him into silence. Back in Santo Domingo, however, the acuerdo treated Manso's claims—including his statement he would rather have led two hundred men to Cuba for a military campaign than face the dangers he did as a judge armed only with papers—with skepticism and allowed his commission to expire. Manso finally returned to Hispaniola in spring 1608 with little to show for his time in Cuba apart from numerous complaints from its residents.[36]

Manso de Contreras's actions may have helped motivate tighter metropolitan restrictions on district investigations. He was likely correct about the extent of foreign commerce in eastern Cuba, which had become indispensable for many inhabitants of the Spanish Caribbean from the sixteenth century onward; however, it was evident that he used the acuerdo's authorization to pursue his own interests and strengthen his network of regional contacts, while also trying to demonstrate extraordinary service to the Crown.[37] Like his efforts to broaden the scope of his investigation and inflate his salaries, this was common, indeed logical, behavior for magistrates on similar assignments. The hostility he encountered was likewise unsurprising; commissioned judges, usually accompanied only by a sympathetic notary plus a bailiff named after arriving, were often right to fear for their personal safety. Locals were not quick to welcome an outsider with an incentive to find proof of illicit trade and the power to levy severe penalties and disrupt customary arrangements they depended on. Provincial authority figures had similar reasons to dislike these investigations, and so the audiencia's delegates frequently sought potential allies after arriving, as Manso had in Havana.

Provincial governors in particular used legal and extralegal means to resist the audiencia's interference in their business. Shortly after Manso de Contreras's return, the audiencia sent another agent who was not a superior minister to eastern Cuba for a case involving twenty-six slaves transported there by fugitives from Hispaniola's depopulations, when working through a local delegate failed. In March 1609, the contador of Bayamo, Francisco de Arceo, wrote fiscal Ruy Gómez to say he had apprehended these slave owners only to have them seized first by an alcalde ordinario and then by Santiago de Cuba's newly appointed governor, Juan de Villaverde Ureta, in order to claim one-third of their property, including the captives. Arceo railed against the alcaldes, who "made themselves kings and popes and devils, and so [he] had no one to protect [him]," while his appeals to Villaverde "went in one ear and out another."[38] The acuerdo met, decided they had jurisdiction, and commissioned Bernardino de Moxica, a trusted local lawyer, to go take custody of the prisoners, likely since he had personal connections in the area. Moxica was also given other orders, one of which was to collect unpaid fees from Manso's investigation to pay his notary Domingo Hernández, who returned to Cuba as Moxica's notary.

Within months both men returned to Santo Domingo to report that Villaverde had neutralized their authority. Moxica and Hernández initially went to the cabildos of Santiago de Cuba and Bayamo to have their commissions recognized, following proper procedure, and took control of the poorly secured prisoners. However, when they went to pay their respects to Villaverde, he stated "I embrace your grace as don Bernardino de Moxica and not as a judge of the audiencia" then physically wrestled Moxica's staff of authority away and ordered the cabildos to reject the Dominican acuerdo's provisions. Their few local supporters were unable to convince the governor to relent, and Moxica was effectively left powerless. Villaverde portrayed this episode quite differently, claiming that the two men—whom he referred to as "two judges or receptors," though he later dismissed Hernández as a "*mulato*"—were pursuing personal interests rather than justice. He further maintained they had attacked his honor by trying to discredit and even imprison him, weakening the region's defense, and called the outstanding fees "excessive salaries that would ruin many of the residents of this island." Like many other regional officials, Villaverde justified his actions using royal orders telling the audiencia not to send special judges for minor matters, in this case issued for Santiago de Cuba in 1594, and noted that he was already dealing with the fugitives on their behalf.[39]

After Moxica returned, the audiencia protested that Villaverde's defiance, together with similar opposition in Puerto Rico and Jamaica, only encouraged additional provincial resistance, as it surely did. However, the Council of the Indies did not validate their assertion that they were representing the king. While they later rebuked Villaverde for denying the audiencia's provisions instead of informing the council and waiting for instructions, they also reminded the audiencia that such commissions were only for "inexcusable cases."[40] The council's fiscal recommended sending someone other than an oidor of Santo Domingo to investigate Villaverde, although this seems to have been left for his residencia. In general, the council members did not see his rejection of the Dominican tribunal's authority as more serious than the audiencia interfering too freely in district affairs. Villaverde's confrontational tactics were repeated elsewhere in the region by local authorities fearful of the Dominican court's involvement; one residencia charge against a later governor of Havana, Sancho de Alquiza, accused him of permitting an agent of the audiencia to use his authority (*alzar vara*; literally, "raise a staff") there.[41]

The Dominican tribunal regularly relied on delegates like Moxica for district errands, and so commissions made in Santo Domingo could offer residents connected to the audiencia—especially lawyers or notaries—a chance to demonstrate exceptional merit to the Crown. In 1633, after their first envoy, Cristóbal González de Benjumea, was blocked from investigating illicit trade in Maracaibo, the acuerdo sent their chief notary Heredia there to look into the abuses of Pedro Fernández Piñero, teniente (in this context, a regional deputy) of the governor in Caracas. Heredia's commission incorporated González de Benjumea's complaint describing how Fernández Piñero and his allies had ignored his royal staff of office, ripped up his papers, and assaulted and imprisoned him, forcing him to flee for his life. It also included similar accusations by a ship captain who confirmed González de Benjumea's story and claimed that Fernández Piñero—who had earlier misappropriated slave ship duties in Angola—had seized his salvaged goods after he wrecked on the nearby coast. By March, Heredia had presented his commissions and staff of justice to Maracaibo's cabildo, which had also written against Fernández Piñero. He eventually captured the former deputy and returned to Santo Domingo to bring him before the audiencia. Like the Council of the Indies, the Dominican tribunal typically had its agents take care of multiple tasks, and while in Maracaibo, Heredia also recovered missing residencia documentation for a temporary deputy governor the audiencia had named for Río de la Hacha.[42] As this episode suggests, support from key residents, usually elites, could be crucial to the success of a special judge's mission, and so understanding factionalism was a survival skill. For Heredia, the Maracaibo cabildo's backing enabled him both to complete his commissions where Benjumea had failed and to arrest Fernández Piñero, who was out of power by then.

Oidor Alcázar de Villaseñor's 1601 efforts to punish individuals on Puerto Rico for stealing treasure from English fugitives were also shaped by local alliance networks. Since Alcázar was already headed to San Juan to audit the situado accounts and carry out other royal commissions, the acuerdo tasked him with taking over this case, which Puerto Rico's governor had started. According to the oidor's later report, four Englishmen had arrived in distress at Utias Island off the southern coast with gold, silver, gems, and coins plundered from Portuguese East Indian shipping, and Juan Ruiz and some companions had killed all but one for their riches. The conspirators tried to hide this treasure, reporting a small part to the governor and bribing the judge he sent; however, Alcázar doggedly continued prying despite their attempts to mislead him, and he even recaptured and interrogated an accomplice who broke out of prison. Eventually, Alcázar sentenced the principal offenders to death and loss of half their property and gave milder punishments to those who aided them. In a postscript, the audiencia noted that several culprits had escaped and taken refuge with the church, but for the Dominican tribunal this investigation was a victory. Alcázar's success in resolving a case the Puerto Rican governor was unable to finish allowed the tribunal's members to emphasize their utility for district management, and they recommended he be given a monetary reward to encourage others to pursue royal justice even where it was "abhorred."[43]

The limits of the audiencia's freedom to act in the region without explicit royal authorization were often unclear to the tribunal's ministers. In 1620, after fiscal Diego Gil de la Sierpe suggested the audiencia send a judge to gather accurate information on resident foreigners throughout their district, the Council of the Indies responded that simply writing to trusted locals would achieve the same ends without additional costs.[44] In other instances, the council members faulted the court or its agents for doing too little. For example, the audiencia complained in 1631 about Venezuelan governor Francisco Núñez Melián, who had jailed their envoy in Caracas and ordered soldiers to stop Coro's cabildo from obeying their orders. Since their instructions were also being ignored in Jamaica, they claimed they could do nothing but send further useless provisions. In response, the council's fiscal remarked sharply, "It does not seem that they lack power but rather resolve," and he argued they had already been conceded all necessary authority and should be held responsible for failing in their obligations. Audiencia members were expected to know when their involvement was appropriate and figure out how to secure effective jurisdiction; that they often fell short on both counts helped keep them reliant on metropolitan guidance.[45]

Although the tribunal faced resistance from a variety of regional authorities, including the bishop of Caracas in 1641, most of its major struggles were with governors or their deputies, who could often command local support and use royal laws to their advantage.[46] In 1608 the audiencia reported that despite their attempts to maintain good relations with Puerto Rican governor

Sancho Ochoa de Castro and avoid interfering with his military decisions, he was flatly refusing to allow judicial appeals and pointedly disrespecting their provisions. Oidor Mejía de Villalobos's 1605 visita of Ochoa and the local treasury officials had only intensified the governor's antipathy toward the audiencia, but continuing complaints of abuses led the acuerdo to send another delegate, Gaspar Fernández de Salazar, a few months later. The new governor, Gabriel de Rojas Páramo, cooperated with Fernández de Salazar to send Ochoa to Santo Domingo as a prisoner after his residencia was finished, though Rojas Páramo also permitted Ochoa to appeal to the Council of the Indies. Opposition to Ochoa in San Juan was instrumental in removing him from Puerto Rico; however, once he reached Spain, he was able to restore his fortunes and was posthumously cleared of most charges.[47]

In some instances metropolitan authorities did at least tacitly accept the audiencia's justification for urgent provincial interventions. Following the death of Puerto Rico's governor Agustín de Silva y Figueroa, the acuerdo—Including oidor Pedro Luis de Salazar, recently returned from San Juan—met in January 1642 to discuss recent unrest there. Although royal orders barred them from naming oidores as interim governors, they decided the situation was dire enough to send oidor Melgarejo to restore order until a replacement could arrive from Spain. On arrival, armed soldiers presented Melgarejo with orders for him to leave immediately from Silva y Figuroa's chosen successor, acting governor Juan de Bolaños, who had been confirmed by San Juan's cabildo. Bolaños claimed that recent enemy activity made allowing a letrado to assume command dangerous, and he had Melgarejo forcibly expelled from the city despite the magistrate's attempt to take sanctuary with the church. The audiencia's pleas to have Bolaños punished for rejecting their commissions and threatening an oidor with violence helped earn the temporary governor two years' suspension from office in his residencia, even if the Council of the Indies later reduced it to one year.[48] From a metropolitan perspective, however, most of these problems vanished once the new governor, Fernando de la Riva Agüero (father of oidor Riva Agüero) reached San Juan.

Military-letrado friction similar to that which drove disputes with their own presidents characterized many of the audiencia's interactions with district governors. These governors regarded their defense responsibilities as paramount, although some also aimed to conceal activities like foreign trade. Yet even with royal laws supporting their military autonomy, they knew that residents' complaints could always offer the Dominican court an entry point for interfering in their affairs. During Riva Agüero's time, the Council of the Indies again upheld Puerto Rico's military independence after the town of San Germán appealed to the audiencia about having to send fifteen soldiers for a campaign in the Virgin Islands. Riva Agüero denied the appeal in 1644 but asked the council to confirm his privileges to prevent additional challenges to his authority. The king duly reminded the audiencia that they were inhibited from reviewing the Puerto Rican governor's military decisions, although they responded they had already declared the appeal invalid. In this case, the Dominican tribunal recognized their limitations, as they also did in 1691 when they declined to take action over an unsigned letter about the abuses of another Puerto Rican governor, Gaspar de Arredondo.[49] More frequently, the court's ministers worried that in fighting their involvement at every turn, district governors and their deputies bolstered their own power and weakened the audiencia's supervisory authority. Faced with the possibility that residents of the areas under their control could seek the audiencia's aid, which might have unpredictable results and set a worrisome precedent, regional officials preferred direct peninsular oversight.

In the late 1640s Margarita's governor, Francisco de Santillán y Argote, exploited divisions among audiencia members to block a special investigation without a direct confrontation. Oidor Pedro Luis de Salazar initially left Santo Domingo in 1647 with two commissions about foreign slave trading, one from the king for Cumaná, and another from the acuerdo for Margarita. When he arrived at Margarita and presented himself to Asunción's cabildo in 1648, he found that Santillán had communicated with the audiencia and convinced them to retract their commission. Salazar was furious, and blamed the governor for dishonesty and the other oidores for abandoning the cause of justice out of personal animosity toward him. While he declared (after holding the new orders over his head in the customary sign of obeisance) that he would continue anyway, it was clear that his work was over before it had started.[50] Santillán likely knew of Salazar's disputes with the rest of the audiencia and used this information to forestall a potentially troublesome judicial inquiry.

During the 1680s, the tribunal succeeded in flexibly managing more serious problems on Margarita to metropolitan approval. In early 1684 residents of that island ousted governor Juan Fermín de Huidobro and replaced him with previous governor Juan Muñoz de Gadea. Fermín traveled to Santo Domingo for help, and the audiencia commissioned relator Gregorio Semillán Campuzano to restore him to office and investigate the unrest. On arriving, Semillán discovered that opposition to Fermín was more widespread than expected, and after being denied entry to Asunción, he sailed to Caracas, though its governor refused to give military support. Semillán next returned to inform the audiencia—at that time only president Robles and oidor Pizarro Cortés—that a more forceful approach was needed. In October 1685, they sent sargento mayor Martín Cabeza de Vaca to Margarita to take over as temporary governor, restore order, and arrest Muñoz de Gadea and his allies. As a military officer, Cabeza de Vaca had better results than Semillán, judging from Muñoz de Gadea's 1691 complaints to the Council of the Indies that he had been practically kidnapped and forced to endure dishonorable imprisonment in Caracas and Santo Domingo.[51]

Meanwhile, the audiencia also sent documentation of these events to the Council of the Indies, leaving them to decide the dispute over the governorship. As a result, in 1686 the Crown ordered oidor-elect Araujo y Rivera to go directly to Margarita and carry out a thorough investigation. Even with Cabeza de Vaca as interim governor, Araujo soon realized he could not reinstate Fermín; indeed, after finding substantial evidence against the former governor, Araujo commandeered a ship and sent him to Santo Domingo as well. Due to Margarita's extreme poverty, Araujo levied moderate fines before traveling to Hispaniola to have the audiencia review his records and pass sentence (once enough oidores were present).[52] Although it took years, in this case the Dominican tribunal changed its response to problems on Margarita as it learned more about local circumstances, and the combination of initiative, prompt communication, and cooperation with Spain resulted in a district intervention that effectively combined judicial and military authority. Moreover, Muñoz de Gadea's shaky legitimacy made it hard for him to outmaneuver the audiencia, especially after they sent a soldier rather than a lawyer to enforce their orders.

More commonly, particularly against a permanent governor like Villaverde, the Dominican tribunal had difficulty getting its authority for extraordinary interventions recognized. In 1697 Severino de Manzaneda—by then the audiencia's president—was declared to have improperly "twisted the meaning" of royal orders barring the court from sending judges for minor matters when he governed Havana to prevent oidor Jerónimo de Córdoba from auditing the situado accounts; the new governor was cautioned against doing the same.[53] By contrast, following a complaint by Venezuela's governor, the Marquis of Casal, the tribunal's ministers were commanded in 1690 to justify sending a delegate to Coro to reinstate an alcalde ordinario at the cost of the accused instead of the petitioner. They responded (with documentation) that the governor's story was untrue and that a deputy the previous governor had illegally placed in Coro had interfered with the cabildo and then disobeyed the audiencia's orders, requiring them to send someone. They had also subsequently fined this representative for proceeding improperly and made him return the excessive salaries Casal complained about. The Council of the Indies appeared to accept the audiencia's reasoning and reprimanded the Venezuelan governor for sending a teniente to Coro.[54]

In the eyes of district governors, the tribunal and its agents deliberately overstepped jurisdictional boundaries to inflate their own importance and enrich themselves at local inhabitants' expense, without concern for the disruption it caused. An earlier Venezuelan governor, Pedro de Porres y Toledo, was rebuked and fined 200 pesos in 1661 for rejecting the audiencia's representative, Salvador de Caseda. However, the king also expressed his displeasure to the audiencia over Caseda's unseemly behavior in selling food in Coro and reminded them they could not investigate emergency ship arrivals without prior metropolitan approval.[55] Oidores on district assignments were sometimes accused of arrogance; Gaspar de Hoyo, governor of Cumaná, complained late in the century that two of them had refused to furnish legal opinions in Caracas, leading to a stern warning to the audiencia that such assistance was compulsory. Shortly afterward, oidor Bravo de Añaya was recalled to Spain over misbehavior in his investigation of the Marquis of Casal.[56]

Yet another Puerto Rican governor, Diego de Aguilera y Gamboa, laid bare his opposing perspective in 1652 when he wrote interim president Pantoja de Ayala about the tribunal's orders for him to stop using the title "lordship" (*señoría*), as it was contrary to royal law and damaging to their authority. Aguilera said he and those around him had to hold back laughter when he read their writ of requirement (*requisitoria*), since the Council of the Indies normally used this very title with him, and suggested the royal seals must have been "very moldy" to be used for trivialities while enemies infested nearby waters. Much like Dominican president-governors, he contrasted his honors "won with a sword in hand" to those letrados gained by "trimming lamps" and afflicting others with lawsuits. He also referred to an oidor in Cumanagotos—presumably Fernando de Cepeda—holding court in a dressing gown and slippers while reminding attendees that they spoke with "the king" himself. Even if exaggerated, Aguilera's letter captures provincial feelings about these magistrates' pompousness. The audiencia humorlessly sent the governor's letter to Spain as evidence of his disrespect (as Aguilera predicted they would), claiming that it could harm their legitimacy throughout the district. The council's fiscal remarked that the audiencia could focus on more pressing matters instead of seeking quarrels, though since Aguilera's response was rather impolitic there was no need to respond.[57]

The audiencia's authority within the broader Caribbean was intimately bound up with that of its president, and their combined judicial, military, and political powers were supposed to facilitate good governance and robust defense. The Dominican president-governor did not command the other district governors but was to coordinate with them and alert them to enemy activity and was also to disseminate information and provide opinions about regional affairs. In 1610 Gómez de Sandoval responded to a royal letter concerning the treatment of Indians around Caracas, which he had forwarded to Venezuelan governor Sancho de Alquiza to announce publicly. He also relayed what Alquiza had told him, that local *encomenderos* had asked him to suspend the royal decree for Indians not to do millwork, which Alquiza had granted after an inspection convinced him laborers were well-treated and not overworked.[58] Routing such orders through the audiencia or its president allowed the Council of the Indies to emphasize accountability by involving a separate district authority that could provide additional information, while also making it harder for regional officials to later claim the Crown had been misinformed.[59]

During the seventeenth century, the president-governors of Santo Domingo had limited patronage rights within the Caribbean, mainly to name interim district governors on the death or absence of the officeholder, ideally after conferring with the acuerdo, although these customary privileges decayed over time. Gómez de Sandoval claimed in 1609 that his predecessors had supervised sales of notary positions in places like

Margarita, which he asked to have confirmed for him, apparently without success. In 1656 ex-president Meneses complained that his successor Zúñiga arbitrarily replaced his well-qualified temporary governors of Venezuela and Trinidad with new and unfit nominees. However, a few years later—as mentioned at the start of this chapter—the alcaldes ordinarios of Caracas received royal confirmation of what they claimed was a sixteenth-century right to the interim government after rejecting oidor Padilla's authority to take over. When president Zayas Bazán named a temporary governor for Puerto Rico in 1674, the Council of the Indies was uncertain whether he had the authority to do so.[60]

In 1681, in the wake of a restitution of the provision of offices to viceroys, president Segura Sandoval requested that his own district privileges be restored. He maintained that Dominican presidents had named interim district governors for over a century, but Havana and Caracas had fought it, and now this right only applied to Puerto Rico and Cumaná. Metropolitan authorities found his arguments unconvincing, and when Pérez Caro tried to nominate corregidores for Caracas in 1691, he was definitively told that neither he nor the audiencia had any jurisdiction there apart from judicial appeals. Oidor Bravo de Añaya served as interim governor of Venezuela two years later, but only because he had authorization directly from the king.[61] By the end of the century, the president-governor had effectively lost this district patronage.

President-governors played a role in assigning district commissions to specific letrado audiencia ministers, although their discretionary power declined over this period as well. In 1605 Antonio Osorio explained that he had picked Mejía de Villalobos for the visita on Puerto Rico because Manso de Contreras had personal ties there and the other two magistrates were new. Presidents' choices might reflect or intensify internal divisions; Osorio had reason to want both men away from Hispaniola around the time of the 1605–6 depopulations, although he later implied that Manso had dishonestly engineered the investigation in Cuba (Osorio admitted to signing the commission without reading it).[62] Ministers chosen for regional tasks were not always pleased about leaving Santo Domingo. Gómez de Sandoval asked in 1609 to be allowed to compel magistrates to carry out the commissions they were given, a sentiment echoed by president Luis Fernández de Córdoba four decades later when oidor Cepeda hid for months in the Mercedarian convent to avoid an assignment on Margarita.[63] By midcentury, though, royal commissions usually named a specific person, with alternate second and third choices, so that the Council of the Indies selected the most appropriate ministers. If reducing personal quarrels was their aim, it was not obviously effective, but it did delay some tasks by limiting the president's ability to adapt to circumstances, as with the investigation in Santiago de Cuba given to oidor Córdoba in 1689, which Oviedo had to carry out in 1693. In asserting greater control over these commissions, metropolitan authorities further reduced the audiencia's options for managing district affairs.

Letrado audiencia ministers regularly assisted the president-governor, whether in the acuerdo or in special juntas, in advising the Crown about regional defense and making decisions on matters outside their judicial duties. When asked for information about Puerto Rico's situado in 1609, for example, Gómez de Sandoval and the other ministers drafted a detailed report that recommended transporting it with Hispaniola's payment to save expenses. After Dutch forces attacked San Juan in 1625, all the tribunal's members worked to send supplies there, ready Santo Domingo's defenses, and update Spain on the siege and the subsequent movements of Dutch ships. The audiencia also wrote as a body about regional challenges to their authority, such as when Porres, the Venezuelan governor, blocked Salvador de Caseda's commission in 1661. President Balboa and his letrado colleagues informed the Council of the Indies that they had evidence about over thirty ships that had arrived in that province from Dutch Curaçao and Aruba within two years. Although they could not investigate it without peninsular approval, their report drove the council's fiscal to recommend a thorough inquiry, along with a sharp warning to Porres that it was up to the audiencia, not him, to determine whether a matter was serious enough to send a judge.[64]

Unsurprisingly, the president-governor and letrados did not always agree about district affairs. Oidor Oviedo reported in 1691 that some of the magistrates criticized president Robles for claiming an overly large share of the prizes taken by two privateers (*capitanes de corso*) in regional waters. In 1689 Robles disagreed with oidores Córdoba and Araujo, who were in favor of suppressing the governorship of Margarita to save money, though three years later president Pérez Caro joined the other ministers in recommending Margarita be reduced to a dependency of Cumaná. Ultimately, the council did not heed their advice, but these responses reflect both their duty to provide regional insights to the Crown and the tension between military and financial needs.[65]

Just the same, president-governors had final responsibility for the defense of the island and region, which is why Segura Sandoval received a death sentence for allowing the pirate Van Hoorn to leave Santo Domingo and sack Veracruz in 1683. Gabriel de Chaves Osorio, Juan Bitrián, and Nicolás de Velasco, in conjunction with the governors of Puerto Rico, sent supplies to maintain the Spanish garrison on Saint Martin before it was dismantled in 1648; Bitrián also drew up a lengthy report about the Dutch in Curaçao when he wrote about these aid shipments in 1640. Despite limited local resources, president Pedro de Carvajal y Cobos provided munitions to Cumaná and Venezuela during the 1660s, while Segura—likely to offset his mishandling of Van Hoorn—put together a list of Dutch, English, French, Danish, and Swedish settlements in the Americas in 1683.[66]

As was readily apparent on both sides of the Atlantic, the seventeenth-century Caribbean was a fundamentally international arena, whether or not the Spanish Crown was prepared to admit it. Although peninsular officials viewed foreigners in the region primarily as enemies, from the early 1500s onward trade forged persistent ties of mutual benefit between Spanish subjects and non-Spanish traders. These pervasive connections are usually only hinted at in the correspondence of audiencia members—for example, in 1608 when Osorio complained that letters he had sent from Santo Domingo wound up in Manso de Contreras's hands in Cuba after being captured by a foreign ship.[67] As other European powers made significant inroads into the Dominican audiencia's district over the course of the century, the Council of the Indies found itself in the awkward position of acknowledging non-Spanish settlement while maintaining that it was both illegal and temporary. This delicate political situation was reflected by peace treaties in 1648, 1659, 1678, and 1697 permitting Dutch, Portuguese, English, and French ships to seek emergency shelter and supplies in Spanish ports while forbidding them to trade.[68]

President-governors were responsible for enforcing these treaties, but particularly in the second half of the century, dealing with other Europeans in the Caribbean as conditional allies who constantly sought to circumvent Spain's commercial restrictions was nearly as much trouble as fighting them. In 1677 the governor of Curaçao, Jan Doncker, wrote Zayas Bazán about the

French fleet that had recently attacked Cayenne; he also sent some powder "just in case [they] were not well provided" and the "latest gazettes" from the Netherlands, a courtesy that may also have been subtle mockery of Hispaniola's poor communications. Another governor of Curaçao, Willem Kerckrinck, sent a ship in 1687 to request provisions after a poor harvest, though it sailed away after not gaining access to the port, confirming Robles's suspicion it was a disguised trade attempt.[69] President-governors also had to handle intelligence about developments in Europe. Pérez Caro was instructed to treat English ships bearing letters patent from the recently defeated James II of England as enemies due to their French ties in 1689, while in late 1698 Manzaneda learned from a slave trading agent in Curaçao about the Scots heading to Darién and duly notified Panama, Mexico, and Spain.[70]

On Hispaniola, the president-governor played a key role in managing relations with the French to the west and north, even after the Nine Years' War and the 1697 Treaty of Ryswick. Although oidor Araujo y Rivera estimated that the French controlled roughly two-thirds of the island, the Spanish Crown steadfastly insisted they had never specifically recognized French possession of Saint-Domingue. The Junta de Guerra explained to Carlos II shortly before his death that "the present situation of Europe obliges much dissimulation in order not to risk everything" and that "if today the monarchy were in a more robust state it might dislodge and punish the French that live on Hispaniola, without infringing the agreed-upon peace." They also reminded Felipe V two years later that the French had "usurped" this territory, though to little practical effect. Manzaneda's 1702 advice to negotiate with France for the entire island was ignored.[71]

Hispaniola's unreliable maritime connections, which worsened over the century, complicated any role the audiencia or its president could play in district supervision. In 1698 Manzaneda claimed that after waiting over two and a half years, he had simply purchased a ship to get there from Cuba.[72] Although irregular arrivals of foreign vessels meant that Santo Domingo was not quite as isolated as the tribunal's ministers reported, they were still dependent on Spanish ships even to send letters to the provinces. The annual Indies fleets made only occasional stops in Santo Domingo for most of the century, and especially in later decades indirect communication caused substantial delays. Segura Sandoval said in 1681 that it took letters three or four months to reach him after the galleons or *aviso* (messenger) ships left them in Puerto Rico. Enemy activity also restricted traffic to and from Hispaniola and sometimes prevented delivery of the situado. In 1626, for example, the audiencia reported that three out of four vessels that departed in April were taken near Saona Island.[73] Large gaps in the audiencia's correspondence during 1621, 1670, 1682, and 1697 testify to the disruption of transatlantic communications caused by foreign attacks, weather, and lack of shipping. Increasingly unpredictable communications shortened the audiencia's reach within its district.[74] In 1684 the tribunal's notaries protested laws in the printed *Recopilación de Indias* that reduced the court's ability to judge local civil suits in first instance, which would seriously reduce their pay since regional appeals were uncommon "due to the lack of embarkations and commerce with the other ports of the district." The audiencia also claimed in 1691 that provincial governors did not properly remit the monetary penalties they levied to Santo Domingo, requiring treasury officials to take a forced loan from the convent of Santa Clara to pay local infantry.[75]

Several audiencia ministers made recommendations for streamlining intra-Caribbean communications. Carvajal y Cobos suggested in 1666 that stamped paper be sent directly to provincial officials to avoid the delays of distribution from Santo Domingo. No change was made, and oidor Riva Agüero was unsure what to do in 1687 when paper from Spain was not delivered to Puerto Rico, though he eventually learned it had ended up in Havana. A decade later, oidor Araujo y Rivera's printed memorial to Carlos II identified a lack of shipping as one of Hispaniola's main problems and proposed the creation of specific transportation circuits to connect Spain's Caribbean territories.[76]

The audiencia's weak relationship with Florida offers one final illustration of how the court's role in district oversight was shaped by the logistical realities of the seventeenth-century Caribbean. Like Guyana, Florida is seldom mentioned in the tribunal's correspondence. Early in the century its ministers believed the province to be part of their jurisdiction, and in 1602 they claimed to be working on a requested report about whether Florida was worth settling. In 1608 they complained that governor Pedro de Ibarra had rejected the audiencia's provision in a case involving amber trading on the basis that Florida was not subject to their authority. They maintained, however, that they had the rights of "determining all the suits and business that come from there" and of receiving and forwarding "the cedulas that [his] majesty sends for it and its governors, as with the others of the other provinces" in their district.[77] This statement seems rather dubious, given that in 1579 governor Pedro Menéndez Márquez told the acuerdo he had not sent news in the two years since his arrival for lack of ships and noted that he usually wrote to Spain via the fleets leaving Havana. While the audiencia was occasionally asked about Florida after 1608 (and forwarded a French plan for its conquest in 1677), they effectively had no direct connection with or authority in Florida, which relied on Havana or New Spain for communication and aid.[78] As was true for other parts of its district to varying degrees, the audiencia had little more than a potential presence there.

For the Council of the Indies, the audiencia's utility as one of numerous tools for managing the Caribbean had to be balanced against its ministers' desire to establish supremacy within the district. In judicial appeals, they were one link in a chain of proper procedure, as the council reminded them in 1697 when sending a 1690 decision by Cumaná's governor back across the Atlantic for the audiencia to sentence, since only then would the council members review it.[79] Metropolitan authorities employed the court and its ministers in numerous other ways in the region, as with all overseas audiencias, though they also recognized challenges that were specific to the tribunal on Hispaniola. In mid-1692, in response to new general orders for audiencias to make regular district visitas, the Dominican ministers argued that limited shipping, problems collecting salaries, and the habitual defiance of regional governors were major obstacles preventing them from carrying out these visitas. The council's fiscal, though generally in favor of district visitas, agreed that in their case the difficulties were "insurmountable."[80]

The repeated complaints of the Dominican audiencia's ministers about provincial disobedience reflect their assumptions that they should have greater authority in the district. In 1661, after Caseda returned from his unsuccessful commission in Venezuela, they claimed most of their instructions to regional authorities were "only good for wasting paper."[81] Six years later, fiscal Juan Pizarro Cajal blamed the audiencia's inability to rectify fraud in the Venezuelan treasury on royal orders those governors had obtained in their favor. Fiscal Garcés de los Fayos and the other ministers recommended in 1677 that the Crown either order yearly inspections of Caracas or move the court there, because they did not receive regular information about Venezuela and could not rely on sending commissioned agents.[82] What none of them acknowledged, however, was that the Crown had intentionally restricted the audiencia's power to intervene in district affairs without first advising the Council of the Indies.

It is hardly surprising that regional officials—even on Hispaniola outside of Santo Domingo—often saw the audiencia as an aggressive intruder. Participation in various forms of unofficial trade fostered alliances between governors and many inhabitants of their provinces to resist external scrutiny, and the tribunal's agents threatened local arrangements.[83] Regional officials dreaded the possibility that their opponents could capitalize on the audiencia's readiness to respond to district problems, knowing it could lead to a costly and disruptive legal process followed by serious punishments. Early in the century, oidor Mejía de Villalobos condemned the treasury officials of Puerto Rico to death and loss of goods over 80,000 ducados missing from their accounts, and he even built gallows to scare them into providing security for their fines.[84] Such dramatic measures may have been celebrated in Santo Domingo, but they hardened local governors' resolve to keep the audiencia at a distance and reduced the likelihood that provincial residents could get effective redress of grievances from the tribunal.

When audiencia members carried out royal commissions within the district, the Crown also reminded provincial governors that there were multiple ways to hold them responsible for their actions, even if it took considerable time. In the early 1660s, oidor Gaspar Vélez Mantilla sentenced Puerto Rican governor José de Novoa y Moscoso to over 300,000 pesos in fines in his residencia and sent him prisoner to Spain, while the following decade fiscal Acosta y Cabrera charged Venezuelan governor Fernando de Villegas with nepotism and contraband trading.[85] Despite ordering San Juan's fort to fire on oidor Francisco de Cárdenas's ship as it entered the harbor in 1679, Puerto Rican governor Juan de Robles Lorenzana was unable to prevent an eventual investigation. He was sent to Santo Domingo in 1683, where he was imprisoned for at least two years (though he apparently avoided a five-year sentence in the presidio of Oran). Indeed, when Cárdenas sent his report and the king ordered the audiencia to proceed against Robles Lorenzana, it was in part to give an "example and lesson in these provinces."[86]

Ambiguity over how much authority the Audiencia of Santo Domingo was supposed to have over regional authorities—which was not unique to the Caribbean—ultimately benefited the Spanish Crown. Outside of military matters, preserving some uncertainty about when and how the tribunal could intervene on its own underscored the importance of the Council of the Indies as mediator and left open the possibility that the king could permanently change this relationship. When the audiencia and provincial officials did clash, both sides tried to convey to the Crown that they were looking after the welfare of district residents, even as they pursued other agendas.

The audiencia retained some supervisory duties within the Caribbean to the end of the century; in 1689, for example, it was instructed to ensure that offices in Puerto Rico, Cumaná, and Margarita were properly sold at public auction.[87] When peninsular authorities used the Dominican tribunal as one of several options for making inquiries or carrying out district commissions, they showed all involved that they were part of a larger imperial system and potentially gained alternate perspectives on regional affairs. Just the same, the Crown was not inclined to give the court's ministers broad autonomy to deal with overseas crises, and the audiencia's freedom to take initiative in the region declined over the century. Despite the opinions of its members and the fears of regional officials, the Audiencia of Santo Domingo was never meant to be an effective administrative center for the Spanish Caribbean. Rather, the tribunal's ministers served as the king's agents in the region to help supervise the district in conjunction with, not in place of, the Council of the Indies. Moreover, their oversight of district residents outside Santo Domingo was usually indirect and depended on either the cooperation of regional authorities or the assistance of local allies.

6

The Audiencia Ministers

Before turning to the relationship between the audiencia and local society in Santo Domingo, it is worth examining the origins, careers, and goals of the tribunal's members as a way to better understand their behavior during their time in office. Eighty-two different men served as superior ministers of the Dominican audiencia between 1600 and 1700: eighteen presidents, fifty-two oidores (including two in deposit from other audiencias), and twelve fiscales (not including seven promoted to oidor). Nearly thirty additional candidates were named to one of these three positions but for various reasons did not take up their offices.[1] While their backgrounds and career paths were quite varied, this group of men represented a numerically tiny part of Spanish society, mostly from the middle elite rather than the higher nobility; all of them came from relatively wealthy families and had access to either a university education or the higher ranks of the military. The biggest differences were between military presidents and the letrado ministers, although some oidores and fiscales came from families of career soldiers, like oidor Fernando de la Riva Agüero, whose father governed Puerto Rico and Panama. Social and racial restrictions, especially purity of blood requirements, were not usually mentioned in the records of their appointments—oidor Francisco de Cárdenas's note in his list of merits about papers proving he was an "hijodalgo and Old Christian" is a rare exception—but most audiencia ministers claimed at least hidalgo (minor noble) status and expected to have their claims to precedence recognized.[2] Their formation and experiences prepared them to wield royal authority and shaped how they perceived themselves in relation to their colleagues and to local residents during their time on the Dominican tribunal, which most hoped was only a temporary stop on a longer journey in the king's service.

* * *

The majority of these men were native to New or Old Castile, although a few came from other territories of the Castilian Crown, like oidor Diego Bartolomé Bravo de Añaya, who was from Vélez (near Málaga) in Andalusia and resided in Córdoba, Seville, Alcalá de Henares, and Granada during his studies. A handful, probably no more than seven or eight, were born in the Indies or had at least one creole parent, but compared to the audiencias of Quito or Lima, this was uncommon, and almost none could be considered "native sons" of the island or district.[3] Fiscal and oidor Francisco Manso de Contreras was a noteworthy exception: he was born in Spain and returned there to study but grew up on Margarita, where his father was from, making him a regional partisan if not technically a creole. Before coming to Hispaniola, he held offices on Margarita and governed Santa Marta and Río de la Hacha, and his widespread network of family and friends in the Caribbean made Antonio Osorio and fiscal Pedro Arévalo Sedeño suspect him of partiality. In his defense, Manso argued that he had made his background clear to the Council of the Indies long before his appointment, and he said because of his knowledge of regional conditions, "There has never been a judge more feared or loved than I." Manso later ascended to alcalde del crimen in Mexico, but his behavior as oidor of Santo Domingo may have strengthened the council's desire to avoid posting candidates to audiencias in their home districts.[4] Oidor Andrés Martínez de Amileta, by contrast, was from Lima but had no Caribbean connections when he was appointed in 1653. Even so, Juan de Balboa criticized him together with Rodrigo Pimentel, since they were "both creoles," and suggested the oidor's career was due to an advantageous marriage. Even less common than creoles were those from Aragón, like president Juan Bitrián de Biamonte, who described himself as an "Aragonese gentleman" in 1647 while lobbying for a seat on the Council of the Indies, or Juan Francisco Montemayor, who was made oidor due to the intercession of the Aragonese *Corts* (parliament).[5]

The social origins of these men were neither humble nor particularly distinguished, though there was a clear shift around the 1610s to oidores and fiscales with hidalgo status who used the honorific "don." A letter from 1608 shows that only president Diego Gómez de Sandoval signed with don, while the names of all the letrado ministers are simply preceded by "licenciado." Although a few oidores and fiscales were addressed with don before that time, over the following decade it became universal. After the appointment of oidor Juan Camacho de Escobar and fiscal Damián Gentil de Párraga in 1620, every letrado minister of Santo Domingo used don, and by 1631 only the long-serving oidor Juan Martínez Tenorio did not have the honorific.[6]

Names and titles were proclamations of occupation and social standing, and these men ensured they were properly observed. In general, letrados used both don and their highest university degree when writing their own names. Usage depended on the individual and the context, so while most used academic titles like "Doctor don Jerónimo de Alzate," oidor Montemayor usually styled himself "don Francisco de Montemayor," likely omitting "Doctor" to emphasize his family's noble background and equate himself with military president-governors. However, he used his full name "Doctor Don Juan Francisco de Montemayor y Córdoba de Cuenca" in a 1677 compilation of laws for New Spain. Oidor Miguel de Otalora's membership in the Order of Santiago, granted after his appointment in 1626, was unusual and reflected his family's prominence, but late in the century such markers of distinction were increasingly sought after, especially as they became available for purchase; oidores Bravo de Añaya, Manuel de la Cruz Ahedo, and Diego Oviedo Baños de Sotomayor all requested military habits in the 1690s.[7]

The pedigrees of the Dominican tribunal's presidents were considerably more varied. Some were sons of relatively important families, and two had noble titles: Bernardino de Meneses, Count of Peñalba, and Félix de Zúñiga, Count of the Holy Empire, the latter earned in the service of the Holy Roman Emperor (although both were far below viceroys in prestige). At the other end of the spectrum were Andrés Pérez Franco—who had soldiered for a half century in Europe, the Philippines, and Mexico—and Ignacio Pérez Caro, a merchant captain whose title, *almirante* (admiral), was an honorary concession rather than an earned military rank.[8] Every permanent president during this period was a don and by midcentury was usually addressed by his highest military rank ("Count" replaced rank for Meneses and Zúñiga). For example, in late 1686, Andrés de Robles became "*general de la artillería* don Andrés de Robles" after learning of his promotion from *maestre de campo*. Fourteen of the eighteen presidents were members of a military order—primarily Santiago but also Calatrava, Alcántara, and San Juan—which was listed with their names in audiencia records; Gabriel de Chaves Osorio reportedly boasted that his habit of San Juan gave him immunity from imprisonment and corporal punishment.[9]

In the seventeenth century, fiscales and oidores of peninsular and overseas audiencias were supposed to have a minimum of ten years of university. Fiscal Francisco Ladrón de Guevara, named in 1689, counted nineteen years of higher studies (*estudios mayores*) in Lima and Salamanca, while oidor Jerónimo Chacón Abarca completed nineteen years at Salamanca before his 1672 nomination. A few other candidates got at least part of their education in Lima or Mexico, though the great majority went to peninsular universities. During this time, they needed to earn at least the degree of *bachiller* in canon or civil law, though only three of Santo Domingo's sixty-four oidores and fiscales stopped there. A further forty-three earned the next rank of *licenciado*, and eighteen went on to the highest level of *doctor*, which opened access to professorial positions in universities while improving their prospects for royal office.[10]

The accomplishments of applicants for posts in the imperial bureaucracy were listed in documents usually called *relaciones de méritos y servicios* that described educational and employment history, services to the Crown, and other qualifications, including relatives' services. Versions of these records used by the Council and Cámara of the Indies, annotated as candidates acquired new merits and occupations, have been preserved for many audiencia ministers appointed from the 1640s onward, while council members' discussions sometimes contain notes about nominees before this point. Those for letrado aspirants included scholarly distinctions, such as graduating *nemine discrepante*, which indicated they had been approved without dissent. Some future ministers pursued multiple degrees, as did oidor-elect Lucas Francisco de Bilbao la Vieja, who became a licenciado and maestro in arts in Seville before switching to Salamanca for degrees of bachiller in both theology and canon law. Recently graduated candidates, or those still at university, often noted other achievements like literary exercises or substitutions for permanent faculty; several future members of Santo Domingo's audiencia described how many times they had competed for temporary and permanent *cátedras* (professorial chairs), whether or not they succeeded.[11]

As a mark of status and a source of personal connections, membership in one of the *colegios* within a European or American university could also benefit candidates, although none of the seventeenth-century oidores or fiscales of Santo Domingo belonged to the six main *colegios mayores* in Spain, as peninsular councilors often did. Those listed for nominees to the

Dominican tribunal included Santa Catalina Mártir de los Verdes, San Felipe y Santiago, and Los Caballeros Manriques at Alcalá de Henares; Santo Tomás, San Miguel, San Pelayo, and La Magdalena at Salamanca; Pan y Carbón at Oviedo; the Colegio Real of Granada; Santa María de Jesús at Seville; and San Martín in Lima. While not all these colegios (or universities) carried the same prestige, admission to a colegio was usually based on a combination of social connections and academic merit, and was clearly regarded as a sign of distinction. However, it is difficult to assess how much help the influence of fellow *colegiales* in positions of power was in gaining an overseas post, especially for lesser colegios. As with honors like military habits, it appears that the proportion of colegiales among the growing numbers of candidates for audiencia openings rose later in the century.[12] Yet for all letrado ministers, having a university education set them apart from most residents of Santo Domingo.

Some letrados had a range of occupations after university prior to obtaining a post on Hispaniola. Bilbao had been a licensed lawyer of the royal councils for about a decade when he was named oidor in 1687, and he had developed useful relationships with council members; his work on special projects like compiling the indices of the *Recopilación* earned an enthusiastic recommendation from a member of the Council of Castile, which was added to his merits, and he was promoted to Chile before reaching Santo Domingo. Riva Agüero practiced law for years in the Audiencia of Galicia after graduating as bachiller from Salamanca in 1671, then in 1680 moved to court at Madrid and became a lawyer of the royal councils. From then until 1686, he carried out commissions for these councils and the Audiencias of Valladolid and Granada (one of which ended in a shootout); his time as alcalde mayor of Málaga, Murcia, and Toledo gave him experience far beyond his education by the time he was made oidor of Santo Domingo. Similarly, oidores Juan Martínez Tenorio, Gaspar Narváez de Valdelomar, Andrés Caballero, and Pedro Álvarez de Toledo Venegas had been, respectively, relator of the House of Trade, *auditor de guerra* of the armada, and alcaldes mayores of Salamanca and Málaga before being named to the Dominican tribunal.[13] Naturally, lists of merits for these candidates usually focused less on university achievements; however, a few including Pedro Sanz Morquecho, Montemayor, and Chacón Abarca reinforced their scholarly credentials by writing books during or after their time in Santo Domingo.[14]

Family history, which varied considerably for letrados, also played a role in qualifying candidates for bureaucratic positions, and relaciones de méritos frequently incorporated the services of fathers and grandfathers. The impressive accomplishments Juan Padilla Guardiola listed in 1689 built on those of his relatives, which helped elevate him to oidor of Mexico and gain him both a habit of Calatrava and a new noble title, Marquis of Santa Fe de Guardiola. These were, in a sense, rewards for his entire family: Padilla's father belonged to the elite colegio mayor of Cuenca at Salamanca and was an oidor in Seville and Granada, two uncles died in military service without heirs, one grandfather was on the Council and Cámara of Castile, and the other grandfather was visitador general in Naples. Fiscal-elect Joseph Merlo de la Fuente was born in Lima and studied there as a colegial of San Martín, becoming a lawyer in that audiencia and securing recommendations from the magistrates and the viceroy. His father, after going to Spain to contest a visita sentence, had offered to renounce several years of unpaid wages as oidor in Charcas in exchange for a supernumerary or future place in an overseas audiencia for his son. This request was not explicitly granted, but it did become part of Merlo de la Fuente's list of merits—along with his grandfather's services in the Audiencias of Panama, Lima, and Chile—and contributed to his nomination as fiscal of Santo Domingo in 1684, followed by a promotion to Panama before leaving.[15]

Overall, would-be appointees to Santo Domingo (and other audiencias) did not have a single, normative career path but rather were expected to meet high standards of merit that could be demonstrated in multiple ways. Fiscal Bruno González de Sepúlveda's long route to the Dominican tribunal offers one final illustration. A native of Aragón, he graduated as bachiller in philosophy and law at Zaragoza, then completed doctoral studies in law at Gandia in 1655. He became a lawyer to the royal councils in 1662 and carried out commissions throughout Spain up to 1670, when he was made alcalde mayor of Málaga. His next major service was auditing the officials in charge of the *millones* tax in the kingdom of Granada in 1681. Two years later, his career path changed when the Aragonese Corts reminded the king of their right to two places in the Indies and recommended González de Sepúlveda. After this was communicated to the Cámara of the Indies, he was named fiscal of Santo Domingo in 1685. González de Sepúlveda's studies and services together with the Corts's intervention did not automatically earn him an overseas post or represent a trajectory that others could follow—it is unclear why the Corts recommended him, and its role in both his and Montemayor's appointments was left unstated—but these factors combined to qualify him for the least prestigious position in the audiencia system, which happened to be available. He might still have ascended further, but he was older than most of his colleagues and died on Hispaniola before hearing of his promotion to oidor.[16]

While the letrados shared roughly similar educational backgrounds, the seventeenth-century president-governors of Santo Domingo had a broader range of experiences. Most had years of military service before arriving on Hispaniola, such as Zayas Bazán, whose list of merits reads like fiction. By 1662, he had served in Flanders and France for over twenty-three years, earning promotions as he fought in numerous sieges and battles. During this time he was once left for dead, seriously wounded at least four more times, had two horses shot out from under him in a single battle in 1655, and was imprisoned by both Dutch and French forces, for about three years each time. Robles did not experience quite as many disastrous battles (though he may have lost more horses) during twenty-six years in Extremadura and Galicia, but he was still wounded four different times in combat against French and Portuguese troops. Several earlier presidents had comparable military services throughout Spain's empire, like Diego Osorio, Chaves Osorio, or Luis Fernández de Córdoba, who boasted fifty years' experience by 1651, including several turns as general of the annual fleets.[17]

These men came to Hispaniola from many different posts and were often just available at a convenient time. Around 1650, early rumors of an English invasion drove the Council of the Indies to seek a high-ranking, seasoned military commander to take charge of Santo Domingo's defense. Fernández de Córdoba and Pérez Franco had extensive experience but died in office, while Meneses's higher status but more limited military achievements made him less than ideal. After two other candidates with years of service declined the post, Felipe IV selected Zúñiga, then governing Alcántara after his time under the Austrian Habsburgs, in 1656. When the council decided in 1658 that Zúñiga needed to be removed, Balboa was hurriedly transferred from the governorship of Gibraltar, in the hopes that he had the necessary military skills and the political acumen to restore order.[18] Likewise, Robles's experience as governor of Buenos Aires qualified him to take over as temporary president when Segura was suspended following Van Hoorn's 1683 sack of Veracruz. There was no requirement that president-governors have experience overseas; Antonio Osorio was corregidor of Jerez de la Frontera in Spain before replacing his deceased brother Diego, who had previously governed Venezuela. Even Gómez de Sandoval, who obtained his office in 1607 through the Duke of Lerma's intercession, had a substantial list of merits. An attendant (*menino*) to Queen Ana of Austria as a boy, he spent years in military service before becoming corregidor in Murcia—where he organized defense efforts against Mediterranean corsair Murat Reis—and was president of the House of Trade before going to Hispaniola.[19] In general, president-governors had more practical experience than letrados before their arrival, though this did not necessarily mean that they were well suited for the position.

Only rarely is the role of alternate qualifications like personal connections or monetary contributions clearly evident in appointments to the Audiencia of Santo Domingo, though they surely influenced many of these nominations, as competitors for scarce positions looked for opportunities to turn the process in their favor. However, going to Hispaniola might be a sign that a candidate did not have enough sway to be named to a more prestigious audiencia. Gómez de Sandoval was the only president-governor to be named by decree, but though he was also given 1,000 ducados in financial assistance, the post was likely a demotion from the House of Trade. Otalora's nomination noted, alongside his academic achievements, that his grandfather was on the Council of the Indies and his uncle was oidor of Mexico and president of Guadalajara, yet his family's influence did not shield him from having to start in Santo Domingo. Montemayor, who claimed he had been named to the "inferior" Dominican tribunal even though he was supposed to go straight to Mexico, was later promoted there thanks to his own service and support from the Aragonese Corts, but his gift of six *arrobas* of cacao to the secretary of New Spain was rejected as an unacceptably direct attempt to cultivate patronage. Many other audiencia ministers also wrote to the council's secretaries, since they perceived personal relationships as a key part of placement and promotion, though these almost always enhanced formal qualifications rather than rendering them superfluous.[20] The only known sale of a post on the Dominican audiencia during this period was to president Pérez Caro. After his 1684 and 1687 voyages to Hispaniola, he was unable to collect his promised compensation and ended up negotiating for the Dominican governorship instead. Although he effectively purchased the post, his canceled debts and monetary contribution were considered another service, to be added to his previous services of ferrying settlers and supplies to Hispaniola. Just the same, this transaction meant that Pérez Caro's military qualifications were the weakest of any permanent president-governor.[21]

After sales of judicial positions began in the 1680s under Carlos II, Santo Domingo did experience a slight increase in supernumerary appointments—two in the early 1690s while several members were away on district commissions, compared to only two others in 1649 and 1661—but the change was not as noticeable as in other overseas audiencias.[22] However, taking into account increasing competition for such places and a rise in requests for honors like military habits, the academic qualifications of Santo Domingo's letrado ministers remained roughly comparable to those of earlier appointees. The same was generally true for president-governors, although Pérez Caro stands out as an unusual (and failed, from a metropolitan perspective) experiment with a president who was not a career military man. Even in this case, while Pérez Caro had difficulties managing active war with the French and was suspended for about eight years over accusations of self-enrichment, his administration was not obviously worse than many previous ones, especially Zúñiga's, and he was later reinstated. Otherwise, Santo Domingo was anomalous in that no other positions were openly sold in the seventeenth century; local elites were not interested, and candidates with money and influence to purchase office had little desire to start on Hispaniola.[23]

Nominations to the Dominican tribunal followed other shifts in metropolitan policies during the century. The Cámara of the Council of the Indies, although it did not drastically change the selection process, gave the monarch and his advisors easier control of patronage. Even so, Felipe IV unilaterally named Alonso de Cereceda oidor in 1624, when the full council handled appointments. Since Cereceda had been auditor general of the army in Italy after doctoral studies at the colegio of San Clemente in Bologna, the reasons for his selection were likely external to the Council of the Indies.[24] After the Cámara's reestablishment in 1644, Felipe occasionally chose nominees other than their proposed candidates, and its members complained to him directly in 1648 about his selection of archbishops for Santo Domingo. He rather curtly responded that he appreciated their counsel but was under no obligation to follow it, though he generally accepted their recommendations regarding Hispaniola from then on.[25]

Beginning in 1631, the ministers of the Audiencia of Santo Domingo were subject to the *media anata*, which required all new secular and ecclesiastical appointees to pay a half year's salary in two installments, one before leaving and the second at the end of the first year in office. A further impost of a quarter-year's salary was added in the early 1640s, so that between the "old" and "new" media anatas, oidores and fiscales of Santo Domingo had to pay a hefty 600 ducados on accepting their nomination and then send the same amount to Spain a year after arriving.[26] This was understandably unpopular among bureaucrats, but though the new media anata was soon repealed, the original duty was kept. Very infrequently, payment terms might be adjusted, but the tax was almost never waived for letrados. In 1666 oidor Pedro de Carvajal was permitted to defer his second payment for a year, since he and his family had been captured in 1663 by "Moors of Algeria" (and then ransomed by Mercedarians) after departing for Hispaniola, but his request to cancel it was denied to avoid setting a precedent. Another plea from oidor Jerónimo de Córdoba in 1688, to be excused from the media anata due to his family's needs and his indebtedness, was simply marked "seen." By contrast, later in the century presidents were usually exempted from the payment, since they were engaged in active warfare, which was also an incentive to accept a nomination. Even so, Zayas Bazán had trouble getting peninsular officials to recognize his claims to the same privileges as his predecessors.[27]

At least in theory, as jurists proved their merit in lower-status positions and vacancies became available, they were moved up the ascenso to more important overseas audiencias. The bottom rung on this ladder was fiscal of Santo Domingo, the least desirable audiencia; an ideal magisterial trajectory would begin there, followed by a turn as oidor of Santo Domingo or fiscal or oidor of a middle-status audiencia like Guadalajara or Panama, and ultimately as alcalde del crimen and then oidor of a viceregal audiencia. Jacinto de Vargas Campuzano, previously a lawyer in the Council of the Inquisition, was a living illustration of this path, moving from fiscal (1658) to oidor (1661) of Santo Domingo, then oidor of Panama (1664) and Santa Fe (1665), and finally alcalde del crimen (1674) and oidor (1685) of Mexico before his death.[28] However, relatively few overseas audiencia ministers started on Hispaniola or were promoted so many times.

An initial posting as fiscal or one of the four oidores of Santo Domingo was often a matter of chance. With the exception of supernumerary appointments, letrado positions could only be filled when promotion, death, or (rarely) retirement left them vacant. The Council of the Indies kept track of a separate line for each oidor; for example, Juan de Retuerta was chosen for the slot vacated when Otalora was named oidor of Panama in 1635 and was in turn replaced by Fernando de Cepeda after receiving the same promotion in 1647. The waiting lists for overseas audiencias could be quite long, as suggested by the council's notes from 1684 identifying González de Sepúlveda as number 94 out of 116 for places in the Audiencia of Mexico. Candidates were not always happy to hear they would begin in Santo Domingo rather than in another lower-tier audiencia like Guadalajara or Manila. Luis Martínez Hidalgo was living in the city of Mexico in 1680 when he accepted a place as fiscal of Santo Domingo "with all resignation," but with the support of the viceregal audiencia, he was upgraded to fiscal of Guadalajara before leaving. Oidor Diego de Orozco, by contrast, was moved to Santo Domingo in 1648 during a visita of the Audiencia of Panama, and though he went to Spain to decline was forced to reembark, while recent nominee Juan Marín de Nava was instead given Orozco's place in Panama. Men such as Cereceda or Montemayor, who felt they deserved better, might openly express disappointment at being posted to Hispaniola, but before 1700 very few could follow careers like that of Juan de Solórzano Pereira, who started in Lima and was promoted to fiscal of the Council of the Indies; not until the next century did the council regularly include members who had served overseas.[29]

Not all nominees were willing to accept a position on the Dominican tribunal. For most of these men, travel to Hispaniola entailed considerable risk en route to a life of less material comfort. Joseph Luna y Peralta was seized by Algerian pirates in 1663, the same year Pedro de Carvajal was captured, after leaving to investigate Balboa. Pedro de Treviño refused the post of oidor due to a "long illness" in 1658. Fiscal-elect Nicolás Baraiz y Molinet explained to the Council of the Indies in 1684 that he was determined to accept even though his frequent, documented health problems made the island's climate a risk to his life; however, despite his "zealous persuasions," his wife refused to go, which (together with his limited funds for the voyage) forced him to decline.[30] Some prospective ministers had alternate career options, as did Marcos Marañon y Lara, who chose to become relator of the Council of the Inquisition after being named oidor in 1699. Still others, like oidor-elect Sebastián Pérez de Moya in 1672, preferred to continue studying instead of gambling on an unknown future overseas. Diego de Sierra Valdez in 1664 and Francisco Sánchez de la Barcena in 1688 simply dragged their feet on needed paperwork for so long—the latter for eleven months, and the former for five years—that the council withdrew their appointments to the understaffed Dominican audiencia.[31]

Since president-governors were considered essential for government and defense, nominees to this post were more likely than letrados to request or be offered additional incentives to accept, including exemption from the media anata. Diego de Acuña was promised 2,000 ducados' assistance, which he claimed his predecessors received, though he was still negotiating for it in 1625 after nearly a year on the island. Metropolitan authorities also tended to handle president-governors more diplomatically—for example, in easing Zúñiga out of office in 1658 without publicly harming his reputation or in denying Antonio Monforte a future place of president in 1697 for the "disconsolation" it might cause Severino de Manzaneda while still in office.[32]

The only other audiencia position filled by the Council of the Indies, though sporadically, was that of relator.[33] While the tribunal required a relator to function, the office was well below the fiscal in status, and relatores were drawn from a different pool of candidates. It was the audiencia's responsibility to ensure the relator's duties were carried out, but the years following Doctor Jerónimo Gutiérrez de Salas's nomination in 1608 illustrate how haphazardly this was done. Gutiérrez de Salas reached Hispaniola but left again in early 1609 to bring his family back from Mexico. When he did not return, the audiencia chose a visiting lawyer from Margarita to fill in temporarily, though he made so many mistakes that the superior ministers eventually made chief notary Gaspar de Azpichueta provisional relator. After the council discovered Azpichueta was not a trained lawyer, they ordered the tribunal in 1615 to find a qualified letrado, though the audiencia responded two years later that they needed a relator from Spain due to a lack of suitable local candidates. The council members' comments about the low salary of the position were confirmed when the audiencia and their new relator, Fulgencio Martínez de Huarte, wrote in 1619 that he needed a pay increase.[34] In 1675 the council selected Gregorio Semillán Campuzano, who had arrived in 1670 as part of oidor Padilla's household and had served provisionally for three years, as proprietary relator. However, by then nobody in Santo Domingo or Madrid knew what the normal salary was. The most recent records they had were for only 53 1/3 ducados per year for Martínez in 1622, and the council approved Semillán's request for 500 ducados.[35]

There was no overlap in career tracks for presidents and letrado ministers, and even successful interim presidents like oidor Padilla had no chance of being named to the office. At least for Santo Domingo, there was also no practical way for the audiencia's relatores, lawyers, notaries, or other supporting staff to become permanent oidores or fiscales. Just the same, during the seventeenth century these secondary officials regularly acted as interim fiscales and auxiliary judges. Although the junior oidor was supposed to do the fiscal's work when necessary, if the audiencia was shorthanded, they could instead choose a temporary fiscal with half pay. Three men in particular—Martínez de Huarte, Semillán Campuzano, and Alonso de Cisneros Laudin, a lawyer who also acted as relator—served in this capacity for extended periods of time. Semillán's 1685 complaint that he was given a stool (which he refused to sit on) rather than a chair suggests that presidents and oidores did not always respect the privileges of their office; however, they performed the same duties and were held to the same standards as permanent fiscales.[36]

Management of the audiencia's secondary personnel—whose vital role in keeping the court running and shaping its decisions is rarely portrayed directly in the superior ministers' correspondence—was handled locally, subject to the later approval of the Council of the Indies. Supporting officials regularly performed multiple functions, and at various times Semillán Campuzano was not only relator and temporary fiscal but also assessor to the president, accompanying judge, interim alcalde mayor of Santiago de los Caballeros, delegate for district commissions, and French translator. A rather opportunistic approach to staffing, driven by limited funds and the court's need for the services of secondary personnel, is evident in Juan Mendes de Carvallo's employment as lawyer after he arrived from Angola in charge of a slaving vessel in 1626 as well as the dispute between president Manzaneda and oidor Sebastián de Cereceda y Girón over lawyer and relator Francisco de la Sota Palacios's suitability for office in 1699. The great majority of the audiencia's supporting officials were native to Hispaniola, especially the notaries who were essential to the court's daily business, while relatores Martínez de Huarte and Semillán, both Spaniards, ended up settling there.[37] Despite being excluded from the tribunal's upper ranks, these men provided institutional continuity for more transient superior ministers and helped anchor the audiencia in the social environment of the city and island, as is discussed in the following chapter.

Candidates who accepted a post as a superior minister of the Dominican tribunal might take months or years to reach Hispaniola. Before departure, they had to be checked for outstanding debts against the royal treasury or other impediments to office. Hipólito de Barrientos, named interim fiscal with full salary while Alarcón Coronado was under investigation, was barred from leaving in 1654 when the Council of Castile's president reported that he had been suspended for two years. In 1689 oidor-elect Bravo de Añaya's voyage was delayed over a lawsuit about a promise of marriage he had made to Catalina Vásquez de la Cuadra about ten years earlier, which he withdrew due to his parents' objections after she had given birth to a daughter. The papal nuncio fined him, to allow doña Catalina to marry, but absolved him of the marriage commitment, and by 1692 Bravo de Añaya was preparing to travel to the Caribbean with his wife Micaela de Aguilar y Ortega and four servants.[38]

Outgoing ministers also faced an embarkation process that involved substantial expenses, including the nonrefundable first media anata payment, fees for passage, and travel to and accommodations in Seville or Cádiz, where they had to present their titles of office issued by the king to the House of Trade. Most, like Bravo de Añaya, traveled with family members—including wives, children, siblings, in-laws, and nephews—and free or enslaved servants or other dependents, who usually had to demonstrate they did not belong to prohibited groups such as conversos or moriscos.[39] These parties varied considerably in size, though presidents were generally allowed larger retinues in keeping with the prestige of their offices. For example, in 1615 oidor Rodrigo de Valcárcel sought passage for his wife, aunt, brother, and six servants, and in 1695 fiscal Pedro Marín y Muñoz traveled with his wife, two children, a brother, and two servants, while fiscal Diego de Acosta y Cabrera brought only two free servants and a *mulato* slave in 1673. By comparison, Gómez de Sandoval crossed with his wife and son, two assistants and their families, and twenty-one servants in 1608. Bitrián asked for twenty-two servants in 1636, though he was given license for only ten (plus weapons and 4,000 ducados' worth of valuables).[40]

The time before departure could be financially and emotionally stressful, particularly for those with larger families, and many of these men had to take out loans against the salaries they would receive in Santo Domingo. After his nomination as fiscal, González de Sepúlveda went to Seville in May 1686, but when the fleet was suspended, he was stuck there with his wife and four daughters without means to either sustain them or return to Madrid. His request for aid was granted by making his salary effective from the date he left the royal court, rather than on taking possession, to give him sufficient credit to arrange financing. Gentil de Párraga, a lawyer in the Audiencia of Mexico chosen as fiscal of Santo Domingo in 1620, was less fortunate. He was allotted six months after receiving the news to move his "seven children and much family" to Hispaniola, but because the only ship leaving Veracruz for Santo Domingo sailed once a year (with the situado), it took him almost eight months, and his salary for that time was forfeit. Gentil de Párraga pleaded for it to be restored, in view of his family's dire financial straits and his hard work and notable accomplishments as fiscal, but the Crown's decision remained firm.[41]

On reaching Santo Domingo, a new minister had to present his titles of office to the acuerdo and treasury officials to be formally admitted to his post and paid, while also dealing with the mundane chores of setting up a household. President-governors were provided with housing in the casas reales, in a separate part of the same building complex where the audiencia met, which they vacated for other quarters when a successor arrived. With a few exceptions like oidor Otalora, who had no resident family and stayed with president Chaves Osorio, oidores and fiscales had to find lodgings in the city.[42] For many this was complicated by their outstanding travel debts and infrequent pay. Fiscal Arévalo Sedeño's 1607 request that newly arrived ministers be permitted to borrow 1,000 ducados from the treasury "to set up their houses" was accepted (unlike his earlier proposal of 2,000 ducados). Three years later, fiscal Herrera criticized the treasury officials for not correctly docking him 1,400 ducados—400 from travel expenses in Seville and 1,000 from his housing advance—and said that oidor Mejía de Villalobos owed over 2,000 ducados. A chronic lack of royal funds meant that later in the century audiencia ministers were forced to rely on personal loans, as the treasury was kept afloat by local elites.[43]

Housing could cause other problems. Some ministers tried to leverage their positions to demand special treatment, according to president Chaves Osorio's 1628 report about oidor Diego Gil de la Sierpe, who had refused to vacate a house owned by regidor Rodrigo de la Bastida. Bastida had planned to give it to his eldest son and brought suit in the audiencia, which eventually ruled in his favor, giving Gil de la Sierpe thirty days to move. However, Chaves Osorio claimed it was common for oidores to remain in rented houses as long as they liked, paying in promises rather than money, and asked for confirmation of a 1581 decree that ministers were not to take or keep houses without the owners' consent. In 1650 the tribunal allowed oidor Retuerta to occupy a property of contador Antonio de Ordas until its auction price was paid, although the Crown disapproved, since Retuerta was also responsible for collecting the payment.[44]

Audiencia ministers' households are seldom described in letters to Spain, but occasional clues—together with repeated royal laws on the subject—indicate that families strongly influenced their decisions and actions. Most of these men were married and were required to live with their wives to set a positive moral example. Early in the century, oidores Manso de Contreras and Mejía de Villalobos were permitted to come to Hispaniola without their spouses for three years, but reports about their scandalous lifestyles confirmed peninsular convictions that they needed the restraining influence of their wives. Villalobos's wife did not want to go, claiming poor health, and backed her husband's unsuccessful request to let her stay in Spain, suggesting she may have had her own reasons to remain apart from her husband. Osorio was also unable to force Manso to go live with his wife on Margarita around this time, and so both oidores were apparently not reunited with their spouses until they moved to Panama.[45]

In Santo Domingo, audiencia members' wives helped shape both litigation and the interpersonal dynamics of the court. This potential power was hinted at in royal orders forbidding ministers or their children from marrying district residents, punishable by removal from office, although compared to other audiencias this was not a major issue for the Dominican tribunal during the seventeenth century. These restrictions might, however, have influenced Antonio Osorio's marriage to his deceased brother's daughter, Leonor María

Osorio, and oidor Cereceda's marriage to Antonia de Villalobos, daughter of the chief constable of Cartagena, outside Santo Domingo's district.[46] No matter where they were from, accusations in residencia and visita investigations suggest ministers' wives were valuable channels of influence to their husbands. Around 1605, Osorio's wife was involved in a lawsuit as a creditor, and in the 1620s Mariana de Orduña, the wife of oidor Juan Parra de Meneses, allegedly arranged favorable verdicts for litigants. Mariana de Palacios y Toledo, sometimes referred to as *la señora presidenta*, came to the defense of her husband, Gómez de Sandoval, in 1610, calling fiscal Herrera a "villain" (*bellaco*) for contradicting him, and she later crossed the Atlantic to intercede on his behalf. Cereceda's open criticism of Ana de Acuña, whom he described as president Acuña's "government" for her interference with audiencia business, provoked Acuña into assaulting the oidor in an unusual episode of physical violence in 1626. These wives were not supposed to be involved in their husbands' duties; however, seeing the audiencia ministers as members of a household shows their wives to be partners who actively pursued family interests in a variety of ways, even though archival sources obscure and distort these women's roles.[47]

Many superior ministers sought advantages for their children in education, marriage, and employment. Indeed, laws against allowing the children to marry in the district reflect contemporary expectations that the fathers would make beneficial local matches for their sons and daughters. In 1622 fiscal Gentil de Párraga asked to be moved to an audiencia of "greater weight" because his salary did not cover his family's needs and because Santo Domingo's lack of teachers limited the education of his seven children. Six decades later, Juan Garcés de los Fayos solicited letters from the president, the archbishop, and the secular and ecclesiastical cabildos to recommend his promotion after eight years as fiscal and oidor in view of his tireless service and financial distress in supporting a wife and four children.[48] Presidents and letrados alike helped their sons into occupations that could lead to stable careers and advancement. Jerónimo Gómez de Sandoval had been a junior officer in the Mediterranean before accompanying his father to Santo Domingo, where he acted as lieutenant and led naval expeditions against enemies "infesting" nearby waters without pay. These services, which president Gómez de Sandoval enabled and then enthusiastically described to the Crown, set his son on a path to becoming commander of the yearly

Indies fleets and member of the Council of War.[49] Around the same time, in 1610, fiscal Herrera complained bitterly when the president and Archbishop Rodríguez removed his son from the chaplaincy of the hospital of San Nicolás. He successfully petitioned the audiencia to annul their decision (which Gómez de Sandoval regarded as an abuse of his office), and the king ordered the son reinstated the following year. Herrera protested again when a different son was passed over for the same position in 1615, claiming that his services and ancestry clearly made him the superior candidate, although shortly afterward Gómez de Sandoval imprisoned Herrera and a third son and shipped them off to Spain.[50]

In general, presidents had greater ability to create opportunities for their sons, though Meneses's rather bold request in 1656 that his son be made governor of Venezuela for fighting the recent English invasion was denied. Yet jurists were no less interested in placing and promoting their children, as shown by the audiencia's 1610 report about the military services of oidor Narváez de Valdelomar's son in Peru and Santo Domingo or by Meneses's commendation of oidor Caballero's son in 1656 for serving in the presidio without salary. Oidor Gil de la Sierpe even got the audiencia to name his son interim governor of Caracas in 1623, though its cabildo prevented him from taking office.[51]

Competition over public recognition of status extended to audiencia ministers' households as well. In 1604 Arévalo Sedeño described a dispute over seating arrangements started by Manso de Contreras, who brought his mother and daughter-in-law to mass in the cathedral and other public events and claimed his wife would precede all the other spouses once she arrived. Senior oidor Marcos Núñez de Toledo's daughter reacted by asking to be seated ahead of the other letrados' wives, while Mejía de Villalobos's mother contended that she should sit first. Arévalo Sedeño himself argued these requests harmed his own wife's reputation and, by extension, the office of fiscal. The Council of the Indies saw this matter as minutia they did not need to respond to and left president Osorio to sort it out. However, in 1610 Gómez de Sandoval—who had previously gotten the audiencia to grant his son a seat with a cushion in "public acts" as his lieutenant—received orders that only wives of the oidores, fiscal, and head bailiff, following their husbands' ranking, were to have seats on carpets in the cathedral. At the same time, he recommended that treasury officials' wives also be allowed some kind of lesser honor, to distinguish them from the "wives of mechanical officials and even *mulatas* who have velvet cushions."[52]

Other royal laws, such as those barring ministers from serving as godparents for local residents but encouraging them to do so for each other, aimed to separate audiencia members' families from the rest of the city's population.[53] This was effectively impossible. Most were not as deeply embedded in the social fabric of the district as Manso de Contreras's relatives (who Arévalo Sedeño claimed were involved in nearly all litigation before the court), but ministers' family members necessarily found places and made connections in Santo Domingo, sometimes lasting ones; Manso himself, responding to accusations about his relatives, pointed out that extended family members of other ministers had also been given posts in the district. The sons of oidores Sanz Morquecho and Juan Melgarejo Ponce de León occupied ecclesiastical positions in the city's cathedral years after their fathers had left. Pérez Caro's descendants intermarried with local families and were prominent during the eighteenth century, although his son died in 1698 while attending to his father in prison in Santiago de los Caballeros. Other dependents who arrived with audiencia members might also become long-term residents and support personnel for the tribunal, like Semillán Campuzano, who also married on the island.[54] The audiencia's correspondence offers only scattered insights into these households, but even fragmentary information strongly suggests that many ministers' actions represented the interests of their entire families and that—royal decrees notwithstanding—their relatives formed multiple connections with the social world of Santo Domingo after their arrival.

Hispaniola's poverty was a more frequent theme in the letters of audiencia members, who described the low value and scarcity of coinage, the high prices and limited availability of European foodstuffs and goods like cloth, and above all the irregularity of their salary payments. The annual situado was often in arrears, especially in the second half of the century, while the audiencia's meager and unreliable revenue from fines and fees was never enough to cover its ministers' pay, and many of these men sank further into debt after taking up office. In 1674 the letrados stressed their difficulty in living with "decency" on Hispaniola: "We see ourselves like exiles in it, and in the utmost state of misery." Their requested raise was denied, however, and new orders for their outstanding salaries to be paid promptly had no effect. Presidents had similar troubles collecting their higher salaries; some found illicit sources of income, although others claimed they had bankrupted themselves to pay for defense needs.[55]

Despite their claims of dire poverty, the superior audiencia ministers—who could earn extra pay for special commissions—were still substantially better off than most of the population of the city and island, including their own supporting personnel. In early 1622 fiscal Gentil de Párraga said the tribunal's chaplain had quit over lack of payment, and he feared the others would soon follow suit. Two years later, the magistrates wrote that because there was no money from fines and fees for the salaries of the "chaplain, doorman, clock-keeper, lawyer, and procurator for the poor and other ministers who serve and constitute the body of this audiencia," they had borrowed from another account. The Council of the Indies offered no guidance for this perennial problem beyond telling the tribunal's members to change nothing and take these salaries from "what was consigned to them." Doorman Miguel de Tafalla protested in 1636 that he was regularly owed over 500 pesos for a salary of less than half that; several decades later Francisco de Oya claimed that ten years' good service as doorman had left him with an "infinity" of unpaid debts.[56]

Although the council sometimes allowed funds to be reassigned, as in 1673 when the audiencia's chaplain was paid from church vacancies in New Spain, they remained unwilling to spend additional money on support personnel. Fiscal Garcés de los Fayos's 1677 claim that the tribunal's secondary officials were ready to abandon their effectively unpaid jobs was met with silence.[57] In 1681 the audiencia did approve Semillán Campuzano's new salary of 500 ducados as relator, despite the treasury officials' objections. The tribunal's notaries had to advocate for themselves, however, and when they wrote in 1684 that limiting local appeals would financially ruin them, they reminded the king that the offices they had purchased came with certain rights. A report from 1689 on the tips and other additional payments that oidores had (mostly improperly) received since 1659 also records how infrequent payments to the auxiliary staff were during this time. While the audiencia habitually relied on some unpaid labor, as temporary judges were not compensated, the secondary officials who made the tribunal's work possible did not expect to work for free.[58]

Relationships between the so-called "inferior" personnel and the higher-status ministers are also rarely described directly in contemporary sources.

In Quito, Tamar Herzog contends that audiencia's notaries, who kept its archives, had considerable control over the experiences of litigants and the decisions of magistrates.[59] However, visita charges against oidores suggest that letrado ministers normally built alliances of mutual benefit with individual notaries rather than being duped by them. In 1663 oidor Caballero was accused of choosing as notaries Francisco Facundo, an "intimate friend," and Mateo Moreno, the audiencia's receptor, and inducing them to cooperate in fraud with presents and favors. Yet superior ministers were also sometimes accused of mistreating supporting officials, and Caballero allegedly slapped doorman Oya's hands for not performing minor chores. Solicitor Juan de Rosados wrote the king directly in 1661 about the persecutions of oidor Gaspar Vélez Mantilla over his ties to Rodrigo Pimentel and others, which had forced him to take refuge in a convent.[60]

When they felt it necessary, other secondary personnel likewise appealed to metropolitan authorities in defense of their own interests. In 1619 head bailiff Baltasar López de Castro y Sandoval (son of the notary involved in the 1605 depopulations) petitioned the Crown, along with his counterpart in the cabildo, to oppose Gómez de Sandoval's decision to name his own bailiff. López de Castro cited relevant royal orders to argue that this was contrary to his office's privileges, which allowed him to either go in person or name a deputy whenever the audiencia needed a bailiff in the city or island. Although the head bailiff's prerogatives eroded over the century, supporting officials continued to communicate directly with the king and even traveled to Spain in pursuit of their own agendas, as did doorman Tafalla in 1641. Longtime chief notary Antonio de Heredia complained about the president and oidores delegating tasks they were supposed to do personally, like reporting on worthy subjects' merits, to those in "low offices," hinting at the resistance superior ministers encountered when they treated the audiencia's supporting staff like personal servants.[61] The letters of the tribunal's ministers often minimized the importance of the secondary officials, but these officials made their own efforts to communicate their perspectives to the Crown.

For the oidores, the process of acquiring seniority and moving up the ascenso to another tribunal normally began immediately on being received into office in Santo Domingo. In theory, and semifrequently in practice, the senior oidor was promoted first, and so observance of rank mattered to these men both for their career goals and as part of a general concern with status distinctions; oidor Gil de la Sierpe strenuously objected to his colleague Parra de Meneses's attempts to move their chairs in 1625 precisely because it negated his seniority. Especially later in the century, some appointees hurried to the island to improve their prospects for promotion, while others negotiated before departure for some advantage over their fellow magistrates. Oidor Caballero claimed he was allowed to take his oath in the Council of the Indies in 1654, giving him a head start on seniority and pay. In 1686, after the annual fleet was canceled, oidor Riva Agüero made his way to Hispaniola anyway via the mercury ships that stopped in Puerto Rico and was the tribunal's sole magistrate for nearly a year. He was understandably upset when Jerónimo de Córdoba showed up in mid-1687 with a royal concession of seniority for carrying out a special commission in Cumaná. In response to Riva Agüero's formal protest, both Córdoba and oidor Cruz Ahedo refused to swear in until the uncertainty over precedence was resolved. The Cámara eventually decided in Córdoba's favor, although Riva Agüero was actually promoted sooner. Just the same, their disagreement demonstrates how important leaving Santo Domingo was to them.[62]

Most letrado ministers hoped to move up the ascenso quickly, but many spent considerable time on Hispaniola. Cereceda, on being stripped of his promotion to Mexico and then robbed by pirates while crossing the Atlantic after a decade there, lamented, "I have not been an oidor in the Indies, but rather in Santo Domingo, the most miserable place there is in them, or in Spain." In 1607 Antonio Osorio recommended increasing oidores' salaries to encourage them to focus on their work instead of waiting to be promoted elsewhere.[63] Reaching senior oidor gave magistrates a chance to become interim president (and by custom acting governor and captain-general) if the permanent president died or was absent, which allowed them to demonstrate extraordinary services worthy of promotion or to line their own pockets more easily. Cereceda in the 1630s and Padilla in the 1670s, for example, launched military efforts that oidores normally had no authority over. Becoming interim president was largely a matter of fortune, however. Juan Alcázar de Villaseñor was away on commissions on Puerto Rico when Diego Osorio died (from a "flow of blood from the mouth"), allowing the more junior Sanz Morquecho to take over, and his report about his accomplishments as president may have helped earn him a promotion to Quito. Oidor Cepeda pressured his senior colleague Melgarejo to share the governorship with him after Nicolás de Velasco died in 1648, without success. Three years later, Cepeda missed another opportunity since he was on Margarita when Fernández de Córdoba died, although he had likely been sent there because the president felt that he was totally unfit to govern, even temporarily.[64]

Successful overseas ministers were not shy about reminding the Crown that their achievements and sacrifices merited promotion. Oidor Montemayor knew this well, and actively sought to distinguish himself, particularly in organizing the 1654 assault on Tortuga as interim president-governor. At the same time, his letters emphasized his qualifications for a better audiencia than Santo Domingo, and he was eventually promoted directly to oidor of Mexico. Fellow oidor Jerónimo de Alzate (in deposit while under investigation as fiscal of Guadalajara) even tried to share Montemayor's glory by declaring that "Santo Domingo, with only two oidores, has conquered the island of Tortuga." Some embellishment was normal, although Cereceda's boasts about the low cost of his 1635 campaign against Tortuga were undercut by a detailed contradiction from the treasury officials. Padilla, by contrast, successfully demonstrated extraordinary services as oidor and as interim governor of both Santo Domingo and Cumaná, and his frequent letters about his efforts combined with favorable residencias aided his rise to oidor of Mexico.[65]

Oidor Martínez Tenorio stands out from his contemporaries as one of very few ministers who did not actively seek promotion. Neither ambitious nor well-connected, he may have simply been promoted as far as possible. Martínez Tenorio served for over two decades in Santo Domingo after his 1604 appointment, and even when he presided following Gómez de Sandoval's death in 1624, he merely asked that a replacement be sent promptly. A year or so later, he took minor clerical orders, making him unable to vote in criminal cases. Shortly after, in view of his illnesses and long service, the Council of the Indies granted his request for retirement—something they rarely did—at age sixty-five with full salary, on the condition he attend acuerdos when he could. (By 1630, he was spending most of his time in bed.) Later in the century, oidor Cárdenas's request to join the church was noted but did not prevent his promotion to Panama. President-governor Meneses's plea to remain with his son in Santo Domingo is also noteworthy, but it was likely related to the Crown's lack of faith in his continued military leadership, plus the high costs of relocating to Charcas, rather than a sign of a permanent commitment to the island.[66]

The great majority of the Dominican audiencia's members, however, vied for advancement throughout their careers. Even those who were suspended from office, like oidores Simón de Meneses, Cereceda, or Caballero, were frequently reinstated after negotiating with the Crown and hoped for further promotions. Most moved from Santo Domingo to another overseas audiencia, with the notable exception of oidor Melgarejo, who stepped off the normal career path by returning to Spain due to illness; his later posting to the peninsular Audiencia of Galicia was likely facilitated by carrying out a visita in the Canary Islands.[67]

Advancement options for fiscales were slightly different. During the seventeenth century eight of them were elevated to oidor in Santo Domingo, while another six were promoted directly to fiscal or oidor of another tribunal. Some of these appointments were due to favorable vacancies, as when Bernardo Trigo de Figueroa was made oidor of Panama after only a few years in the 1650s. However, fiscales could help their prospects by making aggressive use of their office to uncover abuses, particularly by their colleagues. Not only did this demonstrate service to the Crown, but it might also cause enough discord that it was easiest for the Council of the Indies to send them elsewhere; in Trigo's case, his opposition to Zúñiga was part of why he was moved. Fiscal Arévalo Sedeño's detailed accusations against Manso de Contreras and others may have accelerated his promotion to oidor of Guatemala, although fiscal Herrera's tendency to fight with all of his colleagues did not help advance his career. Francisco de Prada argued in 1634 that his investigations in Puerto Rico and Cuba merited a place in Mexico or Lima, and he was named oidor of Quito the following year (despite the misgivings of the council's president about collecting the massive fines he levied).[68]

While some ministers did develop friendships with colleagues, there was little sense of common cause among the seventeenth-century members of the Audiencia of Santo Domingo, outside of conflicts with other authorities. Contemporary conceptions of officeholding meant these men saw their positions as the product of their relationships to the king and influential figures like the secretaries of the Council of the Indies, and they had little reason to develop lasting allegiance to the Dominican court. The differences of opinion that were fundamental to all overseas audiencias easily turned to resentment and encouraged ministers to criticize their colleagues as they represented their own services to the Crown, whether to push for advancement or minimize the damage from charges of misconduct. A promotion off the island depended on available opportunities, as when Mejía de Villalobos's return to Spain over problems with Gómez de Sandoval coincided with the retirement of a seventy-four-year-old oidor in Panama, but with few exceptions Dominican audiencia ministers were only too willing to go wherever else they might be sent.[69]

The time audiencia members spent on Hispaniola varied wildly. Martínez Tenorio lived in the city the longest, at least twenty-six years, while fiscal Alarcón Coronado and president Gómez de Sandoval remained on the tribunal for seventeen and fifteen years, respectively. Presidents Chaves Osorio and Pedro de Carvajal y Cobos both completed full eight-year terms, though oidores, who served indefinitely, usually cycled through in under a decade. Some, like Gil de la Sierpe, Melgarejo, Vélez Mantilla, or Fernando de Araujo y Rivera, stayed longer than this before leaving or dying in office. Others spent only a brief time in their positions, such as Fernández de Córdoba, who lived less than a year as president, or oidor Riva Agüero, who was promoted to Panama within a few years.[70]

Death ended the careers of roughly a third of the presidents of Santo Domingo and perhaps a quarter of the oidores. Diego de Orozco, for example, died about two months after reaching the island. Nominees to the Dominican tribunal were aware of widespread assumptions about Hispaniola's unhealthy climate, and resident ministers regularly blamed it for their chronic illnesses, while periodic epidemics affected the court along with the rest of the island's population.[71] Less than a year after arriving, fiscal González de Sepúlveda claimed that living in Santo Domingo had seriously damaged his entire family's health, providing medical certification of his own "hypochondria, rheumas, intermittent flatulent asthma, and other problems of lesser consideration." He died three months later.[72] In 1640 the audiencia recommended retirement for oidor Pedro Álvarez de Mendoza due to his poor health and lack of vision, while in 1668 fiscal Juan Pizarro Cajal was granted four months off the island to recuperate after seven months of being too sick to attend audiencia meetings; each was dead within a few years. Perennially ill oidor Agustín Félix Maldonado defied expectations, however. Zayas Bazán said in 1675 he had been bedridden on leaving Spain, and preparations for his burial were already underway. Yet although health issues forced him to decline a 1674 promotion to fiscal of Guadalajara, Maldonado was apparently well enough to go as oidor a few years later and soon after became oidor of Mexico. Likewise, oidor Cruz Ahedo lived to enjoy a position in Spain on the Council of Finance, even though Pérez Caro reported in 1694 that he had not had eight days of good health in four years.[73] Maritime violence in the seventeenth-century Caribbean also imperiled the lives and property of overseas ministers. Oidor Cristóbal de la Cerda Sotomayor, traveling to Chile in 1618 after a brief time in Santo Domingo, was robbed of 20,000 ducados' worth of belongings by an English corsair near Portobelo, while oidor Caballero, who survived several Atlantic crossings, died in Coro in 1673 after being attacked on the way to Margarita.[74]

The death of an audiencia minister usually spelled serious difficulties for surviving family members, especially widows and daughters left on Hispaniola with no income and few opportunities to return to Spain. The tribunal was supposed to report on these families, though spouses and children also solicited aid directly from the Crown, often arguing that their poverty was proof of the deceased minister's integrity.[75] In 1605 Ana de Villaseñor listed the services of oidor Alcázar de Villaseñor, who had left her and five children with extensive debts on his death in 1602; the audiencia said she had survived thanks to the kindness of an "honorable" local resident, and she was granted 3,000 ducados. Two decades after his father died, Antonio Osorio's son Diego got his mother's encomienda income continued for himself and his cousin Petronila Osorio de Ayala. Catalina de Vargas, Gil de la Sierpe's widow, fought for access to property (including her dowry) impounded by visitador Alonso Hurtado in the early 1630s, while Alberta Josepha de Mendoza, wife of Bernardino de Meneses, was granted a year of the president of Charcas's salary in 1657 even though he had not taken office before dying. Thanks to Segura Sandoval's redemption in the 1691 assault on the French, his daughter Teresa was able to obtain a year's worth of his former salary to return to Spain.[76]

Perhaps most tenacious of all was González de Sepúlveda's widow, Isabel María de Altamira Cárdenas Manrique de Lara, who wrote about her inability to pay funeral costs or feed their four daughters in 1688 and requested some income plus a military habit for the future husband of one of her daughters to ensure a good marriage. The Council of the Indies decided that they could give her a year's salary and a habit in view of a previous concession to oidor Caballero's wife, but by the time she received the news, doña Isabel had already buried her husband using money from alms and left Hispaniola; she was grateful but asked again for annual income instead of a one-time grant. In response, the council offered her 200 ducados per year in base-metal currency (*vellón*) and two places in royal convents for her daughters. Due to the high entrance costs and lack of openings in these convents, doña Isabel petitioned instead for a place of oidor in Galicia or the Canaries for a future son-in-law, which was given in 1691 (although she continued to negotiate further).[77] Even if her political acumen and apparent influence at court were unusual, she illustrates the active role that spouses often took in advocating for family interests.

Ministers who survived their time on Hispaniola faced some final hurdles before leaving to assume a promotion. A handful—such as fiscal Alarcón Coronado, oidores Simón de Meneses and Parra de Meneses, or presidents Zúñiga, Segura Sandoval, and Pérez Caro—were suspended or otherwise punished while still serving on the tribunal, usually due to a special investigation. Oidor Caballero was recalled to Spain after Ubilla's visita and was barred from office between 1661 and 1671 after being found guilty on several charges. He found work as a minor judge in the Canaries, however, and eventually got the Council of the Indies to restore him to Santo Domingo with his seniority intact.[78] Most audiencia members, by comparison, only had to face residencia investigations of their time in office. Those for letrados were normally carried out by an oidor named by the Crown, while presidents typically had theirs taken by incoming successors and a letrado assistant. The majority of these residencias produced only minor charges, often further reduced on review in Spain, together with the necessary declaration that the minister had performed well and deserved promotion. This was the case for oidor Diego López de la Puerta, whose residencia was done by his colleague Vélez Mantilla in 1665.[79] A few led to substantial fines or suspension for serious crimes, most notably for oidor Cereceda following his time as interim president. Since judges in these and other investigations into conduct received both public and secret accusations, the process could also deepen existing factionalism, as opponents organized testimony about abuses while the accused tried to invalidate witnesses as notorious enemies. Residencias could keep promoted audiencia members on Hispaniola in a state of limbo for several years, as with Montemayor, Martínez de Amileta, or Balboa; further delays caused by lack of transportation motivated Robles to ask in 1684 that outgoing ministers be ordered to continue their duties until leaving. If audiencia members' knowledge that they would go through a residencia before leaving did not deter them from what contemporaries saw as unacceptable behavior, such investigations still served as a regular reminder to all the potential consequences of royal oversight.[80]

For the most part, the presidents, oidores, and fiscales who accepted a place on Hispaniola during the seventeenth century saw the Dominican tribunal primarily as a gateway to more desirable positions. Letrados who made it off the island were normally promoted to other overseas audiencias—usually Panama, Guatemala, Guadalajara, and Santa Fe, less often to more prestigious ones like Quito or Chile, and in only three cases directly to Mexico. Career paths for the president-governors of Santo Domingo during this time are harder to characterize, though they were also likely to remain overseas. Acuña and Bitrián became presidents of Guatemala and Panama, Manzaneda was made governor of Cartagena, and Meneses and Balboa were promoted to Charcas and Chile but were not able to take up their positions. Others are hard to trace after their time on Hispaniola, though the most mysterious may be Carvajal: by 1688 someone named don Pedro de Carvajal y Cobos was a wanted fugitive after transporting goods from English Jamaica to Puerto Rico.[81] Just the same, long-term career goals did not preclude these men or their family members from making a home in Santo Domingo and developing working relationships and close friendships with permanent residents, often soon after arriving. Audiencia ministers might complain about the island's poverty and climate or feel that they deserved a better place in the king's service. However, they also regularly interceded with the Crown for the welfare of Hispaniola's inhabitants, whether as part of their duties, out of self-interest, or from a genuine concern for a society that they also belonged to, despite the largely fictional legal boundaries between them and the local population.

7

The Audiencia and Society

For the seventeenth-century inhabitants of Santo Domingo, the audiencia was simultaneously a privileged royal institution and a collection of individuals who were part of the city's society. Peninsular authorities and resident ministers alike worked to foster an image of the court as a body set apart from the local population, which dispensed royal justice, transmitted the king's will to the city and island, and furnished vital regional information to Spain. Even so, the entire city knew that the men who constituted the audiencia were entangled with the social world of Santo Domingo and reliant on locals for both basic necessities and recognition of their legitimacy. Employing modern conceptions of "state" and "society" to analyze the audiencia or reducing its history to an evolutionary stage in a larger process of state-building ignores contemporary perspectives on the practice of imperial administration, especially in a place where—despite audiencia ministers' insistence on their own importance—the institution was heavily influenced by the city's elites.[1] A close examination of how the audiencia portrayed the city and island to the Crown, and how its performance of royal authority was shaped by its relationships with local inhabitants, can offer a clearer understanding of the tribunal's role in connecting Hispaniola to the metropole.

As the preceding chapters demonstrate, the Dominican audiencia's claims to represent the king did not go uncontested, and the divisions among its ministers were evident on both sides of the Atlantic. Yet their collective identity, which was continually reestablished and reinforced by signs and displays, was what enabled these men to have their judicial pronouncements acknowledged as valid and to exercise some kind of meaningful local oversight. The audiencia's visible presence in the city was perhaps the most fundamental element of its legitimacy; the imposing stone casas reales where they met, in the same building complex that housed the president-governor and the royal treasury, conveyed a message of power and permanence, which justified costly repair work in 1610 and 1611. Likewise, its central location on Santo Domingo's *plaza de armas*, a short walk from the cathedral and cabildo, marked the tribunal as a key feature of the city, which was emphasized by processions linking these sites on holy days and special occasions. The superior ministers' attire also proclaimed their high office. Oidores and fiscales had a distinctive long, dark robe with a short cape, called a *garnacha* or *toga* (to be put on only after they departed for the island), while presidents usually wore clothes that identified them as military commanders. The ceremonial staff (*vara de justicia*) of the magistrates, often carried by the bailiffs who accompanied them, further symbolized their embodiment of royal justice, similar to other kinds of staves carried by a range of authority figures, including the tribunal's commissioned agents.[2] The oidores protested Félix de Zúñiga's new orders for soldiers to accompany them on street patrols in 1656 because they rightly perceived that their public power rested more on customary displays than coercive force. Toward the end of the century, the magistrates lamented that their inability to pay bailiffs meant that during these rounds they had to carry their own staves and apprehend delinquents personally, which was "far from the decency with which [his] majesty orders [his] ministers to behave."[3]

An array of ritual signs such as terms of address or spatial arrangement highlighted the institutional boundaries of the audiencia and the roles of its members whenever they met. Letrado ministers were addressed by colleagues as *vuestra merced* (your grace) and referred to as *señor*, while presidents customarily used the loftier title of *señoría* (lordship) even though royal laws suggested this was only for viceroys. Within the audiencia chambers, the superior ministers' individual chairs in the front of the room set them apart from others present, and seating, speaking, or signing order proceeded from the president through the oidores by seniority down to the fiscal. As the acuerdo, they were jointly addressed as *Vuestra Alteza* (Your Highness), or *muy poderoso señor* (very powerful lord) in petitions, signifying their personification of the king. The royal seal that enabled them to issue provisions in the monarch's name was also treated with fitting veneration; the audiencia was ordered to solemnly destroy Felipe III's seal following his death in 1621, and in 1668 oidor Gaspar Vélez Mantilla had new seals crafted in the presence of the treasury officials and a notary.[4]

None of this is to say that the audiencia's authority was accepted without question or that contemporaries confused the tribunal with the king. Rather, the constant repetition of signs and gestures surrounding these ministers, even by those who challenged the tribunal, represented a declaration of collective belief that the institution was backed by the Crown. This was further reinforced when audiencia members attended mass or walked in religious processions and were again set apart as a body and arranged in order of precedence. Such practices were particularly important to the letrados, who depended on public recognition of their status and were quick to complain when not given due respect. According to Severino de Manzaneda, the audiencia's sole oidor Sebastián de Cereceda y Girón refused to respond to acuerdo business for months because the request did not say "highness." Protocol mattered, since it allowed audiencia ministers to produce decisions that—pending review by the council—had to be accepted as expressions of royal authority, even when the city's residents did not feel their actions were fair or justified.[5]

The tribunal's members sometimes altered established conventions, however, often to undermine their colleagues. In 1604, after being told that the president, oidores, and even the lawyers were personally addressing the fiscal as "señor," Felipe III ordered them to return to previous usage; at the same time, he instructed the oidores not to carry chairs and cushions to the church in imitation of the president. Several presidents targeted fiscales in an effort to distance them from the other ministers, as in 1630 when Gabriel de Chaves Osorio blocked Francisco de Prada's wife from receiving meat that was given to oidores' spouses or in 1640 when Juan Bitrián removed Francisco de Alarcón Coronado's seat next to the junior oidor. Violating protocol could earn a royal rebuke, which would be read aloud by the senior magistrate in the presence of the other ministers, either during normal audiencia sessions or (for more serious matters) in the acuerdo, again emphasizing institutional boundaries. In 1650, for example, oidor Fernando de Cepeda was scolded for speaking out of turn and questioning Juan Melgarejo as senior oidor and interim president. Despite some local changes, ceremonial procedures for the audiencia were tethered to peninsular models and intentions primarily through metropolitan responses to the complaints of resident ministers.[6]

Public events also helped remind the local population of the tribunal's institutional identity but did not reach beyond the city and did not require active acceptance of the court's royal power in the same way that direct interactions did. Festivities in Santo Domingo were always less elaborate than those in cities like Mexico, and they became notably shabbier over the course of the century. A 1602 procession marking the birth of a royal daughter reportedly featured "over forty on horseback with different livery, in their squadrons of Spanish, French, Flemish, Germans, Turks, and Indians" plus a triumphal carriage along with bullfights, games, and fireworks. In 1681, however, Francisco de Segura Sandoval explained that plays were held at night during religious feasts so residents could attend, due to their "extreme poverty and nakedness."

Outside of Santo Domingo, the audiencia's presence was seldom felt, and its ministers rarely mentioned the interior (*tierra adentro*) of the island, which was overseen by the alcalde mayor in Santiago de los Caballeros. According to 1665 and 1666 letters from Pedro de Carvajal y Cobos and Rodrigo Navarro, it included the settlements of Santiago, La Vega, Cotuí, Bayaguana, Monte Plata, Seibo, Higüey, Azua, Guaba (modern Hinche in Haiti), and Boyá.[7] At the start of the century, oidores were supposed to carry out yearly visitas of the interior, though this was reduced to once every three years after 1613, since they were done so haphazardly. In 1622 fiscal Damián Gentil de Párraga reported there had been no such visitas for the past eight years, and—though he promised an oidor would go soon—they were almost unknown from then on. By the end of the century, while the audiencia could still order them in extraordinary cases, even the Council of the Indies' fiscal agreed that regular visitas of Hispaniola were unnecessary.[8]

The tribunal's correspondence, however, did provide a connection between the island's inhabitants and the Crown, especially within Santo Domingo. The audiencia disseminated news about the royal family, such as the deaths of queen Isabel and prince Baltasar Carlos, or Felipe IV's recovery from illness and remarriage, which were all marked by appropriate ceremonies in Santo Domingo and "the places of this island" during the later 1640s. In other ways—by collecting a monetary donation to the Crown in 1625, encouraging clergy and laity to pray for victory over the French in 1636, or having the Duke of Veragua's coat of arms removed from the cathedral in 1668 in recognition of the loss of Jamaica—the tribunal's members brought imperial concerns to the local level.[9] They also had a duty to recommend worthy local subjects to the Crown, as in 1653 when they praised the merits of Gaspar de Carrisosa y Sandoval, a parish priest and the son and grandson of regidores of Santo Domingo; he received a prebendary in 1665. While the audiencia acted as a conduit for benefits to the general population—for example, after the 1655 invasion when they were ordered to propose a suitable reward for the city's defenders—it was primarily elites who asked the tribunal to represent their interests to the Crown. Throughout the seventeenth century, usually in conjunction with the president, archbishop, and treasury officials, the court confirmed a variety of individual and group petitions for aid, such as tax concessions requested by the municipal cabildo. Audiencia ministers also relayed other, less official messages: the celebrated bit of graffiti during Félix de Zúñiga's administration proclaiming that the city knew "no more law nor king" than regidor Rodrigo Pimentel was intended for the eyes of peninsular council members as much as it was for locals. The tribunal was certainly not the only way residents could communicate with the Crown, but it was treated as an important gateway to royal favor and attention.[10]

Moreover, because of their privileged position as royal representatives, audiencia members played a key role in shaping peninsular visions of society on Hispaniola and in mediating between metropolitan expectations and residents' desires. Their reports about their temporary home give a limited and distorted elite view of the city and island but still illustrate contemporary attitudes toward social control in seventeenth-century Spanish America. As Luis Rafael Burset Flores has observed, using sources that "privilege the dominant classes" and reduce most of the population to "an anonymous mass of individuals without order, honor, or importance" is deeply problematic for understanding daily life in the colonial Caribbean, but this was essentially how the Council of the Indies operated.[11] Audiencia ministers distinguished elites (*gente principal*) from the masses (*plebe*) and generally reinforced metropolitan preconceptions of the great majority of Hispaniola's free and enslaved inhabitants as mostly nonwhite and by nature unruly and sinful; this in turn explained why they were afflicted by poverty, disease, natural disasters, and enemies and in dire need of the restraint and correction of secular and ecclesiastical officials. Yet the tribunal's letters contain a wealth of details about the island and show genuine interest in improving residents' lives alongside an obligation to police their behavior following royal expectations.[12]

Audiencia ministers had an official duty to promote the island's spiritual welfare, ideally in collaboration with ecclesiastical authorities, and they also judged some moral crimes in the absence of an Inquisition tribunal. In 1652 they wrote that a recent outbreak of disease was "without doubt" caused by local sins, which they combated by prosecuting those in extramarital relationships instead of merely warning them. Oidor Marcos Núñez de Toledo sentenced one person to burn for sodomy (*el pecado nefando*, the nefarious or heinous sin) in 1603, while in 1664 president Carvajal reflected on the depravity of "people who are so vice-ridden as those of this land" after the audiencia and archbishop had burned four people and exiled two others in a joint effort to punish sodomy (which also produced evidence of sex acts with a mule and a dog).[13]

They also tackled more minor offenses, although presidents in particular might adapt royal orders to local demands. Oidor Pedro Sanz Morquecho said he had halted gaming in regidores' houses in 1601, but eight years later Diego Gómez de Sandoval argued gambling was not a serious problem, since it was limited to private houses for occasions like weddings or baptisms. Likewise, Segura reluctantly reduced the number of bullfights and banned plays held at night because the archbishop had complained, though he understood that residents enjoyed these things; two years later he temporarily suspended royal orders to ship married soldiers to Spain to live with their wives to avoid weakening the island's defense.[14] The audiencia's moralizing campaigns generated popular resistance and resentment, and several archbishops expressed skepticism about its ministers' own piety, but these efforts reinforced local awareness that the tribunal was responsible for keeping them in line with peninsular religious values.

In their letters to Spain, audiencia ministers expressed anxiety over their ability to control a racially diverse and deeply unequal society, even as they lobbied—alongside the city's cabildo, the archbishop, and local monasteries—for increasing Hispaniola's reliance on enslaved African labor. Not long after arriving, Gómez de Sandoval wrote in 1609, "In this island they tell me there are a thousand Spanish and twelve thousand blacks, the largest part slaves and the other free, and as freedom is so sought after, it seems [only] miraculously this republic has maintained itself in peace." He believed the enslaved population's division into different "nations" had helped prevent coordinated uprisings but feared a recent influx of

Angolan captives might upset this balance. At the same time, he reported the exemplary execution of eleven "negros angolas" who had settled in the depopulated zone near Puerto de Plata. A few years earlier, Antonio Osorio had explained that he had required a ship headed to New Spain to sell all 530 captives it carried. He also recommended granting a proposal to bring another thousand slaves to be sold on credit and limiting the use of enslaved individuals for ginger cultivation and personal service to boost mining, cattle ranching, and sugar and indigo production. Gómez de Sandoval himself advocated for renegotiating the monopoly contract to transport enslaved Africans (*asiento de esclavos*) to send substantial numbers of captives to Hispaniola and Venezuela. In 1653, following the end of the Portuguese-controlled asiento in 1640 and a sharp drop-off in the slave trade to Spanish America, the audiencia sent a memorial about the island's desperate need for enslaved labor, written by one of their chief notaries and backed by the municipal and ecclesiastical cabildos. Months later they claimed that a lack of enslaved workers was the root cause of local poverty to justify their decision to let a Dutch privateer sell several hundred captives taken from the Portuguese. Local demand for enslaved African labor meant that audiencia members were often under pressure to approve irregular entries of slaving vessels, which they could also benefit from; one of the charges against Zúñiga and his legal assistant oidor Diego López de la Puerta was for allowing "many Dutch ships with cargoes of black slaves and other goods" to trade in the late 1650s.[15]

Both individual ministers and the audiencia as a whole relied on unfree labor. The tribunal's members, including the president, were legally prohibited from owning more than four slaves, but it was not unusual for them to bring enslaved attendants to the island or to purchase captives in Santo Domingo. Enslaved individuals performed a substantial amount of audiencia-related work that is only rarely visible in reports to the Crown, as with a murder trial in 1642 when Juan Grande, "slave of his majesty," acted as torturer during the questioning of Miguel Angola, a *ladino* (Hispanicized) slave, or in 1687 when Nicolás Francisco, "slave of captain Esteban de Labria," asked for his pay as town crier (*pregonero*) in a suit over seized goods. The same was true for other tasks, like repairs to the audiencia's chapel and the public jail. Fiscal Gentil de Párraga ordered twenty "blacks" to help bail out a ship in the harbor in 1626, while ten years later Cereceda sent captain Antonio

Méndez and "two blacks of his" to spy on Tortuga, where they killed some enemies and took six of their captives.[16]

In characterizing Hispaniola's nonwhite inhabitants, the audiencia offered some clues about local experiences of race, while generally reinforcing the Council of the Indies' convictions about the importance of metropolitan racial restrictions. Their letters provided very little information about the island's remaining Indigenous inhabitants, and tended to use racialized terms like "*mestizo*" in a very general sense. In 1622, responding to general orders about Indian servants, the audiencia said there were no Indian towns at all, although Gómez de Sandoval in 1610 and Segura Sandoval in 1681 mentioned Boyá, a self-governing town composed of a handful of Indigenous families. In 1616, when Portuguese ships from "Maranhão and the Amazon River" made an emergency arrival to Santo Domingo with roughly one hundred Indian captives, the tribunal decided they could not be sold as slaves, and Gómez de Sandoval put them under the temporary care of monasteries, convents, and trustworthy locals.[17]

Audiencia ministers had much more to say about Africans and African descendants on the island, both enslaved and free. For example, in 1613 they reassured the Crown that several local religious brotherhoods "of blacks of different nations" performed good works, manifested charity, included Spanish members, and did not meet without leaders' supervision. Occasionally, they even offered distant insights on those who sought to escape enslavement in the interior. Several campaigns organized by president-governors between the 1640s and 1660s targeted fugitive communities in the Sierra del Maniel for destruction. In 1650 interim president Melgarejo ordered the exemplary execution of a captured maroon leader who had escaped multiple times and relayed news of tensions in "el Maniel" between locally born maroons and Angolas over a belief the latter group was the reason "the whites were going to pursue them in their lands." He also noted reports of "smoke and fires" and missing livestock even farther west, where he planned to send patrols next.[18] Within Santo Domingo, the audiencia was charged to uphold laws on enslaved individuals, though the orders they received in 1665 to ensure that "*mulato* and *mestizo* slaves" did not carry arms (except for those who accompanied bailiffs), and to set an example with their own enslaved attendants, suggest that local observance of such prohibitions was uneven. The court also had a nominal duty to prevent egregious abuses of captives, though their reply in 1684 to general orders about safeguarding the "good treatment of black and *mulato* slaves," which they promised to obey with "care and zeal," was largely formulaic.[19]

The audiencia's members generally embraced negative stereotypes about nonwhites as a threat to peace and order, whether in 1609, in sentencing an enslaved man who had gone on a crime spree in order "to leave a memory of himself" to execution, or in 1644 when Bitrián reported that a "*negro ladino*" had guided the pirates who sacked Azua. At times, however, ministers had to manage local elites' concerns over race and status. Andrés de Robles reported in 1684 that four militia captains had resigned rather than serve under recently deceased captain Juan Domínguez because his first and second wives were black and *mulata* and the "daughters or granddaughters of slaves of some of their fathers or grandparents." Robles commented that such considerations substantially reduced the number of suitable candidates for the post. A few years later, he also wrote that, as ordered, he had verified the Indian and African ancestry of a priest in Azua (who had since died) but noted it was very remote and his family was important there, suggesting the initial complaint stemmed from competition over status.[20]

Only in exceptional cases was the Council of the Indies willing to moderate legal strictures about nonwhites—for example, when they rejected fiscal Francisco Ladrón de Guevara's 1691 request to require all free blacks and *mulatos* on the island, particularly those in the town of San Lorenzo, to pay tribute so they would "live with greater subordination" because they felt those who fled the French deserved a reward. More typical was the council's refusal to grant special dispensation for Jerónimo de Quesada Torres to succeed his father as treasury notary a year later because his mother was nonwhite, despite support from the entire audiencia, which suspended their sentence against him due to the ability he demonstrated as provisional notary; even Ladrón de Guevara felt no one else was "more fitting or of greater intelligence." Yet his grandfather, Jerónimo López de Torres, sometimes described as "*mulato*," had been chief clerk (*oficial mayor*) of the treasury—a potentially more lucrative position—for decades starting in 1626, highlighting the gap between peninsular expectations about race and the social world of Santo Domingo.[21]

The Council of the Indies did partially understand, through the accounts of the tribunal's members, that Hispaniola's racial makeup differed from other parts of Spanish America and that the nonwhite population was important to its defense and preservation, though they tended to minimize the role of Africans and African descendants. Oidor Pedro Álvarez de Mendoza dismissed a 1637 rumor that "blacks and *mulatos*" had written to the Dutch to offer help conquering the island, arguing that they had faithfully fought the Crown's enemies in the past. By contrast, Bernardino de Meneses's claim that he had needed the help of "*mulatas* and free black women" to fight the English in 1655 was meant to illustrate his desperation, and he saw it as "the providence of God, that people so miserable as are the majority of all those of this city" had responded to his call. Juan de Balboa's decision to disband the mixed-race militia companies of lanceros before the 1660 French attack on Santiago de los Caballeros—supposedly on the pretext that "his majesty did not pay blacks or *mulatos*," though likely for financial expediency—was strongly disapproved of in Spain, and they were reconstituted in the 1670s.[22] The Council of the Indies' response to the Council of War's 1658 request that Juan García Fernández, "native of the kingdom of Congo," be given command of a black regiment in Santo Domingo suggests how notions of racial difference on Hispaniola were conveyed across the Atlantic. They declared there were no such companies in that presidio but rather largely ceremonial militias "of free blacks and creole slaves," while the lanceros were "*mestizos* of Indians and other mixtures, different than *mulatos* and *negros* of Congo, Angola, Arda, and other *castas* [ethnic groups] of Africa," who were led by lighter-skinned captains, and so there were no suitable positions for "this black who has been the slave of different owners."[23]

The audiencia also provided some insights into Santo Domingo's multinational European population, in part because they were periodically charged with removing "foreigners" from the island. There were numerous Portuguese residents—although Antonio Osorio's 1606 census listed only six Portuguese *vecinos* (established heads of households), perhaps to emphasize the success of the depopulations—but subjects of several other countries also lived in the city. When Osorio was told to deport nonnaturalized Flemish and Dutch individuals in 1607, he made four crew members of one ship leave but exempted three naturalized residents, plus a clock-keeper who played the organ and two trumpet players because their services were indispensable.[24] A few may have acted as spies; oidor Cristóbal de la Cerda Sotomayor warned against allowing foreigners in port cities after the English pirate who captured him in 1618 boasted about his up-to-date knowledge of Santo Domingo. By contrast, public notary Enrique Franco said he had lived there for twenty-three years and had a wife and children when visitador Alonso Hurtado imprisoned him for being Portuguese and sentenced him to four years' exile in 1631. Oidor Salazar complained in 1642 about president Bitrián's use of Portuguese, English, French, and Irish soldiers, adding that it was scandalous "to hear them speak in different tongues."[25]

Portugal's successful rebellion against Spanish rule in 1640 increased ministers' fears about Portuguese inhabitants, although the audiencia described most as long-term residents in 1642, and the acuerdo decided to suspend drastic action in 1650 when they debated the news (later proven false) of a violent Portuguese uprising in Buenos Aires. Fiscal Alarcón Coronado and oidor Cepeda argued that local Portuguese families had been peaceful and obedient to the Crown, but interim president-governor Melgarejo was more concerned and had 47 unmarried Portuguese soldiers removed from the presidio. Two months later, he also ordered a review of all male foreigners, offering a unique snapshot of Santo Domingo's non-Spanish European population at midcentury, which listed 225 men, 155 of them Portuguese (including 61 soldiers), 33 English, 16 Irish, 9 French, 6 Flemish, 5 Swedish, and 1 Dutch. Some were sailors passing through the port, but most were apparently established residents in a wide variety of occupations, and three were elites with military habits. Compared with canon Luis Jerónimo de Alcocer's rough estimate of 500 vecinos and over 2,000 "blacks and *mulatos*, enslaved and free" that same year, these foreign residents represented a significant proportion of the city's population, and the Crown did not move to have them expelled. There are no easily comparable numbers for later decades, but audiencia ministers usually worried more about the French to the north and west than non-Spaniards living in Santo Domingo, while permanent residents tended to pragmatically ignore questions of national identity, especially in connection to foreign trade.[26]

While the audiencia sought to enforce peninsular gender expectations on the island, there were limits to their ability to regulate women's behavior, including that of their spouses. Gómez de Sandoval was asked in 1621 about reports that the wives of oidores, fiscales, corregidores, treasury officials, and other ministers had been interfering with their husbands' business, instead of living "modestly and Christianly, occupying themselves only in the education of their children and the management of their houses behind closed doors." He responded that his careful investigation had found no problems, so he had thanked the husbands and urged them to have their wives continue their good example. Although the court could punish women for crimes like infidelity, their efforts to correct the "bad way of living" of doña Isabel de Ledesma around 1667 were frustrated by local opposition. The audiencia ministers wrote that, even after being sequestered in the convent of Santa Clara following her husband's death, she had been the cause of an attempted murder, and so they sentenced her to exile from the island. However, the nuns of Santa Clara had allowed doña Isabel to take their habit, effectively granting her permanent sanctuary, and the acuerdo's decision to use soldiers to force her out of the convent generated widespread public indignation. The Council of the Indies later fined and reprimanded the acuerdo members while permitting doña Isabel to remain.[27]

Audiencia ministers also sporadically described class distinctions within the city or revealed their own preconceptions about social order. President Balboa reported on his 1659 efforts to stop the spread of leprosy (*mal de San Lázaro*) in the city and island by ordering everyone affected, even "the very powerful and principal people" accustomed to special treatment, to be moved out of their houses to the hospital of San Lázaro. By contrast, toward the end of the century, the tribunal's members advised against putting a foundling house in the hospital of San Nicolás because the infantry "and other poor people" went there, and "the restlessness of these people and those who go to visit them" would be too disturbing; they instead recommended the hospital of San Andrés, "where poor people only rarely go to recover." Such observations, even when read alongside other surviving sources, act as a reminder that written records from this period offer only fleeting glimpses of the lives of most of the inhabitants of Spanish Hispaniola.[28]

While the audiencia's correspondence emphasizes its supervisory role, it also illustrates the extent to which its members were embedded in local society. The court's supporting personnel were instrumental in connecting the institution to the city, though their importance was usually downplayed by the superior ministers. The notaries, bailiffs, lawyers, doormen, chaplains, relatores, jailers, and other secondary officials of the court, who acted as its institutional memory, were essential to its operation, and it was generally understood that they directly influenced decisions produced by the more transient ministers. The majority were permanent residents, although some began as dependents of superior officials. Fiscal Juan Vela Núñez Vote reported in 1636 that he had stopped oidores from appointing their own servants as bailiffs using royal orders from 1623; however, magistrates' servants increasingly performed these duties later in the century because there was no money for salaries. In addition to making his son an officer and giving ten servants places of soldiers, president Gómez de Sandoval employed Antonio Pérez de Ledesma, who arrived with him in 1608, as personal secretary, notary, administrator of salt, military captain, and official in charge of retrieving the situado. Those who benefited from such patronage could put down roots in the city, like longtime doorman and bailiff Gabriel Marañon, who also came to Hispaniola as Gómez de Sandoval's servant and remained with the audiencia after the president's death.[29]

Some of the occasional references to support personnel show them to be independent actors with their own affiliations and interests. Temporary relator Juan de las Mariñas, for example, was also alcalde ordinario of the cabildo and the archbishopric's legal advisor in 1649. Chief notary Antonio de Heredia joined the tribunal when his Portuguese father-in-law—Manuel González de Melo, also a cabildo and treasury official—transferred the office of registrar to him in 1633. Although Heredia was promoted to a position of trust, he did not get along with all the superior ministers. Bitrián reported that Heredia and lawyer Alonso de Cisneros Laudin had verbal confrontations with oidor Retuerta and fiscal Alarcón Coronado in 1642, the same year that oidor Salazar wrote that Bitrián used outside notaries because Heredia was "not his friend." In 1655 Heredia was fined fifty ducados for commenting that it was a "bad joke [*chasco*] to make [them] leave for every little thing" as he was sent out of the acuerdo, since he was already privy to its secrets. Oidor Andrés Caballero claimed in 1661 that he had ended Heredia's habit of "governing the audiencia" and had required lawyer Baltasar Méndez to work for the 100 ducados per year he was paid as an attorney for the poor. According to Caballero, this had turned them into his worst enemies on the island, and they coached witnesses and took their testimony while visitador Sancho de Ubilla courted women. However, both men enjoyed the favor of Caballero's opponents, oidores Vélez Mantilla and Martínez de Amileta.[30] Fiscal Alarcón Coronado wrote in 1637 that lawyers regularly failed to treat him with suitable decorum and that he had to chase down notaries for papers; however, decades later oidor Diego de Orozco maintained that notaries and relatores had useful insights to defend his consultation with chief notary Diego Méndez in a decision about Rodrigo Pimentel. In 1699 president Manzaneda even personally wrote a report about oidor Cereceda y Girón for fear that local notaries would inform the magistrate.[31]

The benefits that support staff hoped to gain from their association with the audiencia were not limited to their unreliable salaries. Chief notaries Heredia and Méndez got recommendations for family members, while head bailiff Baltasar López de Castro's fight to have his "preeminences" restored in 1627 was related to his status within the city. Relator Fulgencio Martínez de Huarte was able to delay a suit over a rural estate and continue using the land, though this may also have been why he and another (unnamed) notary were reported to the Council of the Indies for illicit affairs.[32] Accusations against notaries Francisco Facundo de Carvajal and Diego Franco de Quero (also a constable of the cabildo) for collusion with presidents Bitrián and Zúñiga also reflect opportunities for patronage and profit that such alliances offered secondary officials. For some, however, working for the court was hardly worth the trouble. Bitrián reportedly jailed Cisneros Laudin at age sixty over his friendship with a regidor, ultimately costing him a hefty 2,100 pesos and the hearing in one ear, while in 1684 interim fiscal Gregorio Semillán Campuzano complained that acting as treasury prosecutor in Segura's visita had only earned him new enemies, despite years of faithful service in multiple capacities.[33]

These references to the court's staff also reveal some of the personal relationships presidents, oidores, and fiscales developed during their time in Santo Domingo, even though they were charged by royal laws to remain aloof from the city's population. Even those with an inflated sense of their importance as superior ministers needed support and assistance from the city's residents. Many also joined or helped build alliances that included the audiencia's secondary personnel along with regidores, clergy members, merchants, treasury officials, military officers, and many others whose goals were generally compatible with their own.[34] As Tamar Herzog observes, those affected by sentences and other decisions of the acuerdo or president perceived them as declarations of favor or disfavor, and so incoming audiencia ministers were quickly identified with existing social networks.[35] Fiscal

Herrera's list of his main enemies in 1618—including Gómez de Sandoval, the president's secretary Pérez de Ledesma, lawyer Cisneros Laudin, notary and interim relator Gaspar de Azpichueta, attorney Juan Pérez de Urraca, constable (and later regidor) of the cabildo Francisco Rodríguez Franco, clergy member Diego de Alvarado, and residents Diego Valera and Bartolomé de Cuellar—captures his sense of an opposing network of interests.[36]

Even the Council of the Indies recognized that overseas officials' feelings would shape their actions. For example, in 1614 they decided not to return Mejía de Villalobos to Santo Domingo to prevent him from "avenging himself on those he understands deposed against him . . . and favoring the causes of those who swore in his defense" in the recent inquiry into his alleged drunkenness. The judicial process had two main mechanisms to account for the emotional and political relationships of both litigants and magistrates: *tachas*, by which unfriendly witnesses were disqualified, and recusations, by which judges were excluded from specific decisions. These involved demonstrating conflicting interests or enmity, and although they did not usually require rigorous proof, they could substantially affect legal suits and other business, as was the case with the recusations resulting from the 1618 visita against Herrera and Gómez de Sandoval. President Fernández de Córdoba sent testimony of multiple recusations against oidores Cepeda and Salazar in 1651 to show locals felt their decisions were unfair, while a decade later visitador Navarro went through most of the letrados in the city before finding a suitable and willing accompanying judge for Rodrigo Pimentel's suit against Balboa. Together with a recurring shortage of oidores, recusations also meant that some residents might vote in the tribunal's judicial decisions, especially later in the century. In 1681 oidor Juan Garcés de los Fayos said he was postponing difficult and important cases until new oidores arrived, because he could only sentence them with canon Diego de Medrano as second judge or with relator Semillán Campuzano when Medrano was ineligible.[37]

Audiencia ministers were not necessarily the dominant figures within their social networks, and many were indebted to local residents, as oidor López de la Puerta confessed in his 1655 residencia. The city's elites usually maintained working partnerships with the tribunal's members, something hinted at in fiscal Arévalo Sedeño's 1606 claim that several oidores conspired with "some regidores and rich men" to suppress any negative testimony in case there were a visita, allowing them to freely defraud the treasury.[38]

Influential locals did have numerous ways to get what they wanted from ministers, including exploiting the divisions between them. In 1625 oidor Gil de la Sierpe described a dispute in which regidor Santiago Rodríguez slashed Cisneros Laudin with a sword. Since at the time Cisneros was an alcalde ordinario of the cabildo, this was really a conflict of local elites that happened to include one of the audiencia's lawyers, and Rodríguez's father worked through president Acuña and his wife to get oidor Juan Parra de Meneses to vote for a split decision in the lawsuit. In 1687, when the regidores petitioned the audiencia to send a representative to Spain to report on the island's "miserable state," they managed to offset the opposition of fiscal Bruno González de Sepúlveda by lobbying his colleagues and soliciting funds from city residents, and by 1691 Francisco Franco de Torrequemada was in Madrid arguing the cabildo's case.[39]

During the seventeenth century, no one achieved more influence over the tribunal than Rodrigo Pimentel, especially in the later 1650s when he united with Zúñiga—who Juan José Ponce Vázquez suggests initially sought out the regidor—and used his family and friends to establish unchallenged control of the treasury and the yearly situado. Pimentel's entire career illustrates how president-governors and other audiencia ministers were integrated into existing social and political relationships in the city. During Zúñiga's time, one of Pimentel's local opponents, Salvador de Caseda, attempted to outmaneuver both men by traveling to Spain to report their misdeeds in person, which was one of the reasons Balboa and Ubilla were sent to the island to investigate abuses. However, even though they forcibly shipped Pimentel across the Atlantic, his wealth and connections ensured his prompt return. Once back on Hispaniola, Pimentel used the judicial system to harass and imprison Caseda and his associates, while his new allies president Carvajal and Archbishop de la Cueva dismissed Caseda as a troublemaker.[40]

Previously, Pimentel had gotten help from other audiencia members to embarrass fiscal Alarcón Coronado in 1650 for bringing criminal charges against him. In his response, Pimentel included a copy of a royal reprimand against Alarcón from 1640 and asked that the fiscal be taken to task "for slandering persons of [Pimentel's] quality with the pretext and color of the office he exercises, being only for his personal passions." Alarcón was livid: the reprimand could only have come from the acuerdo's archives, controlled by the notaries, and despite his objections oidor Montemayor, a friend of Pimentel, admitted it into the case.[41] From the 1630s to the 1680s Pimentel judiciously maintained similar relations with audiencia ministers that limited the threat of effective prosecution and gave him and his adherents a great deal of power within and beyond Santo Domingo. Yet while the degree to which Pimentel affected the audiencia was unique, his example shows how the economic and social predominance of the city's elites gave the tribunal's ministers strong reasons to partner with them soon after arriving.[42] Those who either failed to attract allies or chose the wrong ones—notably Balboa, whose residencia dragged on for years—might face real consequences.

Although president-governors had the greatest ability to demonstrate effectiveness as patrons, particularly in relation to trade opportunities, letrado ministers' willingness to offer favors also attracted supporters, as suggested by Melgarejo's 1650 comment that there was always "a judge where the malcontents go."[43] Audiencia members did not just advance the interests of individual elites but also acted as transatlantic intermediaries for the city and island, in a variety of ways. Sometimes this meant flexibly interpreting royal orders—for example, in responding to popular demand to allow a Dutch ship to sell enslaved Africans in 1653 or contributing their own funds instead of taking a forced donation from locals in 1666. More often, it meant amplifying the city cabildo's claims and advocating for broader policy changes. In 1678 the audiencia wrote at the cabildo's behest, "[A lack of ships] has reduced these vassals to extreme poverty, we see it with our eyes, and that many nobles live withdrawn for most of the year in the countryside, for not having enough to buy clothes, we see them sell their slaves voluntarily to sustain their families, or under pressure to pay their debts." A few years earlier, the tribunal's members coordinated with other local institutions to request relief from nearly all royal duties for at least two decades, which incidentally benefited them as well.[44]

While audiencia ministers' affiliations and sympathies were public knowledge in Santo Domingo, their infighting and squabbles with other institutions also provided city residents with a certain kind of free entertainment. A sense of being perpetually on display is reflected in frequent references to "scandal" in ministers' letters, usually meant to evoke concern among metropolitan council members, as when oidor Vélez Mantilla claimed in 1656 that "the *plebe* was scandalized" by Zúñiga's misdeeds. In 1611 fiscal

Herrera's shouting and scolding in the audiencia reportedly caused "much scandal and murmuration in this city," while Herrera described how Gómez de Sandoval sent soldiers with live matches on their firearms to his house to imprison him "with notable scandal" in 1616. According to Gómez de Sandoval, Herrera tried to provoke him to violence by attacking his honor whenever possible—for example, by not taking off his hat when passing by in public.[45] Contemporary understanding of the seriousness of such challenges made the feud between these two men no less compelling as a spectacle.

A few ministers, like oidor Cereceda, reveled in gossip. His colleagues' accusations to this effect seem to be confirmed by the story he told visitador Hurtado about oidor Miguel de Otalora dancing in the house of some women "who put a *moño* [hairpiece or hair ornament] on him since he was bald." (He apologized, probably disingenuously, that Hurtado should have to hear such things.)[46] Others saw danger in popular interest in their lives. Fiscal Garcés de los Fayos expressed his fears of Santo Domingo's mixed-race population in 1677 in reporting Archbishop Escalante's slanderous claims about him and the audiencia: "Among people of reason (even were they not noble) [such claims] could be borne; but, señor, among *negros* and *mulatos* who make up most of this population, what a noisy impression these injurious rumors will not have made coming from the mouth of a consecrated man, especially where there is no other knowledge of who I am than the royal seal with which your majesty deigned to honor me, which is so effaced as is manifest in so many occurrences of contempt and insult of this audiencia."[47] What audiencia members wrote about one another offers some clues about their public reputations—for example, that fiscal Alarcón Coronado' motives were "always the children of the hate or the love" for those involved or that he owned no books and never cited any laws but had grown wealthy after fifteen years in office as he and his wife conducted business from their house. However, Bitrián's account of a notary finding oidor Retuerta casually watching gambling in the house of a Portuguese man was likely taken less seriously in Santo Domingo than in Madrid. Locals generally judged whether audiencia ministers' behavior crossed the line from personal foibles into abuse of office not by the laws they violated but by the harm it caused them.[48]

Specific grievances against audiencia members were most often brought to light during residencia or visita investigations. Oidor Simón de Meneses allegedly caused the death of Miguel de Reynoto, an "honorable man," by imprisoning him while he was sick, while president Robles jailed two brothers from the Canaries and forced them to work on the city wall without pay or the food given to foreign prisoners. Reports that oidor Cereceda habitually pressured residents to loan or give him money, household items, livestock, slaves, and more, denouncing those who sued for repayment, were the basis for visitador Hurtado's condemnations for verbal and physical mistreatment of litigants and creditors.[49]

Some presidents also conducted inquiries that allowed locals to register their disapproval of individual ministers' behavior, though they do not prove that these feelings were widespread. The testimony Antonio Osorio sent in 1606 about Mejía de Villalobos's sexual misconduct, which included keeping mistresses and bullying litigants or their family members into sexual liaisons, was likely retaliation for the oidor's opposition to the depopulations; however, it indicates there were numerous such complaints against Villalobos, which resurfaced in the visita Osorio took of him two years later. Bitrián sent documentation about oidor Salazar that revealed the magistrate's harassment of Antonio Cuello, a long-term Portuguese resident, in late 1643, to the disapproval of many locals and the rest of the audiencia. More serious was Fernández de Córdoba's 1651 report about Salazar's "obscene appetites," in which witnesses testified that he had negotiated with the mother, sister, and neighbors of a twelve- or thirteen-year-old girl so he could "enjoy her" as his mistress. Their accounts suggest he was using his office to prey on their poverty, though all refused, and the mother warned that news of his bizarre request would get out. Salazar died shortly afterward, and the Council of the Indies took no further action.[50]

Anger at such kinds of abusive behavior was usually directed at individual ministers rather than the entire tribunal, but two unusual episodes of open popular resistance from 1609 and 1648 illustrate how public opinion did set practical limits on royal authorities. In the first, Gómez de Sandoval described his difficulties imprisoning Tomás Justinián, "*mulato*," over a complaint by a Spanish woman, Leonor Collantes, that he called her "dirty pig, villain, despicable old woman" (*puerca sucia, bellaca, vieja ruin*), and more when he saw her beat an enslaved boy. After the audiencia's bailiffs failed to capture Justinián, who was not actively hiding, for over a month, Gómez de Sandoval said he sent presidio soldiers to apprehend the accused.

However, "his mother and another infinity of women and some monks and residents took him away" from them, permitting him to reach the refuge of the Mercedarian convent. During the scuffle, Justinián and others even insulted and drew swords against the soldiers. Justinián's defenders included two cabildo members and a *mulato* slave of his mother, hinting at local relationships that did not neatly align with metropolitan conceptions of race or status. The audiencia's bailiffs surely understood that Justinián (likely from a moderately wealthy family, though identified here only as *mulato* in appearance) was more well-liked than his accuser and chose not to track him down; rather, it was the new president-governor's attempt to force compliance with legal procedures that turned city residents against garrison soldiers. Although he gave no further information about Justinián's fate, Gómez de Sandoval imprisoned regidor Álvaro Caballero Pimentel, along with other accomplices, and saved face by making him apologize for his role in the unrest. Yet as the president must have known, the "great quantity of women" who showed up to stop Justinián's arrest represented a much greater threat to his authority.[51]

The second episode occurred under Nicolás de Velasco, after the audiencia sentenced Andrea de la Cruz and Juan Angola, a Spanish woman and an enslaved African man who lived near La Vega in the interior, to be hanged for murdering de la Cruz's husband. As the two were being taken through the streets to be executed, their procession reached the hospital of San Nicolás, where the clergy attending the prisoners and others who joined them seized de la Cruz and pulled her into the sanctuary of the hospital's chapel, while another group did the same with Angola, who had been left unguarded. Francisco de Oya, the tribunal's head bailiff, claimed that he had called out the king's name for aid, but it went unheeded by the clergy and soldiers who were present, while some other residents with swords kept him from taking action. After senior oidor Melgarejo arrived, he was insulted and threatened with excommunication as he tried to have the prisoners removed; worse, when he spotted and grabbed de la Cruz, who was disguised in the habit of a Mercedarian monk, clergy members again snatched her away, pushing the oidor to the ground and trampling his staff of justice. Unlike the incident with Justinián, this was a direct and serious challenge to the audiencia's judicial authority.

However, the audiencia's subsequent investigation showed there had been a plan by specific clergy members to prevent de la Cruz's execution, which also allowed them to make a show of defending ecclesiastical privilege. Locals, including soldiers, hesitated when asked to choose between assisting the tribunal or offending the church, and a number of them took the rebellious clerics' side. The absence of an archbishop, which left the cathedral's provisor nominally in charge, heightened the tension, especially when the regular clergy still resented Melgarejo's 1639 invasion of the convent of Regina Angelorum. Although he allowed the cathedral bells to be rung to announce excommunication after Melgarejo entered the chapel, the provisor would not permit the communion host to be carried to the hospital, which some witnesses felt could have thrown the city into chaos. Even the audiencia's acting relator Juan de las Mariñas, who primarily worked for the archbishopric, defended the chapel's right to shelter the convicts, which Melgarejo had to overlook because no one else could perform his job. When president Velasco died a few months later, Melgarejo also had difficulty effectively punishing presidio soldiers as his interim successor. On receiving the tribunal's report, sent nearly a year later, the Council of the Indies called for severe penalties for both clergy and soldiers, to be carried out by the new archbishop and president. Even so, it was uncomfortably clear that a group of the city's inhabitants had essentially rejected a judicial sentence of execution they considered unjust.[52]

Yet neither of these episodes constituted a political crisis comparable to riots in the city of Mexico in 1624 or 1692, and despite the fears of audiencia ministers and peninsular council members they did not signify a general repudiation of the authority of the president-governor or the tribunal.[53] When Santo Domingo's residents defied the king's agents, knowing they might later face consequences, they did so for locally understandable reasons in situations where they felt that what was legally justified was not what was fair. In the metropole, these challenges to royal officials were reduced to disobedience meriting heavy-handed punishment, but the audiencia's members must have known why city residents fought them on these specific issues, reminding them that their limited coercive power was dependent on local cooperation. It is even possible that they quietly avoided similar problems at other times, as the tribunal's bailiffs tried to do with Justinián. The audiencia's ministers might claim these incidents proved that respect for royal justice was on the brink of collapse, yet there was no indication they represented a popular rejection of the court's jurisdiction. For the most part, the inhabitants of

Santo Domingo, particularly elites, accepted and even benefited from the tribunal's authority, but they expected it to operate within a local context.

The visita general of 1630 offers one final illustration of how the city provided an arena for the performances of royal officials and royal authority. Hurtado, in attempting to visibly demonstrate his superiority to president Chaves Osorio as visitador, managed to draw audiencia ministers and influential city residents closer together in opposition against him. Within Santo Domingo, Chaves Osorio succeeded in promoting the narrative he later spelled out in formal complaints, that the arrogant and erratic visitador repeatedly and publicly slighted him to raise his own standing from the moment of arrival. For example, he claimed that when he tried to make his deposition at Hurtado's lodgings, the visitador disrespectfully but deliberately received him in a suit "all of different colors" and angrily insisted on being addressed as "caballero" rather than "licenciado" to show they were social equals. While the Council of the Indies' fiscal was more inclined to believe that Chaves Osorio was looking for any pretext to derail the visita, local elites and soldiers largely sided with the president. For months, the two men carried on a symbolic struggle over precedence in full view of the city's population, in which the visitador was at a considerable disadvantage.[54]

The element of popular theater in this visita reached its height with the outrageous public demonstrations or cantaletas against Hurtado in early 1631, after he suspended Chaves Osorio. Although the president suggested they were spontaneous expressions of public disapproval, they were transparently meant to destroy the visitador's reputation and show support for Chaves Osorio. In the first cantaleta, a soldier representing Hurtado was whipped through the streets on a donkey as a crier announced he was being punished "as a *puto* ['faggot'; literally, 'male whore'] and bad visitador," to which the rider responded, "Yes as a *puto* but not as a visitador, that it was better to be a *puto* than a visitador." The rider also proclaimed that "when he died they should bury him among *mulatas* of Santo Domingo, since he got along well with them." The second cantaleta involved a group of soldiers standing outside Hurtado's house, shouting for him to send his wife out so they could cuckold him.[55] Even if these unforgivably offensive demonstrations (which Hurtado was certain were orchestrated by oidor Otalora and the general of the Tierra Firme fleet to please Chaves Osorio) did not reflect popular opinion, it appeared they did, and the president prevented

Hurtado from punishing them. The cantaletas succeeded in demoralizing the visitador and undermining his standing as an authority figure who could judge the president. When Hurtado's house was smeared with excrement in June, Rodrigo Pimentel's leading role (early in his political career) signaled his alliance with Chaves Osorio, and the visitador's orders to the cabildo to send militia soldiers to round up the guilty played right into the president's hands. Claiming Hurtado was trying to seize power, Chaves Osorio ordered him confined, effectively ending his visita.[56]

None of this means, however, that most of the city's population liked the president. Even before he heard from witnesses in the city, Hurtado was given a list of accusations in Spain that portrayed Chaves Osorio as a violent, greedy, and sacrilegious man who mocked local elites' claims to nobility, openly carried on an affair with a widow, and commanded soldiers to shoot a neighbor's dog after it bit his own dog. Apart from Otalora, the letrado ministers did not automatically follow the president's lead, and after Hurtado was placed under guard, oidores Cereceda and Parra de Meneses took him to their own lodgings for protection. Yet the visitador perfectly understood the gravity of having his doors and windows covered in "shit" (*mierda*) in full public view, arguing, "It would have been much better if they had killed and stabbed me to death in my house." The participation of Santo Domingo's residents as observers was a crucial part of this contest between president and visitador. Each man criticized the other for scandalizing the city, but the gestures they made only carried weight because they were witnessed and discussed by others.[57]

While his role as visitador general put him on a collision course with the president, Hurtado faced choices that were comparable to those confronting the audiencia's letrado ministers. He arrived as an unknown outsider, with papers to show he represented the king but little to offer locals beyond the hope of eventual redress of any abuses he might be able to prove. Although he tried to aggressively publicize his supremacy over Chaves Osorio, he failed to attract powerful allies. One of Hurtado's more serious mistakes was trying to compete with the president in terms of status and honor when he was clearly a bureaucrat. Chaves Osorio claimed that Hurtado remarked "If the oidores were men they would have had that president imprisoned" and even challenged him to a duel to the death; however, conflicts between Acuña and oidores Gil de la Sierpe and Cereceda a few years earlier had convincingly shown that letrados could not match the coercive power of military presidents. Hurtado's description of soldiers outside his house shouting "Here they didn't know any king other than the president!" reflects how firmly established Chaves Osorio's social standing and legitimacy were within Santo Domingo. The visitador had a few supporters—including his wife, doña Hipólita de Alarcón, who was accused of suborning witnesses and helped broker a dramatic but temporary reconciliation with Chaves Osorio when her husband fell ill—but his public shaming left him isolated and unable to complete his commissions. Two later (and less combative) judges, Fernando de Salazar and Diego de la Rasa, eventually succeeded in fining, suspending, sentencing to death, or otherwise punishing a wide range of individuals for charges made by Hurtado, although after Chaves Osorio's death in 1634 his fines could only be applied to his estate.[58] Just the same, the main lesson learned within Santo Domingo was that support from soldiers and local elites in particular gave the president a kind of power that was more tangible than authority based only on respect for the distant monarch.

Throughout the seventeenth century, metropolitan authorities continued to conceive of the Dominican audiencia primarily as an institution that dispensed justice and helped supervise and control the inhabitants of Hispaniola, despite abundant evidence about the agendas of specific ministers and their relationships with the island's inhabitants. In Santo Domingo, however, the tribunal's institutional boundaries looked much more permeable and situational; city residents readily understood the difference between the court as a corporate entity and the men who constituted it, which informed their strategies for advancing their own interests. Even if superior ministers hoped for speedy promotions, during their time on the island they and their families became enmeshed in local society and reliant on permanent residents, from lower-status colleagues who did much of the audiencia's work to wealthy elites who provided housing and made loans to officials and the treasury. Both as individuals and as a group, the court's members played a key role in shaping the Council of the Indies' understanding of the island and its inhabitants and in mediating between the Crown and local residents, as they adapted peninsular expectations to local conditions and kept Hispaniola connected to a larger imperial framework.

Conclusion

In view of the complaints its own ministers made throughout the seventeenth century, it might seem surprising that the Audiencia of Santo Domingo was not moved somewhere like Cuba long before 1795 or even suppressed, as the short-lived Audiencia of Buenos Aires was in 1671. Periodically torn by internal factionalism, the court was unable to pay its staff, indebted to and in league with wealthy city residents, and openly defied by other authorities in the rest of its district. When its judicial work was not hindered by a shortage of magistrates, its members sometimes suggested they had little to do; in his 1665 residencia, Diego López de la Puerta claimed that even when he had missed audiencia sessions due to illness during his eleven years as an oidor, it had never delayed business: "Only by a miracle does there happen to be a suit, and many times it has happened that I go to work and there is not even a single petition to respond to."[1]

Yet audiencia members' letters overemphasize the problems they faced and paint an incomplete picture of an institution that, for the most part, functioned as intended.[2] Despite its poverty, limited reach, and low prestige, the Dominican audiencia was a key piece of Spain's administrative structure overseas, and its utility to both peninsular authorities and overseas residents lay in something more than the volume of suits it handled. The tribunal provided at least the possibility of access to royal justice, not in the form of convincingly reasoned judicial sentences, but in decisions that were, with very few exceptions, publicly accepted as binding. Wealthier litigants' ability to appeal many of these decisions to the Council of the Indies also strengthened their ties to the metropole. The information the audiencia's ministers sent about district conditions heavily influenced peninsular conceptions of Hispaniola and the Spanish Caribbean, while royal orders to these men made them primarily responsible for a successful outcome within the limits of available resources. For residents of Santo Domingo, the tribunal was not a faceless entity that dispensed impartial decisions and inflicted royal government upon them. Rather, locals navigated the allegiances and interests of its ministers even as they recognized their utility as a two-way channel to the monarchy. Litigants, who were mostly from the city, used the court as one of several tools for dispute resolution (one potential reason for de la Puerta's claims about a lack of business) and knew that individual ministers' help could be crucial to ensuring the acuerdo produced a favorable decision.[3] Residents from elsewhere in the district continued to complain to the audiencia about provincial officials throughout the century because they perceived the tribunal as a disruptive force, which is also why these officials fought its involvement in their affairs.

Most of the problems described in audiencia members' correspondence were, from the Crown's perspective, manageable ones. Although it did not pay for itself, the Dominican tribunal was a relatively minor imperial expense, held in check by steadfastly denying its ministers' requests for a raise, and the decision early in the century to use the situado to support Hispaniola ensured that funds from Mexico or Cartagena, not Spain, covered the costs of justice and defense. The island's poverty may even have helped encourage cooperation with other authorities in the city, particularly in their mutual requests for royal aid. Personnel issues were an occasional headache for the Council of the Indies, exacerbated by slow communications with Hispaniola, but when necessary the court could be kept afloat for extended periods with a single magistrate. Conflicts among audiencia members, an enduring feature of government throughout Spain's empire and beyond, usually required no more than strongly worded letters and were often resolved when these men died or were promoted. More direct interventions were rarely necessary, and—apart from the visita general of 1630 and Sancho de Ubilla's investigations—did not usually cause lasting disturbances. Even the protracted hostilities between Diego Gómez de Sandoval and Jerónimo de Herrera that led to a short visita in 1619 did not prevent Herrera's promotion to Panama in 1620. Although reprimands, residencias, or special investigations were generally unsuccessful at curbing misbehavior, they reminded all observers of the audiencia's dependence on the monarch, and peninsular authorities continued to believe in the basic soundness of the institution.[4]

Some brief comparisons with other overseas audiencias indicate that, while the situation of Hispaniola and the Spanish Caribbean during the seventeenth century was unique, many of the issues facing the Dominican tribunal were not. Its district was under the greatest threat of foreign encroachment, but the audiencias of Santa Fe, Panama, Guatemala, and Mexico were responsible for other parts of the Caribbean and Gulf of Mexico where attacks by sea and land were common, and Chile and the Philippines were also often active war zones. The military-letrado friction that characterized the court in Santo Domingo was duplicated in all other praetorian tribunals, where career soldiers had to manage bureaucrats; indeed, even in subordinate tribunals letrado presidents clashed with the other ministers. Military men, especially those who cared little about legal technicalities, typically had an advantage in disputes with jurists, at least in the short term. In the early 1620s Alonso Fajardo, the president-governor of Manila, was accused of abuses like interfering with outgoing mail and imprisoning oidores, anticipating Félix de Zúñiga's efforts to establish total control over the Dominican audiencia in the 1650s. Chile was unusual in that its president-governor normally resided in Concepción, while the audiencia was in Santiago, helping limit competition between them.[5]

For the most part, warfare within Santo Domingo's district was more important for its effects on the audiencia's relationship with the president-governor than for its direct impact on their work. The loss of Jamaica to England in 1655, or even the rise of Saint-Domingue in the second half of the century, did not fundamentally change how the Dominican court operated, even if they did increase hostilities and opportunities for foreign commerce. This warfare, and the geography of the Caribbean, contributed to the audiencia's weak authority outside of Santo Domingo, but even other audiencias that received more regional appeals and made more frequent district visitas typically had no more than an occasional presence in most of their territories.[6]

Economic decline affecting Hispaniola and the Spanish Caribbean was reflected in the correspondence of the Dominican tribunal's members, and in a growing inability to pay support personnel. However, the shift from export production to subsistence agriculture that intensified in the second half of the century affected most of the island's permanent population much more deeply than it did the court's superior ministers. Claims of poverty, isolation, and reliance on contraband were by no means limited to Hispaniola—in 1660 Puerto Rico's governor claimed that not one registered ship had arrived in eleven years—and the presence of the audiencia likely mitigated some of the effects of population loss and limited commerce by attracting greater royal attention to the island or by keeping the port mostly receptive to non-Spanish vessels claiming distress. Occasional tensions aside, the Dominican tribunal generally cooperated with the municipal cabildo in local tax decisions. In Guatemala, by contrast, the audiencia declared in 1667 that Santiago's cabildo should no longer collect the alcabala.[7]

While Santo Domingo was unquestionably poorer than Charcas or Lima, oidores in these places also complained their salaries did not cover their expenses and requested additional pay. When royal officials' and soldiers' salaries in Panama were briefly suspended in 1662, its audiencia—including a former Dominican fiscal, oidor Bernardo Trigo de Figueroa—complained that the high cost of living there made the lack of income worse than in Santo Domingo, Havana, or San Juan, since those were "lands abundant in produce, and their vecinos and inhabitants more giving," where soldiers could live for months without pay. A few years later, the president-governor of Panama imprisoned the treasury officials after they protested his use of irregular funds to pay the tribunal's staff. The doorman of Guadalajara's audiencia said in 1661 that he was owed some 7,000 pesos in back pay (though he likely had other income). Salary issues were not as pressing for Manila's audiencia, but even so its chaplain, relator, and doorman had to petition the court for their wages late in the century when revenue from monetary penalties ran low. Chile also relied on a situado—which was likewise affected by periodic delays, seizures, and fraud—and its soldiers were similarly unhappy about being paid in clothing instead of coin. The absence of buyers for audiencia positions in Santo Domingo between 1687 and 1712 likely means that its magistrates' claims about their relative poverty were not wholly inaccurate, but a comparative perspective shows why their complaints did not seem exceptional to peninsular authorities.[8]

The limited resources of the Dominican tribunal did mean it projected a less impressive image of judicial authority within its city than did most other overseas audiencias. It is not always possible to verify which supporting personnel worked for the court in any given year, but especially later in the century it operated with a reduced staff. In Santa Fe, by comparison, eleven *receptores* handled the court's paperwork in 1688.[9] However, for all of them protocol and ceremony—in forms of address, careful observation of seniority, or ministers' spatial arrangement and behavior—were essential to their perpetual relegitimation. Santo Domingo's example suggests that the repetition of these symbolic gestures was more important than their visual grandeur for promoting public acceptance of audiencia members' connection to the Crown. Even audiencia magistrates' periodic quarrels over precedence, with ecclesiastical authorities or with their own presidents, in Santo Domingo or in Mexico, underscore their need for others to witness the performance of royal authority.[10]

In all of these places, ministers quickly became enmeshed in the society of the cities where they lived rather than remaining outsiders. Although in Santo Domingo formal marriage to district residents was uncommon compared to Quito, both these tribunals' members developed and maintained very similar kinds of friendships and working relationships with locals, which often deepened their opposition to specific colleagues. Guadalajara's fiscal argued in 1634 that city residents had strong incentives to develop personal or business connections to oidores and their families. More permanent supporting personnel including relatores, notaries, lawyers, or doormen also facilitated the integration of superior ministers into the surrounding social environment. Yet despite their considerable power to shape the work of these tribunals, at least in Santo Domingo, it seems that these secondary officials generally worked within rather than subverting the audiencia, even as they pursued their own agendas. Public respect may have been more inconsistently observed for Dominican magistrates—especially those who opposed local elite Rodrigo Pimentel—than for their counterparts in Mexico or Charcas, but even members of these tribunals relied on local acceptance and assistance to perform their duties.[11]

A direct reference to Santo Domingo's place in a broader system from 1654 reveals the beliefs of two ministers about the other tribunals they hoped to be promoted to. In criticizing the city's cabildo for not accompanying them in public functions (at the encouragement of recently deceased president Andrés Pérez Franco), interim president Francisco de Montemayor and oidor Jerónimo de Alzate argued that as the oldest audiencia and "being praetorian and dispatching provisions sealed with the royal seal of [his] majesty, it merits no less than the other chancelleries." The larger courts in Mexico and Lima, they said, were given due honor, but with "fewer inferior ministers than in any of them," the Dominican audiencia needed royal orders to shore up the public prestige of a "tribunal that so immediately represents the person of [his] majesty." Neither man maintained a lasting association with Santo Domingo; Alzate was a fiscal from Guadalajara temporarily deposited there, and four years later Montemayor was made oidor of Mexico, where he stayed for over two decades. Most of the letrado ministers moved on to other audiencias, where they drew on their earlier experiences, formed new attachments, and sometimes repeated past behavioral patterns. Although they might complain about starting in the Dominican tribunal, over the course of the century at least eight reached Mexico, four ended up in Lima, and three became peninsular council members. Some ministers did have the advantage of starting their overseas careers in more prestigious audiencias, but there is little evidence to show their behavior was substantially different from colleagues who were promoted from lesser courts like the one on Hispaniola.[12] The men who staffed all these tribunals came from very similar backgrounds, which helped keep this institution roughly coherent across the Atlantic.

Ultimately, the seventeenth-century Audiencia of Santo Domingo offers insight into some practical aspects of mature Habsburg administration, the goals of which were not minimal Crown involvement, the construction of a perfectly consistent legal structure, or the total elimination of conflict. Rather, peninsular authorities sought to maintain and defend Spain's territorial claims, meet the material and spiritual needs of the king's subjects, and gain revenue or minimize expenditures, all within the limits of insufficient resources and the logistical difficulties of overseas communications. Royal legislation—together with the seeming conservatism of a system in which, from the metropolitan to the local level, innovations (*novedades*) were met with disapproval—offers an overly rigid impression of governmental practices that were constantly changing and adapting.[13] Conditions in all audiencias were often quite different from plans laid in Spain, but these plans were updated as the Council of the Indies received new information. The tribunal in Santa Fe, for example, had six oidores and separate civil and criminal chambers for part of the seventeenth century, and both letrado and capa y espada candidates were considered for its presidency, although the 1680 *Recopilación* specified five oidores and a military president. Quito, which gained a permanent protector of Indians around midcentury, sometimes had only two oidores available to handle business. The Dominican audiencia went through very few structural changes between 1600 and 1700, but the transfer of Maracaibo to Santa Fe's district in 1676, or the creation of the cabo subalterno position in 1697, show that adjustments were always possible. Bigger projects like the 1605 depopulations or the importation of Canary Islanders beginning in 1687 likewise demonstrate that the council could be convinced to support more radical reforms in response to specific regional issues.[14]

This willingness to experiment throughout the seventeenth century suggests that later Habsburg governance at least contained the potential for reforms similar to those carried out under the Bourbon monarchs of the following century. In particular, the 1686 junta to discuss Hispaniola, led by the president of the Council of the Indies, reflects a desire to find creative solutions to pressing problems overseas. However, even in the later part of Carlos II's reign, when metropolitan advisors backed new policies—including the 1695 joint campaign with the English against French Saint-Domingue—they generally articulated them in terms of preservation or restoration rather than as system-wide reforms or a rupture with the past.[15] For example, from at least the 1640s onward the council sought to select seasoned military commanders for the position of president-governor of Santo Domingo, signaling their general acceptance of its strategic importance. Financial exigency led them to negotiate merchant captain Ignacio Pérez Caro's purchase of the office in 1689, but the council members quickly came to see this as a mistake, which they addressed by naming a cabo subalterno and returning to military nominees. By contrast, the move to end purchases and install military governors for the circum-Caribbean in the second decade of Felipe V's reign was a more comprehensive policy shift that involved circumventing the council's normal decision-making process. I am inclined to agree with Francisco Eissa-Barroso's contention that administrative reforms in the early Bourbon period were qualitatively different from more piecemeal changes implemented under Carlos II, yet they were still built on this earlier impulse to identify and confront major problems facing the monarchy.[16]

The example of the seventeenth-century Dominican audiencia also suggests that, in comparison to its European rivals, the Spanish Crown created a more comprehensive colonial system that connected its overseas territories to each other and to the figure of the monarch across the Atlantic in a flexible and durable fashion. As one of a number of like institutions in major cities throughout Spanish America, the Dominican tribunal followed a common model that allowed for substantial adaptation to different settings, populations, and geographies. From the perspective of the metropole, it provided access to royal justice by permitting appeals from local judicial authorities across a large region, even if this principally benefited wealthier residents of Santo Domingo. In conjunction with its president, the audiencia provided information about the residents of its district and helped elevate some local concerns to the Council of the Indies and incorporate them into administrative discussions and decisions.[17]

By the later seventeenth century, the Caribbean territories of other European countries were also part of formal colonial systems, though these remained more partial when set against Spain's larger and older administrative structure. The Dutch colonial project in the region continued as a commercial venture even after the 1674 collapse of the first West India Company, while England's territories were marked by strong local power rather than shared institutions. Starting in the late 1660s, France was able to exert greater royal control over its colonies, but in part tensions between intendants and governors-general limited the elaboration of a common framework across its American possessions. Portuguese Brazil offers the closest comparison, and the High Court (*Relaçao*) in Bahia was in many ways analogous to Spain's colonial audiencias; its judges likewise built strong local connections after arriving as outsiders. However, it was suppressed for a quarter-century in 1626 (while under Spanish rule) and was the only court of its kind up until 1751, and so it represented a more restricted kind of system compared to Spanish America's.[18] The reach and impact of Spain's audiencia system should not be overstated, and many individuals and groups of people were untouched by these courts in any more than an indirect or theoretical way. Yet the circulation of magistrates through this colonial judicial system helped keep these territories tied to peninsular norms and expectations, and the courts helped sustain an image of a Spanish monarch who was interested in the welfare of his overseas subjects.

Within Santo Domingo itself, the audiencia was largely accepted as the voice of royal justice. The tribunal's ministers never faced the kind of widespread rioting that the viceroy in the city of Mexico did in 1624 and 1695, or the shouts of "death to the oidores" that greeted oidor Juan Padilla in Caracas around 1675, or even the open ridicule directed at visitador general Alonso Hurtado in 1630.[19] To be sure, there were recurring conflicts with other institutions and instances of resistance; however, these were uncommon, and even the 1648 street riot that forcibly took two condemned prisoners away from the audiencia did not signal a wholesale rejection of the court's authority. Local residents, especially elites, had numerous options for influencing the tribunal and using it to further their own interests, but their relations with audiencia members over the course of the seventeenth century were more like mutual dependence than simple domination or cooptation. Even when the criminal or civil decisions or personal behavior of these magistrates were criticized, it did not harm the unseen monarch's role as the final arbiter of justice.

The Dominican tribunal had little impact on the daily lives of most of the people in its district, yet even outside the city there was a general understanding that the audiencia was a conduit to Madrid, where its ministers' reports carried substantial weight. Contemporary attitudes toward the court in Santo Domingo are hard to reconcile with Pierre Chaunu's contention that the audiencia as an institution represented "efficacy and honesty," but the Dominican incarnation still helped keep its city, island, and district linked to the Crown.[20] Ultimately, while it was smaller and shabbier than the viceregal tribunals of Mexico or Lima, over the course of the seventeenth century the Audiencia of Santo Domingo demonstrated a kind of enduring adequacy at meeting the expectations of the monarchy and local residents. The tribunal on Hispaniola was not moved to Havana or Caracas partly because peninsular authorities strongly believed it was essential to preserving a Spanish presence on the island but mainly because there was no compelling reason to make a major change to an institution that was working as effectively as it needed to.

APPENDIX

Ministers of the Audiencia of Santo Domingo, 1600–1700

Years listed here are best estimates of when ministers served in the Audiencia of Santo Domingo. For further information, see Schäfer, *El Consejo Real*, vol. 2 appendixes; Barrientos Grandon, *Guía prosopográfica de la judicatura letrada indiana*; and *Diccionario Biográfico electrónico de la Real Academia de la Historia* at https://dbe.rah.es/db~e.

Presidents

- **Don Diego Osorio:** 1597–1600; previously governor of Venezuela; died in office.
- Doctor Pedro Sanz Morquecho: 1600–1602 (interim as senior oidor).
- **Don Antonio Osorio:** 1602–8; previously corregidor of Jerez de la Frontera; died returning to Spain.
- **Don Diego Gómez de Sandoval:** 1608–23; previously president of House of Trade; died in office.
- Licenciado Juan Martínez Tenorio: 1623–24 (interim as senior oidor).
- **Don Diego de Acuña:** 1624–26; previously governor of Cartagena; promoted to president-governor of Guatemala.
- **General Don Gabriel de Chaves Osorio:** 1627–34; previously general of Flota of New Spain; completed term and died in office.
- Doctor Don Alonso de Cereceda: 1634–36 (interim as senior oidor).
- [Don Iñigo Hurtado de Corcuera: named 1634, declined.]
- **Don Juan Bitrián de Biamonte y Navarra:** 1636–45; previously governor of Havana; promoted to president-governor of Panama.
- **Don Nicolás de Velasco Altamirano:** 1645–48; previously *castellano* of San Juan de Ulúa; died in office.

- Licenciado Don Juan Melgarejo Ponce de León: 1649–50 (interim as senior oidor).
- **General Don Luis Fernández de Córdoba:** 1650–51; previously governor of Cartagena; died in office.
- Licenciado Don Pedro Luis de Salazar: 1651 (interim as senior oidor).
- Licenciado Don Francisco Pantoja de Ayala: 1651–52 (interim as senior oidor).
- **Maestro de Campo Don Andrés Pérez Franco:** 1652–53; previously alcalde mayor of Tacuba; died in office.
- Doctor Don Juan Francisco de Montemayor y Córdoba de Cuenca: 1653–55 (interim as senior oidor).
- **Don Bernardino Hurtado de Meneses Bracamonte y Zapata, Conde de Peñalba:** 1655–56; previously corregidor of Toledo; promoted to president of Charcas (died en route).
- [Don Sebastián Hurtado de Corcuera: named ca. 1655, declined.]
- [Don Martín Carlos de Mencos: named ca. 1655, offer withdrawn.]
- **Don Félix de Zúñiga y Avellaneda, Conde del Sacro Imperio:** 1656–59; previously governor of Alcántara; recalled to Spain.
- **Maestro de Campo Don Juan de Balboa Mogrovejo:** 1659–61; previously governor of Gibraltar; promoted to president-governor of Chile (suspended).
- **Maestro de Campo Don Pedro de Carvajal y Cobos:** 1661–71; previously maestro de campo in Flanders; completed eight-year term.
- **Maestro de Campo Don Ignacio de Zayas Bazán:** 1671–77; previously maestro de campo in Flanders; died in office.
- Doctor Don Juan Padilla Guardiola y Guzmán: 1677–78 (interim as senior oidor).
- **Maestro de Campo Don Francisco de Segura Sandoval y Castilla:** 1678–84; previous military position unknown; suspended; died on Hispaniola ca. 1691.
- **General de la Artillería Don Andrés de Robles:** 1684–90 (interim); previously governor of Buenos Aires; returned to Spain 1690.
- **Almirante Don Ignacio Pérez Caro:** 1690–96; previously merchant captain; suspended (restored to office 1705).
- Don Gil Correoso Catalán: 1696–98 (interim as cabo subalterno).

- **Maestro de Campo Don Severino de Manzaneda Salinas y Rozas de Zumalabe:** 1698–1702 (interim); previously governor of Havana; promoted to governor of Cartagena (died before taking office).

Oidores

- **Doctor Don Simón de Meneses:** 1593–1600; previously lawyer of Audiencia of Lima; suspended, deprived of office (rehabilitated 1605).
- **Licenciado Juan Alcázar de Villaseñor:** 1597–1602; previous position unknown; died in office.
- **Doctor Pedro Sanz Morquecho:** ca. 1597–1605; previous position unknown; promoted to oidor of Quito.
- **Licenciado Marcos Núñez de Toledo:** 1601–6; previously regidor of Cebreros; promoted to oidor of Guatemala (died on commission in Havana).
- **Licenciado Gonzalo Mejía de Villalobos:** 1603–13; previous position unknown; licensed to go to Spain 1612; promoted to oidor of Panama.
- **Licenciado Francisco Manso de Contreras:** 1604–9; previously fiscal-elect; promoted to oidor of Panama.
- **Licenciado Juan Martínez Tenorio:** 1605–27; previously relator of House of Trade; allowed to take clerical orders 1619; granted retirement; died on Hispaniola.
- **Doctor Gaspar Narváez de Valdelomar:** 1605–21; previously corregidor of Lima; promoted to oidor of Chile.
- **Licenciado Ruy Gómez:** 1608–ca. 1614; previously fiscal; died in office.
- **Licenciado Don Rodrigo de Valcárcel:** ca. 1615–18; previously at University of Osma; promoted to oidor of Guatemala.
- **Doctor Don Cristóbal de la Cerda y Sotomayor:** ca. 1615–17; previously fiscal (interim) of Audiencia of Seville; promoted to oidor of Chile.
- **Licenciado Jerónimo de Herrera:** 1617–20; previously fiscal; promoted to oidor of Panama.
- **Licenciado Hernando Ibáñez de Albendea:** 1618–20; previously at University of Sigüenza; promoted to oidor of Panama.
- **Licenciado Don Juan Parra de Meneses:** 1620–31; previously alcalde mayor of El Escorial; licensed to go to Spain; suspended 1633 (suspension lifted 1636).

- **Licenciado Juan Camacho de Escobar:** 1620–25; previously lawyer of Audiencia of Granada; promoted to oidor of Guatemala.
- **Licenciado Diego Gil de la Sierpe:** 1621–ca. 1633; previously fiscal; died in Cartagena (en route to Spain).
- **Doctor Don Alonso de Cereceda:** 1625–37; previously auditor general of Lombardy; promoted to oidor of Mexico (suspended).
- **Licenciado Don Miguel de Verastegui y Otalora:** 1627–35; previously *juez apostólico*; moved to oidor of Panama (died before arriving).
- **Doctor Don Cristóbal de Torres:** 1634–38; previously lawyer of Audiencia of Mexico; promoted to oidor of Guadalajara.
- **Licenciado Don Juan Melgarejo Ponce de León:** 1635–51; previously lawyer of royal councils; licensed to go to Spain.
- **Licenciado Don Juan de Retuerta:** 1635–48; previously lawyer of royal councils; promoted to oidor of Panama.
- **Doctor Don Pedro Álvarez de Mendoza:** 1636–41; previously at University of Alcalá; died in office.
- **Licenciado Don Pedro Luis de Salazar:** 1640–49 (returned to Spain without license), 1650–51; previous position unknown; died in office.
- [Licenciado Don Juan de Grijota: named 1643, declined.]
- **Licenciado Don Francisco Pantoja de Ayala:** 1644–52; previous position unknown; promoted to oidor of Guatemala.
- **Licenciado Don Fernando de Cepeda:** 1648–53; previously relator of Audiencia of Mexico; died in office.
- [Licenciado Don Juan Marín de Nava: named 1648, transferred to Panama before leaving Spain.]
- **Doctor Don Diego de Orozco:** 1653; previously oidor of Panama (moved during visita); died on Hispaniola.
- **Doctor Don Juan Francisco de Montemayor y Córdoba de Cuenca:** 1650–57 (initially supernumerary); previously auditor general of Aragón; promoted to oidor of Mexico (supernumerary).
- **Doctor Don Jerónimo de Alzate:** 1653–56; previously fiscal of Guadalajara (moved to Santo Domingo in deposit); ordered to Spain.
- **Doctor Don Andrés Martínez de Amileta:** 1655–ca. 1664; previously lawyer of royal councils; promoted to oidor of Panama (departure delayed due to visita).

- **Licenciado Don Diego López de la Puerta:** 1655–66; previously lawyer of royal councils; promoted to oidor of Santa Fe.
- [Don Fernando Jiménez Paniagua: named 1654, declined.]
- [Don Luis de Mendoza y Guzmán: named 1654, declined.]
- **Licenciado Don Gaspar Vélez Mantilla:** 1655–68; previously at University of Salamanca; died in office.
- **Licenciado Don Andrés Caballero:** 1655–62 (suspended), 1672–73; previously alcalde mayor of Salamanca; died in office.
- [Licenciado Don Pedro de Treviño: named 1658, declined.]
- [Licenciado Don Sancho de Ubilla: named 1658; promoted to visitador of future oidor of another audiencia before leaving Spain.]
- **Bachiller Don Pedro Álvarez de Toledo Venegas:** 1659–62; previously alcalde mayor of Málaga; died in office.
- **Licenciado Don Jacinto de Vargas Campuzano:** 1661–66; previously fiscal; promoted to oidor of Santa Fe.
- [Licenciado Don Manuel Bernardo de Quiros: named 1662, declined.]
- **Licenciado Don Pedro de Carvajal y Vargas:** 1665–72; previously commissioned judge of Council of Finance; promoted to fiscal of Guatemala.
- [Licenciado Don Diego de Sierra Valdez: named 1664, did not respond.]
- **Licenciado Don Agustín Félix Maldonado de Salazar:** 1666–77; previously at University of Salamanca; promoted to fiscal of Guadalajara [declined]; promoted to oidor of Guadalajara.
- **Doctor Don Juan Padilla Guardiola y Guzmán:** 1670–80; previously at University of Alcalá; promoted to oidor of Guadalajara.
- **Licenciado Don Juan Pizarro Cajal y Monrroy:** 1669–71; previously fiscal; died in office.
- **Doctor Don Jerónimo Chacón Abarca:** 1673–77; previously at University of Salamanca; promoted to oidor of Guatemala (interim/supernumerary).
- [Doctor Don Sebastián Pérez de Moya: named 1672, declined.]
- [Licenciado Don Tomás de Oña: named 1673, promoted to fiscal of Panama before leaving Spain.]
- **Bachiller Don Francisco de Cárdenas:** ca. 1676–83; previously alcalde mayor of Castilla la Vieja; promoted to oidor of Panama.

- [Doctor Don Juan Palacios de la Bastida: named 1676, moved to interim oidor of Guatemala before leaving Spain.]
- [Don Benito de Novoa Salgado: oidor of Guatemala ordered to Santo Domingo in deposit 1678, restored to Guatemala before arriving.]
- **Doctor Don Thomás Pizarro Cortés de Monrroy:** 1683–86; previously oidor of Guadalajara (ordered in deposit to Santo Domingo 1680); restored to position.
- **Licenciado Don Juan Garcés de los Fayos:** 1680–84; previously fiscal; promoted to oidor of Santa Fe.
- **Licenciado Don Francisco López de Dicastillo:** 1682–84; previously at University of Alcalá; promoted to oidor of Santa Fe.
- **Licenciado Don Jerónimo de Córdoba:** 1687–92; previously auditor general of Armada; promoted to oidor of Panama.
- **Licenciado Don Joseph de Salazar:** 1684–85; previously fiscal; promoted to fiscal of Quito; died before leaving Spain.
- [Licenciado Don Lucas Francisco de Bilbao la Vieja: named 1684, promoted to oidor of Chile before leaving Spain.]
- **Licenciado Don Fernando de la Riva Agüero:** 1686–88; previously alcalde mayor of Toledo; promoted to oidor of Panama.
- **Licenciado Don Fernando de Araujo y Rivera:** 1686–ca. 1705; previously at University of Salamanca; promoted to oidor of Santa Fe.
- **Licenciado Don Manuel de la Cruz Ahedo:** 1687–95; previously at University of Alcalá; given license to go to Spain; promoted to Council of Finance.
- [Doctor Don Bruno González de Sepúlveda y Coronel: named oidor 1688; died as fiscal before receiving notification.]
- **Doctor Don Diego Bartolomé Bravo de Añaya:** 1692–99 (ordered to Spain); previously lawyer of Audiencia of Granada; promoted to Council of Finance.
- **Licenciado Don Diego Antonio de Oviedo Baños de Sotomayor:** 1690–ca. 1702 (supernumerary until 1692); previously auditor general of Armada del Mar del Sur; promoted to oidor of Guatemala.
- **Licenciado Don Sebastián de Cereceda y Girón:** 1695–1722 (supernumerary until 1697); previously lawyer of royal councils; promoted to oidor of Mexico (1710).
- [Licenciado Don Marcos Marañon y Lara: named 1699, declined.]

- [Don Felipe García de Valdez: named 1700, appointed to post in Spain before leaving.]
- **Bachiller Don Nicolás Fernández Molinillo:** 1701–2; previously at University of Salamanca; died in office.
- [Bachiller Don Nicolás Chirino Vandeval: given alternative place in 1700.]

Fiscales

- **Licenciado Buenaventura Cuadrado Solanilla:** 1596–1603; previously *juez de registros* of Canary Islands; promoted to fiscal of Santa Fe.
- [Licenciado Francisco Manso de Contreras: named 1602, promoted to oidor before leaving Spain.]
- **Licenciado Pedro de Arévalo Sedeño:** 1603–6; previously corregidor of Villa de Palma; promoted to oidor of Guadalajara.
- **Licenciado Ruy Gómez:** 1606–8; previously lawyer of Audiencia of Galicia; promoted to oidor.
- **Licenciado Jerónimo de Herrera:** 1609–17; previously lawyer of Audiencia of Granada; promoted to oidor.
- **Licenciado Diego Gil de la Sierpe:** 1618–21; previously relator of Audiencia of Seville; promoted to oidor.
- **Doctor Damián Gentil de Párraga:** 1621–ca. 1626; previously lawyer of Audiencia of Mexico; promoted to fiscal of Guadalajara.
- **Licenciado Don Francisco de Prada:** 1627–ca. 1634; previously relator of Audiencia of Valladolid; promoted to oidor of Quito.
- **Licenciado Don Juan Vela Núñez Vote:** 1635–36; previous position unknown; died in office.
- [Doctor Don Juan de Manjares: named 1637, declined.]
- **Doctor Don Francisco de Alarcón Coronado:** 1637–54 (ordered to Spain); previously juez de registros of Gran Canaria; died in office.
- [Licenciado Don Hipólito de Barrientos: named interim 1654, found ineligible.]
- **Licenciado Don Bernardo Trigo de Figueroa:** 1655–58 (went to Spain); previous position unknown; promoted to oidor of Panama.
- [Licenciado Don Sancho de Ubilla: named 1658; promoted to oidor before leaving Spain.]

- **Licenciado Don Jacinto de Vargas Campuzano:** 1659–61; previously at University of Toledo; promoted to oidor.
- **Licenciado Don Juan Pizarro Cajal y Monrroy:** 1661–69; previously at University of San Marcos (Lima); promoted to oidor.
- [Licenciado Don Manuel García de Olivera: named 1669; died before leaving Spain.]
- [Licenciado Don Carlos Romeo: named 1672, had already died.]
- **Licenciado Don Diego de Acosta y Cabrera:** 1674–76; previous position unknown; promoted to fiscal of Guadalajara.
- **Licenciado Don Juan Garcés de los Fayos:** 1675–80; previously lawyer of royal councils; promoted to oidor.
- [Doctor Don Luis Martínez Hidalgo: named 1680, promoted to fiscal of Guadalajara before leaving Spain.]
- [Licenciado Don Alfonso Castellanos de la Torre: named 1681, declined.]
- **Licenciado Don Joseph de Salazar:** 1683–84; previous position unknown; promoted to oidor.
- [Licenciado Don Nicolás Baraiz y Molinet: named 1684, declined.]
- [Licenciado Don Francisco Joseph Merlo de la Fuente: named 1684, promoted to oidor of Panama before leaving Spain.]
- **Doctor Don Bruno González de Sepúlveda y Coronel:** 1687–88; previously visitador of Granada; promoted to oidor (died before receiving notification).
- [Don Francisco Sánchez de la Barcena: named 1688, offer withdrawn.]
- **Licenciado Don Francisco Ladrón de Guevara:** 1690–94; previously at University of Salamanca; died in office.
- **Licenciado Don Pedro Marín Muñoz:** 1695–98; previously lawyer of royal councils; died in office.
- **Licenciado Don Mauricio de la Torre y Ángulo:** ca. 1702–ca. 1717; previously lawyer of royal councils; permitted to take ecclesiastical post.

NOTES

Abbreviations

ACA	Archivo de la Corona de Aragón, Barcelona
AGI	Archivo General de Indias, Seville
AHN	Archivo Histórico Nacional, Madrid
BP	Biblioteca del Palacio Real, Madrid
BNE	Biblioteca Nacional de España, Madrid
CA	Consejo de Aragón
Cod	Códices
Ctdra	Contaduría
Cttn	Casa de la Contratación
DC	Diversos-Colecciones
Esc	Escribanía de Cámara de Justicia
Filipinas	Gobierno: Audiencia de Filipinas
Guadalajara	Gobierno: Audiencia de Guadalajara
Guatemala	Gobierno: Audiencia de Guatemala
Indif	Gobierno: Indiferente General
Mexico	Gobierno: Audiencia de México
OM-CS	Órdenes Militares–Caballeros Santiago
Panama	Gobierno: Audiencia de Panamá
Patr	Patronato Real
Quito	Gobierno: Audiencia de Quito
SD	Gobierno: Audiencia de Santo Domingo
SF	Gobierno: Audiencia de Santa Fe
VE	Various Especiales

1. Introduction

1. AGI-Esc 33B, visita of Audiencia of Santo Domingo (1630), pza. 11, fol. 17v.
2. AGI-SD 2, R. 1, no. 73, 75 (consultas, 19 and 20 December 1658).
3. Moreta Castillo, *La Real Audiencia de Santo Domingo*, 165.
4. Schäfer, *El Consejo Real*, 2:86–88, 94–99; García Gallo, "Las Audiencias de Indias," 387–88; Cauzzi, *Historia de la primera Audiencia*; Valenzuela Márquez, *Las liturgias del poder*, 37; Eagle, "Restoring Spanish Hispaniola," 400; Burkholder, "Spain's America," 125–27.
5. Ponce Vázquez, "Unequal Partners," 706. However, for new work on seventeenth-century Spanish Hispaniola, see González de Peña, *Historia general del pueblo dominicano*; Ponce Vázquez, *Islanders and Empire*; and the recent issue of *Clío* 92, no. 205 (January–June 2023).
6. See, for example, Silva i Molina, "Oidores de la Real Audiencia," 5–75; Ruíz Guiñazú, *La magistratura indiana*; Cunningham, *Audiencia in the Spanish Colonies*; Schäfer, *El Consejo Real*, especially vol. 2; Parry, *Audiencia of New Galicia*; Phelan, *Kingdom of Quito*; Moreno, *La Audiencia de Charcas*; Burkholder and Chandler, *From Impotence to Authority*; Cauzzi, *Historia de la primera Audiencia*; Arregui Zamorano, *La Audiencia de México*; Suárez, *Las reales audiencias indianas*; Mayorga García, *La Audiencia de Santafé*; Jiménez Núñez, *Antropología histórica*; Martiré, *Las Audiencias*; and Rosenmüller, *Corruption and Justice*. See also Schwartz, *Sovereignty and Society*. On Santo Domingo, see Malagón Barceló, *El distrito*; Herrera, "La Real Audiencia de Santo Domingo," 3–14; Vega Boyrie, "La Real Audiencia de Santo Domingo," 91–104; Gil-Bermejo García, *La Española*; Peña Pérez, *Cien años de miseria*; Aranda Mendíaz, *Visiones*; Moreta Castillo, *La Real Audiencia de Santo Domingo*; and Paredes Vera, "Justicia y gobierno," 279–303.
7. Jiménez Núñez, "Sistema político," 296; Cañeque, *King's Living Image*, 7–13; Herzog, *Upholding Justice*, 1–8.
8. For eighteenth-century records transferred to Cuba, see Malagón Barceló, *El distrito*, 65–66, 107–258; see also Sánchez Lustrino, "Los Archivos Dominicanos," 3–7; and Moreta Castillo, *La Real Audiencia de Santo Domingo*, 146–47.
9. Malagón Barceló, *El distrito*, 39; García Gallo, "Las Audiencias de Indias," 366–77; Planas Rosselló, *La Real Audiencia de Mallorca*, 18–19.
10. Schäfer, *El Consejo Real*, 2:66; Herrera, "La Real Audiencia de Santo Domingo," 7–10; García Gallo, "Las Audiencias de Indias," 378–80; Vega Boyrie, "La Real Audiencia de Santo Domingo," 93–96.
11. Herrera, "La Real Audiencia de Santo Domingo," 11–13; Vega Boyrie, "La Real Audiencia de Santo Domingo," 93.

12. García Gallo, "Las Audiencias de Indias," 366, 381–82; Malagón Barceló, *El distrito*, 73–79, 81–98; Pietschmann, *El estado*, 132–37; Tau Anzoátegui, "La idea de Derecho," 30–31.
13. Schäfer, *El Consejo Real*, 2:68; Nesvig, *Promiscuous Power*, 6.
14. García Gallo, "Las Audiencias de Indias," 382–83; Barrientos Grandon, "La Real Audiencia de Concepción," 134–37, 169–71; Valenzuela Márquez, *Liturgias del poder*, 37.
15. García Gallo, "Las Audiencias de Indias," 361; Nesvig, *Promiscuous Power*, 178–81; Díaz Ceballos, *Poder Compartido*, 36–37; cf. Malagón Barceló, *El distrito*, 39–40.
16. Solórzano Pereira, *Política Indiana*, L. 5, cap. 3, no. 8–14; Pietschmann, *El estado*, 113–18; Calvo, *Poder, religión y sociedad*, 33–34; Cañeque, *King's Living Image*, 57–59.
17. Schäfer, *El Consejo Real*, 2:94–99; García Gallo, "Las Audiencias de Indias," 382–83; Valenzuela Márquez, *Liturgias del poder*, 83; Cañeque, *King's Living Image*, 53–54.
18. Ruíz Guiñazú, *La magistratura indiana*, 41–44; Sarfatti, *Spanish Bureaucratic-Patrimonialism*, 27.
19. AGI-SD 58, R. 3, no. 42 (Meneses to king, 28 July 1656); *Recopilación*, L. 2, T. 15, ll. 1, 46–47, 49–54; T. 16, l. 87; Phelan, *Kingdom of Quito*, 18–19, 107–8; Moreno, *La Audiencia de Charcas*, 37–44; Calvo, *Poder, religión y sociedad*, 32; Rosenmüller, "Two Kingdoms," 2.
20. AGI-Panama 21, R. 4, no. 26 (audiencia of Panama to king, 5 August 1650); *Recopilación*, L. 2, T. 15, l. 46; Schäfer, *El Consejo Real*, 2:505; Muro Romero, *Las Presidencias-Gobernaciones*, 3, 65–71; García Gallo, "Las Audiencias de Indias," 387–92; Mayorga García, *La Audiencia de Santafé*, 162; Rosenmüller, "Two Kingdoms," 4.
21. Phelan, *Kingdom of Quito*, 131–33; Burkholder and Chandler, *From Impotence to Authority*, 3–4; Castejón, "Un *cursus honorum*," 438, 446–47.
22. Cunningham, *Audiencia in the Spanish Colonies*, 291–92; Bridikhina, *Theatrum mundi*, 114–15; Hernández González, "La organización de la colonia, 1500–1795," 387; Castejón, "Un *cursus honorum*," 447; see also Moreno, *La Audiencia de Charcas*, 32; and Burkholder, "Honest Judges," 264n6.
23. *Recopilación*, L. 5, T. 2, l. 1; Schäfer, *El Consejo Real*, 2:115–16, 557; Muro Romero, *Presidencias-Gobernaciones*, 2–3, 181; Lane, *Pillaging the Empire*, 51–53.
24. Schäfer, *El Consejo Real*, 2:99–108; Muro Romero, *Presidencias-Gobernaciones*, 24, 33–34, 41, 54, 181; Vega Boyrie, "La Real Audiencia de Santo Domingo," 96–100; Eagle, "Beard-Pulling and Furniture-Rearranging," 492–93.

25. *Recopilación*, L. 2, T. 15, ll. 22, 34, 66, 68, 71, 75–76, 88, 121–22; L. 5, T. 12, 13; Phelan, *Kingdom of Quito*, 122; Cañeque, *King's Living Image*, 55–57; Herzog, *Upholding Justice*, 24–40, 43–44.
26. *Recopilación*, L. 2, T. 15, ll. 21, 24–28, 30–31; Bravo Lira, "Símbolos de la función judicial," 249–51; Cañeque, *King's Living Image*, 133–37; Herzog, *Upholding Justice*, 44–47.
27. *Recopilación*, L. 2, T. 15, ll. 57, 61, 139, 156, 159; L. 7, T. 7; Herzog, *Upholding Justice*, 46–47.
28. Solórzano Pereira, *Política Indiana*, L. 5, cap. 3, 10, 12–14, 58–62; *Recopilación*, L. 2, T. 15, ll. 110, 117, 119; L. 7, T. 1, ll. 1, 3–4, 6, 13. See also García Gallo, "Las Audiencias de Indias," 385–86; Sánchez Bella, "Las audiencias," 164–65; Bravo Lira, "Símbolos de la función judicial," 247.
29. Cutter, *Legal Culture*, 34.
30. Cutter, *Legal Culture*, 34–38; Herzog, *Upholding Justice*, 6–8, 19–24; see also Nuzzo, "Between America and Europe," 161–91.
31. AGI-SD 57, R. 1, no. 17 (petition of Alarcón Coronado, 21 May 1649); AGI-Esc 1181 (visita sentence vs. Cereceda, 9 January 1635); Phelan, "Authority and Flexibility," 54–60; Herzog, "'Recopilación de Indias,'" 143–46; Barrientos Grandon, "Juan Francisco Montemayor," 142–50; Tau Anzoátegui, "Provincial and Local Law," 238–39; Tau Anzoátegui, *El Jurista*, 17–19; Tau Anzoátegui, "Entre leyes, glosas y comentos," 152.
32. Jiménez Núñez, *Antropología histórica*, 21; Herzog, *Upholding Justice*, 10–11, 157; see also Burset Flores, "Cotidianidad en el Caribe colonial," 737.
33. Herzog, *Upholding Justice*, 47–48; see also Honores, "Litigación en la Audiencia Arzobispal de Lima," 70–72.
34. *Recopilación*, L. 2, T. 15, ll. 20, 168; T. 20–30; Schäfer, *El Consejo Real*, 2:120–21; Moreta Castillo, *La Real Audiencia de Santo Domingo*, 73.
35. *Recopilación*, L. 3, T. 3, ll. 38, 39, 41.
36. *Recopilación*, L. 2, T. 15, l. 83; T. 18, l. 4; L. 3, T. 3, l. 45; Herzog, *Upholding Justice*, 66.
37. Jiménez Núñez, "Sistema político," 297, 305.

2. President-Governors, 1600–1653

1. AGI-SD 71, L. 1, fol. 219 (cabildo to king, 25 October 1563); Rodríguez Morel, "Sugar Economy of Española," 89, 105–7; Cassá, *Historia social y económica*, 160–61; De la Fuente, *Havana and the Atlantic*, 3, 52, 136; Eagle, "Restoring Spanish Hispaniola," 390.
2. Lockhart and Schwartz, *Early Latin America*, 65; Peña Pérez, *Cien años de miseria*, 9; Ponce Vázquez, *Islanders and Empire*, 9–10.

3. For a few examples, see AGI-Panama 14, R. 13, no. 88 (audiencia to king, 27 October 1597); AGI-Quito 26, no. 56 (Ocampo to king, 20 April 1606); AGI-Filipinas 20, R. 4, no. 31 (Alvarado Bracamonte to king, 10 July 1610); Cunningham, *Audiencia in the Spanish Colonies*, 59; and Vila Vilar, *Historia de Puerto Rico*, 36.
4. Andrews, *Spanish Caribbean*, 150–51; Moutoukias, *Contrabando y control colonial*, 116–17; Deive, *Tangomangos*, 142–43; Lane, *Pillaging the Empire*, 51–52; Cassá, *Historia social y económica*, 176; Ponce Vázquez, *Islanders and Empire*, 58–59.
5. Muro Romero, *Presidencias-Gobernaciones*, 181; Moreta Castillo, *La Real Audiencia de Santo Domingo*, 145.
6. AGI-SD 52, R. 1, no. 2 (Sanz Morquecho to king, 20 February 1601); *Recopilación*, L. 2, T. 15, l. 180.
7. AGI-SD 868, L. 3, fols. 148v–149r (king to Villagra, 22 September and 29 December 1593); Deive, *Tangomangos*, 152–53, 159–63; Moya Pons, *La otra historia dominicana*, 61; Aranda Mendíaz, *Visiones*, 160–61; Ponce Vázquez, *Islanders and Empire*, 76–77, 96–97. See also AGI-Esc 133B (Puerto Rico, 1594); AGI-Esc 150A-B (Margarita, 1595); AGI-Esc 364A–B (Veracruz and Honduras, 1595); AGI-Esc 585A–586C (Tierra Firme, 1594); AGI-Esc 647A (Cumaná, 1596); and AGI-Esc 32, nos. 4–9 (Santo Domingo, 1593–98).
8. AGI-SD 51, R. 16, no. 127 (audiencia to king, 20 September 1594); AGI-SD 1, R. 1, no. 13 (consulta, 31 March 1596); AGI-SD 51, R. 17, no. 140 (Varela to king, 20 November 1595); AGI-Indif 433, L. 2, fols. 277r–278v (decree, 8 March 1595); AGI-Esc 1181 (visita sentence vs. Meneses, 21 February 1601); Deive, *Tangomangos*, 152–57, 163–66; Aranda Mendíaz, *Visiones*, 161–62; Ponce Vázquez, *Islanders and Empire*, 82–87; see also AGI-Esc 17A–20B.
9. AGI-SD 1, R. 1, no. 66 (consulta, 7 October 1605); AGI-Panama 1, no. 242a (consulta, 6 October 1609); Herzog, *Ritos de control*, 175–79; Eagle, "Portraits of Bad Officials," 100–101.
10. Sluiter, "Dutch-Spanish Rivalry," 175–81; Peña Pérez, *Antonio Osorio*, 100; Lane, *Pillaging the Empire*, 64–66; Klooster, *Dutch Moment*, 21, 59–60.
11. Schäfer, *El Consejo Real*, 1:177–88, 227–31. See also Phelan, *Kingdom of Quito*, 129; Feros, *Kingship and Favoritism*, 132; and Williams, *Great Favourite*, 111–13.
12. AGI-SD 1, R. 1, no. 32 (consulta, 30 March 1601); AGI-SD 52, R. 2, no. 3 (king to audiencia, 11 March 1602); *Recopilación*, L. 2, T. 15, l. 39; Ponce Vázquez, *Islanders and Empire*, 109–10.
13. AGI-SD 52, R. 2, no. 4 (audiencia to king, 8 July 1602); Gil-Bermejo García, *La Española*, 11.
14. AGI-Cttn 5792, L. 2, fols. 171r–173r (title of governor, 15 January 1592); AGI-SD 1, R. 1, no. 48 (consulta, 17 April 1603); Gil-Bermejo García, *La Española*, 230–31;

Burset Flores, "'Cosas indebidas,'" 96–153; Ponce Vázquez, *Islanders and Empire*, 110–12. See also Burkholder, *Spaniards in the Colonial Empire*, xi–xiv.

15. AGI-Cttn, 5792, L. 2, fols. 330v–331v (title for Sanz Morquecho, 30 October 1604); AGI-SD 52, R. 6, no. 82a, fols. 11v–12r (testimony, 10 September 1603); AGI-Patr 293, no. 23, R. 28 (title for Mejía de Villalobos, 9 October 1601).
16. Juan José Ponce Vázquez offers a detailed overview of this literature in "Casting Traitors and Villains" and *Islanders and Empire*, 100–133. See also Peña Pérez, *Antonio Osorio*.
17. AGI-SD 868, L. 3, fols. 165r–168r (king to Osorio and Dávila Padilla, 6 August 1603); AGI-SD 52, R. 6, no. 73 (Osorio to king, 12 October 1606); Rodríguez Morel, "Las Devastaciones de Osorio," 296–97, 309; Ponce Vázquez, *Islanders and Empire*, 107–9, 117–25.
18. AGI-SD 868, L. 3, fol. 179r (king to audiencia, 12 December 1603); AGI-SD 1, R. 1, no. 59 (consulta, 29 December 1604); AGI-SD 52, R. 5, no. 27 (Manso to king, 2 July 1605). See also Deive, *Tangomangos*, 195–203.
19. Ugarte, *Estampas Coloniales*, 1:20; Peña Pérez, *Antonio Osorio*, 115–17; Ponce Vázquez, "Casting Traitors and Villains," 160–62; Rodríguez Morel, "Las Devastaciones de Osorio," 311, 313.
20. AGI-Esc 3A, fiscal vs. Agüero Bardecí (1606), pza. 1, fol. 11; Peña Batlle, *La Isla de Tortuga*, 41–43; Klooster, *Dutch Moment*, 29n92.
21. AGI-SD 52, R. 6, no. 29 (Osorio to king, 20 October 1605); AGI-Esc 1181 (visita sentence vs. Mejía de Villalobos, 16 May 1608); Ponce Vázquez, *Islanders and Empire*, 110.
22. AGI-SD 1, no. 78b (consulta, 20 January 1607); AGI-SD 52, R. 8, no. 102 (Osorio to king, 4 January 1608); Ponce Vázquez, *Islanders and Empire*, 126–27.
23. AGI-SD 52, R. 4, no. 18 (Arévalo Sedeño to king, 20 December 1604); R. 5, no. 34, 44 (Arévalo Sedeño and Osorio to king, 12 and 20 October 1605); Phelan, "Authority and Flexibility," 53–57.
24. AGI-SD 52, R. 5, no. 44 (Osorio to king, 20 October 1605); Deive, *Tangomangos*, 194; Burset Flores, "'Cosas indebidas,'" 102, 111; Ponce Vázquez, *Islanders and Empire*, 112–13.
25. AGI-SD 52, R. 5, no. 30, 30c (Manso to king and testimony, 22 August and 10 October 1605).
26. AGI-SD 52, R. 5, no. 30a, 50 (Osorio to king, 20 October 1605); no. 40 (Manso to king, 16 October 1605); R. 6, no. 81a (Osorio to king, 5 November 1606); Macías Domínguez, *Cuba en la primera mitad del siglo XVII*, 337–43; Burset Flores, "'Cosas indebidas,'" 117–18.
27. AGI-SD 52, R. 5, no. 54 (Manso to king, 3 December 1605); no. 55 (Osorio to king, 4 December 1605); R. 6, no. 68 (Manso to king, 15 June 1606); no. 81 (Osorio to

king, 5 November 1606); no. 81a (Manso to acuerdo, 17 December 1604); Ponce Vázquez, *Islanders and Empire*, 127.

28. AGI-SD 52, R. 6, no. 72, 81 (Osorio to king, 12 October and 5 November 1606); R. 8, no. 113 (Osorio to king, 27 March 1608); Burset Flores, "'Cosas indebidas,'" 120–29; Ponce Vázquez, *Islanders and Empire*, 128.
29. AGI-SD 52, R. 8, no. 116 (Osorio to king, 7 May 1608); no. 117 (Gómez de Sandoval to king, 8 August 1608); AGI-SD 53, no. 6 (Gómez de Sandoval to king, 30 April 1609); AGI-Esc 1181 (visita sentence vs. Manso, 13 April 1616).
30. AGI-SD 52, R. 4, no. 6, 7 (Arévalo Sedeño to king, 20 August 1604); R. 5, no. 24, 33, 35 (Arévalo Sedeño to king, 18 February, 12 October, and 13 October 1605); no. 29 (Osorio to king, 20 October 1605); R. 6, no. 64, 66 (Arévalo Sedeño to king, 2 March 1606); R. 7, no. 93, 93d (Ruy Gómez to king, 1 July and 26 August 1607); Burset Flores, "'Cosas indebidas,'" 100, 104–6.
31. AGI-SD 52, R. 6, no. 82 (audiencia to king, 18 November 1606); R. 7, no. 85 (Osorio to king, 23 March 1607); R. 8, no. 141 (audiencia to king, 1 December 1608); see also AGI-SD 52, R. 7, no. 95 (audiencia to king, 1 July 1607); R. 8, no. 101, 105, 115 (audiencia to king, 4 January, 10 January, and 2 May 1608).
32. AGI-SD 1, R. 1, no. 78b, 85 (consultas, 20 January and 10 November 1607); AGI-SD 52, R. 5, no. 45 (Osorio to king, 20 October 1605); R. 8, no. 122 (Osorio to king, 20 August 1608); Sluiter, "Dutch-Spanish Rivalry," 190–91; Klooster, *Dutch Moment*, 30–31.
33. AGI-SD 53, R. 1, no. 51 (Gómez de Sandoval to king, 20 October 1609).
34. AGI-SD 869, L.5, fols. 111v–112v (king to treasury officials, 2 September 1607); AGI-SD 53, R. 1, no. 9, 9a (Gómez de Sandoval to king and testimony, 8 May and 10 March 1609); Moya Pons, *Historia colonial*, 135; Peña Pérez, *Cien años de miseria*, 231–33; Ponce Vázquez, *Islanders and Empire*, 137–40, 192–93. See also Marichal and Souto Mantecón, "Silver and Situados," 587–89; and Reichert, *Sobre las olas*, 44–45, 99.
35. AGI-SD 1, R. 1, no. 87, 108 (decrees, 30 December 1607 and 6 May 1612); no. 91, 100, 107 (consultas, 21 February 1608, 23 April 1609, and 12 February 1612); AGI-SD 54, R. 9, no. 123a (decree, 8 September 1618); Feros, *Kingship and Favoritism*, 186–87, 245–46; Williams, *Great Favourite*, 234–36.
36. AGI-SD 52, R. 8, no. 117, 131 (Gómez de Sandoval to king, 8 August and 3 October 1608); no. 122 (Osorio to king, 20 August 1608); no. 125 (audiencia to king, 20 August 1608); AGI-SD 53, R. 1, no. 2, 36 (Gómez de Sandoval to king, 15 August and 17 September 1609); Moya Pons, *Historia colonial*, 134; Peña Pérez, *Antonio Osorio*, 189–94; Gil-Bermejo García, *La Española*, 54–60, 212–13; Deive, *Tangomangos*, 200.
37. AGI-SD 52, R. 8, no. 117 (Gómez de Sandoval to king, 8 August 1608); AGI-SD 53, R. 1, no. 8 (Gómez de Sandoval to king, 8 May 1609); no. 24 (Mejía de Villalobos to king, 28 May 1609).

38. AGI-SD 54, R. 1, no. 8 (Gómez de Sandoval to king, n.d.); no. 9 (Gómez de Sandoval to king, 20 March 1610); no. 9b (testimony, 16 May 1610); R. 2, no. 55, 78 (Gómez de Sandoval to king, 15 June and 12 October 1611).

39. AGI-SD 1, R. 1, no. 109 (consulta, 13 May 1612); R. 2, no. 117 (consulta, 8 April 1614); AGI-SD 54, R. 3, no. 98 (Gómez de Sandoval to king, 31 August 1612); AGI-SD 869, L. 6, fols. 144v–146v (king to Bohórquez, Mejía de Villalobos, and Gómez de Sandoval, 6 June 1612); AGI-Panama 1, no. 281 (consulta, 8 April 1614); Schäfer, *El Consejo Real*, 2:154; Gil-Bermejo García, *La Española*, 233; Eagle, "Portraits of Bad Officials," 92.

40. AGI-SD 1, R. 1, no. 108a (Rodríguez to king, n.d.); AGI-SD 53, R. 1, no. 33, 34 (audiencia to king, 16 September 1609); no. 51 (Gómez de Sandoval to king, 21 October 1609); AGI-SD 54, R. 2, no. 80b (audiencia to king, 28 November 1611).

41. AGI-SD 1, R. 1, no. 106 (consulta, 29 August 1611); R. 2, no. 143 (consulta, 13 December 1617); AGI-SD 54, R. 8, no. 117 (Gómez de Sandoval to king, 22 April 1617); AGI-Cttn 342B, no. 1, R. 18 (estate of Solier, 1620); Herrera, *Historia del Convento*, 398.

42. AGI-SD 52, R. 8, no. 122 (Osorio to king, 20 August 1608); Chaunu and Chaunu, *Seville et l'Atlantique*, 6:498–502.

43. AGI-SD 53, R. 1, no. 5 (Jerónimo Gómez de Sandoval to king, 23 April 1609); no. 9, 36 (Gómez de Sandoval to king, 8 May and 17 September 1609); AGI-SD 54, R. 1, no. 2, 21 (Gómez de Sandoval to king, 23 January and 6 July 1610); R. 2, no. 49, 75, 77 (Gómez de Sandoval to king, 29 May and 12 October 1611); R. 6, no. 112 (Gómez de Sandoval to king, 30 March 1615); Torres Ramírez, *La Armada de Barlovento*, 29–33.

44. AGI-SD 54, R. 1, no. 20, 20a, 37 (Gómez de Sandoval to king and testimony, 6 July, 26 June, and 31 October 1610); R. 2, no. 44 (Gómez de Sandoval to king, 20 March 1611); Gil-Bermejo García, *La Española*, 213–15.

45. AGI-SD 72, R. 5, no. 12a (testimony, 2 January 1610); AGI-SD 54, R. 2, no. 73 (Gómez de Sandoval to Ruiz de Contreras, 18 July 1611); R. 3, no. 88, 88a, 100 (Herrera to king and testimony, 23 May 1612, 24 May 1610, and 30 November 1612).

46. AGI-SD 869, L. 6, fols. 112r–112v (king to Gómez de Sandoval and Herrera, 7 June 1611); L. 7, fol. 18r (king to Herrera, 17 June 1617); AGI-SD 54, R. 4, no. 106 (Narváez de Valdelomar to San Juan de la Corte, 12 December 1613); AGI-SD 1, R. 2, no. 132 (consulta, 15 September 1616); AGI-SD 54, R. 8, no. 118 (audiencia to king, 20 May 1617); AGI-SD 869, L. 7, fols. 25r–30r (king to Ibarra, 10 April 1618).

47. AGI-SD 72, R. 5, no. 12c, 12d (petitions of Herrera, 13 and 15 January 1618); no. 12j (petition of Gómez de Sandoval, 18 August 1618); no. 12l, fols. 65v–72r (petition of Gómez de Sandoval, 6 March 1619); Gil-Bermejo García, *La Española*, 213–14.

48. AGI-Cttn 5359, no. 16 (license for Herrera, 23 June 1618); AGI-SD 54, R. 10, no. 124 (audiencia to king, 5 February 1619); AGI-SD 72, R. 5, no. 12i (petition of Gómez de Sandoval, 18 August 1618); no. 12l, fols. 1r–2r, 5r, 57r–57v (testimony, 3 September 1619); no. 12ñ (Gómez de Sandoval to king, 20 November 1619).
49. AGI-SD 72, R. 5, no. 12 (petition of Gómez de Sandoval, 19 February 1620); AGI-SD 55, R. 1, no. 1 (Gil de la Sierpe to king, 27 February 1620); AGI-SD 1, R. 2, no. 152 (consulta, 18 March 1620); AGI-Panama 229, L. 2, fols. 179v–180r (king to Vivero y Velasco, 13 February 1627); Aranda Mendíaz, *Visiones*, 162–63. See also AGI-Esc 4, Herrera vs. Gómez de Sandoval (1616).
50. AGI-SD 72, R. 5, no. 12l, fols. 49r–51v (acuerdo, 5 August 1619); no. 12m (testimony, 9 September 1619).
51. AGI-SD 72, R. 5, no. 12l, fols. 13r–14v (testimony, 3 September 1619); Solórzano Pereira, *Política Indiana*, L. 5, cap. 3, no. 44; Eagle, "Beard-Pulling," 487–88.
52. AGI-SD 54, R. 7, no. 115, 115b (audiencia to king, 8 May 1616 and n.d.); AGI-SD 869, L. 7, fols. 16r–16v (king to oidores and Gómez de Sandoval, 17 September 1616).
53. *Recopilación* L. 2, T. 16, l. 12; Phelan, "Authority and Flexibility," 48–49; Jiménez Núñez, "Sistema político," 297.
54. Goslinga, *Dutch in the Caribbean*, 141; Andrews, *Trade, Plunder and Settlement*, 300–303; Butel, *Histoire des Antilles françaises*, 27–30; Kamen, *Empire*, 320–23; Klooster, *Dutch Moment*, 40–41.
55. AGI-SD 54, R. 6, no. 113 (Gómez de Sandoval to king, 1 July 1615); AGI-SD 55, R. 3, no. 13, 14 (Gómez de Sandoval to king, 29 January and 10 February 1623).
56. AGI-SD 55, R. 4, no. 18, 20 (Martínez Tenorio and Acuña to king, 2 January and 5 October 1624); R. 5, no. 24 (Martínez Tenorio to king, 8 February 1625); no. 30, 32, 33 (Acuña to king, 3 October, 12 October, and 18 November 1625); AGI-SD 1, R. 2, no. 191 (consulta, 16 November 1626); Goslinga, *Dutch in the Caribbean*, 159–62; Gil-Bermejo García, *La Española*, 233–35; Lynch, *Hispanic World in Crisis*, 101; Klooster, *Dutch Moment*, 42.
57. AGI-SD 55, R. 5, no. 37, 38 (audiencia and Acuña to king, 23 and 25 December 1625); R. 6, no. 41, 44, 45 (Acuña to king, 28 March, 22 May, and 29 May 1626); R. 8, no. 55a (audiencia to king, 20 September 1628); AGI-SD 870, L. 8, fols. 126v–127r (king to Chaves Osorio, 28 June 1628); Goslinga, *Dutch in the Caribbean*, 186–90; Phillips, *Six Galleons*, 3–5; Elliott, *Count-Duke of Olivares*, 362–64; Klooster, *Dutch Moment*, 45–48.
58. AGI-SD 55, R. 5, no. 25, 29 (Acuña and Gil de la Sierpe to king, 13 February and 16 May 1625); R. 6, no. 42 (Cereceda to king, 24 April 1626); Eagle, "Beard-Pulling," 467–70, 481–83.
59. AGI-SD 55, R. 6, no. 46, 47, 48, 49 (Cereceda, Acuña, Gentil de Párraga, and audiencia to king, 14 and 15 June 1626); AGI-Esc 33B, visita of Audiencia of

Santo Domingo (1630), pza. 11, fols. 8r–17v (testimony, 28 November 1630); Eagle, "Beard-Pulling," 491–92.

60. AGI-SD 1, R. 1, no. 135 (consulta, 5 December 1626); AGI-SD 55, R. 5, no. 29c (notes of Consejo, 10 December 1626); R. 8, no. 56 (Chaves Osorio to king, 20 September 1628); AGI-Esc 34A, visita of Audiencia of Santo Domingo (1630), pza. 18, fol. 15; AGI-Indif 112, no. 123 (merits of Juan de Acuña, 20 August 1645).

61. AGI-SD 55, R. 5, no. 32, 37 (Acuña and audiencia to king, 12 October and 23 December 1625); Camus, *L'île de la Tortue*, 27–31, 47–48; Butel, *Histoire des Antilles françaises*, 27–39; Klooster, *Dutch Moment*, 60.

62. AGI-SD 55, R. 9, no. 57 (audiencia to king, 30 November 1629).

63. Hussey, "Spanish Reaction," 299; Moya Pons, *Historia colonial*, 144–45; Peña Pérez, *Cien años de miseria*, 28; Elliott, *Count-Duke of Olivares*, 518; Phillips, *Six Galleons*, 181–86; Klooster, *Dutch Moment*, 60–61.

64. AGI-SD 55, R. 13, no. 74b (Chaves Osorio to Fernando Ruiz de Contreras, 9 August 1633); AGI-SD 56, R. 1, no. 1 (Bitrián to king, 10 February 1641); R. 6, no. 46 (Velasco to king, 31 March 1646); Mathews, "Spanish Domination"; Vila Vilar, *Historia de Puerto Rico*, 159–60.

65. AGI-SD 55, R. 13, no. 74 (Chaves Osorio to king, 10 August 1633; see also 74a–74r); Eagle, "Restoring Spanish Hispaniola," 388; Ponce Vázquez, *Islanders and Empire*, 134–35; Flores Sasso, "El comercio," 115–17. See also Peña Pérez, *Cien años de miseria*, 242; and Gil-Bermejo García, *La Española*, 262–64.

66. Phelan, *Kingdom of Quito*, 217, 222–24, 302–7; Arregui Zamorano, *La Audiencia de México*, 53; Pietschmann, *El estado*, 158–59, 167–68; Herzog, *Ritos de control*, 7–10, 69, 175–78; Martiré, *Las Audiencias*, 210–19; Eagle, "Portraits of Bad Officials," 101.

67. AGI-SD 55, R. 8, no. 56 (Chaves Osorio to king, 20 September 1628); AGI-Cttn 5789, L. 1, fols. 46r–48r (king to Hurtado, 28 May 1630); AGI-Esc 33B, visita of Audiencia of Santo Domingo (1630) pza. 12, fols. 1r–1v; Gil-Bermejo García, *La Española*, 216–18. For Quito, see Phelan, *Kingdom of Quito*; on visitas generales, see Céspedes del Castillo, "La visita como institución indiana," 985–91, 998; Sánchez Bella, "Visitas a Indias," 163–208; Herzog, *Ritos de control*, 53, 178.

68. AGI-Esc 33A, visita of Audiencia of Santo Domingo (1630), pza. 1, cuad. 2, fols. 28v–29r (testimony, 18 October 1630); fols. 80v, 81v, 92r (testimony, 1 November 1630); fols. 116, 120r, 124r–126v (testimony, 7 November 1630); fols. 128v–134v (testimony, 8 November 1630). See also AGI-SD 55, R. 10, no. 61 (Chaves Osorio to king, 12 July 1630); R. 14, no. 78 (Chaves Osorio to king, 20 August 1634); and Eagle, "Beard-Pulling," 475–76, 483–84.

69. AGI-Esc 33A, visita of Audiencia of Santo Domingo (1630), pza. 1, cuad. 2, fol. 109v (testimony, 4 November 1630).

70. AGI-Esc 33A, visita of Audiencia of Santo Domingo (1630), pza. 7, fol. 7r (petition of Chaves Osorio, 18 November 1630); AGI-Esc 33B, pza. 12, fols. 54r–55r (testimony, 31 October–1 November 1630).
71. AGI-Esc 33A, visita of Audiencia of Santo Domingo (1630), pza. 7, fols. 1r–4v (petition of Chaves Osorio, 28 April 1631).
72. AGI-Esc 33A, visita of Audiencia of Santo Domingo (1630), pza. 4, fol. 2r (auto of Chaves Osorio, 12 June 1631); pza. 7, fol. 106r (king to Chaves Osorio, 28 June 1630); AGI-Esc 33B, pza. 9, fols. 1r–10r (autos of Hurtado, 5 June 1631); fol. 226r (king to Chaves Osorio, 14 January 1631); fols. 232v–233r (Salazar to king, 23 August 1631).
73. AGI-SD 870, L. 8, fols. 222v–223r (king to Fernández Valdivieso, 3 June 1631); AGI-Esc 33A, visita of Audiencia of Santo Domingo (1630), pza. 5, fol. 4r (auto of Hurtado, 17 June 1631); fols. 64r–65v (Salazar to king, 15 December 1632); AGI-Esc 33B, pza. 9, fols. 234r–236r (Salazar to king, 23 August 1631); pza. 10, fols. 1r–2r (petition of Salazar, n.d.); fols. 3r–4v (king to Hurtado, 6 and 10 June 1631); pza. 14, fol. 62r (auto of Hurtado, 12 October 1631).
74. La Rasa also appears as Larrasa. AGI-Panama 2, no. 39 (consulta, 29 March 1635); AGI-Esc 33A, visita of Audiencia of Santo Domingo (1630), pza. 7, fols. 195r–196v (Bautista Larrea to Consejo, 6 October 1638); fol. 220v (notes of Consejo, 7 July 1644); AGI-Esc 33B, pza. 12, fols. 1r–6r (king to De la Rasa, 17 April 1635); fol. 7 (auto of De la Rasa, 29 December 1635); fols. 52v–53r (Facundo de Torres to De la Rasa, 1 February 1636); AGI-SD 55, R. 16, no. 85 (Cereceda to king, 8 May 1636); AGI-Cttn 5785, L. 1, fols. 118r–119v (king to Hurtado, 10 May 1637).
75. AGI-Esc 1181 (visita sentences vs. Cereceda, Gil de la Sierpe, Otalora, and Parra de Meneses, 9 January 1635); AGI-SD 1, R. 3, no. 236 (consulta, 12 January 1635); no. 258 (consulta, 10 May 1636); AGI-Esc 33A, visita of Audiencia of Santo Domingo (1630), pza. 2, fol. 95 (petition of fiscal of Consejo, 31 October 1633); AGI-Esc 33B, pza. 4 (Catalina de Vargas vs. fiscal of Consejo, 1633–37); AGI-SD 55, R. 14, no. 78 (Chaves Osorio to king, 20 August 1634); R. 15, no. 79 (Cereceda to king, 12 June 1635). See also Eagle, "Portraits of Bad Officials," 87, 90, 93–94.
76. AGI-SD 870, L. 8, fols. 223v–224r (king to Hurtado, 17 June 1631); AGI-Esc 33A, pza. 1, fols. 21r–22v (autos of Consejo, 20 October 1630); pza. 7, fols. 193r–196v (petition of Bautista de Larrea, 6 October 1638), 217r–220v (autos of Consejo, 15 March–7 June 1644); Gil-Bermejo García, *La Española*, 218.
77. Céspedes del Castillo, "La visita como institución indiana," 1021; Phelan, *Kingdom of Quito*, 217, 224, 243–64, 305–7; Arregui Zamorano, *La Audiencia de México*, 61–62, 97–107; Elliott, *Count-Duke of Olivares*, 676; Herzog, *Ritos de control*, 5–10, 37.
78. AGI-SD 55, R. 15, no. 79 (Cereceda to king, 12 June 1635); no. 80 (Torres to king, 15 August 1635); no. 80a (testimony, 14 August 1635); R. 16, no. 86 (Vela Núñez to king, 9 May 1636); see also *Recopilación*, L. 2, T. 15, ll. 34, 35.

79. Morfo also appears as Morfa. AGI-Patr 273, R. 1–2 (reports on Tortuga, 1635); AGI-SD 1, R. 3, no. 255a (testimony, 30 April 1635), no. 255b (printed memorial of Morfo, n.d.), 255d (consulta, 11 February 1636); AGI-SD 55, R. 15, no. 79 (Cereceda to king, 12 June 1635). See also Camus, *L'île de la Tortue*, 31–35; Castillo Lara, *Las acciones militares*, 22–23; and Pérez Tostado, "'Buscando el amparo,'" 55–57.
80. AGI-Indif 453, L. A18, fols. 251r–253v (king to Cereceda, 11 January 1636).
81. AGI-SD 55, R. 18, no. 91 (printed memorial of Cereceda, n.d.); AGI-SD 1, R. 3, no. 281 (consulta, 14 August 1640); AGI-Cttn 5793, L. 2, fols. 460r–461v (king to Cereceda, 26 April 1641); Gil-Bermejo García, *La Española*, 239–40.
82. Historians' assessment of Bitrián's service in Havana has been mixed; Macías Domínguez, *Cuba en la primera mitad del siglo XVII*, 225–28; Gil-Bermejo García, *La Española*, 225.
83. Torres Ramírez, *La Armada de Barlovento*, 44–47; Elliott, *Count-Duke of Olivares*, 518–19; Kupperman, *Providence Island*, 336–39; Kamen, *Empire*, 393.
84. AGI-SD 72, R. 6, no. 17 (testimony, 9 June 1640); AGI-SD 56, R. 3, no. 16 (audiencia to king, 30 January 1643); AGI-SD 56, R. 4, no. 34 (Bitrián to king, 31 July 1644); AGI-SD 1, R. 3, no. 304 (consulta, 9 May 1645); Moya Pons, *Historia colonial*, 153. There was another Tortuga expedition in 1636, but a 1638 assault on "Tortuga" was against the Dutch settlement on an island off the coast of Venezuela; compare AGI-SD 870, L. 10, fols. 11r–11v (king to Bitrián, 23 March 1637); fol. 12v (king to Vargas Machuca, 23 March 1637); AGI-SD 55, R. 19, no. 115 (Bitrián to king, 1639); Camus, *L'île de la Tortue*, 35–36; Klooster, *Dutch Moment*, 60; Antczak, Antczak, and Antczak, "Risky Business," 202–4; with Peña Batlle, *La Isla de Tortuga*, 129; Peña Pérez, *Cien años de miseria*, 31–32; Matibag, *Haitian-Dominican Counterpoint*, 38–39; and Pestana, "Early English Jamaica without Pirates," 344, 346.
85. Studnicki-Gizbert, *Nation upon the Ocean Sea*, 26, 43–44; Ponce Vázquez, *Islanders and Empire*, 228.
86. AGI-SD 56, R. 2, no. 11 (audiencia to king, 19 July 1642); AGI-SD 870, L. 11, fols. 114v–115r (king to audiencia, 30 April 1643); Ponce Vázquez, *Islanders and Empire*, 228.
87. AGI-SD 56, R. 2, no. 13c (municipal cabildo to king, 6 February 1643); R. 3, no. 18 (Bitrián to king, 2 February 1643); no. 22 (Bitrián to king, 6 August 1643); R. 5, no. 38 (Bitrián to king, 29 June 1645); AGI-SD 58, R. 1, no. 11 (Francisco de Montemayor to king, 28 July 1654); Gil-Bermejo García, *La Española*, 95; Pérez Tostado, "'Buscando el amparo,'" 48–50, 56; Block and Shaw, "Subjects without an Empire," 38–44.
88. AGI-SD 56, R. 3, no. 20 (audiencia to king, 5 February 1643).

89. AGI-SD 52, R. 7, no. 100 (Osorio to king, 31 December 1607); AGI-SD 55, R. 8, no. 55a, 56 (audiencia and Chaves Osorio to king, 20 September 1628); Chaunu and Chaunu, *Seville et l'Atlantique*, 6:498, 502; Gil-Bermejo García, *La Española*, 67–77; Peña Pérez, *Cien años de miseria*, 159, 172–73.

90. AGI-SD 55, R. 20, no. 120 (Bitrián to king, 29 June 1640); Gil-Bermejo García, *La Española*, 284–85; Peña Pérez, *Cien años de miseria*, 244.

91. Nolasco, *Días de la colonia*, 88–113; Peña Pérez, *Cien años de miseria*, 248–50; Ponce Vázquez, *Islanders and Empire*, 196–98.

92. AGI-SD 55, R. 19, no. 105 (Álvarez de Mendoza to king, 24 March 1639); Eagle, "Chasing the *Avença*," 101.

93. AGI-SD 55, R. 20, no. 124 (Alarcón Coronado to king, 30 June 1640).

94. AGI-SD 56, R. 2, no. 10 (Salazar to king, 15 July 1642).

95. AGI-SD 55, R. 20, no. 123 (Bitrián to king, 30 June 1640); AGI-SD 870, L. 11, fols. 55r–56r (king to Bitrián, 8 March 1641); Ponce Vázquez, *Islanders and Empire*, 181.

96. AGI-SD 55, R. 20, no. 129 (audiencia to king, 3 November 1640).

97. AGI-SD 56, R. 2, no. 9 (audiencia to king, 30 June 1642); Vila Vilar, *Historia de Puerto Rico*, 50–54.

98. AGI-SD 870, L. 11, fols. 61r–62r (king to audiencia and Melgarejo, 8 March 1641); AGI-SD 56, R. 2, no. 8 (Melgarejo to king, 5 April 1642).

99. AGI-Indif 192, no. 103 (merits of Guevara, 1 March 1641); AGI-SD 1, R. 3, no. 306a, 318 (consultas of Cámara, 22 September 1645 and 28 March 1648); Schäfer, *El Consejo Real*, 2:600; Peña Pérez, *Cien años de miseria*, 170–71. The Cámara de Indias sharply criticized the king's rejection of their proposed candidates in 1648.

100. AGI-SD 56, R. 5, no. 40, 40a, 40b (Salazar, audiencia, and Salazar, Pantoja, and Alarcón Coronado to king, 7 August, 8 August, and 12 August 1645); R. 6, no. 47a (Alarcón Coronado to king, 26 February 1646); Deive, *La esclavitud del negro*, 298–301; Gil-Bermejo García, *La Española*, 227–28.

101. AGI-SD 56, R. 6, no. 44a (sentence of Velasco vs. Bitrián, 8 March 1646); no. 47, 52 (Alarcón Coronado and Velasco to king, 20 October and 2 November 1646); R. 7, no. 53a (Melgarejo to king, 14 January 1647); AGI-SD 1, R. 3, no. 316 (consulta of Cámara, 20 October 1647); AGI-Cttn 5794, L. 1, fols. 15r–16r (king to Bitrián, 16 December 1648); AGI-Panama 21, R. 4, no. 32 (Carlos Romeo to king, 22 August 1650); see also Ponce Vázquez, *Islanders and Empire*, 184–85.

102. AGI-SD 56, R. 5, no. 37 (Bitrián to king, 25 March 1645); R. 7, no. 57 (audiencia to king, 24 January 1647).

103. AGI-SD 56, R. 6, no. 50 (Velasco to king, 2 November 1646); Block and Shaw, "Subjects without an Empire," 43–44.

104. AGI-SD 56, R. 7, no. 60, 60a (Velasco to king, 10 October 1647); AGI-SD 871, L. 12, fols. 120v–121v (king to Velasco, 17 June 1648); see also Clapham, "Charles Louis, Elector Palatine," 387–88; Moya Pons, *Historia colonial*, 172.

105. AGI-SD 57, R. 1, no. 1 (audiencia to king, 12 February 1649).

106. AGI-SD 57, R. 1, no. 2, 3, 6, 8, 12, 15 (audiencia to king, 12 February, 1 March, 3 March, and 17 April 1649).

107. AGI-SD 57, R. 2, no. 27, 30 (Melgarejo to king, 18 and 29 March 1650).

108. AGI-SD 57, R. 2, no. 23, 31 (audiencia to king and testimony, 14 March and 18 May 1650); AGI-Mexico 76, R. 7, no. 39 (audiencia to king, 21 July 1650); no. 39a (notes of Consejo, 13 February 1651); no. 39c (king to audiencia, n.d.); AGI-Mexico 1068, L. 14, 346v–348r (king to Alba de Liste, 25 February 1651); Serrano Mangas, *La Encrucijada Portuguesa*, 159–61; Ponce Vázquez, *Islanders and Empire*, 230–31.

109. AGI-SD 57, R. 1, no. 21 (Melgarejo to king, 31 May 1649); R. 3, no. 41c (Melgarejo to king, 18 March 1650); no. 44j, 44l (Melgarejo and Cepeda to king, 30 and 31 May 1649); no. 44ll, 44ñ (Melgarejo and cabildo to king, 18 and 19 March 1650).

110. AGI-SD 57, R. 1, no. 10 (audiencia to king, 3 March 1649).

111. Nolasco, *Días de la colonia*, 89, Ponce Vázquez, *Islanders and Empire*, 184–85.

112. AGI-SD 57, R. 2, no. 32 (Fernández de Córdoba to king, 5 August 1650).

113. AGI-SD 57, R. 3, no. 40, 41, 44, 44s, 44x (Fernández de Córdoba to king, 30 January, 12 February, 20 February, 26 February, and 2 March 1651).

114. AGI-SD 57, R. 3, no. 38, 48 (Fernández de Córdoba and Pantoja to king, 30 January and 31 March 1651).

115. AGI-SD 57, R. 3, no. 52 (Figueroa y Castilla to king, 31 December 1651); Ponce Vázquez, *Islanders and Empire*, 201.

116. AGI-SD 57, R. 4, no. 61 (audiencia to king, 22 August 1652); AGI-SD 57, R. 5, no. 72, 73 (Montemayor and Pantoja to king, 26 and 27 April 1653); AGI-SD 58, R. 1, no. 4 (audiencia to king, 16 April 1654).

117. AGI-SD 57, R. 5, no. 75–75c (testimony, 20 August 1653); Ponce Vázquez, *Islanders and Empire*, 204–6.

118. AGI-SD 2, R. 1, no. 35a (consulta of Junta de Guerra, 1653); Aranda Mendíaz, *Visiones*, 140–41.

119. AGI-SD 2, R. 1, no. 36, 36a, 36b (consultas, 10 November, 27 August, and 22 October 1653); AGI-SD 57, R. 5, no. 71, 72 (Pérez Franco and Montemayor to king, 23 and 26 April 1653).

120. Another visita had been suggested in 1647; AGI-SD 56, R. 7, no. 58 (Velasco to king, 25 January 1647).

121. Eagle, "Beard-Pulling," 468–69, 486–87.

3. President-Governors, 1653–1700

1. AGI-Indif 116, no. 3 (merits of Montemayor, 7 February 1651); Peña Batlle, *La Isla de Tortuga*, 161–62; Rodríguez-Sala and Erice, "Juan Francisco de Montemayor y Córdoba de Cuenca," 193–233; Barrientos Grandon, "Juan Francisco Montemayor"; Cruz Barney, *Una visión indiana*.
2. AGI-SD 58, R. 1, no. 1, 5 (audiencia to king, 16 April 1654); AGI-SD 2, R. 1, no. 49 (consulta, 18 September 1654).
3. AGI-SD 58, R. 1, no. 7 (Montemayor to king, 22 April 1654); Peña Pérez, *Cien años de miseria*, 254–55; Ponce Vázquez, *Islanders and Empire*, 203–5.
4. AGI-SD 58, R. 1, no. 11 (Montemayor to king, 28 July 1654); no. 11a (testimony, 14 January 1655); no. 11b (Baltasar Calderon de Espinosa to Montemayor, 27 April 1654); AGI-Patr 273, R. 7, no. 2 (Montemayor to king, 30 March 1654); R. 8, no. 16 (Morfo to king, 2 January 1655); Pérez Tostado, "'Buscando el amparo,'" 58; Polo y La Borda, "Representando la experiencia," 74–80.
5. AGI-Patr 273, R. 7, no. 2 (Montemayor to king, 30 March 1654); no. 15 (notes of Junta de Guerra, 9 April 1655); Peña Batlle, *La Isla de Tortuga*, 161–75. See also oidor Fernando de Araujo y Rivera's 1699 "Descripción de la Isla Española, o de Santo Domingo," BP Ms. 2, no. 2835, fol. 16 (reprinted in *Boletín del Archivo General de la Nación* 5, no. 22 [June 1942]: 215–16); and Nolasco, *Días de la colonia*, 95–96.
6. For recent accounts, see Vega, *La derrota de Penn y Venables*; Pestana, *English Conquest of Jamaica*.
7. AGI-SD 2, R. 1, no. 39 (consulta, 6 March 1654); AGI-Patr 273, R. 7, no. 11, fol. 212 (notes of Junta de Guerra, 1 October 1654); no. 14 (Montemayor to king, 8 November 1654); R. 8, no. 12 (treasury officials to king, 5 June 1655); Jekabson-Lemanis, "Balts in the Caribbean," 35–40.
8. The countship is usually spelled "Peñalva," though Meneses used "Peñalba." AGI-Cttn 5431, no. 1, R. 33 (passenger list, 23 February 1655); AGI-Patr 273, R. 8, no. 7 (Meneses to Gregario de Leguía, 24 May 1655).
9. AGI-SD 58, R. 3, no. 17 (Meneses to king, 20 February 1656); Vega, *La derrota de Penn y Venables*, 114–15; Block, *Ordinary Lives*, 122–23.
10. AGI-Patr 273, R. 7, no. 12 (treasury officials to king, 5 June 1655); AGI-SD 2, R. 1, no. 63a (consulta of Junta de Guerra, 1657); AGI-SD 58, R. 3, no. 38 (audiencia to king, 12 May 1656); no. 39 (Bernardo Trigo de Figueroa to Leguía, 26 May 1656); Taylor, *Western Design*, 31–32.
11. Schmitt, "Centering Spanish Jamaica," 718–20.
12. AGI-Patr 273, R. 8, no. 8 (Meneses to king, 30 September 1655); no. 8, fols. 379v–385r (testimony, 26–27 July 1655); cf. Pestana, *English Conquest of Jamaica*, 192.

13. See the 1691 "Representación" of Francisco Franco de Torrequemada, BP Ms. 2, no. 2835, fols. 334v–335v (reprinted in *Boletín del Archivo General de la Nación* 4, no. 17 [August 1941]: 206–7); Araujo, "Descripción," 216; and Hernández González, "Santo Domingo en el contexto internacional," 369–70.

14. AGI-Patr 273, R. 7, no. 8 (Meneses to king, 30 September 1655); no. 12 (Montemayor to king, 2 December 1656); AGI-SD 58, R. 3, no. 19, 40 (Meneses to king and Leguía, 20 March and 1 June 1656).

15. AGI-SD 871, L. 13, fols. 186v–196r (king to Meneses, 13 September 1654). See also Peña Batlle, *La Isla de Tortuga*, 194–202.

16. AGI-Patr 273, R. 7, no. 20 (Zapata to king, 6 February 1655).

17. AGI-SD 871, L. 13, fols. 196r–197v (king to Montemayor, 13 September 1654); AGI-SD 2, R. 1, no. 48 (consulta of Cámara, 21 August 1654).

18. AGI-SD 58, R. 3, no. 18, 40 (Meneses to Leguía, 20 March and 1 June 1656); no. 40a (index of orders to Meneses, 28 April 1656). See also AHN-DC 27, no. 30–32 (1655).

19. AGI-SD 58, R. 3, no. 14 (Meneses to king, 20 January 1656); no. 40, 42 (Meneses to Leguía, 1 June and 28 July 1656); no. 43, 53 (Meneses to king, 28 July 1656 and n.d.); 53a (merits of Meneses, 6 August 1656); AGI-Esc 12A, no. 2, residencia of Montemayor (1655), fols. 62r–63r; Ponce Vázquez, *Islanders and Empire*, 208.

20. AGI-Patr 273, R. 9, no. 1 (Zúñiga to Leguía, 30 July 1656); AGI-SD 2, R. 1, no. 54, 70 (consultas, 4 February 1656 and 28 August 1658).

21. AGI-SD 58, R. 3, no. 40 (Meneses to Leguía, 1 June 1656); no. 17, 42 (Meneses to king and Leguía, 20 February and 28 July 1656); AGI-Patr 273, R. 9, no. 1, 2 (Zúñiga to Leguía and king, 30 July and 3 December 1656); AGI-Panama 2, no. 213 (consulta of Cámara, 20 August 1657).

22. AGI-SD 58, R. 3, no. 45, 48 (Vélez Mantilla and Trigo de Figueroa to Leguía, 28 and 29 July 1656).

23. AGI-SD 58, R. 3, no. 42 (Meneses to Leguía, 28 July 1656); no. 51, 52 (Zúñiga to king, 30 July 1656).

24. AGI-SD 2, R. 1, no. 70 (consulta, 28 August 1658); Ponce Vázquez, *Islanders and Empire*, 208–13. See also Veitia y Linage, *Norte de la Contratación*, L. I, cap. 32, 249.

25. AGI-SD 2, R. 1, no. 70 (consulta, 28 August 1658); Peña Pérez, *Cien años de miseria*, 261–63; Ponce Vázquez, *Islanders and Empire*, 212–13; Paredes Vera, "'No hay más Ley,'" 392.

26. AGI-SD 58, R. 3, no. 57 (Montemayor to Leguía, 3 November 1656); R. 4, no. 62 (Zúñiga to king, 14 February 1657); R. 5, no. 72 (Martínez de Amileta to king, 4 November 1658); AGI-SD 2, R. 1, no. 71 (consulta, 28 August 1658); AGI-Esc 1182 (visita sentences vs. Martínez de Amileta and Caballero, 9 June 1668 and 8 August 1671).

27. AGI-SD 2, R. 1, no. 70 (consulta, 28 August 1658).
28. AGI-SD 57, R. 5, no. 74c (notes of Consejo, 29 November 1653); AGI-SD 2, R. 1, no. 66, 71–73 (consultas, 16 June, 15 October, 23 November, and 19 December 1658); Peña Pérez, *Cien años de miseria*, 264.
29. AGI-SD 58, R. 3, no. 14 (Meneses to king, 20 January 1656); R. 4, no. 63 (Zúñiga to king, 30 November 1657); Ponce Vázquez, *Islanders and Empire*, 209.
30. AGI-SD 58, R. 6, no. 79 (Balboa and Ubilla to king, 31 October 1659); no. 80 (Balboa to king, 7 November 1659); R. 8, no. 92 (Balboa to king, 8 February 1661).
31. AGI-Esc 24B, no. 3, commission of Ubilla (1658), fols. 63r–65v; AGI-SD 58, R. 8, no. 92 (Balboa to king, 8 February 1661); AGI-SD 88, R. 3 [1658] (decree, 1 July 1661); Ponce Vázquez, *Islanders and Empire*, 214–15.
32. AGI-SD 58, R. 6, no. 80 (Balboa to king, 7 November 1659).
33. AGI-SD 58, R. 8, no. 92 (Balboa to king, 8 February 1661); no. 93a (Ubilla to Leguía, 10 February 1660).
34. AGI-SD 58, R. 8, no. 90 (Vargas Campuzano to king, 6 January 1661); no. 90a (Vélez Mantilla to Subiza, 6 February 1661); no. 90b-90e (Martínez de Amileta to king, 15 December 1660 and 15, 16, and 20 January 1661); no. 90f (Caballero to king, 27 January 1661); AGI-SD 59, R. 1, no. 1 (Rosados to king, 25 January 1661); no. 2 (Caballero to king, 27 January 1661).
35. AGI-SD 58, R. 8, no. 92 (Balboa to king, 8 February 1661).
36. Morales Padrón, *Jamaica Española*; Lane, *Pillaging the Empire*, 104–5; Pestana, "Early English Jamaica without Pirates," 329–36; Schmitt, "Centering Spanish Jamaica," 721–25.
37. In Spain, this was mischaracterized as a 1661 English attack; AGI-SD 2, R. 2, no. 90 (consulta, 9 October 1662); no. 90c (summary of residencia charges vs. Balboa, 4 October 1662); AGI-SD 59, R. 2, no. 16 (Carvajal to king, 26 May 1662); Ponce Vázquez, *Islanders and Empire*, 243–44.
38. Stradling, *Philip IV*, 295–99; Malcolm, *Royal Favouritism*, 212–16, 235–37, 242. See also Pincus, *Protestantism and Patriotism*, 258–59.
39. Klooster, *Dutch Moment*, 174–75.
40. AGI-SD 8, R. 1, no. 1 (consulta, 5 July 1657); no. 3a (memorial of Jansen, 1657); no. 3b (States General to king, 22 August 1657); no. 11, 14 (consultas, 30 August 1664 and 21 May 1669); AGI-Esc 12C, residencia of Balboa, no. 1 (1666), pza. 15, fols. 18v–28v (Navarro to king, 28 July 1667); see also AGI-SD 2, R. 1, no. 78 (consulta, 26 May 1660).
41. AGI-SD 58, R. 6, no. 79 (Balboa and Ubilla to king, 31 October 1659); AGI-SD 58, R. 8, no. 92 (Balboa to king, 8 February 1661); AGI-SD 88, R. 3 [1658] (decree, 1 July 1661); AGI-Cttn 5789, L. 2, fols. 264r–266v (king to Carvajal, 11 April 1661);

AGI-SD 2, R. 2, no. 90b (memorial of Piñel y Monrroy, n.d.); Peña Pérez, *Cien años de miseria*, 266–67; Ponce Vázquez, *Islanders and Empire*, 216–18.

42. AGI-SD 2, R. 2, no. 88 (consulta, 30 July 1661); no. 89 (sentence of Ubilla vs. Balboa, 11 December 1661); no. 90 (consulta, 9 October 1662).

43. AGI-SD 59, R. 2, no. 10 (audiencia to king, 25 May 1662); AGI-Esc 12A, no. 4, residencia of Balboa (1661), pza. 2, fols. 2r–9r (De la Cueva to king, 1 September 1663); no. 5, residencia of Balboa (1666), pza. 2, fols. 193r–194r (cabildo to king, 18 May 1662); Ponce Vázquez, *Islanders and Empire*, 218.

44. AGI-SD 2, R. 2, no. 95 (consulta, 29 October 1669); no. 95a, 95k (memorials of Balboa, 19 September 1669 and 3 December 1670); no. 129, 132, 132a, 139 (consultas, 19 November 1664 and 31 March, 10 May, and 19 November 1666); AGI-Esc 12A, no. 4, residencia of Balboa (1661), pza. 1, fol. 1 (queen regent to Navarro, 29 May 1666); no. 5, residencia of Balboa (1666), pza. 2, fols. 217r–238v; AGI-Esc 12C, no. 1, residencia of Balboa (1666), pza. 15, fols. 18v–28v (Navarro to king, 28 July 1667); AGI-Esc 24B, no. 4, commission of Navarro (1666), pza. 1, fol. 231.

45. AGI-Esc 12C, no. 1, residencia of Balboa (1666), pza. 10, fols. 46r–49v (Pimentel to Balboa, 9 December 1659, 2 November 1660, and 7 June 1661); Ponce Vázquez, *Islanders and Empire*, 218–19.

46. AGI-Esc 12C, no. 1, residencia of Balboa (1666), pza. 15, fols. 18v–28v (Navarro to king, 28 July 1667); Peña Pérez, *Cien años de miseria*, 291; Ponce Vázquez, *Islanders and Empire*, 219–21; Paredes Vera, "'No hay más Ley,'" 403–7.

47. AGI-SD 60, R. 1, no. 6 (Carvajal to Ramos del Manzano, 30 August 1663); AGI-SD 2, R. 2, no. 136 (consulta, 17 August 1666).

48. AGI-SD 60, R. 1, no. 3 (Carvajal to king, 30 August 1663); AGI-SD 62, R. 2, no. 20, fols. 300r–301r (auto of Navarro, 6 February 1668); AGI-Esc 12C, no. 1, residencia of Balboa (1666) pza. 15, fols. 18v–28v (Navarro to king, 28 July 1667). See also AGI-SD 61, R. 1 (1665–66).

49. Malcolm, *Royal Favouritism*, 230–34; Peña Pérez, *Cien años de miseria*, 56–58; Cassá, *Historia social y económica*, 219; Garrigus, *Before Haiti*, 25; Boucher, *France and the American Tropics*, 180–81; Hernández González, "Santo Domingo en el contexto internacional," 370; Ponce Vázquez, "Colaboraciones fronterizas," 266–67.

50. AGI-SD 59, R. 1, no. 5 (Carvajal to king, 10 October 1661); R. 2, no. 16 (Carvajal to king, 26 May 1662).

51. AGI-SD 60, R. 1, no. 1 (Carvajal to king, 15 February 1663); no. 1c (letters patent of "don Thomás, conde de Vindesor," 20 September 1662); no. 2 (audiencia to king, 16 February 1663); Lane, *Pillaging the Empire*, 107; Schmitt, "Centering Spanish Jamaica," 725. See also Pincus, *Protestantism and Patriotism*, 254.

52. AGI-SD 60, R. 1, no. 1d (Carvajal to king, 16 September 1662); R. 2, no. 13 (Carvajal to king, 12 September 1666); AGI-SD 62, R. 2, no. 18 (Carvajal to king, 14 August 1668); AGI-SD 63, R. 3, no. 56 (audiencia to king, 21 October 1677).
53. AGI-SD 62, R. 3, no. 22 (Carvajal to king, 16 September 1669); Lane, *Pillaging the Empire*, 111.
54. AGI-SD 59, R. 2, no. 18 (Carvajal to king, 26 May 1662); AGI-SD 60, R. 2, no. 14 (audiencia and treasury officials to king, 25 July 1664); AGI-SD 61, R. 2, no. 12 (audiencia to king, 15 March 1666).
55. AGI-SD 62, R. 1, no. 8 (audiencia to king, 4 August 1667); no. 8a (Carvajal to king, 12 September 1666); Sáez Ramo, "La epidemia de viruelas en Santo Domingo," 67–88. See also Sánchez Belén, *La política fiscal*, 259.
56. Utrera, *Santo Domingo: Dilucidaciones históricas*, 361–64, 429; Peña Pérez, *Cien años de miseria*, 183–84; García-Herrera et al., "New Records of Atlantic Hurricanes from Spanish Documentary Sources," 5; Cassá, *Historia social y económica*, 220; Gutiérrez Escudero, "La estructura económica de Santo Domingo," 77–78; Ponce Vázquez, "Atlantic Peripheries," 304–5.
57. AGI-SD 61, R. 2, no. 8 (Carvajal to king, 6 March 1666); AGI-SD 2, R. 2, no. 143 (consulta, 5 March 1668); no. 143a (Carvajal to king, 28 July 1667); Moya Pons, *Historia colonial*, 204; Deive, *Los guerrilleros negros*, 85–89; Landers, "Central African Presence," 236; Schwaller, "Contested Conquests," 636–37. Maroons continued to inhabit the island's interior long after these campaigns.
58. AGI-SD 62, R. 1, no. 10 (audiencia to queen regent, 4 August 1667); AGI-SD 873, L. 18, fols. 433r–435r (queen regent to audiencia, 26 September 1668).
59. AGI-SD 2, R. 2, no. 156 (consulta of Cámara, 28 April 1670); no. 176 (consulta, 1 August 1672).
60. AGI-SD 2, R. 2, no. 170 (consulta of Cámara, 4 November 1671).
61. AGI-SD 3, R. 1, no. 5 (consulta of Cámara, 11 August 1674); no. 12, 12a (consultas of Cámara, 19 May and 2 June 1677); AGI-SD 62, R. 6, no. 53 (audiencia to king, 14 September 1673); AGI-SD 63, R. 1, no. 5 (Zayas Bazán to king, 28 April 1675); AGI-Panama 3, no. 132 (consulta of Cámara, 9 October 1674); AGI-Indif 130, no. 78 (merits of Maldonado, 9 April 1685); Burkholder and Chandler, *From Impotence to Authority*, 3–4.
62. AGI-SD 62, R. 5, no. 31 (Zayas Bazán to king, 27 January 1672); no. 31a, fols. 7v–11r (testimony, 20 and 30 June 1671); Lane, *Pillaging the Empire*, 117–22; Ponce Vázquez, *Islanders and Empire*, 236. See also Gould, "Entangled Histories, Entangled Worlds," 770–72.
63. AGI-SD 62, R. 5, no. 31b (Zayas Bazán to king, 27 January 1672); R. 7, no. 56 (Zayas Bazán to king, 13 May 1674); see also R. 5, no. 33 (Zayas Bazán to king, 27 January 1672); R. 7, no. 62, 62a (Maldonado and Padilla to king, 20 May and 10 July 1674).

64. AGI-SD 63, R. 3, no. 28, 28a (Padilla and cabildo to king, 15 August and 12 September 1677).

65. AGI-SD 3, R. 1, no. 18a (Doncker to Zayas Bazán, 2 April 1677); no. 18c (Zayas Bazán to king, 11 April 1677); no. 34 (consulta, 3 October 1678); AGI-SD 63, R. 3, no. 32c (Padilla to king, 24 August 1677); no. 32e (French memorial, 20 February 1676); no. 32g, 32l (Padilla to king, 1 February and 12 June 1678); AGI-SD 3, R. 1; Pritchard, *In Search of Empire*, 290–94; Boucher, *France and the American Tropics*, 206; Klooster, *Dutch Moment*, 110–11. See also Hernández González, "Sociedad en la Española," 221.

66. AGI-SD 63, R. 3, no. 32b (Padilla to king, 1 February 1678); see also no. 32–32al.

67. AGI-SD 63, R. 3, no. 62 (Padilla to king, 25 October 1677); AGI-SD 64, R. 1, no. 5 (Garcés de los Fayos to king, 24 March 1679); no. 34 (Padilla to king, 24 July 1679); AGI-SD 874, L. 21, fol. 60r (king to Padilla, 25 November 1679); Schäfer, *El Consejo Real*, 2:448, 458, 496; Moya Pons, *Historia colonial*, 219–20; Deive, *Los guerrilleros negros*, 93–100; Landers, "Central African Presence," 235–36; Garrigus, *Before Haiti*, 29–30; Julián, "La fuga de esclavos," 41–42.

68. AGI-SD 63, R. 3, no. 32ñ (Padilla to king, 12 June 1678); no. 41 (Garcés de los Fayos to king, 2 September 1677); no. 49 (audiencia to king, 8 October 1677).

69. AGI-SD 63, R. 3, no. 32q, 32r (audiencia and cabildo eclesiástico to king, 18 August 1678); no. 32u (archbishop to king, 4 April 1679); AGI-SD 874, L. 21, fol. 72 (king to audiencia, 22 February 1680); fols. 83v–84r (king to archbishop, 22 February 1680).

70. AGI-SD 3, R. 1, no. 24 (consulta of Cámara de Indias, 2 April 1678); AGI-SD 64, R. 1, no. 16 (Segura to king, 28 March 1679); R. 2, no. 42 (Segura to king, 7 November 1680).

71. AGI-Indif 124, no. 106 (merits of Palacios, 10 July 1674); AGI-Indif 130, no. 53 (merits of Chacón Abarca); AGI-Guatemala 26, R. 1, no. 43 (Palacios to Joseph Veitia Linaje, 8 January 1679); AGI-SD 3, R. 1, no. 42 (consulta of Cámara, 13 May 1680); AGI-SD 64, R. 1, no. 25, 25b (Segura to count of Medellín and king, 22 April 1679); R. 3, no. 45, 93 (Cárdenas to king, 10 April and 24 December 1681); no. 48, 68 (Segura to king, 3 and 8 June 1681); no. 85 (audiencia to king, 30 June 1681).

72. AGI-SD 3, R. 2, no. 57 (consulta of Cámara, 6 October 1683); R. 3, no. 86 (consulta of Cámara, 13 February 1686); AGI-SD 64, R. 5, no. 99 (Segura to king, 17 April 1683); no. 99a (notes of Cámara, n.d.); no. 107, 107c (Pizarro Cortés to king, 18 August and 30 March 1683); AGI-SD 65, R. 2, no. 43 (audiencia to king, 13 December 1686); AGI-Indif 130, no. 53 (merits of Chacón Abarca, 18 August 1684).

73. AGI-SD 65, R. 1, no. 14 (audiencia to king, 20 May 1685); Burkholder and Chandler, *From Impotence to Authority*, 21–22. See also Herzog, *Los ministros de la Audiencia de Quito*, 22.

74. AGI-SD 64, R. 1, no. 17 (Segura to king, 28 March 1679); see also AGI-SD 92, s.no. (audiencia to king, 22 April 1683); AGI-SD 63, R. 3, no. 32s (memorial of Martínez de Quixano, n.d.); Eagle, "Restoring Spanish Hispaniola," 389.

75. AGI-SD 64, R. 1, no. 3, 11 (Segura to king, 26 February and 28 March 1679); R. 5, no. 98 (Segura to king, 7 February 1683); no. 101 (king to Segura, 27 July 1683); AGI-SD 874, L. 21, fol. 72 (king to audiencia, 22 February 1680); Peña Pérez, *Cien años de miseria*, 244–45; Reichert, *Sobre las olas*, 113.

76. AGI-SD 63, R. 3, no. 32y (Segura to king, 20 November 1680). See also no. 32v (Segura to king, 22 July 1680); Charlevoix, *Histoire de l'isle Espagnole*, vol. 2, L. 8, 123; Boucher, *France and the American Tropics*, 206–7; and Hrodej, "Défense statique et défense dynamique," 43–44.

77. AGI-SD 63, R. 3, no. 32z (testimony, 13 November 1680); AGI-SD 92, s.no. (testimony, 28 May 1681); Peña Pérez, *Cien años de miseria*, 74–80, 97. See also Pritchard, *In Search of Empire*, 295; Peña Battle, *Historia de la cuestión fronteriza*, 101–6; and Ponce Vázquez, "Atlantic Peripheries," 308–9.

78. AGI-SD 3, R. 2, no. 66a (consulta, 17 December 1683); no. 66b (summary, 13 December 1683); no. 70 (consulta, 7 February 1684); AGI-SD 76, R. 3, s.no. (treasury officials to king, 29 November 1684); Torres Ramírez, *La Armada de Barlovento*, 126–27; Lane, *Pillaging the Empire*, 166; Ponce Vázquez, "Contrabandistas, piratas y diplomacia," 291–99.

79. AGI-SD 3, R. 2, no. 68 (consulta of Cámara, 27 January 1684); AGI-SD 64, R. 6, no. 132 (Robles to king, 10 July 1684); AGI-SD 930, s.no. (king to audiencia, 10 May 1685); Nolasco, *Días de la colonia*, 111–12; Ponce Vázquez, *Islanders and Empire*, 256. See also AGI-Esc 25A–25C.

80. AGI-SD 64, R. 6, no. 161 (Robles to king, 29 November 1684); no. 162 (Semillán to Diego de Valverde, 1 December 1684); no. 163 (Semillán to king, 1 December 1684).

81. Garrigus, *Before Haiti*, 30; Pritchard, *In Search of Empire*, 424. See also AGI-SD 65, R. 3, no. 50 (Robles to king, 16 May 1687).

82. AGI-SD 2, R. 2, no. 119 (consulta, 20 April 1663); AGI-SD 3, R. 2, no. 61, 63, 64, 74 (consultas, 23 November, 6 December, 7 December, and 5 October 1684); no. 75 (consulta, 8 March 1685); R. 4, no. 149 (consulta, 3 March 1693); R. 5, no. 179 (consulta, 11 September 1699); AGI-SD 65, R. 1, no. 1 (Robles to king, 5 March 1685); R. 5, no. 173 (Robles to king, 13 August 1689); AGI-SD 72, R. 10, no. 26a, fol. 4v (testimony, 7 March 1686); Gutiérrez Escudero, "Inmigración canaria a América," 129–30. See also Gutiérrez Escudero, "Vicisitudes de una villa de canarios," 707–11; Hernández González, *El sur dominicano*, 169–84; Moya Pons, "Evolución de la población dominicana," 34–36; Paredes Vera, "El cabildo de Santo Domingo," 242–47.

83. AGI-SD 3, R. 3, no. 118a (Pérez Caro to king, 30 September 1689).

84. AGI-SD 65, R. 1, no. 17 (Robles to king, 26 April 1685); Sluiter, "Word *Pechelingue*," 691–92; Moutoukias, *Contrabando y control colonial*, 105.

85. AGI-SD 65, R. 3, no. 69 (Robles to king, 22 July 1687); see also no. 49, 66 (Robles to king, 15 May and 20 July 1687); Ponce Vázquez, "Colaboraciones fronterizas," 274–75.

86. AGI-SD 65, R. 1, no. 23d (notes of Consejo, 18 January 1686); R. 3, no. 80 (Robles to king, 22 August 1687); R. 5, no. 165 (Robles to king, 4 April 1689); Peña Pérez, *Cien años de miseria*, 299–303.

87. AGI-SD 3, R. 3, no. 87 (Vélez to king, 4 March 1686); no. 107 (consulta, 3 December 1687); AGI-SD 876, L. 25 (king to Robles, 29 January 1690); Everaert, "Comment récupérer la 'Isla Colombina'?," 79–81; Ponce Vázquez, *Islanders and Empire*, 254–55. See also Eagle, "Restoring Spanish Hispaniola," 398–99; Aranda Mendíaz, *Visiones*, 64–65.

88. AGI-SD 64, R. 6, no. 138 (Robles to king, 22 July 1684); AGI-SD 65, R. 1, no. 14 (audiencia to king, 20 March 1685); AGI-SD 875, L. 22, fols. 147v–148r (king to Robles, 1 June 1685).

89. AGI-SD 65, R. 1, no. 22 (Robles to king, 1 July 1685); R. 2, no. 43 (Robles to king, 13 December 1686); R. 3, no. 82 (Robles to king, 22 August 1687).

90. Nolasco, *Días de la colonia*, 108; Ponce Vázquez, *Islanders and Empire*, 221–22.

91. AGI-SD 64, R. 5, no. 97a, 110, 117 (Segura, audiencia, and Segura to king, 17 April, 20 August, and 25 August 1683); R. 6, no. 150, 155 (audiencia to king, 28 July and 11 August 1684); AGI-SD 65, R. 4, no. 102, 154 (Robles to king, 21 March and 8 September 1688); AGI-SD 72, R. 10, no. 25 (Robles to king, 15 March 1686).

92. AGI-SD 65, R. 4, no. 117, 117a (Robles to king, 15 April 1688 and 24 July 1687); R. 6, no. 214 (Pérez Caro to king, 4 August 1690); R. 7, no. 232c (Oviedo to king, 28 May 1691); AGI-Esc 13A, no. 3, residencia of Robles (1690), pza. 1, fols. 619r–639r; AGI-Esc 1192 (sentence vs. Robles, 12 May 1692).

93. AGI-SD 3, R. 3, no. 118 (consulta, 3 October 1689); no. 118a, 118b (memorials, 30 September and 11 October 1689); no. 126 (Ortiz to Fuentehermosa, 11 October 1689); Burkholder and Chandler, *From Impotence to Authority*, 59.

94. AGI-SD 65, R. 7, no. 227, 227a, 228 (audiencia to king, 9 and 10 March 1691).

95. AGI-SD 66, R. 1, no. 3 (Pérez Caro to king, 24 August 1692); R. 4, no. 91 (Pérez Caro to king, 21 November 1695); Burkholder and Chandler, *From Impotence to Authority*, 23–24.

96. AGI-SD 65, R. 5, no. 187 (Robles to king, 15 September 1689); R. 6, no. 208–11, 215, 215a (Pérez Caro to king, 2 June, 4 June, 12 June, 6 August, and 12 October 1690); R. 7, no. 241 (Pérez Caro to king, 28 May 1691); Pritchard, *In Search of Empire*, 314; Ponce Vázquez, *Islanders and Empire*, 223–25.

97. AGI-SD 65, R. 7, no. 223a (report of battle of Puerto Real, 14 February 1691); Peña Pérez, *Cien años de miseria*, 305; Sigüenza y Góngora, "Trofeo de la justicia española," 49–92; Pritchard, *In Search of Empire*, 315, Boucher, *France and the American Tropics*, 221; Ponce Vázquez, *Islanders and Empire*, 256–57.
98. AGI-SD 65, R. 7, no. 223, 223a (Pérez Caro to king, 22 and 14 February 1691); no. 223b, 223c (cabildo to king, n.d. and 4 March 1691); no. 229, 244 (Araujo and Ladrón de Guevara to king, 24 April and 29 May 1691); AGI-SD 66, R. 1, no. 1 (letter "que parece de Araujo" to los Vélez, 18 April 1692); R. 2, no. 20 (decree, 6 February 1693); R. 3, no. 54 (Pérez Caro to king, 6 July 1695); AGI-SD 76, R. 3, s.no. (memorial of Consejo, 16 February 1692); R. 5, s.no. (treasury officials to king, 2 July 1694); AGI-SD 91, R. 6, s.no. (petition of Theresa Francisco Agustina de Segura Sandoval y Castilla, 28 February 1697); Ponce Vázquez, "Colaboraciones fronterizas," 278–79. See also López Cantos, *Historia de Puerto Rico*, 33.
99. AGI-SD 66, R. 2, no. 20 (decree, 6 February 1693); no. 20a (Galve to king, 18 August 1692); no. 20b (Pérez Caro to Galve, 10 and 16 April 1692); no. 20c (Galve to Pérez Caro, 15 August 1692).
100. AGI-SD 65, R. 7, no. 233 (Pérez Caro to king, 28 May 1691).
101. AGI-SD 3, R. 4, no. 148 (consulta, 13 February 1693); AGI-SD 876, L. 27, fols. 138r–141r (king to Pérez Caro, 18 February 1693); Ponce Vázquez, *Islanders and Empire*, 259–60.
102. AGI-Indif 132, no. 141, 141 (2) (merits of Correoso, 11 July 1691 and 21 October 1691); AGI-SD 66, R. 2, no. 39 (Pérez Caro to king, 22 November 1693).
103. AGI-Patr 271, R. 9 (3) (Pérez Caro to king, 18 March 1696); AGI-SD 67, R. 1, no. 37 (Manzaneda to king, 3 July 1699).
104. AGI-SD 3, R. 4, no. 150 (consulta of Junta de Guerra, 21 April 1693); AGI-SD 66, R. 3, no. 42 (Pérez Caro to king, 10 February 1694); no. 42a (title of Correoso, 10 February 1694); R. 4, no. 85 (Pérez Caro to king, 16 November 1695); no. 85a (petition of Correoso, n.d.).
105. AGI-Patr 271, R. 9 (2) (Carvajal to Galve, 20 September 1695); AGI-SD 66, R. 2, no. 39a (consulta of Junta de Guerra, 14 February 1696); R. 3, no. 58 (Pérez Caro to king, 22 December 1694).
106. AGI-Patr 271, R. 9 (2) (Carvajal to Galve, 20 September 1695); see also R. 5–9 (1692–96); Morgan, "British West Indies," 400–402; Moya Pons, *Historia colonial*, 197–98; Torres Ramírez, *La Armada de Barlovento*, 156–57; Pritchard, *In Search of Empire*, 319–20; Garrigus, *Before Haiti*, 25; Boucher, *France and the American Tropics*, 221–22; Hrodej, "Défense statique et défense dynamique," 44–46, 48–49.
107. AGI-Patr 271, R. 8 (1) (Pérez Caro to king, 30 October 1695); R. 9 (3) (Pérez Caro to king, 18 March 1696); AGI-SD 66, R. 4, no. 60 (audiencia to king, 16 October 1695); no. 88b (Pérez Caro to Galve, 16 September 1695).

108. AGI-SD 3, R. 5, no. 161 (consulta, 19 January 1696); AGI-SD 877, L. 28, fols. 175v–199r (king to Manzaneda, Correoso, and audiencia, 9 May 1696); AGI-SD 72, R. 11, no. 50 (Arredondo to Pardiñas, 1 August 1696); AGI-SD 66, R. 6, no. 107 (Manzaneda to king, 26 September 1698); López Cantos, *Historia de Puerto Rico*, 202–3; Sanz Tapia, *¿Corrupción o necesidad?*, 44, 438.

109. AGI-SD 76, R. 3, s.no. (memorial of Consejo, 16 February 1692); AGI-SD 66, R. 2, no. 33 (Pérez Caro to king, 20 June 1693).

110. AGI-SD 3, R. 5, no. 161 (consulta, 19 January 1696); AGI-SD 65, R. 5, no. 170 (Robles to king, 28 July 1689); no. 170b (Pérez Caro to king, 20 April 1691); AGI-SD 66, no. 41, 53 (Pérez Caro to king, 28 November 1693 and 25 June 1694).

111. AGI-SD 3, R. 4, no. 155, 158 (consultas of Cámara, 23 March and 18 June 1695); AGI-SD 66, R. 4, no. 60, 91 (audiencia and Pérez Caro to king, 15 October and 21 November 1695).

112. Sánchez Belén, *La política fiscal*, 248; Storrs, *Resilience*, 112–19.

113. AGI-SD 66, R. 4, no. 64 (Pérez Caro to king, 17 October 1695); R. 5, no. 71 (Pérez Caro to king, 17 October 1695); no. 71a (certification of salaries, 26 October 1695).

114. AGI-SD 72, R. 11, no. 55 (Correoso to Bernardino Antonio Pardiñas, 22 May 1698); no. 56 (Correoso to king, 22 May 1698); R. 12, no. 59 (Correoso to king, 10 January 1699); AGI-SD 67, R. 1, no. 37 (Manzaneda to king, 3 June 1699).

115. AGI-SD 3, R. 5, no. 163b (Carvajal y Rivera to king, 10 January 1697).

116. AGI-SD 72, R. 11, no. 53, 54 (Correoso to king, 22 May 1698); AGI-SD 3, R. 5, no. 179 (consulta, 11 September 1699); no. 179e (memorial of Consejo, 15 August 1699); no. 179g (memorial of Carvajal y Rivera, n.d.); no. 180 (consulta of Cámara, 5 October 1699); no. 180a (petition of Carvajal y Rivera, 23 September 1699); Pérez Memén, *El Arzobispo Fernando Carvajal y Rivera*, 15–29; Mir, *La noción de período en la historia dominicana*, 143–46.

117. Pritchard, "French West Indies," 57; Eagle, "Restoring Spanish Hispaniola," 399.

118. AGI-SD 66, R. 1, no. 31 (Manzaneda to king, 30 May 1699); AGI-SD 236, s.no. (consultas of Junta de Guerra, 26 August 1700 and 31 May 1702); Peña Pérez, *Cien años de miseria*, 96–102; Boucher, *France and the American Tropics*, 228; Ponce Vázquez, "Colaboraciones fronterizas," 280–81.

119. AGI-SD 66, R. 6, no. 108, 109 (Cereceda y Girón to king and Sierralta, 3 and 4 October 1698); AGI-Esc 964 (sentences of vista and revista vs. Pérez Caro, 21 July 1704 and 15 September 1704); Schäfer, *El Consejo Real*, 2:534. See also AGI-Esc 26A-29B.

120. AGI-SD 67, R. 1, no. 1, 19, 21a (audiencia to king, 18 February, 27 April, and 4 May 1699); no. 21b, 32e (Cereceda y Girón to king, 23 May and 16 April 1699); no. 23 (Manzaneda to king, 20 May 1699); no. 24 (testimony, 20 May 1699); no. 39 (Manzaneda to king, 4 June 1699).

121. AGI-SD 67, R. 1, no. 16 (audiencia to king, 28 March 1699); no. 20, 21, 23, 32, 34, 39 (Manzaneda to king, 20 May, 30 May, and 4 June 1699); AGI-SD 68, R. 1, no. 20 (audiencia to king, 15 September 1700).
122. AGI-SD 67, R. 1, no. 2, 14 (audiencia to king, 4 and 26 March 1699); AGI-SD 68, R. 1, no. 4, 5 (audiencia to king, 3 and 4 July 1700).
123. AGI-SD 72, R. 11, no. 51 (Arredondo to king, 1 January 1697); Hernández González, "Sociedad en la Española," 256; Torres Agudo, "Élites y grupos de poder," 102, 113–14; Eissa-Barroso, "'Having Served,'" 330–33.
124. Burkholder and Chandler, *From Impotence to Authority*, 32–33.
125. Torres Agudo, "Élites y grupos de poder," 88–91; Ponce Vázquez, *Islanders and Empire*, 9–14.
126. Valenzuela Márquez, *Liturgias del poder*, 24, 80–81; Galván Rodríguez, *Tríptico*, 195–210; Mawson, "Convicts or *Conquistadores*?," 120–24.
127. See for example Phelan, *Kingdom of Quito*, 149–50; Cañeque, *King's Living Image*, 170–71; Herzog, *Upholding Justice*, 17, 69–70; Bertrand, *Grandeur et misère*, 37–41, 361–63, 366; Goode, "Merchant-Bureaucrats, Unwritten Contracts," 180–82, 188–91.
128. Moutoukias, "Power, Corruption, and Commerce," 775–77; Eagle, "Restoring Spanish Hispaniola," 397–400; Ponce Vázquez, *Islanders and Empire*, 261–62.
129. Herzog, *Upholding Justice*, 161–62; Galván Rodríguez, *Tríptico*, 91–92; Eagle, "Beard-Pulling," 487–90.

4. Local Institutions

1. Herzog, *Upholding Justice*, 153–54; Cañeque, *King's Living Image*, 7–11, 13.
2. AGI-Indif 118, no. 54, fol. 11r (merits of Heredia, 30 December 1659).
3. *Recopilación*, L. 2, T. 15, l. 44; Schäfer, *El Consejo Real*, 2:533; Muro Romero, *Presidencias-Gobernaciones*, 83–84.
4. *Recopilación*, L. 2, T. 15, ll. 32, 36, 43, 176; Solórzano Pereira, *Política Indiana*, L. 5, cap. 12, no. 1; Pietschmann, *El estado*, 137–39; Cañeque, *King's Living Image*, 17–18.
5. Phelan, *Kingdom of Quito*, 227–33; Herzog, *Upholding Justice*, 229; Eagle, "Beard-Pulling," 470–75.
6. *Recopilación*, L. 2, T. 15, ll. 34–36, 38, 42–43; Solórzano Pereira, *Política Indiana*, L. 5, cap. 3, no. 29–30; Sánchez Bella, "Las audiencias," 170–73; Arregui Zamorano, *La Audiencia de México*, 36–37.
7. Ponce Vázquez, *Islanders and Empire*, 179, 193–96.
8. AGI-SD 53, R. 1, no. 31, 35 (audiencia to king, 24 August and 16 September 1609); AGI-SD 869, L. 6, fols. 78r (king to Gómez de Sandoval, 20 March 1610).
9. AGI-SD 54, R. 1, no. 24 (Gómez de Sandoval to king, 30 September 1610).

10. AGI-SD 869, L. 6, fols. 121v–122r (king to audiencia, 3 September 1611); Sánchez Bella, "Las audiencias," 177–82; Andrés Santo, "Los proyectos de recopilación," 65.

11. AGI-SD 54, R. 3, no. 85 (Gómez de Sandoval to king, 10 March 1612).

12. AGI-SD 869, L. 6, fols. 94v–95v (decree, 28 August 1610); AGI-SD 54, R. 1, no. 17 (Gómez de Sandoval to king, 20 May 1610); AGI-SD 54, R. 2, no. 73 (Gómez de Sandoval to Ruíz de Contreras, 18 July 1611); *Recopilación*, L. 3, T. 11, ll. 2, 4; Solórzano Pereira, *Política Indiana*, L. 5, cap. 13, no. 41.

13. AGI-SD 54, R. 1, no. 24 (Gómez de Sandoval to king, 30 September 1610); R. 7, no. 115 (audiencia to king, 8 May 1616); AGI-SD 72, R. 5, no. 12n (Gómez de Sandoval to king, 9 September 1619).

14. AGI-SD 55, R. 20, no. 124 (Alarcón Coronado to king, 30 June 1640); AGI-SD 56, R. 1, no. 10 (Salazar to king, 15 July 1642); AGI-SD 57, R. 1, no. 1, 2 (audiencia to king, 12 February 1649); *Recopilación*, L. 2, T. 18, l. 2.

15. AGI-SD 57, R. 1, no. 3 (audiencia to king, 12 February 1649); no. 3a (testimony, 3 February 1649); R. 2, no. 32 (Fernández de Córdoba to king, 5 August 1650); R. 4, no. 61 (audiencia to king, 22 August 1652).

16. Paredes Vera, "Ejército, milicias y sociedad," 397–98.

17. AGI-SD 58, R. 5, no. 72 (Martínez de Amileta to king, 4 November 1658); AGI-SD 64, R. 1, no. 16 (Segura to king, 28 March 1679); Eagle, "Beard-Pulling," 474–75; Harden, *Arms and Letters*, 15–16.

18. AGI-SD 54, R. 2, no. 73 (Gómez de Sandoval to Ruíz de Contreras, 18 July 1611).

19. AGI-SD 55, R. 6, no. 42 (Cereceda to king, 24 April 1626); AGI-Esc 33B, visita of Audiencia of Santo Domingo (1630), pza. 11, fols. 8r–17v; Eagle, "Beard-Pulling," 467–68, 482.

20. AGI-SD 72, R. 5, no. 12l, fol. 14 (testimony, 4 February 1619); AGI-SD 55, R. 5, no. 29 (Gil de la Sierpe to king, 16 May 1625); R. 6, no. 42 (Cereceda to king, 24 April 1626); Eagle, "Beard-Pulling," 475–76.

21. AGI-Esc 1181 (sentence of Consejo vs. Meneses, 21 February 1601); AGI-SD 1, R. 1, no. 66 (consulta of Consejo, 7 October 1605); AGI-SD 63, R. 3, no. 24 (Garcés de los Fayos to king, 15 January 1677).

22. AGI-SD 58, R. 1, no. 4 (audiencia to king, 16 April 1654).

23. AGI-SD 56, R. 1, no. 10 (Salazar to king, 15 July 1642); AGI-SD 57, R. 5, no. 72 (Montemayor to king, 26 April 1653); AGI-SD 58, R. 3, no. 45 (Vélez Mantilla to king, 28 July 1656); AGI-Esc 12A, no. 5, residencia of Balboa (1666), pza. 2, fols. 235v–236r; Eagle, "Beard-Pulling," 473–75.

24. AGI-SD 72, R. 5, no. 12l, fols. 57r–57v (testimony, 3 September 1619); AGI-SD 55, R. 10, no. 61 (Chaves Osorio to king, 12 July 1630); R. 14, no. 78 (Chaves Osorio to king, 20 August 1634); AGI-SD 86, R. 1, s.no. (Bitrián to king, 30 January 1637); Pelorson, *Les "Letrados,"* 203, 237, 302–3.

25. AGI-SD 64, R. 1, no. 13, 13a (Segura and Padilla to king, 28 March 1679 and 20 August 1677); no. 13b (king to Zayas Bazán, 29 January 1676); R. 3, no. 53 (Segura to king, 8 June 1681).

26. AGI-SD 52, R. 8, no. 103 (Osorio to king, 5 January 1608); AGI-SD 869, L. 6, fol. 15r (king to Gómez de Sandoval, 13 May 1609); *Recopilación*, L. 2, T. 16, l. 14.

27. AGI-SD 56, R. 2, no. 10 (Salazar to king, 15 July 1642); R. 5, no. 40b (audiencia to king, 8 August 1645); AGI-SD 57, R. 3, no. 45 (Fernández de Córdoba to king, 25 February 1651); AGI-SD 64, R. 5, no. 127 (Salazar to king, 30 August 1683); AGI-SD 65, R. 4, no. 154 (Robles to king, 8 September 1688); AGI-SD 72, R. 10, no. 25a (autos, 19 September 1685).

28. AGI-SD 56, R. 4, no. 34 (Bitrián to king, 31 July 1644); AGI-SD 57, R. 3, no. 38 (Fernández de Córdoba, 30 January 1651).

29. AGI-SD 55, R. 15, no. 80 (Torres to king, 15 August 1635); AGI-SD 57, R. 3, no. 44 (testimony, 27 March 1649); AGI-SD 65, R. 5, no. 170 (Robles to king, 28 July 1689); *Recopilación* L. 2, T. 15, l. 57; Sánchez Bella, "Las audiencias," 165–66.

30. AGI-SD 54, R. 1, no. 9 (Gómez de Sandoval to king, 20 March 1610); no. 9a, 9b (testimony, 14 March and 16 May 1610); no. 38 (Gómez de Sandoval to king, 1 November 1610); AGI-SD 72, R. 5, no. 12l, fols. 49r–51v (testimony, 3 September 1619).

31. AGI-SD 57, R. 2, no. 32 (Fernández de Córdoba to king, 5 August 1650); R. 4, no. 61 (audiencia to king, 22 August 1652); AGI-SD 58, R. 1, no. 4 (audiencia to king, 16 April 1654); R. 4, no. 62 (Zúñiga to king, 14 February 1657); AGI-SD 871, L. 13, fols. 128v–131r (king to Meneses, 12 May 1654).

32. AGI-SD 874, L. 20, fols. 528r–529v (king to audiencia, 13 May 1678); AGI-SD 64, R. 1, no. 16 (Segura to king, 28 March 1679).

33. AGI-SD 55, R. 10, no. 61 (Chaves Osorio to king, 12 July 1630); R. 14, no. 78 (Chaves Osorio to king, 20 August 1634); Eagle, "Beard-Pulling," 475–76.

34. AGI-Esc 33A, visita of Audiencia of Santo Domingo (1630), pza. 1, cuad. 2, fol. 120r (testimony, 7 November 1630); AGI-SD 56, R. 3, no. 17 (Bitrián to king, 2 February 1643); AGI-SD 65, R. 4, no. 125 (González de Sepúlveda to king, 26 April 1688); Crahan, "Spanish and American Counterpoint," 487–88.

35. Valenzuela Márquez, *Liturgias del poder*, 80–82; Herzog, *Upholding Justice*, 224–25; Cañeque, *King's Living Image*, 60–65, 143–45.

36. AGI-SD 58, R. 3, no. 52 (Zúñiga to king, 20 July 1656); no. 52a (king to Pérez Franco, 5 March 1653); no. 52b (audiencia to king, 26 February 1649); AGI-SD 872, L. 16, fols. 37r–38r (king to audiencia, 24 April 1659).

37. AGI-SD 869, L. 6, fols. 66r–67r (king to audiencia, 8 February 1610); AGI-SD 870, L. 8, fols. 101v–102v (king to audiencia, 3 September 1627); *Recopilación*,

L. 8, T. 6, l. 2; Sánchez Bella, *La organización financiera*, 121–27; Paredes Vera, "'No hay más Ley,'" 405–6.

38. AGI-Filipinas 339, L. 1, fol. 112 (decree, 9 June 1584); AGI-SD 1, R. 1, no. 55, 58 (consultas, 11 February and 8 October 1604); no. 81 (consulta of Cámara, 2 August 1607); AGI-SD 869, L.5, fol. 158r (king to Osorio, 13 February 1608); AGI-SD 75, R. 1, s.no. (treasury officials to king, 30 June 1640); AGI-SD 76, R. 2, s.no. (treasury officials to king, 4 July 1681); Sánchez Bella, *La organización financiera*, 29; Bertrand, *Grandeur et misère*, 50–56, 72–73.

39. AGI-Cttn 5371, no. 29 (license for Tajagrano, 31 March 1620); AGI-SD 1, R. 3, no. 309, 325 (consultas of Cámara, 22 June and 23 September 1649); Sáez, *Libro de bautismos de esclavos*, 48.

40. AGI-SD 869, L. 5, fols. 154v–157r (king to audiencia and treasury officials, 28 January 1608); AGI-SD 72, R. 5, no. 12a (testimony, 2 January 1610); R. 12, no. 59 (Correoso to king, 10 January 1699); AGI-SD 76, R. 2, s.no. (treasury officials to king, 9 September 1677); *Recopilación*, L. 2, T. 15, l. 132.

41. AGI-SD 74, R. 4, no. 188, 190, 225 (treasury officials to king, 4 January and 15 June 1635 and 30 November 1638); AGI-SD 75, R. 4, s.no. (treasury officials to king, 24 October 1658); R. 6, s.no. (treasury officials to king, 20 May 1662); AGI-SD 76, R. 1, s.no. (treasury officials to king, 16 September 1669 and 3 November 1670); R. 2, s.no. (treasury officials to king, 15 May 1676 and 4 July 1681); R. 3, s.no. (treasury officials to king, 15 March, 13 September, and 13 September 1685); R. 5, s.no. (treasury officials to king, 2 July 1694 and 9 November and 1 December 1695).

42. AGI-SD 74, R. 4, no. 212, 216, 221 (treasury officials to king, 14 October and 30 November 1638); AGI-SD 75, R. 1, s.no. (treasury officials to king, 30 June 1640); *Recopilación*, L. 5, T. 12, l. 14; Sánchez Bella, *La organización financiera*, 190–91; Eagle, "Chasing the *Avença*," 101, 103, 107.

43. AGI-SD 57, R. 1, no. 18, 18a (Melgarejo to king, 24 May and 28 February 1649); AGI-SD 74, R. 4, no. 191, 197 (treasury officials to king, 11 August 1635 and 30 April 1636); AGI-SD 75, R. 2, s.no. (treasury officials to king, 3 April 1646); R. 3, s.no. (treasury officials to king, 12 May 1652).

44. AGI-SD 53, R. 1, no. 10 (audiencia to king, 8 May 1609). See also Sánchez Bella, *La organización financiera*, 171–82.

45. AGI-SD 55, R. 5, no. 22 (Gentil de Párraga to king, 15 January 1625); no. 23 (audiencia to king, 7 February 1625); AGI-SD 76, R. 1, s.no. (treasury officials to king, 8 May 1671).

46. Andrien, *Crisis and Decline*, 121–28; Sánz Tapia, "Provisión, beneficio y venta de oficios," 167; Bertrand, *Grandeur et misère*, 14; Rosenmüller, *Corruption and Justice*, 9, 75–78; Eagle, "Informal Entrepôts," 14, 16, 19.

47. AGI-SD 1, R. 3, no. 325 (consulta of Cámara, 23 September 1649); AGI-Esc 24B, no. 2, commission of Carvajal y Cobos (1661), fols. 5v–9r; Ponce Vázquez, *Islanders and Empire*, 209–10; Paredes Vera, "'No hay más Ley,'" 384.
48. AGI-SD 52, R. 4, no. 17 (Arévalo Sedeño to king, 20 December 1604); AGI-SD 55, R. 5, no. 29e (decree, 4 July 1626); AGI-Esc 33B, visita of Audiencia of Santo Domingo (1630), pza. 11, fol. 13v (petition of Cereceda, 28 November 1630); AGI-SD 57, R. 5, no. 78 (Montemayor to king, 12 December 1653); AGI-SD 64, R. 5, no. 117 (Segura to king, 25 August 1683); AGI-SD 65, R. 1, no. 20 (Robles to king, 29 April 1685); R. 4, no. 123 (Robles to king, 25 April 1688). See also AGI-Ctdra, 1056–57, 1059–62, 1064, and 1068; Sánchez Bella, *La organización financiera*, 66–68; Bertrand, *Grandeur et misère*, 106–11; Paredes Vera, "'No hay más Ley,'" 394.
49. AGI-Esc 1181 (sentences of Hurtado vs. treasury officials, 9 January 1635); AGI-SD 75, R. 4, s.no. (Izquierdo to king, 23 April 1656); R. 5, s.no. (treasury officials to king, 3 August 1660); AGI-Esc 1182 (sentences of Navarro vs. treasury officials, 3 February 1672); AGI-SD 874, L. 20, fols. 531v–534r (king to treasury officials, 13 May 1678); AGI-SD 76, R. 2, s.no. (treasury officials to king, 28 April 1679); R. 3, s.no. (treasury officials to king, 28 November 1684); AGI-SD 66, R. 1, no. 14 (Ladrón de Guevara to king, 12 September 1692).
50. AGI-SD 53, R. 1, no. 9 (Gómez de Sandoval, 8 May 1609); AGI-SD 54, R. 1, no. 7 (Gómez de Sandoval to king, 20 February 1610).
51. Ponce Vázquez, *Islanders and Empire*, 144–45.
52. *Recopilación*, L. 4, T. 11, ll. 3–5; AGI-SD 1, R. 2, no. 213 (consulta, 30 April 1631); AGI-SD 2, R. 1, no. 84 (consulta of Cámara); R. 2, no. 175, 176 (consultas, 7 April and 1 August 1672); AGI-SD 3, R. 5, no. 173 (consulta of Cámara, 26 May 1698); Eagle, "Restoring Spanish Hispaniola," 396. See also Rodríguez Morel, *Cartas del cabildo*.
53. AGI-SD 868, L. 4, fol. 71 (king to Osorio, 24 July 1602); AGI-SD 52, R. 8, no. 103 (Osorio to king, 5 January 1608); Ponce Vázquez, *Islanders and Empire*, 146–47, 150–51. See also AGI-SD 1, R. 2, no. 195 (consulta, 28 August 1627); Paredes Vera, "El cabildo de Santo Domingo," 234.
54. AGI-SD 54, R. 1, no. 12 (Gómez de Sandoval, 2 May 1610).
55. AGI-SD 56, R. 1, no. 3 (Bitrián to king, 10 February 1641); AGI-SD 870, L. 11, fols. 80v–81r (king to audiencia and cabildo, 30 December 1641); AGI-SD 65, R. 4, no. 102d (cabildo proceedings, 31 October 1687); Gil-Bermejo García, *La Española*, 246–47; Ponce Vázquez, *Islanders and Empire*, 150–54.
56. AGI-SD 868, L. 4, fol. 68 (king to Osorio, 30 May 1602); Rodríguez Morel, *Cartas del cabildo*, 224.
57. AGI-SD 52, R. 7, no. 95 (audiencia to king, 1 July 1607); R. 8, no. 101 (audiencia to king, 4 January 1608); see also *Recopilación*, L. 3, T. 15, l. 37; Valenzuela Márquez,

Liturgias del poder, 25; Curcio-Nagy, *Great Festivals*, 28–32; Cañeque, *King's Living Image*, 129–31.

58. Herzog, *Upholding Justice*, 124; cf. Valenzuela Márquez, *Liturgias del poder*, 85–86.
59. AGI-SD 57, R. 5, no. 72 (Montemayor to king, 26 April 1653); AGI-SD 58, R. 1, no. 5 (audiencia to king, 16 April 1654); AGI-Patr 273, R. 7, no. 5 (Montemayor to king, 3 April 1654).
60. AGI-SD 65, R. 1, no. 19 (Robles to king, 29 April 1685).
61. AGI-SD 52, R. 5, no. 54 (Manso to king, 3 December 1605); AGI-SD 57, R. 3, no. 44ñ, 44p, 44aa (cabildo to king, 19 March 1650, 15 January and 30 March 1651); AGI-Esc 12A, leg. 2, no. 5, pza. 2, fols. 193r–194r (cabildo to king, 18 May 1662); Rodríguez Morel, *Cartas del cabildo*, 218–19, 305–8, 355, 361, 400.
62. AGI-SD 55, R. 19, no. 105 (Álvarez de Mendoza to king, 24 March 1639); AGI-SD 73, no. 225 (cabildo to king, 1 October 1637).
63. AGI-SD 67, R. 1, no. 39, 39j, 39m, 39n (Manzaneda, audiencia, cabildo, and Carvajal Campofrío to king, 4 June, 15 June, 15 May, and 12 May 1699); AGI-SD 68, R. 1, no. 2 (testimony, 5 June 1700).
64. AGI-SD 52, R. 1, no. 2 (Sanz Morquecho to king, 20 February 1601); R. 6, no. 82a (testimony, 1603); AGI-SD 53, R. 1, no. 16 (audiencia to king, 8 May 1609); AGI-SD 56, R. 7, no. 57 (audiencia to king, 24 January 1647); AGI-SD 58, R. 1, no. 7 (Montemayor to king, 22 April 1654); AGI-SD 62, R. 7, no. 59, 59a, 59c (Zayas Bazán, audiencia, and Chacón Abarca to king, 16 and 24 May 1674); AGI-SD 64, R. 2, no. 37 (Segura to king, 8 October 1680); Peña Pérez, *Cien años de miseria*, 169–70; Rodríguez Morel, *Cartas del cabildo*, 227–28, 263–64; Eagle, "Restoring Spanish Hispaniola," 389, 393–94.
65. AGI-SD 57, R. 5, no. 75a (testimony, 20 August 1653); Ponce Vázquez, *Islanders and Empire*, 205–6.
66. Solórzano Pereira, *Política Indiana*, L. 5, cap. 3, no. 27; *Recopilación*, L. 1, T. 6, l. 39; T. 10, ll. 9, 11, 12; L. 2, T. 15, ll. 134–36, 142–43; Bruno, *El derecho público*, 81–82; Pietschmann, *El estado*, 54–55; Hera, *Iglesia y corona*, 389–90; Arregui Zamorano, *La Audiencia de México*, 33–34; Herzog, *Upholding Justice*, 57–58; Cañeque, *King's Living Image*, 81–94; Moreta Castillo, *La Real Audiencia de Santo Domingo*, 60.
67. *Recopilación*, L. 3, T. 15, ll. 5–9, 13–18, 22, 25–32; Herzog, *Upholding Justice*, 44.
68. AGI-SD 1, R. 1, no. 106 (consulta, 29 August 1611); R. 2, no. 201, 215 (consultas, 22 May 1629 and 13 June 1631); AGI-SD 7, R. 2, no. 92b (consulta of Cámara, 31 May 1649); AGI-SD 3, R. 1, no. 10 (consulta of Cámara, 29 March 1677); Rodríguez Souquet, *El Concilio Provincial Dominicano*, 7.
69. AGI-SD 1, R. 1, 108a (memorial of Rodríguez, n.d.); see also Rodríguez Souquet, *El Concilio Provincial Dominicano*, 34–37.

70. AGI-SD 869, L 6, fol. 78v (king to Rodríguez, 20 March 1610); AGI-SD 54, R. 2, no. 80, 80b (audiencia to king, 28 November 1611); *Recopilación*, L 1, T. 8, l. 6.

71. AGI-Esc 4, no. 9, Archbishop vs. Chaves Osorio (1629); Hernández González, "La organización de la colonia," 382.

72. AGI-SD 1, R. 3, no. 318d (note of Consejo, n.d.); AGI-SD 57, R. 5, no. 74 (report of fiscal of Consejo, 18 May 1653); AGI-SD 2, R. 1, no. 36b (consulta, 22 October 1653).

73. AGI-SD 58, R. 3, no. 56 (Montemayor to king, 24 September 1656).

74. AGI-SD 63, R. 1, no. 3 (audiencia to king, 4 February 1675); AGI-SD 874, L. 20, fols. 219, 261v–264r (king to audiencia, 10 December 1675 and 8 March 1676).

75. AGI-SD 63, R. 2, no. 23 (audiencia to king, 12 August 1676); R. 3, no. 24, 42 (Garcés de los Fayos and audiencia to king, 15 January and 6 September 1677).

76. AGI-SD 63, R. 2, no. 23 (audiencia to king, 12 August 1676); no. 23i (Maldonado and Padilla to count of Medellín, 14 August 1676); R. 3, no. 42 (audiencia to king, 6 September 1677).

77. AGI-SD 61, R. 1, no. 1, 1c, 1f (audiencia, De la Cueva, and Pizarro Cajal to king, 25 September, 24 September, and 30 September 1665). See also Cañeque, *King's Living Image*, 79–80, 102.

78. AGI-SD 55, R. 2, no. 7 (audiencia to king, 18 September 1622); no. 11 (Gómez de Sandoval to king, 29 September 1622); R. 3, no. 12 (audiencia to king, 26 January 1623); Rodríguez Souquet, *El Concilio Provincial Dominicano*, 113–16; cf. Hernández González, "La organización de la colonia," 382.

79. AGI-SD 55, R. 13, no. 75 (audiencia to king, 6 September 1633); AGI-SD 64, R. 1, no. 28 (Segura to king, 26 April 1679); R. 3, no. 94 (audiencia to king, 27 December 1681).

80. AGI-SD 54, R. 2, no. 43 (audiencia to king, 2 February 1611); AGI-SD 57, R. 3, no. 43 (Fernández de Córdoba to king, 17 February 1651); AGI-SD 58, R. 7, no. 86, 86a (audiencia and Balboa to king, 6 and 8 August 1660).

81. AGI-SD 54, R. 8, no. 117 (Gómez de Sandoval to king, 22 April 1617); AGI-SD 55, R. 12, no. 71 (Martínez de Huarte to king, 28 January 1632); AGI-SD 58, R. 7, no. 82 (audiencia to king, 8 April 1660).

82. AGI-Esc 33A, visita of Audiencia of Santo Domingo (1630), pza. 1, cuad. 1, fol. 21v; Rodríguez Souquet, *El Concilio Provincial Dominicano*, 48–50.

83. AGI-SD 870, L. 11, fols. 61r–62r (king to audiencia and Melgarejo, 8 March 1641); AGI-SD 56, R. 2, no. 8 (Melgarejo to king, 5 April 1642); AGI-SD 57, R. 1, no. 10 (audiencia to king, 3 March 1649); AGI-SD 62, R. 1, no. 10 (audiencia to queen regent, 4 August 1667); AGI-SD 873, L. 18, fols. 433r–435r (queen regent to Audiencia of Santo Domingo, 26 September 1668); Rodríguez Souquet, *El Concilio Provincial Dominicano*, 153–54; Luque Talaván, "La inmunidad del sagrado," 259–62. See also chapter 7.

84. Deive, *Heterodoxia e inquisición*, 253–54; Aranda Mendíaz, *Visiones*, 58–59.

85. AGI-SD 1, R. 3, no. 323 (consulta, 24 April 1649).

86. AGI-SD, R. 1, no. 29 (Gómez de Sandoval to king, 20 September 1610).

87. AGI-SD 52, R. 7, no. 88 (Osorio to king, 23 March 1607).

88. AGI-SD 62, R. 1, no. 7 (Pizarro Cajal to king, 31 July 1667); AGI-SD 66, R. 3, no. 51 (Pérez Caro to king, 23 June 1694); AGI-SD 877, L. 28, fol. 366 (king to audiencia, 3 June 1697).

89. AGI-SD 55, R. 14, no. 77 (Chaves Osorio to king, 31 July 1634); AGI-SD 870, L. 9, fols. 153r–154r (king to Cereceda, 10 August 1635); AGI-SD 2, R. 2, no. 117 (consulta of Cámara, 17 February 1663); AGI-SD 64, R. 5, no. 128 (audiencia to king, 1 September 1683).

90. AGI-SD 66, R. 3, no. 53 (Pérez Caro to king, 25 June 1694).

91. AGI-SD 57, R. 5, no. 75d (testimony, 26 August 1653); AGI-SD 66, R. 3, no. 53 (Pérez Caro to king, 25 June 1694); AGI-Esc 33A, visita of Audiencia of Santo Domingo (1630), pza. 1, cuad. 1, fol. 21v.

92. AGI-SD 868, L. 4, fols. 69v–71r (king to audiencia, archbishop, and treasury officials, 7 June 1602).

5. District Supervision

1. AGI-SD 63, R. 1, no. 10 (Padilla to king, n.d.); AGI-SD 874, L. 20, fols. 293v–295r (decree, 2 April 1676); fols. 387r–390r, 391v–394v (king to Padilla, Zayas Bazán, Chacón Abarca, and audiencia, 18 September 1676); Llavador Mira, *La gobernación de Venezuela*, 36; Vaccari, *Sobre gobernadores y residencias*, 30.

2. AGI-SD 63, R. 3, no. 36 (Garcés to king, 24 August 1677); Vaccari, *Juicios de residencia*, 32–34.

3. *Recopilación*, L. 2, T. 15, l. 2; L. 5, T. 2, l. 1; Malagón Barceló, *El distrito*, 50–53; Mayorga García, *La Audiencia de Santafé*, 149, 153; Montoya Salas, *Evolución político-territorial*, 69–75.

4. AGI-SD 62, R. 1, no. 9 (Carvajal to king, 5 August 1667); no. 9a (testimony, 10 September 1666).

5. AGI-SD 62, R. 5, no. 38 (audiencia to king, 13 August 1672); AGI-SD 63, R. 3, no. 49 (audiencia to king, 8 October 1677); see also AGI-SD 874, L. 20, fols. 242v–243r (king to Acosta, 29 January 1676); Gil-Bermejo García, *La Española*, 201–2; Rodríguez Morel, *Cartas del cabildo*, 263–64; Hernández González, "La organización de la colonia," 382.

6. AGI-Patr 273, R. 7, no. 8a (Montemayor to Albuquerque, 25 March 1654); AGI-SD 58, R. 3, no. 14 (Meneses to king, 20 January 1656); AGI-SD 63, R. 3, no. 32g (Padilla to king, 1 February 1678); AGI-SD 64, R. 3, no. 62 (Segura to king, 8 June 1681); AGI-SD 65, R. 1, no. 24a (Robles to La Laguna, 18 August 1685);

R. 3, no. 66 (Robles to king, 20 July 1687); Cañeque, *King's Living Image*, 157–58; Paredes Vera, "Ejército, milicias y sociedad," 399; Rosenmüller, *Corruption and Justice*, 134–36.

7. See *Recopilación*, L. 5, T. 12, ll. 7, 8, 9, 13, 14, 19, 20, 23; T. 13, l. 8.
8. AGI-SD 869, L. 7, fols. 227r–228r (king to audiencia and decree, 12 August 1623); Herzog, *Upholding Justice*, 40.
9. AGI-SD 65, R. 6, no. 217 (Robles to king, 24 August 1690); Hera, *Iglesia y corona*, 200; MacLachlan, *Spain's Empire*, 32.
10. AGI-SD 869, L. 5, fols. 101v–102v (king to Ochoa de Castro and audiencia, 8 June 1607); fols. 204r–205r (decree, 2 December 1608); Vila Vilar, *Historia de Puerto Rico*, 57–59; Pietschmann, *El estado*, 138–40; Cazull, "Conflicto, alianza y disociación," 58.
11. Araujo, "Descripción," 233–34; Vila Vilar, *Historia de Puerto Rico*, 62–64.
12. AGI-Esc 1181 (visita sentence vs. Mejía de Villalobos, 16 May 1608); AGI-SD 877, L. 29, fol. 35v (king to audiencia, 12 November 1697); AGI-SD 67, R. 1, no. 4 (audiencia to king, 12 March 1699), 4a (testimony, 16 December 1693); Eagle, "Portraits of Bad Officials," 91.
13. AGI-SD 18, no. 11 (report on Cumanagotos, 1608); AGI-SD 869, L. 5, fol. 180v (king to audiencia, 12 October 1608); AGI-SD 55, R. 20, no. 118c (king to audiencia, 8 November 1638); AGI-SD 873, L. 18, fols, 211r–212r (king to audiencia, 17 June 1665); AGI-SD 61, R. 2, no. 12 (audiencia to king, 15 March 1666); Andrews, *Trade, Plunder and Settlement*, 285–86.
14. AGI-SD 66, R. 5, no. 100 (audiencia to king, 8 March 1696); AGI-SD 67, R. 1, no. 2, 5–13 (audiencia to king, 4 March and 15–24 March 1699).
15. AGI-SD 55, R. 20, no. 116 (audiencia to king, 24 June 1640).
16. AGI-SD 873, L. 19, fols. 109r–110r (queen to audiencia, 3 October 1671); AGI-SD 62, R. 5, no. 36 (Zayas Bazán to king, 10 August 1672); cf. Mayorga García, *La Audiencia de Santafé*, 150.
17. AGI-SD 56, R. 3, no. 25 (Melgarejo to king, 6 November 1643); AGI-SD 57, R. 1, no. 5 (Melgarejo to king, 28 February 1649).
18. AGI-SD 877, L. 29, fols. 121r–121v (king to "oidor decano," 30 December 1697).
19. See Elliott, *Count-Duke of Olivares*, 513; Pérez Aínsua Méndez, *De sellos, heráldica y alegorías*, 47–50.
20. AGI-Indif 118, no. 54, fols. 1r, 15r (merits of Heredia, 30 December 1659); AGI-SD 66, R. 2, no. 41 (Pérez Caro to king, 28 November 1693); see also AGI-SD 62, R. 1, no. 9c (audiencia to king, 6 September 1666).
21. AGI-SD 64, R. 5, no. 110 (audiencia to king, 20 August 1683); no. 110a (testimony, 17 August 1683).
22. Phelan, "Authority and Flexibility," 53–56.

23. AGI-SD 52, R. 1, no. 2 (Sanz Morquecho to king, 20 February 1601); R. 4, no. 11 (Osorio to king, 15 December 1604); R. 6, no. 66, 68 (Arévalo Sedeño and Manso to king, 2 March and 15 June 1606); AGI-SD 2, R. 1, no. 86 (consulta, 22 November 1660); AGI-SD 64, R. 3, no. 85c (Diego de Medrano to king, 30 June 1681); AGI-SD 65, R. 1, no. 26 (audiencia to king, 30 October 1685); R. 2, no. 43 (audiencia to king, 13 December 1686); Macías Domínguez, *Cuba en la primera mitad del siglo XVII*, 192–94.
24. AGI-SD 1, R. 1, no. 109 (consulta, 13 May 1612); R. 2, no. 141b (consulta, 20 February 1618); AGI-SD 874, L. 20, fols. 98r–106v (instructions to Mata, 19 January 1675); fols. 106v–109r (queen regent to Mata, 21 January 1675); AGI-SF 30, R. 6, no. 18 (Mata to Fernández de Madrigal, 12 July 1675); Vaccari, *Juicios de residencia*, 65–73.
25. AGI-SD 57, R. 5, no. 72 (Montemayor to king, 26 April 1653).
26. AGI-SD 2, R. 2, no. 132 (consulta, 10 May 1666); AGI-SD 873, L. 18, ff. 406v–407v (king to Navarro, 13 April 1668).
27. AGI-SD 874, L. 20, fols. 4r–8r (queen regent to Acosta, 30 January 1674); *Recopilación*, L. 5, T. 15, ll. 20–22; Llavador Mira, *La gobernación de Venezuela*, 88.
28. AGI-SD 64, R. 2, no. 41 (Padilla to king, 31 October 1680); R. 5, no. 130b (autos, 23 August 1683); AGI-SD 187, R. 15, no. 79 (Padilla to king, 20 March 1681); AGI-Indif 130, no. 52 (merits of Padilla, 13 June 1682).
29. AGI-SD 58, R. 3, no. 55g (notes of Consejo, n.d.); see also Malcolm, *Royal Favouritism*, 125–26, 151.
30. AGI-SD 55, R. 11, no. 64 (Prada to king, 23 January 1631); AGI-Esc 34A, visita of Audiencia of Santo Domingo (1630), pza. 9, fol. 225; López Cantos, *Historia de Puerto Rico*, 172; Macías Domínguez, *Cuba en la primera mitad del siglo XVII*, 222–23; Eagle, "Portraits of Bad Officials," 94.
31. AGI-SD 3, R. 1, no. 1 (consulta of Cámara, 10 January 1673); AGI-SD 873, L. 19, fols. 245v–246r (queen regent to Oña, 4 March 1673); AGI-Panama 3, no. 109 (consulta of Cámara, 12 June 1673); no. 132 (consulta of Cámara, 9 October 1674); López Cantos, *Historia de Puerto Rico*, 198–99.
32. AGI-SD 875, L. 22, fols. 280r–282r, 293v–294v (king to Pizarro Cortés, 14 June 1686); AGI-SD 876, L. 25 (king to Oviedo, 23 February 1690); AGI-SD 112, R. 2, no. 30 (Oviedo to king, 2 June 1693).
33. *Recopilación*, L. 2, T. 15, l. 16; L. 7, T. 1, ll. 1–6, 8, 10–17, 19–25; Bravo Lira, "Símbolos de la función judicial," 247; Hernández García, "Clasificación diplomática," 170–71; Gómez Gómez, *El sello y registro*, 242, 248–49.
34. *Recopilación*, L. 7, T. 1, l. 1.
35. Phelan, "Authority and Flexibility," 63–64; Herzog, *Ritos de control*, 175–76.
36. AGI-SD 52, R. 5, no. 40, 50 (Manso and Osorio to king, 16 and 20 October 1605); R. 6, no. 68, 81 (Manso and Osorio to king, 15 June and 5 November 1606);

no. 81a (Manso to Álvarez and acuerdo, 17 December 1604 and 30 August 1606); R. 8, no. 109 (Osorio to king, 11 January 1608); Wright, "Rescates," 353–56; Gil-Bermejo García, *La Española*, 231; Macías Domínguez, *Cuba en la primera mitad del siglo XVII*, 337–43; Burset Flores, "'Cosas indebidas,'" 125, 138–39; Ponce Vázquez, *Islanders and Empire*, 127–28.

37. Deive, *Tangomangos*, 250–53; Burset Flores, "'Cosas indebidas,'" 118–25.
38. Ureta is also spelled Ozeta, Urreta, or Uzeta. AGI-SD 53, R. 1, no. 26 (audiencia to king, 6 June 1609); no. 26a (Arceo to Ruy Gómez, 22 March 1609). See also Macías Domínguez, *Cuba en la primera mitad del siglo XVII*, 181–85.
39. AGI-SD 53, R. 1, no. 26o (testimony, 5 June 1609); no. 26q (Villaverde to king, 22 April 1609); AGI-SD 100, R. 4, no. 166 (Villaverde to king, 15 June 1610).
40. AGI-SD 53, R. 1, no. 26 (audiencia to king, 6 June 1609); AGI-SD 869, L. 6, fol. 53r (king to Villaverde and audiencia, 22 October 1609).
41. Macías Domínguez, *Cuba en la primera mitad del siglo XVII*, 206.
42. AGI-Indif 118, no. 54, fols. 2v–6v (commissions of Heredia, 31 January and 1 February 1633); fols. 6r–7v (testimony); see also Estevan de Prado, *Por Francisco Nuñez Melian*, fol. 18r.
43. AGI-SD 52, R. 1, no. 2 (Sanz Morquecho to king, 20 February 1601); R. 2, no. 4 (audiencia to king, 8 July 1602); no. 4a (Alcázar to acuerdo, 5 December 1601); see also Astley, *New General Collection*, 1:252–54; Vila Vilar, *Historia de Puerto Rico*, 231–32; Cardona Bonet, *Shipwrecks*, 203–12.
44. AGI-SD 55, R. 1, no. 1 (Gil de la Sierpe to king, 27 February 1620).
45. AGI-SD 55, R. 11, no. 66 (audiencia to king, 11 February 1631); Phelan, "Authority and Flexibility," 56–57.
46. Castillo Lara, *Las acciones militares*, 154–55. See also Eagle, "Chasing the Avença," 109.
47. AGI-SD 52, R. 8, no. 115, 134 (audiencia to king, 2 May and 24 August 1608); no. 135 (testimony, 22 August 1608); AGI-SD 53, R. 1, no. 26 (6 June 1609); AGI-SD 155, R. 15, no. 198 (Ochoa to king, 28 October 1608); R. 16, no. 202 (Rojas to king, 6 January 1609); AGI-SD 869, L. 6, fol. 39 (king to Mejía de Villalobos, 19 February 1606); AGI-Cttn 5303, no. 11 (license for Fernández de Salazar, 28 May 1608); Vila Vilar, *Historia de Puerto Rico*, 62–63, 72–73; Cazull, "Conflicto, alianza y disociación," 54–61.
48. AGI-SD 56, R. 2, no. 7, 9 (audiencia to king, 22 January and 30 June 1642); AGI-Esc 1189 (residencia sentences vs. Bolaños, 12 October and 7 November 1645). See also Vila Vilar, *Historia de Puerto Rico*, 50–54.
49. AGI-SD 56, R. 8, no. 64 (audiencia to king, 20 February 1648); no. 64a (Riva Agüero to king, 20 February 1646); AGI-SD 65, R. 7, no. 252, 252a (Pérez Caro to king, 6 June and 28 May 1691); Vila Vilar; *Historia de Puerto Rico*, 34.

50. AGI-SD 57, R. 1, no. 4 (audiencia to king, 26 February 1649); no. 4a (testimony, 24 November 1648).

51. AGI-SD 65, R. 1, no. 2a (Muñoz de Gadea to king, 30 May 1691); no. 25 (audiencia to king, 13 October 1685); Britto García, *Señores del Caribe*, 442.

52. AGI-SD 65, R. 3, no. 76 (Araujo to king, 26 July 1687).

53. AGI-SD 877, L. 29, fol. 49 (king to Córdoba Lasso, 27 November 1697).

54. AGI-SD 876, L. 25, fols. 181v–183v (king to Casal and audiencia, 3 February 1690); AGI-SD 65, R. 7, no. 231 (audiencia to king, 20 May 1691); Vaccari, *Sobre gobernadores y residencias*, 90.

55. AGI-SD 59, R. 1, no. 3 (audiencia to king, 6 February 1661); AGI-SD 872, L. 17, fols. 135v–136r (king to Porres, 6 September 1661); fols. 136v–139r (king to audiencia, 20 September 1661); Llavador Mira, *La gobernación de Venezuela*, 62–63.

56. AGI-SD 877, L. 28, fols. 173v–174r (king to Pérez Caro, 22 June 1696); L. 29, fol. 42 (king to audiencia, 27 November 1697); AGI-SD 67, R. 1, no. 20 (Manzaneda to king, 20 May 1699).

57. AGI-SD 57, R. 4, no. 62 (audiencia to king, 20 September 1652); no. 62a (Aguilera to Pantoja, 20 February 1652); R. 3, no. 44aa (cabildo of Santo Domingo to king, 30 March 1651).

58. AGI-SD 54, R. 1, no. 12, 33 (Gómez de Sandoval to king, 2 May and 30 September 1610); no. 33a (testimony, 26 June 1610).

59. *Recopilación*, L. 2, T. 1, l. 22; MacLachlan, *Spain's Empire*, 22.

60. AGI-SD 53, R. 1, no. 50 (Gómez de Sandoval to king, 20 October 1609); AGI-SD 58, R. 3, no. 42 (Meneses to Leguía, 28 July 1656); AGI-SD 62, R. 7, no. 60 (Zayas Bazán to king, 18 May 1674); AGI-SD 63, R. 3, no. 36 (Garcés to king, 24 August 1677). See also Vaccari, *Sobre gobernadores y residencias*, 30, 81–82.

61. AGI-SD 64, R. 3, no. 47 (Segura Sandoval to king, 2 June 1681); AGI-SD 66, R. 2, no. 21 (Bravo de Añaya to king, 15 February 1693); AGI-SD 877, L. 28, fols. 162v–163v (king to Pérez Caro, 30 December 1695). See also Vaccari, *Sobre gobernadores y residencias*, 90–92.

62. AGI-SD 52, R. 5, no. 46 (Osorio to king, 20 October 1605); R. 6, no. 81 (Osorio to king, 5 November 1606).

63. AGI-SD 53, R. 1, no. 50 (Gómez de Sandoval to king, 20 October 1609); AGI-SD 57, R. 3, no. 44s (Córdoba to king, 2 February 1651).

64. AGI-SD 54, R. 1, no. 4 (audiencia to king, 12 February 1610); AGI-SD 55, R. 2, no. 5 (Parraga to king, 28 January 1622); AGI-SD 55, R. 5, no. 33, 37 (Acuña and audiencia to king, 18 November and 23 December 1625); AGI-SD 59, R. 1, no. 3a, 3d (audiencia to king, 6 February 1661).

65. AGI-SD 65, R. 7, no. 232 (Oviedo to king, 27 May 1691); AGI-SD 66, R. 2, no. 21b, 21ñ (audiencia to king, 2 September 1692 and 6 September 1698).

66. AGI-Patr 274, R. 4, no. 1a (Bitrián to king, 6 November 1640); no. 1f (testimony, 5 November 1640); AGI-SD 75, R. 1, s.no. (treasury officials and Bitrián to king, 3 and 6 November 1640); AGI-SD 60, R. 1, no. 1d (Carvajal to king, 16 September 1662); AGI-SD 62, R. 2, no. 18 (Carvajal to king, 14 August 1668); AGI-SD 63, R. 3, no. 32s, 32t (memorials, n.d.); Mathews, "Spanish Domination," 12–22; Eagle, "Restoring Spanish Hispaniola," 395–96.

67. AGI-SD 52, R. 8, no. 113 (Osorio to king, 27 March 1608); Deive, *Tangomangos*, 81–84; Rupert, *Creolization and Contraband*, 99; Ponce Vázquez, *Islanders and Empire*, 59–65.

68. Lynch, *Hispanic World in Crisis*, 166, 170, 373, 381.

69. AGI-SD 3, R. 1, no. 18a (Doncker to Zayas Bazán, 2 April 1677); AGI-SD 65, R. 3, no. 56 (Robles to king, 10 July 1687); no. 56a ("Henri Chrinel" to Robles, 29 June 1687). See also AGI-SD 66, R. 7, no. 110b (Bernagie to Robles, 18 March 1699); Goslinga, *Short History*, 53; Rupert, *Creolization and Contraband*, 74, 79–80.

70. AGI-SD 65, R. 7, no. 248 (Pérez Caro to king, 30 May 1691); AGI-SD 67, R. 1, no. 29 (Manzaneda to king, 30 May 1699).

71. Araujo, "Descripción de la Isla Española," 220; AGI-SD 236 (consultas of Junta de Guerra, 26 August 1700 and 31 May 1702). See also Gutiérrez Escudero, "Cuestión de límites," 65–69; and Eagle, "Restoring Spanish Hispaniola," 399–400.

72. AGI-SD 66, R. 7, n 107 (Manzaneda to king, 26 September 1698).

73. AGI-SD 55, R. 5, no. 28, 37 (Acuña and audiencia to king, 12 March and 23 December 1625); R. 6, no. 43 (audiencia to king, 14 May 1626); AGI-SD 56, R. 3, no. 29 (Bitrián to king, 4 December 1643); AGI-SD 64, R. 3, no. 88 (Segura to king, 3 July 1681); López Cantos, *Historia de Puerto Rico*, 116–17; Torres Ramírez, *La Armada de Barlovento*, 59–62, 90–94, 117; Peña Pérez, *Cien años de miseria*, 188, 280–84; Cartay A., *Ideología, desarrollo e interferencias*, 165–74; De la Fuente, *Havana and the Atlantic*, 12–13; Reichert, *Sobre las olas*, 145–50; Eagle, "Restoring Spanish Hispaniola," 391; Ponce Vázquez, *Islanders and Empire*, 88–91.

74. AGI-SD 60, R. 1, no. 1 (Carvajal y Cobos, 15 February 1663); AGI-SD 66, R. 1, no. 11 (Pérez Caro to king, 6 September 1692).

75. AGI-SD 64, R. 6, no. 155a (notaries to king, 9 August 1684); AGI-SD 65, R. 7, no. 243 (audiencia to king, 29 May 1691); see also AGI-SD 877, L. 29, fols. 111v–112r (king to Arancibia, 11 December 1697).

76. AGI-SD 61, R. 2, no. 3 (Carvajal y Cobos to king, 6 March 1666); AGI-SD 65, R. 3, no. 84 (Riva Agüero to king, 11 November 1687); no. 84a (certification, 1 November 1687); Eagle, "Restoring Spanish Hispaniola," 393.

77. AGI-SD 52, R. 2, no. 4 (audiencia to king, 8 July 1602); R. 8, no. 129 (audiencia to king, 24 August 1608).

78. AGI-SD 224, R. 2, no. 13(bis) (Menéndez Márquez to acuerdo, 2 April 1579); AGI-SD 58, R. 5, no. 72 (Martínez de Amileta to king, 4 November 1658); AGI-SD 873, L. 18, fols. 408v–409v (queen regent to audiencia, 6 May 1668); Kapitzke, *Religion, Power, and Politics*, 56–63; De la Fuente, *Havana and the Atlantic*, 45; Grady, *Anglo-Spanish Rivalry*, 50, 57, 65–66, 79–80, 82.
79. AGI-SD 877, L. 29, fol. 70 (king to audiencia, 27 November 1697).
80. AGI-SD 66, R. 1, no. 2, 2c (Pérez Caro and audiencia to king, 6 August and 30 July 1692), no. 2a (notes of 23 January 1697).
81. AGI-SD 59, R. 1, no. 3d (audiencia to king, 6 February 1661).
82. AGI-SD 62, R. 1, no. 6 (Pizarro Cajal to king, 30 July 1667); AGI-SD 63, R. 3, no. 41, 49 (Garcés de los Fayos and audiencia to king, 2 September and 8 October 1677).
83. *Recopilación*, L. 7, T. 1, l. 25; Vila Vilar, *Historia de Puerto Rico*, 64.
84. AGI-SD 52, R. 6, no. 76 (Mejía de Villalobos to king, 14 October 1606); Vila Vilar, *Historia de Puerto Rico*, 202.
85. AGI-SD 59, R. 2, no. 9 (audiencia to king, 25 May 1662); AGI-SD 872, L. 17, fols. 166r–168r (king to Biedma y Carvajal, 6 April 1662); López Cantos, *Historia de Puerto Rico*, 173–74; Vaccari, *Sobre gobernadores y residencias*, 84–85.
86. AGI-SD 874, L. 21, fols. 85v–86r, 313r–315r (king to audiencia, 22 February 1680 and 17 October 1681); AGI-SD 64, R. 6, no. 131 (Pizarro Cortés to king, 4 May 1684); López Cantos, *Historia de Puerto Rico*, 163, 191–93.
87. AGI-SD 65, R. 6, no. 213 (audiencia to king, 18 July 1690).

6. Audiencia Ministers

1. See Appendix.
2. AGI-Indif 124, no. 73 (merits of Cárdenas, 11 November 1673); Kagan, *Students and Society*, 95–96; Burkholder and Chandler, *From Impotence to Authority*, 19, 21; Pelorson, *Les "Letrados,"* 195–98, 203–4, 236; Jiménez Núñez, "Sistema político," 308–9.
3. AGI-SD 3, R. 4, no. 132f (sentence vs. Bravo de Añaya, 1 February 1690); AGI-SD 8, R. 2, no. 93b (merits of Bravo de Añaya, 28 March 1688). Tamar Herzog lists twelve definite and twenty-one possible American-born appointees to Quito for 1650–1700 in *Los ministros de la Audiencia de Quito*; see also Burkholder and Chandler, *From Impotence to Authority*, 4–5.
4. AGI-SD 1, R. 1, no. 48 (consulta of Cámara, 17 April 1603); AGI-SD 52, R. 4, no. 18 (Arévalo to king, 20 December 1604); R. 5, no. 27 (Manso to king, 2 July 1605); Schäfer, *El Consejo Real*, 2:460; Burkholder and Chandler; *From Impotence to Authority*, 5–9; Burset Flores, "'Cosas indebidas,'" 99–110.
5. ACA-CA, leg. 43, no. 6 (petition of Bitrián, 1647); AGI-SD 57, R. 3, no. 49 (Montemayor to king, 20 July 1651); AGI-SD 58, R. 8, no. 92 (Balboa to king,

8 February 1661); Macias Domínguez, *Cuba en la primera mitad del siglo XVII*, 224; Pelorson, *Les "Letrados,"* 289–91; Pérez Collados, *Una aproximación histórica*, 309, 319; Barrientos Grandon, "Juan Francisco Montemayor," 133–34; Quiles García, "Casos y cosas," 145–46.

6. AGI-SD 52, R. 8, no. 120 (audiencia to king, 20 August 1608); AGI-SD 55, R. 11, no. 65 (audiencia to king, 26 January 1631); Pelorson, *Les "Letrados,"* 217–19, 314–16.
7. AGI-SD 8, R. 2, no. 86a, 93a, 95a (petitions of Cruz Ahedo, Bravo de Añaya, and Oviedo, 1692 and 1695); AGI-Esc 1181 (visita sentence vs. Otalora, 9 January 1635); AHN-OM-CS, exp. 8808Bis (genealogy of Otalora, 1630); Wright, "Military Orders," 51–55; Domínguez Ortiz, *Las clases privilegiadas*, 143–45; Burkholder, "Honor and Honors," 27; Barrientos Grandon, "Juan Francisco Montemayor," 153; Herzog, *Upholding Justice*, 122–24; Polo y La Borda, "Representando la experiencia," 75–83.
8. "Conde del Sacro Imperio" was a military honor, so Zúñiga was "conde don Félix de Zúñiga," while Meneses was "conde de Peñalba." AGI-Esc 12C, residencia of Pérez Franco, no. 2 (1661), pza. 2, fols. 1r–4v (merits of Pérez Franco, n.d.); AGI-SD 2, R. 1, no. 36a (consulta, 27 August 1653); AGI-SD 3, R. 1, no. 2 (consulta, 3 March 1673); R. 3, no. 118 (consulta 3 October 1689).
9. AGI-Esc 33B, visita of Audiencia of Santo Domingo (1630), pza. 11, fols. 35r–36r; AHN-Cod, L. 892, fols. 4r–6v (testimony, 30 November 1624); AGI-SD 65, R. 2, no. 41, 42 (Robles to king, 6 September and 12 December 1686).
10. AGI-Indif 131, no. 128 (merits of Ladrón de Guevara, 2 July 1688); AGI-Indif 132, no. 102 (merits of Martínez Hidalgo, 8 October 1690); AGI-Indif 161, no. 425 (merits of Chacón Abarca, 14 December 1690); Pelorson, *Les "Letrados,"* 38–39.
11. AGI-SD 1, R. 2, no. 192 (consulta, 2 December 1626); AGI-Indif 129, no. 134 (merits of Bilbao, 3 October 1682); AGI-Indif 130, no. 78 (merits of Maldonado, 21 January 1698); AGI-Indif 132, no. 41 (merits of López de Dicastillo, 16 May 1689); AGI-Indif 161, no. 425 (merits of Chacón Abarca, 14 December 1690); AGI-SD 3, R. 3, no. 102 (consulta of Cámara, 8 February 1687); MacLeod, "Self-Promotion," 26–28; Aranda Mendíaz, *Visiones*, 174–215; Folger, *Writing as Poaching*, 20–25.
12. AGI-Indif 130, no. 12 (merits of Martínez de Amileta, 9 February 1652); AGI-Indif 161, no. 317 (merits of Venegas, 19 May 1654); Burkholder and Chandler, *From Impotence to Authority*, 9–10; Richard Kagan, *Students and Society*, 112, 193–95; Castejón, "Un *cursus honorum*," 449.
13. AGI-SD 1, R. 1, no. 48 (consulta of Cámara, 17 April 1603); AGI-SD 2, R. 1, no. 75 (consulta of Cámara, 20 December 1658); AGI-Indif 122, no. 132 (merits of Caballero, 27 April 1670); AGI-Indif 129, no. 134 (merits of Bilbao, 3 October 1682); AGI-Indif 131, no. 38 (merits of Riva Agüero, 11 September 1686); AGI-Indif 161,

no. 69 (merits of Luis de Narváez, 20 April 1622); no. 317 (merits of Venegas, 19 May 1654).

14. Sanz Morquecho, *Practica quotidiana*; Montemayor de Cuenca, *Discurso político-histórico-jurídico*; Chacón Abarca y Tiedra, *Decissiones*, BNE-VE 1346/2; Barrientos Grandon, "Juan Francisco Montemayor," 134–57.

15. AGI-SD 63, R. 3, no. 47 (Padilla to king, 13 September 1677); AGI-Indif 130, no. 19 (merits of Merlo de la Fuente, 26 April 1683); AGI-Indif 132, no. 66 (merits of Padilla, 3 September 1689); Ortega y Pérez Gallardo, *Historia genealógica*, VI: "Marqueses de Santa Fe de Guardiola," 1–10; Pelorson, *Les "Letrados,"* 192–93.

16. AGI-SD 3, R. 2, no. 71, 76 (consultas of Cámara, 16 February 1684 and 30 April 1685); AGI-Indif 161, no. 433 (merits of González, 15 December 1693). See also Pérez Collados, *Una aproximación histórica*, 310–15.

17. AGI-Indif 111, no. 22 (merits of Fernández de Córdoba, 19 February 1619); AGI-Indif 118, no. 125 (merits of Zayas Bazán, 17 December 1679); AGI-Indif 122, no. 63 (merits of Robles, 10 January 1669); AGI-SD 1, R. 2, no. 135 (consulta, 5 December 1626); AGI-SD 57, R. 3, no. 42 (Fernández de Córdoba to king, 15 February 1651); Rilova Pérez, "De Sasamón a América," 79–81, 84–88; Harden, *Arms and Letters*, 13–14.

18. AGI-SD 2, R. 1, no. 54 (consulta of Cámara, 4 February 1656); no. 70, 71 (consultas, 28 August and 15 October 1658).

19. AGI-SD 1, R. 1, no. 32 (consulta of Cámara, 30 March 1601); AGI-SD 3, R. 2, no. 68 (consulta of Cámara, 27 January 1684); AGI-SD 15, no. 7 (report, Osorio, 28 July 1593); AGI-SD 72, R. 5, no. 14 (petition of Gómez de Sandoval, 31 August 1623); Schäfer, *El Consejo Real*, 2:533; Gil-Bermejo Garcia, *La Española*, 211–12; Aranda Mendíaz, *Visiones*, 134.

20. AGI-SD 1, R. 1, no. 87 (decree, 30 December 1607); R. 2, no. 192 (consulta, 2 December 1626); AGI-SD 2, R. 1, no. 48 (consulta of Cámara, 21 August 1654); AGI-SD 53, R. 1, no. 20 (Gómez de Sandoval to king, 12 May 1609); AGI-SD 57, R. 3, no. 49 (Montemayor to king, 20 July 1651); R. 4, no. 60 (Montemayor to Leguia, 28 April 1652); Panamá 2, no. 39, 47 (Ruiz de Contreras to king, 29 March and 10 December 1635); Schäfer, *El Consejo Real*, 1:186–87; Herzog, *Upholding Justice*, 126–27; Eagle, "Portraits of Bad Officials," 90; Castejón, "Un *cursus honorum*," 446–47.

21. AGI-Indif 130, no. 12 (merits of Martínez de Amileta, 9 February 1652); AGI-SD 3, R. 3, no. 92, 118 (consultas, 5 July 1686 and 3 October 1689); no. 119 (memorial of Pérez Caro, 16 September 1689); no. 125 (Calzada to Ortiz, 10 September 1689); no. 126 (Ortiz to Fuentehermosa, 11 October 1689); R. 5, no. 171 (consulta of Cámara, 23 September 1697); Ponce Vázquez, "Atlantic Peripheries," 312.

22. AGI-SD 2, R. 1, no. 86 (consulta, 22 November 1649); R. 2, no. 101 (consulta of Cámara, 22 February 1661). See also Burkholder and Chandler, *From Impotence to Authority*, 33–36.
23. AGI-SD 3, R. 5, no. 161 (consulta, 19 January 1696); AGI-Esc 964 (sentences of vista and revista vs. Pérez Caro, 21 July 1704 and 15 September 1704); Burkholder and Chandler, *From Impotence to Authority*, 20–22; Torres Agudo, "Élites y grupos de poder," 100–103, 168–75.
24. AGI-SD 1, R. 2, no. 172 (consulta, 18 May 1624); Cuart Moner, "Algunas notas sobre los colegiales de San Clemente," 815.
25. AGI-SD 1, R. 3, no. 318 (consulta of Cámara, 28 March 1648); Schäfer, *El Consejo Real*, 1:227–34.
26. AGI-SD 1, R. 3, no. 290a (memorial of Consejo, 27 July 1643); Schäfer, *El Consejo Real*, 1:224; Rodríguez Vicente, "El derecho de Media Anata," 466–67, 473–74.
27. AGI-SD 2, R. 2, no. 133, 157 (consultas, 3 July 1666 and 28 May 1670); AGI-SD 60, R. 3, no. 35 (notes of Consejo, 17 March 1665); AGI-SD 65, R. 4, no. 127 (Córdoba to king, 28 April 1688).
28. AGI-Indif 130, no. 80 (merits of Vargas Campuzano, 4 April 1685); Schäfer, *El Consejo Real*, 2:447, 450, 458, 462, 470, 502.
29. AGI-Cttn 5789, L. 1, fols. 223v–225r (title for Retuerta, 4 May 1635); AGI-SD 1, R. 3, no. 315 (consulta, 5 July 1647); AGI-Panama 21, R. 5, no. 36 (file on Orozco, 1651); AGI-SD 3, R. 2, no. 71b (notes of Cámara, n.d.); AGI-Indif 132, no. 102 (merits of Martínez Hidalgo, 8 October 1690); Schäfer, *El Consejo Real*, 2:469, 482; Castejón, "Un *cursus honorum*," 438–42.
30. AGI-SD 2, R. 1, no. 75 (consulta of Cámara, 20 December 1658); R. 2, no. 92 (decree, 21 April 1664); no. 129 (consulta, 19 September 1664); AGI-SD 3, R. 2, no. 71 (consulta of Cámara, 16 February 1684); no. 71a (Baraiz to Gonzaga, 19 March 1684); Pincus, *Protestantism and Patriotism*, 241; Martínez Torres, *Prisioneros de los infieles*, 49, 144.
31. AGI-SD 2, R. 2, no. 128, 152, 192 (consultas of Cámara, 28 July 1664, 8 July 1669, and 7 December 1672); no. 192b (Pérez de Moya to Consejo, 21 December 1672); AGI-SD 3, R. 3, no. 109 (consulta of Cámara, 28 June 1688), no. 116 (consulta, 22 June 1689); R. 5, no. 181 (consulta of Cámara, 5 October 1699); no. 181b (Marañon to Consejo, 29 July 1703).
32. AGI-SD 55, R. 5, no. 31 (Acuña to Ruiz de Contreras, 11 October 1625); AGI-SD 3, R. 5, no. 171 (consulta of Cámara, 23 September 1697).
33. By the seventeenth century, the doorman was effectively named locally; see Utrera, *Noticias históricas de Santo Domingo*, 2:178.
34. AGI-Cttn 5302, no. 83, fol. 21v (passenger list, 27 January 1608); AGI-SD 869, L. 6, fol. 215 (king to audiencia, 13 June 1615); AGI-SD 54, R. 8, no. 119 (audiencia

to king, 20 May 1617); AGI-Cttn 5788, L. 2, fols. 196v–197r (king to Martínez, 3 December 1618); AGI-Cttn 5365, no. 4 (license for Martínez, 18 June 1619); AGI-SD 54, R. 10, no. 128, 129 (audiencia and Martínez to king, 19 and 23 September 1619).

35. AGI-SD 64, R. 1, no. 29 (audiencia to king, 27 April 1679).

36. AGI-SD 65, R. 1, no. 21 (Semillán to king, 2 May 1685); AGI-Cttn 5416, no. 71 (license for Cisneros, 27 April 1635); AGI-Esc 33A, pza. 1, fol. 1 (visita proceedings, 1630); AGI-Esc 1181 (visita sentences vs. Martínez and Cisneros, 9 January and 12 May 1635); AGI-SD 55, R. 11, no. 65 (audiencia to king, 26 January 1631); R. 12, no. 71 (Martínez to king, 28 January 1632); Eagle, "Portraits of Bad Officials," 99. See also Phelan, *Kingdom of Quito*, 141–45.

37. AGI-Esc 21D, commission of Prada (1626), pza. 28, fols. 179r–197v; AGI-Cttn 5427, no. 1, R. 48 (license for Padilla, 4 July 1670); AGI-Indif 130, no. 95 (merits of Semillán, 18 August 1685); AGI-SD 67, R. 1, no. 23 (Manzaneda to king, 20 May 1699); Torres Agudo, "Los Campuzano-Polanco," 38; Hernández González, "Sociedad en la Española," 256–57; Burset Flores, "'Cosas indebidas,'" 98.

38. AGI-SD 2, R. 1, no. 43 (consulta of Cámara, 18 May 1654); no. 43f (notes of Consejo, 19 June 1654); AGI-SD 3, R. 4, no. 132 (consulta of Cámara, 7 February 1690); no. 132f (Camarino to Consejo, 1 February 1690); no. 133a (petition of Vásquez de la Cuadra, n.d.); no. 133h (petition of Bravo de Añaya, 1 February 1690); AGI-Cttn 5454, no. 2, R. 22 (license for Bravo de Añaya, 18 March 1692); Seed, *To Love, Honor, and Obey*, 4–11.

39. Cook, *Forbidden Passages*, 58–63.

40. AGI-Cttn 5343, no. 7 (license for Valcárcel, 13 March 1615); AGI-Cttn 5439, no. 56 (license for Acosta, 4 July 1673); AGI-Cttn 5456, no. 3, R. 10 (license for Marín, 8 July 1695); AGI-Cttn 5417, no. 56 (license for Bitrián, 21 April 1636); AGI-Cttn 5302, no. 83, fol. 25 (passenger list, 27 January 1608); AGI-Indif 2077, no. 279 (license for Bitrián, 1636).

41. AGI-SD 55, R. 2, no. 5 (Gentil de Párraga to king, 28 January 1622); R. 3, no. 16 (notes of Consejo, n.d.); R. 5, no. 22 (Gentil de Párraga to king, 16 January 1625); AGI-SD 3, R. 3, no. 93 (consulta of Cámara, 15 July 1686).

42. AGI-Cttn 5397, no. 59 (license for Otalora, 1627); AGI-Esc 33A, visita of Audiencia of Santo Domingo (1630), pza. 1, cuad. 2, fol. 120r.

43. AGI-SD 1, R. 1, no. 84 (consulta, 5 November 1607); AGI-SD 52, R. 4, no. 17 (Arévalo to king, 20 December 1604); AGI-SD 54, R. 3, no. 88a (Herrera to king, 24 May 1610); Peña Pérez, *Cien años de miseria*, 270–71, 274–76, 282–85; Paredes Vera, "'No hay más Ley,'" 396.

44. AGI-SD 55, R. 8, no. 56 (Chaves Osorio to king, 20 September 1628); AGI-SD 57, R. 2, no. 24 (15 March 1650); *Recopilación*, L. 2, T. 16, l. 78.

45. AGI-SD 52, R. 4, no. 14 (Arévalo to king, 20 December 1604); R. 5, no. 53 (notes of Cámara, 2 December 1605), 53a (certification, n.d.); R. 6, no. 70 (Osorio to king, 12 October 1606); no. 76, 83 (Mejía de Villalobos to king, 14 October and 22 November 1606); R. 8, no. 113, 124 (Osorio and Gómez de Sandoval to king, 27 March and 20 August 1608); AGI-SD 1, R. 1, no. 109 (consulta, 13 May 1612); R. 2, no. 117 (consulta, 8 April 1614); AGI-Cttn 5348, no. 72 (license for Mejía de Villalobos, 6 February 1615); Gil-Bermejo García, *La Española*, 321–22.

46. AGI-SD 52, R. 5, no. 48 (Osorio to king, 20 October 1605); AGI-SD 1, R. 1, no. 102 (consulta, 31 July 1609); *Recopilación*, L. 2, T. 16, ll. 82–86; Phelan, *Kingdom of Quito*, 152; Gil-Bermejo García, *La Española*, 237; Mayorga García, *La Audiencia de Santafé*, 88; Herzog, "Identidades colectivas, fronteras comunitarias," 1425–29; Valenzuela, *Liturgias del poder*, 63.

47. AGI-SD 52, R. 5, no. 27 (Manso to king, 2 July 1605); AGI-SD 72, R. 5, no. 12a, fol. 22v (testimony, 2 January 1610); no. 12j (petition, 18 August 1618); AGI-SD 55, R. 6, no. 42 (Cereceda to king, 24 April 1626); AGI-Esc 33A, visita of Audiencia of Santo Domingo (1630), pza. 1, cuad. 2, fols. 28v–29r (testimony of Cereceda, 18 October 1630); López Beltrán, "La buena vecindad," 224–25; Socolow, *Women of Colonial Latin America*, 85; Eagle, "Beard-Pulling," 467–70, 483.

48. AGI-SD 55, R. 2, no. 5 (Gentil de Párraga to king, 28 January 1622); AGI-SD 64, R. 5, no. 113–113c (Segura, ecclesiastical cabildo, Navarrete, and municipal cabildo to king, 24 August, 20 August, 25 August, and 25 August 1683).

49. AGI-SD 52, R. 8, no. 119 (Gómez de Sandoval to king, 17 August 1608); AGI-SD 54, R. 1, no. 21 (Gómez de Sandoval to king, 6 July 1610); AGI-Indif 161, no. 548 (merits of Jéronimo Gómez de Sandoval, n.d.); Panamá 19, R. 6, no. 65 (memorial of Jéronimo Gómez de Sandoval, 9 May 1640); Panamá 238, L. 17, fols. 43v–45r (king to treasury officials, 9 August 1648).

50. AGI-SD 54, R. 1, no. 37 (Gómez de Sandoval to king, 31 October 1610); R. 6, no. 114 (Gómez de Sandoval to king, 31 October 1615); AGI-SD 869, L. 6, fols. 123v–124r (king to Gómez de Sandoval, 17 September 1611); L. 7, fols. 25r–30r (king to Ibarra, 10 April 1618).

51. AGI-SD 18, no. 24 (report on Alonso Narváez y Valdelomar, 1610); AGI-SD 58, R. 3, no. 21, 23, 25 (Meneses to king, 20 and 30 March 1656); Vaccari, *Sobre gobernadores y residencias*, 82.

52. AGI-SD 52, R. 4, no. 6 (Arévalo to king, 20 August 1604); AGI-SD 53, R. 1, no. 19 (Gómez de Sandoval to king, 12 May 1609); AGI-SD 54, R. 1, no. 7 (Gómez de Sandoval to king, 20 February 1610).

53. *Recopilación*, L. 2, T. 16, ll. 48–50, 53.

54. AGI-SD 52, R. 4, no. 15, 18 (Arévalo to king, 20 December 1604); AGI-SD 52, R. 5, no. 27 (Manso to king, 2 July 1605); AGI-SD 1, R. 2, no. 120 (consulta,

2 June 1614); AGI-Indif 196, no. 34 (merits of Francisco Melgarejo, 6 April 1661); AGI-SD 2, R. 2, no. 105 (consulta of Cámara, 29 July 1661); AGI-SD 72, R. 11, no. 57 (Correoso to king, 22 May 1698); Torres Agudo, "Élites y grupos de poder," 271; Torres Agudo, "Los Campuzano-Polanco."

55. AGI-SD 54, R. 2, no. 61 (Gómez de Sandoval, 15 July 1611); AGI-SD 55, R. 5, no. 25 (Chaves Osorio to king, 13 February 1625); R. 20, no. 128b (Álvarez de Mendoza to king, 28 June 1640); AGI-SD 57, R. 4, no. 63 (Zúñiga to king, 30 November 1657); R. 8, no. 92 (Balboa to king, 8 February 1661); AGI-SD 62, R. 7, no. 64 (audiencia to king, 30 May 1674); Peña Pérez, *Cien años de miseria*, 160–62, 231–33, 274–77, 297–301; Reichert, *Sobre las olas*, 140–44; Ponce Vázquez, *Islanders and Empire*, 192–99; Paredes Vera, "No hay más Ley," 403–4.

56. AGI-SD 55, R. 2, no. 5 (Gentil de Párraga to king, 28 January 1622); R. 4, no. 19 (audiencia to king, 11 January 1624); AGI-SD 869, L. 7, fols. 242v–243r (king to audiencia, 16 September 1624); AGI-SD 872, L. 16, fols. 86r–87v (king to treasury officials of Puerto Rico, 6 June 1659); AGI-SD 903, L. 16, fols. 265r–266r (king to audiencia, 10 May 1665); Schäfer, *El Consejo Real*, 2:120–21; Peña Pérez, *Cien años de miseria*, 244, 272–73. See also AGI-SD 869, L. 5, fols. 154r–155v (king to audiencia, 28 January 1608); Utrera, *Noticias históricas*, 1:306.

57. AGI-SD 62, R. 7, no. 63b (Zayas Bazán to king, 24 May 1674); AGI-SD 63, R. 3, no. 41 (Garcés de los Fayos to king, 2 September 1677).

58. AGI-SD 76, R. 2, s.no. (treasury officials to king, 27 December 1681); AGI-SD 64, R. 3, no. 85 (audiencia to king, 30 June 1681); R. 6, no. 155a (escribanos de cámara to king, 9 August 1684); AGI-SD 65, R. 5, no. 169b (certification, 13 June 1689).

59. Herzog, *Upholding Justice*, 47–53; see also Alonso Romero, "El proceso penal," 211–12.

60. AGI-Esc 1182 (visita sentence vs. Caballero, 8 August 1671); AGI-SD 59, R. 1, no. 1 (Rosados to king, 25 January 1661); see also Utrera, *Noticias históricas*, 2:177.

61. AGI-SD 84, R. 5, s.no. (file on alguaciles of audiencia, 31 December 1619); AGI-SD 57, R. 4, no. 61 (audiencia to king, 22 August 1652); AGI-SD 64, R. 5, no. 126 (audiencia to king, 26 August 1683); AGI-Cttn 5403, no. 40 (license for Tafalla, 1 July 1628); AGI-Cttn 5424, no. 1, R. 4 (license for Tafalla, 29 May 1641); AGI-Indif 118, no. 54, fols. 12r–14v (merits of Heredia, 30 December 1659).

62. AGI-SD 62, R. 4, no. 28 (petition of Caballero, n.d.); AGI-SD 65, R. 3, no. 82 (Robles to king, 22 August 1687); Eagle, "Beard-Pulling," 477–78.

63. AGI-SD 52, R. 7, no. 85 (Osorio to king, 23 March 1607); AGI-SD 55, R. 18, no. 91 (memorial of Cereceda, 1638).

64. AGI-SD 1, R. 1, no. 65 (consulta of Cámara, 4 July 1605); AGI-SD 52, R. 1, no. 2 (Sanz Morquecho to king, 20 February 1601); R. 5, no. 52 (Sanz Morquecho to

king, 7 November 1605); AGI-SD 57, R. 3, no. 44ñ (cabildo to king, 19 March 1650); no. 44q, 44s (Fernández de Córdoba to king, 30 January and 26 February 1651).

65. AGI-SD 75, R. 1, s.no. (treasury officials to king, 24 June 1640); AGI-Indif 115, no. 2 (merits of Alzate, June 1653); AGI-Indif 116, no. 3 (merits of Montemayor, 7 February 1651); AGI-Patr 273, R. 7, no. 18 (Alzate to Leguía, 16 April 1654); R. 12 (Montemayor to king, 2 December 1656); AGI-SD 187, R. 15, no. 79 (Padilla to king, 20 March 1681); Barrientos Grandon, "Juan Francisco Montemayor," 160–90.

66. AGI-SD 55, R. 4, no. 18 (Martínez Tenorio to king, 2 January 1624); R. 6, no. 50, 51, 52 (Martínez Tenorio, audiencia, and Acuña to king, 4 and 5 September 1626); AGI-SD 1, R. 2, no. 191 (consulta, 16 November 1626); AGI-Esc 33A, visita of Audiencia of Santo Domingo (1630), pza. 1, cuad. 2, fol. 109v (testimony of Martínez Tenorio, 4 November 1630); AGI-SD 58, R. 3, no. 14 (Meneses to king, 20 January 1656); AGI-SD 64, R. 3, no. 93 (Cárdenas to king, 24 December 1681).

67. AGI-SD 58, R. 3, no. 41b (Melgarejo [draft], 6 March 1658); Agulló Cobo, "Juan Gómez de Mora," 78.

68. AGI-SD 52, R. 4, no. 18 (Arévalo to king, 20 December 1604); AGI-Indif 113, no. 29 (merits of Arévalo [son], 14 December 1646); AGI-Panamá 66, no. 12 (testimony about Trigo, 28 May 1660); AGI-SD 1, R. 3, no. 233 (consulta, 25 November 1634); no. 233a (petition of Prada, 18 September 1634); no. 233b (Castrillo to king, 4 December 1634); no. 237 (Alarcón to king, 19 January 1635); Eagle, "Portraits of Bad Officials," 98–99.

69. AGI-SD 1, R. 2, no. 117 (consulta, 8 April 1614); Cañeque, *King's Living Image*, 60–65; Herzog, *Upholding Justice*, 129–32; Eagle, "Beard-Pulling," 480.

70. AGI-SD 1, R. 3, no. 230 (consulta, 19 October 1634); AGI-SD 2, R. 2, no. 156 (consulta of Cámara, 28 April 1670); AGI-SD 57, R. 2, no. 32 (Fernández to king, 5 August 1650); R. 3, no. 44aa (cabildo to king, 30 March 1651); AGI-SD 65, R. 3, no. 82c (Riva Agüero to king, 22 August 1687); R. 4, no. 164 (Robles to Ortiz, 21 October 1688). See also Pelorson, *Les "Letrados,"* 60–62.

71. AGI-SD 57, R. 5, no. 72 (Montemayor to king, 26 April 1653); Gómez, *Experiential Caribbean*, 41–442.

72. AGI-SD 65, R. 4, no. 119 (González to king, 22 April 1688); no. 119a (certification, 26 April 1688); no. 147 (Robles to king, 30 August 1688).

73. AGI-SD 55, R. 20, no. 128 (audiencia to king, 2 July 1640); AGI-SD 62, R. 1, no. 5 (Pizarro Cajal to king, 30 July 1667); AGI-SD 2, R. 2, no. 192a (note from Carvajal y Cobos, 5 November 1671); AGI-SD 874, L. 20, fols. 86r–87r (queen regent to Zayas Bazán, 5 November 1674); AGI-SD 63, R. 1, no. 5 (Zayas Bazán to king, 28 April 1675); R. 3, no. 28 (Padilla to king, 15 August 1677); AGI-Indif 130, no. 78

(merits of Maldonado, 9 April 1685); AGI-SD 3, R. 4, no. 158c (Pérez Caro to king, 28 June 1694); AGI-Indif 133, no. 94 (merits of Cruz Ahedo, 23 January 1694).

74. AGI-SD 62, R. 7, no. 55 (Zayas Bazán to king, 9 February 1674); Panamá 17, R. 2, no. 25 (De la Cerda to king, [1618]).

75. *Recopilación*, L. 2, T. 16, l. 95; Phelan, *Kingdom of Quito*, 149; López Beltrán, "La buena vecindad," 225; Burkholder, "Honest Judges," 247–48.

76. AGI-SD 52, R. 6, no. 82a (testimony, 8 November 1603); AGI-SD 1, R. 1, no. 65 (consulta of Cámara, 4 July 1605); R. 2, no. 211 (consulta, 8 August 1630); AGI-Cttn 438, no. 7(2) (petition of Catalina de Vargas, 10 May 1633); Panamá 2, no. 213 (consulta of Cámara, 20 August 1657); AGI-SD 66, R. 3, no. 54 (Pérez Caro to king, 6 July 1694); AGI-SD 76, R. 5, s.no. (treasury officials to king, 2 July 1694); AGI-SD 91, R. 6, s.no. (petition from Teresa de Segura, 28 February 1697).

77. AGI-SD 3, R. 3, no. 130 (consulta of Cámara, 25 November 1689); R. 4, no. 134, 137 (consultas of Cámara, 9 June 1690 and 22 August 1691); see also AGI-SD 91, R. 4–6.

78. AGI-SD 2, R. 1, no. 75 (consulta of Cámara, 20 December 1658); R. 2, no. 127 (consulta, 14 June 1664); no. 169 (consulta of Cámara, 14 October 1671); AGI-SD 58, R. 8, no. 90f (Caballero to king, 27 January 1661); AGI-Esc 12C, no. 1, residencia of Balboa (1666), pza. 15, fols. 18v–28v (Navarro to king, 28 July 1667).

79. AGI-Esc 12C, no. 5, residencia of López de la Puerta (1665), pza. 1, fol. 192 (sentence vs. López de la Puerta, 14 November 1665).

80. AGI-SD 58, R. 3, no. 57 (Montemayor to Leguía, 3 November 1656); AGI-SD 2, R. 2, no. 95, 136 (consultas, 17 August 1666 and 29 October 1669); AGI-SD 64, R. 6, no. 138 (Robles to king, 22 July 1684); AGI-SD 65, R. 7, no. 232c (Oviedo to king, 28 May 1691); Herzog, *Ritos de control*, 51–52; Eagle, "Portraits of Bad Officials," 88–91, 103.

81. AGI-SD 875, L. 24, fols. 100r–101v (king to Riva Agüero, 14 April 1688); AGI-SD 65, R. 4, no. 145 (Robles to king, 28 August 1688); no. 145d (Cerdeño to king, 13 October 1689).

7. Audiencia and Society

1. Bertrand, *Grandeur et misère*, 360–61; Herzog, *Upholding Justice*, 1–8; Cañeque, *King's Living Image*, 4–13; Masters, "Thousand Invisible Architects," 379–83; Ponce Vázquez, *Islanders and Empire*, 175–76, 222.

2. AGI-SD 54, R. 1, no. 18, 35 (Gómez de Sandoval to king, 20 May and 31 October 1610); R. 2, no. 66 (Gómez de Sandoval to king, 15 July 1611); *Recopilación*, L. 2, T. 16, ll. 97, 98; Bravo Lira, "Símbolos de la función judicial," 240–44, 253–54; Herzog, *Upholding Justice*, 6–8, 180–81, 229–31; Cañeque, *King's Living Image*, 120–21, 141–52.

3. AGI-SD 58, R. 3, no. 52 (Zúñiga to king, 20 July 1656); AGI-SD 872, L. 16, fols. 37r–38r (king to audiencia, 24 April 1659); AGI-SD 65, R. 7, no. 228 (audiencia to king, 10 March 1691); see also AGI-SD 67, R. 1, no. 21 (Manzaneda to king, 20 May 1699).
4. AGI-SD 55, R. 1, no. 6 (audiencia to king, 7 February 1622); AGI-SD 62, R. 2, no. 11 (audiencia to king, 10 August 1668); *Recopilación*, L. 3, T. 15, ll. 57, 60–62; Bravo Lira, "Símbolos de la función judicial," 247–49; Valenzuela Márquez, *Liturgias del poder*, 315–21; Herzog, *Upholding Justice*, 221–22; Cañeque, *King's Living Image*, 120; Gómez Gómez, *El sello y registro*, 252–63.
5. AGI-SD 67, R. no. 39, fol. 2r (Manzaneda to king, 4 June 1699); Sánchez Bella, "Las audiencias," 182–83; Herzog, *Upholding Justice*, 46–48, 257; Eagle, "Beard-Pulling," 488–89.
6. AGI-SD 868, L. 3, fol. 184v (king to audiencia, 30 October 1604); AGI-Esc 33A, visita of Audiencia of Santo Domingo (1630), pza. 1, fol. 22r; AGI-SD 55, R. 20, no. 124 (Alarcón Coronado to king, 30 June 1640); AGI-SD 57, R. 3, no. 44ll (Melgarejo to king, 18 March 1650); AGI-SD 871, L. 12, fols. 250v–251v (king to Cepeda, 10 December 1650); *Recopilación*, L. 2, T. 16, l. 51; Moreta Castillo, *La Real Audiencia de Santo Domingo*, 78; Eagle, "Beard-Pulling," 472–73, 477, 488.
7. AGI-SD 52, R. 2, no. 4 (audiencia to king, 8 July 1602); AGI-SD 61, R. 2, no. 7a (report of Carvajal, 19 April 1665); AGI-Esc 12A, no. 5, residencia of Balboa (1666), pza. 1, fol. 94r; AGI-SD 64, R. 3, no. 63 (Segura to king, 8 June 1681); Hernández González, "Sociedad en la Española," 221.
8. AGI-SD 54, R. 4, no. 107 (audiencia to king, 12 December 1613); AGI-SD 55, R. 2, no. 5 (Gentil to king, 28 January 1622); AGI-SD 66, R. 1, no. 2, 2a, 2c (Pérez Caro and audiencia to king, 6 August and 30 July 1692).
9. AGI-SD 55, R. 5, no. 22 (Gentil to king, 15 January 1625); R. 16, no. 84 (Cereceda to king, 8 May 1636); AGI-SD 56, R. 6, no. 49 (Velasco to king, 2 November 1646); R. 8, no. 67 (Velasco to king, 29 February 1648); AGI-SD 57, R. 2, no. 36 (Fernández de Córdoba to king, 15 November 1650); AGI-SD 62, R. 3, no. 24 (audiencia to king, 26 September 1669).
10. AGI-SD 1, R. 2, no. 195 (consulta, 28 August 1627); R. 3, no. 292, 300 (consultas, 31 July 1643 and 16 March 1645); R. 3, no. 326 (consulta of Cámara, [1608]); AGI-SD 2, R. 2, no. 131 (consulta of Cámara, 15 June 1665); AGI-SD 58, R. 3, no. 40a (index of letters, 28 April 1656); AGI-Indif 118, no. 93 (merits of Carrisosa, 9 December 1660); AGI-SD 62, R. 7, no. 59, 59a (Zayas Bazán and audiencia to king, 16 and 24 May 1674); *Recopilación*, L. 2, T. 33; MacLeod, "Self-Promotion," 27.
11. Burset Flores, "Cotidianidad en el Caribe colonial," 736–77.
12. Cope, *Limits of Racial Domination*, 22–24; Moya Pons, "Evolución de la población dominicana," 31–35; Ponce Vázquez, "Unequal Partners," 705–6, 716–17.

13. AGI-SD 82, R. 3, no. 34 (Núñez de Toledo to king, 30 September 1603); AGI-SD 57, R. 4, no. 57 (audiencia to king, 21 January 1652); AGI-SD 60, R. 2, no. 18 (Carvajal to king, 26 July 1664); Tau Anzoátegui, "La idea de Derecho," 26–30. See also AGI-SD 872, L. 16, fols. 281v–282v (king to audiencia, 9 September 1660); AGI-SD 59, R. 2, no. 30 (Vargas to king, 25 October 1662); Tortorici, *Sins against Nature*, 63–64, 72–73.
14. AGI-SD 52, R. 1, no. 2 (Sanz Morquecho to king, 20 February 1601); 53, R. 1, no. 52 (Gómez de Sandoval to king, 30 December 1609); AGI-SD 874, L. 21, fol. 82 (king to Segura, 22 February 1680); AGI-SD 64, R. 3, no. 63 (Segura to king, 8 June 1681); R. 5, no. 127 (Salazar to king, 30 August 1683); see also AGI-SD 868, L. 4, fol. 56 (king to audiencia, 16 August 1601).
15. AGI-SD 52, R. 6, no. 74 (Osorio to king, 12 October 1606); AGI-SD 1, R. 1, no. 80 (consulta, 2 August 1607); AGI-SD 53, R. 1, no. 9, 27 (Gómez de Sandoval, 8 May and 20 August 1609); AGI-SD 57, R. 5, no. 69, 69a, 69d (audiencia to king and testimony, 1 March, 18 April, and 6 December 1653); AGI-SD 2, R. 1, no. 71 (consulta, 15 October 1658); AGI-Esc 12C, no. 5, residencia of López de la Puerta (1665), pza. 1, fols. 142r–144v, 153r; Vila Vilar, *Hispanoamérica y el comercio de esclavos*, 32–54, 169–72. See also AGI-SD 58, R. 7, no. 85 (audiencia to king, 3 August 1660); AGI-SD 59, R. 2, no. 8 (audiencia to king, 25 May 1662); AGI-SD 236, s.no. (consulta, 26 July 1700); Eagle, "Restoring Spanish Hispaniola," 391–93.
16. AGI-SD 55, R. 6, no. 48 (Gentil to king, 15 June 1626); R. 16, no. 82, 86 (Cereceda and Vela Núñez to king, 8 and 9 May 1636); AGI-SD 56, R. 2, no. 8 (Melgarejo to king, 5 April 1642); AGI-SD 62, R. 4, no. 29 (petition of Olivera, 16 December 1671); AGI-Esc 12A, no. 1, residencia of Melgarejo (1649), pza. 2, fol. 143v; AGI-Esc 13A (residencia of Robles, 1690), pza. 1, fol. 304; AGI-Esc 33A, visita of Audiencia of Santo Domingo (1630), pza. 2, fol. 81r; *Recopilación*, L. 2, T. 16, l. 65.
17. AGI-SD 54, R. 1, no. 31 (Gómez de Sandoval to king, 30 September 1610); R. 7, no. 116 (Gómez de Sandoval to king, 20 December 1616); AGI-SD 55, R. 2, no. 6 (audiencia to king, 7 February 1622); AGI-SD 64, R. 3, no. 50 (Segura to king, 8 June 1681); Rappaport, *Disappearing Mestizo*, 15–20.
18. AGI-SD 54, R. 4, no. 105 (audiencia to king, 12 December 1613); AGI-SD 56, R. 6, no. 44a (sentence of Velasco vs. Bitrián, 8 March 1646); R. 7, no. 60a (Velasco to king, 10 October 1647); AGI-SD 57, R. 2, no. 27 (Melgarejo to king, 18 March 1650); Ponce Vázquez, "Unequal Partners," 715; Wheat, *Atlantic Africa*, 41–43.
19. AGI-SD 60, R. 3, no. 33 (audiencia to king, 4 January 1665); AGI-SD 64, R. 6, no. 145 (audiencia to king, 28 July 1684).
20. AGI-SD 53, R. 1, no. 50 (Gómez de Sandoval to king, 20 October 1609); AGI-SD 56, R. 4, no. 34 (Bitrián to king, 31 July 1644); AGI-SD 64, R. 6, no. 139 (Robles

to king, 27 July 1684); AGI-SD 65, R. 3, no. 47 (Robles to king, 1 May 1687); R. 4, no. 137 (Robles to king, 15 May 1688); Ponce Vázquez, *Islanders and Empire*, 243.

21. AGI-SD 2, R. 1, no. 70 (consulta, 28 August 1658); AGI-SD 55, R. 20, no. 122 (Bitrián to king, 30 June 1640); AGI-SD 58, R. 3, no. 22 (Meneses to king, 20 March 1656); AGI-SD 65, R. 7, no. 244 (Ladrón de Guevara to king, 29 May 1691); AGI-SD 66, R. 1, no. 8, 8a, 8b (Pérez Caro, audiencia, and Ladrón de Guevara to king, 29 August, 19 August, and 12 September 1692); AGI-Esc 12A, no. 4, residencia of Balboa (1661), pza. 2, fols. 2r–9r; AGI-SD 75, s.no. (treasury officials to king, 30 June 1640); Rodríguez Demorizi, "Familias Hispanoamericanas," 50–53; Deive, *La esclavitud del negro*, 2:535–43; Julián, "La fuga de esclavos," 40–54.
22. AGI-SD 55, R. 17, no. 89 (Álvarez de Mendoza to king, 8 September 1637); AGI-SD 58, R. 3, no. 17 (Meneses to king, 20 February 1656); AGI-Esc 12A, no. 5, residencia of Balboa (1666), pza. 2, fols. 227r–228r; Ponce Vázquez, "Unequal Partners," 716; Ponce Vázquez, *Islanders and Empire*, 243–44.
23. AGI-SD 2, R. 1, no. 65 (consulta, 29 April 1658).
24. AGI-SD 52, R. 7, no. 99 (Osorio to king, 29 November 1607); AGI-SD 57, R. 5, no. 77 (audiencia to king, 11 December 1653); Ots Capdequi, *El Estado español*, 20–22; Wheat, *Atlantic Africa*, 112; Ponce Vázquez, *Islanders and Empire*, 225–27.
25. AGI-Panama 17, R. 2, no. 25 (De la Cerda to king, [1618]); AGI-Esc 34A, visita of Audiencia of Santo Domingo (1630), pza. 11, fols. 79r–81r, 127r; AGI-SD 56, R. 2, no. 10 (Salazar to king, 15 July 1642); no. 13c (municipal cabildo to king, 6 February 1643); Ponce Vázquez, *Islanders and Empire*, 233–34.
26. AGI-SD 55, R. 4, no. 18 (Martínez Tenorio to king, 2 January 1624); AGI-SD 56, R. 2, no. 11 (audiencia to king, 19 July 1642); AGI-SD 57, R. 2, no. 23, 31 (audiencia to king and testimony, 14 March and 18 May 1650); Alcocer, "Relación Sumaria," 50–51; Gil-Bermejo García, *La Española*, 95–96; Eagle, "Chasing the *Avença*," 110; Paredes Vera, "La decadencia," 98–100; Ponce Vázquez, *Islanders and Empire*, 227–31, 236–37, 261–62.
27. AGI-SD 55, R. 2, no. 4 (Gómez de Sandoval to king, 20 January 1622); AGI-SD 62, R. 1, no. 10 (audiencia to king, 4 August 1667); Socolow, *Women of Colonial Latin America*, 6–8; Beck, "Women's Power," 40–42.
28. AGI-SD 58, R. 6, no. 80 (Balboa to king, 7 November 1659); AGI-SD 66, R. 4, no. 83 (audiencia to king, 15 November 1695); Burset Flores, "Cotidianidad en el Caribe colonial," 753.
29. AGI-Cttn 5302, no. 83, fol. 25 (passenger list, 27 January 1608); AGI-SD 52, R. 8, no. 131a (residencia sentence, 16 September 1608); AGI-SD 54, R. 3, no. 88a (Herrera to king, 24 May 1610); R. 8, no. 118 (audiencia to king, 20 May 1617); AGI-SD 55, R. 5, no. 29 (Gil de la Sierpe to king, 16 May 1625); R. 6, no. 86 (Vela

Núñez to king, 9 May 1636); AGI-SD 64, R. 5, no. 126, 126b, 126a (audiencia and Segura to king, testimony, 28 August, 26 June, and 28 July 1683); AGI-SD 65, R. 7, no. 228 (audiencia to king, 10 March 1691); Herzog, *Upholding Justice*, 47–48.

30. AGI-SD 56, R. 2, no. 10 (Salazar to king, 15 July 1642); no. 14, 14d (Bitrián to king and testimony, 22 and 19 July 1642); AGI-SD 57, R. 3, no. 44k, fol. 4r (testimony, 27 March 1649); AGI-Indif 118, no. 54, fol. 2r (merits of Heredia, 30 December 1659); AGI-SD 59, R. 1, no. 2, 2a (Caballero to king and testimony, 27 January 1661 and 26 August 1655); see also Herzog, *Upholding Justice*, 49–50.

31. AGI-SD 55, R. 17, no. 90 (Alarcón Coronado to king, 20 September 1637); AGI-SD 870, L. 10, fol. 82 (king to Alarcón Coronado, 6 April 1638); AGI-SD 67, R. 1, no. 39 (Manzaneda to king, 4 June 1699); Ponce Vázquez, *Islanders and Empire*, 204.

32. AGI-Indif 118, no. 54, fol. 37 (merits of Heredia, 30 December 1659); AGI-Indif 196, no. 22 (merits of Francisco Méndez de Salazar, 7 February 1661); AGI-SD 870, L. 8, fol. 88 (king to Chaves Osorio, 7 May 1627); L. 10, fols. 79v–81r (king to Bitrián, 6 April 1638); Gil-Bermejo García, *La Española*, 109; Calvo, *Poder, religión y sociedad*, 26.

33. AGI-SD 56, R. 5, no. 40b (audiencia to king, 8 August 1645); AGI-SD 2, R. 2, no. 70 (consulta, 28 August 1658); AGI-SD 64, R. 6, no. 163 (Semillán Campuzano to king, 1 December 1684).

34. Valenzuela Márquez, *Liturgias del poder*, 84–85; Cañeque, *King's Living Image*, 160–62; Eagle, "Beard-Pulling," 483–84; Rosenmüller, *Corruption and Justice*, 37.

35. Herzog, *Upholding Justice*, 129–34.

36. AGI-SD 869, L. 7, fols. 25–30r (king to Ibarra, 10 April 1618).

37. AGI-Esc 3A, no. 2, fiscal vs. Agüero Bardecí (1606), pza. 1, fols. 262r–269v, 277r–308v; AGI-Panama 1, no. 281 (consulta, 8 April 1614); AGI-SD 72, R. 5, no. 12e (petition of Herrera, 31 January 1618); no. 12l (testimony, 3 September 1619); AGI-SD 57, R. 3, no. 44 (Fernández de Córdoba to king, 20 February 1651); AGI-Esc 12C, no. 1, residencia of Balboa (1666), pza. 9, fols. 1r–2v; pza. 10, fols. 1r–9r; AGI-SD 64, R. 3, no. 85, 85c (audiencia and Medrano to king, 30 June 1681); AGI-SD 876, L. 27, 150r (king to audiencia, 9 April 1693); Herzog, *Upholding Justice*, 33–34, 146–52.

38. AGI-SD 52, R. 6, no. 66 (Arévalo Sedeño to king, 2 March 1606); AGI-Esc 12C, residencia of De la Puerta (1665), no. 9, pza. 1, fols. 64–65r; Ponce Vázquez, *Islanders and Empire*, 175–76, 180–81. See also AGI-SD 67, R. 1, no. 24 (testimony, 20 May 1699).

39. AGI-SD 55, R. 5, no. 29 (Gil de la Sierpe to king, 16 May 1625); AGI-SD 65, R. 4, no. 125 (González to king, 26 April 1688); no. 131, fols. 160v–110r (testimony, 8 May 1688); Eagle, "Restoring Spanish Hispaniola," 389.

40. AGI-SD 2, R. 1, no. 70 (consulta, 28 August 1658); AGI-SD 62, R. 1, no. 2a, 4 (De la Cueva and Carvajal to king, 15 and 28 July 1667); AGI-Esc 12C, no. 1, residencia of Balboa (1666), pza. 15, fol. 21v; Ponce Vázquez, *Islanders and Empire*, 208–19.

41. AGI-Esc 12A, no. 1, residencia of Melgarejo (1649), pza. 1, ff. 82r–84v, 93r–100v; Herzog, *Upholding Justice*, 48–50. See also AGI-SD 57, R. 3, no. 44k, fols. 12r–13v (testimony, 27 March 1649).

42. AGI-SD 57, R. 3, no. 52 (Figueroa y Castilla to king, 31 December 1651); AGI-SD 58, R. 3, no. 60 (Pimentel to Leguía, 6 November 1656), no. 60a, 60b (Meneses and Zúñiga to king, 20 April and 30 June 1656); AGI-Esc 12A, no. 4, residencia of Balboa (1661), pza. 2, fols. 2r–9r; AGI-Esc 12C, no. 1, residencia of Balboa (1666), pza. 10, fols. 51r–52v; AGI-SD 63, R. 1, no. 8 (Chacón to king, 12 July 1675); Herzog, *Ritos de control*, 10; Herzog, *Upholding Justice*, 135–40; Ponce Vázquez, *Islanders and Empire*, 172–75, 180–81, 204–5.

43. AGI-SD 871, L. 12, fols. 326r–328r (king to audiencia, 28 February 1652); Ponce Vázquez, *Islanders and Empire*, 196.

44. AGI-SD 55, R. 5, no. 25 (Acuña to king, 13 February 1625); AGI-SD 62, R. 1, no. 8, 8a (audiencia and Carvajal to king, 4 August and 12 September 1667); AGI-SD 63, R. 3, no. 32q (audiencia to king, 18 August 1678); AGI-SD 64, R. 5, no. 112 (Garcés to king, 23 August 1683); AGI-SD 3, R. 2, no. 62 (consulta, 25 September 1683); Moya Pons, *Historia colonial*, 212; Peña Pérez, *Cien años de miseria*, 241–42; Eagle, "Restoring Spanish Hispaniola," 395–99, 402.

45. AGI-SD 54, R. 3, no. 90, 90a (Gómez de Sandoval to king and testimony, 4 June 1612 and 16 November 1611); AGI-SD 869, L. 7, fols. 25r–30r (king to Ibarra, 10 April 1618); AGI-SD 72, R. 5, no. 12n (Gómez de Sandoval to king, 10 November 1619); AGI-SD 58, R. 3, no. 45 (Vélez Mantilla to Leguía, 28 July 1656); Cañeque, *King's Living Image*, 154.

46. AGI-Esc 33A, visita of Audiencia of Santo Domingo (1630), pza. 1, cuad. 2, fols. 22v–29r, 111v–127v; Eagle, "Beard-Pulling," 475.

47. AGI-SD 63, R. 3, no. 24 (Garcés to king, 15 January 1677).

48. AGI-SD 56, R. 2, no. 14c (testimony, 21 June 1642); AGI-SD 870, L. 11, fols. 113v–114v (king to Bitrián, 30 April 1643); AGI-SD 57, R. 3, no. 41 (Fernández de Córdoba to king, 12 February 1651); R. 5, no. 74 (report of fiscal of Consejo, 18 May 1653); Cañeque, *King's Living Image*, 183; Martiré, *Las Audiencias*, 171–78; Eagle, "Portraits of Bad Officials," 88–90.

49. AGI-SD 55, R. 10, no. 61 (Chaves Osorio to king, 12 July 1630); R. 11, no. 63 (Ortiz de Sandoval to king, 8 January 1631); AGI-Esc 1181 (visita sentences vs. Meneses and Cereceda, 21 February 1601 and 9 January 1635); AGI-Esc 13A, no. 3, residencia of Robles (1690), fols. 1r–3v.

50. AGI-SD 17, no. 12 (report, 1606); AGI-Esc 1181 (visita sentence vs. Mejía de Villalobos, 16 May 1608); AGI-SD 22, no. 19 (testimony, 10 November 1643); AGI-SD 56, R. 7, no. 53a (Melgarejo to king, 14 January 1647); AGI-SD 57, R. 3, no. 40, 40a (Fernández de Córdoba to king and testimony, 30 and 18 January 1651); AGI-SD 58, R. 3, no. 40 (Meneses to Leguía, 1 June 1656); Gil-Bermejo García, *La Española*, 227, 321–32, 324; Eagle, "Portraits of Bad Officials," 91–92; Ponce Vázquez, *Islanders and Empire*, 229–30.

51. AGI-SD 53, R. 1, no. 14, 14a (Gómez de Sandoval to king and testimony, 8 and 5 May 1609); Rappaport, *Disappearing Mestizo*, 39–42; Ponce Vázquez, "Unequal Partners," 705. See also AGI-Patr 50, R. 12 (merits of Justinián, 2 April 1579); Rodríguez Morel, "Sugar Economy of Española," 92, 95.

52. AGI-SD 57, R. 1, no. 10, 10a (audiencia to king and testimony, 3 and 2 March 1649); AGI-SD 871, L. 12, fols. 315v–317r (king to audiencia, 28 February 1652).

53. Exbalin, "Riot in Mexico City," 230; Ballone, *1624 Tumult of Mexico*, xxiii–xxviii.

54. AGI-Esc 33A, visita of Audiencia of Santo Domingo (1630), pza. 7, fols. 1r–4v.

55. AGI-Esc 33A, visita of Audiencia of Santo Domingo (1630), pza. 2, fol. 3; pza. 7, fol. 135; AGI-Esc 33B, visita (1630), pza. 9, fols. 231r–232v; Nesvig, *Promiscuous Power*, 214–15, no. 53.

56. Ponce Vázquez, *Islanders and Empire*, 166; see also Andrien, *Crisis and Decline*, 193.

57. AGI-Esc 33A, visita of Audiencia of Santo Domingo (1630), pza. 2, fols. 21r–22v; AGI-Esc 33B, visita of Audiencia of Santo Domingo (1630), pza. 9, fol. 14r, 233v; Boyer, "Respect and Identity," 494–96.

58. AGI-Esc 33A, visita of Audiencia of Santo Domingo (1630), pza. 3, fol. 1r–2v; pza. 4, fol. 2r; pza. 5, fols. 64v–65v; pza. 7, fol. 135v, 193r–194r; AGI-Esc 1181 (visita sentences, 1635); Eagle, "Beard-Pulling," 482–83.

Conclusion

1. AGI-Esc 12C, no. 5, residencia of López de la Puerta (1665), pza. 1, fol. 156.

2. Crahan, "Spanish and American Counterpoint," 56; Eagle, "Beard-Pulling," 487. See also Calvo, *Poder, religión y sociedad*, 27–28.

3. Phelan, "Authority and Flexibility," 60–62; Herzog, *Ritos de control*, 166–68; Herzog, *Upholding Justice*, 53, 133–36; Ponce Vásquez, "Unequal Partners," 714–15; Eagle, "Portraits of Bad Officials," 92.

4. Phelan, *Kingdom of Quito*, 306–7; Domínguez Ortiz, *Política y hacienda*, 5–9; Eagle, "Beard-Pulling," 492–93; Eagle, "Portraits of Bad Officials," 101.

5. Cunningham, *Audiencia in the Spanish Colonies*, 261–67; Parry, *Audiencia of New Galicia*, 112–15; Cauzzi, *Historia de la primera Audiencia*, 133–34; Mayorga García, *La Audiencia de Santafé*, 122, 135–36; Calvo, *Poder, religión y sociedad*,

24, 47–48; Valenzuela Márquez, *Liturgias del poder*, 80–83; Herzog, *Upholding Justice*, 131–32.

6. Mayorga García, *La Audiencia de Santafé*, 134–36; Calvo, *Poder, religión y sociedad*, 385–86; Herzog, *Ritos de control*, 36.
7. López Cantos, *Historia de Puerto Rico*, 117; Santos Pérez, "La práctica del autogobierno en Centroamérica," 76; Gutiérrez Escudero, "Estructura económica," 77–79; Julián, "Situación económica, demográfica," 61–62, 80–91; Ponce Vázquez, *Islanders and Empire*, 144–45, 266–67.
8. AGI-Panama 23, R. 2, no. 65 (audiencia to king, 14 September 1663); AGI-Panama 24, R. 2, no. 54 (treasury officials to king, 7 November 1669); AGI-Filipinas 17, R. 1, no. 30 (Cruzat to king, 14 June 1699); Burkholder and Chandler, *From Impotence to Authority*, 22–36; Calvo, *Poder, religión y sociedad*, 26; Martiré, *Las Audiencias*, 116; Rodríguez Ridao, "La administración del Real Situado," 105–10.
9. Utrera, *Noticias históricas*, 4:142–43; Mayorga García, *La Audiencia de Santafé*, 172; Calvo, *Poder, religión y sociedad*, 27.
10. Calvo, *Poder, religión y sociedad*, 66, 272; Herzog, *Upholding Justice*, 245–46; Cañeque, *King's Living Image*, 60–65, 106–12, 123–24, 141–44; Ballone, *1624 Tumult of Mexico*, 61–62.
11. Moreno, *La Audiencia de Charcas*, 28–29; MacLachlan, *Spain's Empire*, 40; Calvo, *Poder, religión y sociedad*, 33–34, 47, 287–88, 385; Valenzuela Márquez, *Liturgias del poder*, 85–86; Herzog, *Upholding Justice*, 136–50; Martiré, *Las Audiencias*, 100–103; Ponce Vázquez, *Islanders and Empire*, 221–22.
12. AGI-SD 58, R. 1, no. 5 (audiencia to king, 16 April 1654); Schäfer, *El Consejo Real*, 2:448, 456–66, 481–92, 495, 497, 501; Barrientos Grandon, "Juan Francisco Montemayor," 176–77; Castejón, "Un *cursus honorum*," 446–47.
13. Calvo, *Poder, religión y sociedad*, 47; Jiménez Núñez, "Sistema político," 297, 305; Eagle, "Restoring Spanish Hispaniola," 402.
14. *Recopilación*, L. 2, T. 15, l. 8; Sánchez Bella, "Las audiencias," 165–66; Mayora García, *La Audiencia de Santafé*, 46–47, 161–64; Bonnett, *Los protectores de naturales*, 25–28; Herzog, *Ritos de control*, 155–57; Eagle, "Restoring Spanish Hispaniola," 396–97.
15. Sánchez Belèn, *La política fiscal*, 322–26; Storrs, *Resilience*, 164–66; Eagle, "Spanish Hispaniola," 395.
16. Gutiérrez Escudero, "Acerca del proyectismo," 46–48; Eissa-Barroso, "'Having Served,'" 351–53; Eissa-Barroso, *Spanish Monarchy*, 10.
17. Jiménez Núñez, "Sistema político," 299.
18. Schwartz, *Sovereignty and Society*, 220–21, 228–31, 314–15; Boucher, *France and the American Tropics*, 209–10, 228; Russell-Wood, "Portuguese Atlantic," 100–101;

Burnard, "British Atlantic," 117, 119–20, 127; Schmidt, "Dutch Atlantic," 176–77, 180; Klooster, *Dutch Moment*, 112; Castejón, "Un *cursus honorum*," 452.

19. Exbalin, "Riot in Mexico City," 217; Ballone, *1624 Tumult of Mexico*, 6.
20. *L'Espagne de Charles Quint*, 2:430–31; Elliott, "King and *Patria* in the Hispanic World," 177–78; Ponce Vázquez, *Islanders and Empire*, 222.

BIBLIOGRAPHY

Archives

Archivo de la Corona de Aragón, Barcelona, Spain

Archivo General de Indias, Seville, Spain

- Casa de la Contratación
- Contaduría
- Escribanía de Cámara de Justicia
- Gobierno
- Patronato Real

Archivo Histórico Nacional, Madrid, Spain

- Códices
- Diversos-Colecciones
- Órdenes Militares

Biblioteca del Palacio Real, Madrid, Spain

Biblioteca Nacional de España, Madrid, Spain

Published Works

Agulló Cobo, Mercedes. "Documentos para la biografía de Juan Gómez de Mora." *Anales del Instituto de Estudios Madrileños* 9 (1973): 55–80.

Alcocer, Luis Jerónimo. "Relación Sumaria del estado presente de la Isla Española en las Yndias Occidentales." *Boletín del Archivo General de la Nación* [1650] (Dominican Republic) 5, nos. 20–21 (January–April 1942): 31–101.

Alonso Romero, María Paz. "El proceso penal en la Castilla moderna." *Estudis: Revista de historia moderna* 22 (1996): 199–216.

Andrés Santo, Francisco J. "Los proyectos de recopilación del derecho indiano en época de Felipe IV." *Anuario da Facultade de Dereito da Universidade da Coruña* 11 (2007): 45–69.

Andrews, Kenneth R. *The Spanish Caribbean: Trade and Plunder 1530–1630*. New Haven CT: Yale University Press, 1978.

———. *Trade, Plunder and Settlement: Maritime Enterprise and the Genesis of the British Empire, 1480–1630*. Cambridge: Cambridge University Press, 1984.

Andrien, Kenneth. *Crisis and Decline: The Viceroyalty of Peru in the Seventeenth Century*. Albuquerque: University of New Mexico Press, 1985.

Antczak, Andrzej, Konrad A. Antczak, and María Magdalena Antczak. "Risky Business: Historical Archaeology of the Dutch Salt Enterprise on La Tortuga Island, Venezuela (1624–38)." *Post-Medieval Archaeology* 49, no. 2 (2015): 189–219.

Aranda Mendíaz, Manuel. *Visiones sobre el primer tribunal de justicia de la América Hispana: La Real Audiencia de Santo Domingo*. Madrid: Campillo Nevado, 2007.

Araujo y Rivero, Fernando. "Descripción de la Isla Española, o de Santo Domingo." BP Ms. 2, n. 2835, 1–44. Originally printed Madrid, 1699. Reprinted in *Boletín del Archivo General de la Nación* (Dominican Republic) 5, no. 22 (June 1942): 199–248.

Arregui Zamorano, Pilar. *La Audiencia de México según los visitadores: Siglos XVI y XVII*. Mexico City: Universidad Nacional Autónoma de México, 1985.

Astley, Thomas, ed. *A New General Collection of Voyages and Travels*. Vol. 1. London: Thomas Astley, 1745.

Ballone, Angela. *The 1624 Tumult of Mexico in Perspective (c. 1620–1650): Authority and Conflict Resolution in the Iberian Atlantic*. Leiden: Brill, 2018.

Barrientos Grandon, Javier. *Guía prosopográfica de la judicatura letrada indiana (1503–1898)*. In *Nuevas Aportaciones a la historia jurídica de Iberoamérica*, edited by José Andrés Gallego, 1–1640. Madrid: Fundación Hernando de Larramendi-Mapfre, 2000. CD-ROM.

———. "Juan Francisco Montemayor de Cuenca (1618–1685): Entre derecho indiano, derecho común y derecho foral." *Revista de Estudios Histórico-Jurídicos* 23 (2001): 125–208.

———. "La Real Audiencia de Concepción (1565–1575)." *Revista de Estudios Histórico-Jurídicos* 15 (1992–93): 131–78.

Beck, Lauren. "Women's Power and Material Exchange in Transatlantic Spain, 1550s–1650s." *Journal of Women's History* 30, no. 1 (Spring 2018): 35–55.

Bertrand, Michel. *Grandeur et misère de l'office: Les officiers de finances de Nouvelle-Espagne (XVIIe–XVIIIe siècles)*. Paris: Publications de la Sorbonne, 1999.

Block, Kristen. *Ordinary Lives in the Early Caribbean: Religion, Colonial Competition, and the Politics of Profit*. Athens: University of Georgia Press, 2012.

Block, Kristen, and Jenny Shaw. "Subjects without an Empire: The Irish in the Early Modern Caribbean." *Past & Present* 210, no. 1 (February 2011): 33–60.

Boucher, Philip P. *France and the American Tropics to 1700: Tropics of Discontent?* Baltimore: Johns Hopkins University Press, 2008.

Bonnett, Diana. *Los protectores de naturales en la Audiencia de Quito: Siglos XVII y XVIII*. Quito: Facultad Latinoamericana de Ciencias Sociales, 1992.

Boyer, Richard. "Respect and Identity: Horizontal and Vertical Reference Points in Speech Acts." *The Americas* 54, no. 4 (April 1998): 491–509.

Bravo Lira, Bernardino. "Símbolos de la función judicial en el Derecho indiano." In *Poder y presión fiscal en la América española. Siglos XVI, XVII y XVIII: Trabajos del VI Congreso del Instituto Internacional de Historia del Derecho Indiano en homenaje al Dr. Alfonso García-Gallo*, 235–54. Valladolid: Universidad de Valladolid, 1986.

Bridikhina, Eugenia. *Theatrum mundi: Entramados del poder en Charcas colonial*. Lima: Plural, 2007.

Britto García, Luis. *Señores del Caribe: Indígenas, conquistadores, piratas y corsarios en el mar colonial*. Havana: Editorial de Ciencias Sociales, 2006.

Bruno, Cayetano. *El derecho público de la iglesia en Indias: Estudio histórico-jurídico*. Salamanca: Consejo Superior de Investigaciones Científicas, 1967.

Burkholder, Mark. "Honest Judges Leave Destitute Heirs: The Price of Integrity in Eighteenth-Century Spain." In *Virtue, Corruption, and Self-Interest: Political Values in the Eighteenth Century*, edited by Richard K. Matthews, 247–69. Bethlehem PA: Lehigh University Press, 1994.

———. "Honor and Honors in Colonial Spanish America." In *The Faces of Honor: Sex, Shame, and Violence in Colonial Latin America*, edited by Lyman L. Johnson and Sonya Lipsett-Rivera, 18–44. Albuquerque: University of New Mexico Press, 1998.

———. "Spain's America: From Kingdoms to Colonies." *Colonial Latin American Review* 25, no. 2 (September 2016): 125–53.

———. *Spaniards in the Colonial Empire: Creoles vs. Peninsulars?* Chichester UK: Wiley-Blackwell, 2013.

Burkholder, Mark, and D. S. Chandler. *From Impotence to Authority: The Spanish Crown and the American Audiencias, 1687–1808*. Columbia: University of Missouri Press, 1977.

Burnard, Trevor. "The British Atlantic." In *Atlantic History: A Critical Appraisal*, edited by Jack P. Greene and Philip D. Morgan, 111–36. Oxford: Oxford University Press, 2009.

Burset Flores, Luis Rafael. "¿'Cosas indebidas' o 'siembra de mala voz'?: Los conflictos internos de la Real Audiencia de Santo Domingo, 1605–1608." *Clío* 84, no. 189 (January–June 2015): 96–153.

———. "Cotidianidad en el Caribe colonial, 1590–1620." *Revista de Indias* 78, no. 274 (2018): 735–56.

Butel, Paul. *Histoire des Antilles françaises, XVIIe–XXe siècle*. Paris: Perrin, 2002.

Calvo, Thomas. *Poder, religión y sociedad en la Guadalajara del siglo XVII*. Mexico City: CEMCA–Ayuntamiento de Guadalajara, 1992.

Camus, Michel Christian. *L'île de la Tortue au coeur de la flibuste caraïbe*. Paris: l'Harmattan, 1997.

Cañeque, Alejandro. *The King's Living Image: The Culture and Politics of Viceregal Power in Colonial Mexico*. New York: Routledge, 2004.

Cardona Bonet, Walter A. *Shipwrecks in Puerto Rico's History: 1502–1650*. Vol. 1. San Juan: Model, 1989.

Cartay A., Rafael. *Ideología, desarrollo e interferencias del comercio caribeño durante el siglo XVII*. Caracas: Fuentes Para la Historia Colonial de Venezuela, 1988.

Cassá, Roberto. *Historia social y económica de la República Dominicana*. 6th ed. Vol. 1. Santo Domingo: Editora Alfa & Omega, 2006.

Castejón, Philippe. "Un *cursus honorum* entre dos mundos: Los magistrados borbónicos del gobierno de Indias (1701–1808)." *Colonial Latin American Review* 31, no. 3 (September 2022): 433–59.

Castillo Lara, Lucas Guillermo. *Las acciones militares del Gobernador Ruy Fernández de Fuenmayor, 1637–1644*. Caracas: Academia Nacional de la Historia, 1978.

Cauzzi, Teresa Beatriz. *Historia de la primera Audiencia de Buenos Aires (1661–1672)*. Rosario: Universidad Católica Argentina, 1984.

Cazull, Héctor Santiago. "Conflicto, alianza y disociación en el Puerto Rico del siglo XVII: Las redes sociales del capitán general Sancho Ochoa de Castro y el sargento mayor Jerónimo de Mieses (1602–1608)." *Revista Complutense de Historia de América* 34 (2008): 43–62.

Céspedes del Castillo, Guillermo. "La visita como institución indiana." *Anuario de Estudios Americanos* 3 (1946): 984–1025.

Chacón Abarca y Tiedra, Jerónimo. *Decissiones de la Real Audiencia y Chancillería de Santo Domingo*. Salamanca: Antonio Cossio, 1676.

Charlevoix, Pierre François Xavier. *Histoire de l'isle Espagnole ou de S. Domingue*. 2 vols. Paris: Jacques Guerin, 1730–31.

Chaunu, Huguette, and Pierre Chaunu. *Seville et l'Atlantique (1504–1650)*. 8 vols. Paris: SEVPEN, 1956.

Chaunu, Pierre. *L'Espagne de Charles Quint*. 2 vols. Paris: Société d'édition d'enseignement supérieur, 1973.

Clapham, J. H. "Charles Louis, Elector Palatine, 1617–1680: An Early Experiment in Liberalism." *Economica* 7, no. 28 (November 1940): 381–96.

Cook, Karoline. *Forbidden Passages: Muslims and Moriscos in Colonial Spanish America*. Philadelphia: University of Pennsylvania Press, 2016.

Cope, R. Douglas. *The Limits of Racial Domination: Plebeian Society in Colonial Mexico City, 1660–1720*. Madison: University of Wisconsin Press, 1994.

Crahan, Margaret E. "Spanish and American Counterpoint: Problems and Possibilities in Spanish Colonial Administrative History." In *New Approaches to Latin American History*, edited by Richard Graham and Peter H. Smith, 36–70. Austin: University of Texas Press, 1974.

Cruz Barney, Óscar. *Una visión indiana de la justicia de la guerra*. Mexico City: Universidad Nacional Autónoma de México, 2014.

Cuart Moner, Baltasar. "Algunas notas sobre los colegiales de San Clemente en la administración americana (siglos XVI–XVIII)." *Studia Historica: Historia Moderna* 7 (1989): 799–823.

Cunningham, Charles H. *The Audiencia in the Spanish Colonies as Illustrated by the Audiencia of Manila (1583–1800)*. Berkeley: University of California Press, 1919.

Curcio-Nagy, Linda A. *The Great Festivals of Colonial Mexico City: Performing Power and Identity*. Albuquerque: University of New Mexico Press, 2004.

Cutter, Charles R. *The Legal Culture of Northern New Spain, 1700–1810*. Albuquerque: University of New Mexico Press, 1995.

Deive, Carlos Esteban. *Heterodoxia e inquisición en Santo Domingo, 1492–1822*. Santo Domingo: Taller, 1983.

———. *La esclavitud del negro en Santo Domingo (1492–1844)*. 2 vols. Santo Domingo: Museo del Hombre Dominicano, 1980.

———. *Los guerrilleros negros: Esclavos fugitivos y cimarrones en Santo Domingo*. Santo Domingo: Taller, 1989.

———. *Tangomangos: Contrabando y piratería en Santo Domingo, 1522–1606*. Santo Domingo: Fundación Cultural Dominicana, 1996.

De la Fuente, Alejandro, with César García del Pino and Bernardo Iglesias Delgado. *Havana and the Atlantic in the Sixteenth Century*. Chapel Hill: University of North Carolina Press, 2008.

Díaz Ceballos, Jorge. *Poder Compartido: Repúblicas urbanas, Monarquía y conversación en Castilla del Oro, 1508–1573*. Madrid: Marcial Pons, 2020.

Domínguez Ortiz, Antonio. *Las clases privilegiadas en el Antiguo Régimen*. 2nd ed. Madrid: Ediciones ISTMO, 1979.

———. *Política y hacienda de Felipe IV*. 2nd ed. Madrid: Ediciones Pegaso, 1983.

Eagle, Marc. "Beard-Pulling and Furniture-Rearranging: Conflict Within the Seventeenth-Century Audiencia of Santo Domingo." *The Americas* 68, no. 4 (April 2012): 467–93.

———. "Chasing the *Avença*: An Investigation of Illicit Slave Trading in Santo Domingo at the End of the Portuguese *Asiento* Period." *Slavery & Abolition* 35, no. 1 (2014): 99–120.

———. "Informal Entrepôts: Witness Testimony about Slave Ship *Arribadas* to Santo Domingo and San Juan in the 1620s." *Colonial Latin American Review* 32, no. 1 (March 2023): 11–33.

———. "Portraits of Bad Officials: Malfeasance in *Visita* Sentences from Seventeenth-Century Santo Domingo." In *Corruption in the Iberian Empires: Greed, Custom, and Colonial Networks*, edited by Christoph Rosenmüller, 87–109. Albuquerque: University of New Mexico Press, 2017.

———. "Restoring Spanish Hispaniola, the First of the Indies: Local Advocacy and Transatlantic Arbitrismo in the Late Seventeenth Century." *Colonial Latin American Review* 23, no. 3 (December 2014): 384–412.

Eissa-Barroso, Francisco A. "'Having Served in the Troops': The Appointment of Military Officers as Provincial Governors in Early Eighteenth-Century Spanish America, 1700–1746." *Colonial Latin American Historical Review* 18, no. 4 (Fall 2013): 329–59.

———. *The Spanish Monarchy and the Creation of the Viceroyalty of New Granada (1717–1739): The Politics of Early Bourbon Reform in Spain and Spanish America.* Leiden: Brill, 2017.

Elliott, J. H. *The Count-Duke of Olivares: The Statesman in an Age of Decline*. New Haven CT: Yale University Press, 1986.

———. "King and *Patria* in the Hispanic World." In *Spain, Europe and the Wider World, 1500–1800*, 173–92. 2004. Reprint, New Haven CT: Yale University Press, 2009.

Everaert, John. "Comment récupérer la 'Isla Colombina'? Un projet flamand de repeuplement à Santo-Domingo (1699–1701)." In *Vlamingen overzee*, Collectanea Maritima 6, 77–88. Brussels: Koninklijke Academie voor Wetenschappen, Letteren en Schone Kunsten van België, 1995.

Exbalin, Arnaud. "Riot in Mexico City: A Challenge to the Colonial Order?" *Urban History* 43, no. 2 (2016): 215–31.

Feros, Antonio. *Kingship and Favoritism in the Spain of Philip III, 1598–1621*. Cambridge: Cambridge University Press, 2000.

Flores Sasso, Virginia. "El comercio de la madera y la construcción naval en el siglo XVII en la isla Española." *Clío* 92, no. 205 (January–June 2023): 85–121.

Folger, Robert. *Writing as Poaching: Interpellation and Self-Fashioning in Colonial Relaciones de Méritos y Servicios*. Leiden: Brill, 2011.

Franco de Torrequemada, Francisco. "Representación de Don Francisco Franco de Torquemada [*sic*]." BP Ms. 2, n. 2835, 334r–346r. Originally printed Madrid, ca. 1690. Reprinted in *Boletín del Archivo General de la Nación* (Dominican Republic) 4, no. 17 (August 1941): 204–17.

Galván Rodríguez, Eduardo. *Tríptico de la Real Audiencia de Manila (1583–1700)*. Las Palmas de Gran Canaria: Universidad de Las Palmas de Gran Canaria, 2007.

García Gallo, Alfonso. "Las Audiencias de Indias: Su origen y caracteres." In *Memoria del segundo congreso Venezolano de Historia, del 18 al 23 de noviembre de 1974*, vol. 3, 359–432. Caracas, Academia Nacional de la Historia, 1975.

García-Herrera, Ricardo, Luis Gimeno, Pedro Ribera, and Emiliano Hernández. "New Records of Atlantic Hurricanes from Spanish Documentary Sources." *Journal of Geophysical Research* 110, no. D3109 (2005): 1–7. http://doi.org/10.1029/2004JD005272.

Garrigus, John D. *Before Haiti: Race and Citizenship in French Saint-Domingue*. New York: Palgrave Macmillan, 2006.

Gil-Bermejo García, Juana. *La Española: Anotaciones históricas (1600–1650)*. Seville: Escuela de Estudios Hispano-Americanos, 1983.

Gómez, Pablo. *The Experiential Caribbean: Creating Knowledge and Healing in the Early Modern Atlantic*. Chapel Hill: University of North Carolina Press.

Gómez Gómez, Margarita. *El sello y registro de Indias: Imagen y representación*. Cologne: Böhlau, 2008.

González de Peña, coord. *Historia general del pueblo dominicano*. Vol. 2, *Configuración de la sociedad criolla: Siglos XVII y XVIII*. Santo Domingo: Academia Dominicana de la Historia, 2018.

Goode, Catherine Tracy. "Merchant-Bureaucrats, Unwritten Contracts, and Fraud in the Manila Galleon Trade." In *Corruption in the Iberian Empires: Greed, Custom, and Colonial Networks*, edited by Christoph Rosenmüller, 171–95. Albuquerque: University of New Mexico Press, 2017.

Goslinga, Cornelis Ch. *The Dutch in the Caribbean and on the Wild Coast, 1580–1680*. Gainesville: University of Florida Press, 1971.

———. *A Short History of the Netherlands Antilles and Surinam*. The Hague: Martinus Nijhoff, 1979.

Gould, Eliga H. "Entangled Histories, Entangled Worlds: The English-Speaking Atlantic as a Spanish Periphery." *American Historical Review* 112, no. 3 (June 2007): 764–86.

Grady, Timothy Paul. *Anglo-Spanish Rivalry in Colonial South-East America, 1650–1725*. London: Pickering & Chatto, 2010.

Gutiérrez Escudero, Antonio. "Acerca del proyectismo y del reformismo borbónico en Santo Domingo." *Temas Americanistas* 13 (1997): 45–79.

———. "Cuestión de límites en la isla Española, 1690–1777." *Temas Americanistas* 1 (1982): 63–72.

———. "Inmigración canaria a América: Avatares de los isleños en Santo Domingo, 1684–1764." In *VI Coloquio de Historia Canario-Americana*, coordinated by Francisco Morales Padrón, vol. 1, 116–33. Las Palmas: Cabildo de Gran Canaria, 1984.

———. "La estructura económica de Santo Domingo, 1500–1795." In *Historia de la República Dominicana*, coordinated by Frank Moya Pons, 57–94. Madrid: Consejo Superior de Investigaciones Científicas, 2010.

———. "Vicisitudes de una villa de canarios en La Española: San Carlos de Tenerife, 1684–1750." In *IX Coloquio de Historia Canario-Americana*, vol. 1, 706–16. Las Palmas: Cabildo de Gran Canaria, 1990.

Harden, Faith S. *Arms and Letters: Military Life Writing in Early Modern Spain*. Toronto: University of Toronto Press, 2020.

Hera, Alberto de la. *Iglesia y corona en la América Española*. Madrid: Editorial MAPFRE, 1992.

Hernández García, Ángel. "Clasificación diplomática de los documentos reales en la edad moderna." *Norba: Revista de Historia* 15 (2001): 169–86.

Hernández González, Manuel V. *El sur dominicano (1680–1795): Cambios sociales y transformaciones económicas*. Santo Domingo: Editora Búho, 2008.

———. "La organización de la colonia, 1500–1795." In *Historia de la República Dominicana*, coordinated by Frank Moya Pons, 377–91. Madrid: Consejo Superior de Investigaciones Científicas, 2010.

———. "Santo Domingo en el contexto internacional, 1610–1795." In *Historia de la República Dominicana*, coordinated by Frank Moya Pons, 367–76. Madrid: Consejo Superior de Investigaciones Científicas, 2010.

———. "Sociedad en la Española, 1492–1795." In *Historia de la República Dominicana*, coordinated by Frank Moya Pons, 205–61. Madrid: Consejo Superior de Investigaciones Científicas, 2010.

Herrera, César A. "La Real Audiencia de Santo Domingo." *Clío* 29–30, no. 118–19 (January 1961–December 1962): 3–14.

Herrera, Thomás de. *Historia del Convento de San Agustín de Salamanca*. Madrid: Gregorio Rodríguez, 1652.

Herzog, Tamar. "Identidades colectivas, fronteras comunitarias y derecho: La domiciliación de mujeres de oidores quiteños durante el siglo XVII." *Anuario de historia del derecho español* 67 (1997): 1423–31.

———. *Los ministros de la Audiencia de Quito (1650–1750)*. Quito: Ediciones Libri Mundi Enrique Grosse-Luemern, 1995.

———. "The 'Recopilación De Indias' and Its Discourse. The Spanish Monarchy, the Indies and the Seventeenth Century." *Ius Commune* 20 (1993): 143–63.

———. *Ritos de control, prácticas de negociación: Pesquisas, visitas y residencias y las relaciones entre Quito y Madrid (1650–1750)*. In *Nuevas Aportaciones a la historia jurídica de Iberoamérica*, edited by José Andrés Gallego, 1–198. Madrid: Fundación Hernando de Larramendi-Mapfre, 2000. CD-ROM.

———. *Upholding Justice: Society, State, and the Penal System in Quito (1650–1750)*. Ann Arbor: University of Michigan Press, 2004.

Honores, Renzo. "Litigación en la Audiencia Arzobispal de Lima: Abogados y procuradores de causas en la litigación canónica, 1600–1650." In *Normatividades e instituciones eclesiásticas en el virreinato del Perú, siglos XVI–XIX*, edited by Otto Danwerth, Benedetta Albani, and Thomas Duve, 69–108. Frankfurt: Max Planck Institute for European Legal History, 2019. http://dx.doi.org/10.12946/gplh12.

Hrodej, Philippe. "Défense statique et défense dynamique, le cas de Saint-Domingue dans le seconde moitié du XVIIe siècle." In *Défense et colonies dans le monde atlantique, XVe–XXe siècle*, edited by David Plouviez, 41–53. Rennes: Presses Universitaires de Rennes, 2014.

Hussey, Roland D. "Spanish Reaction to Foreign Aggression in the Caribbean to about 1680." *Hispanic American Historical Review* 9, no. 3 (August 1929): 286–302.

Jekabson-Lemanis, Karen. "Balts in the Caribbean: The Duchy of Courland's Attempts to Colonize Tobago Island, 1638 to 1654." *Caribbean Quarterly* 46, no. 2 (June 2000): 25–44.

Jiménez Núñez, Alfredo, comp. *Antropología histórica: La audiencia de Guatemala en el siglo XVI*. Seville: Universidad de Sevilla, 1997.

———. "Sistema político y legislación en la América colonial hispana: Una interpretación desde la antropología cultural." In *Antropología histórica: La audiencia de Guatemala en el siglo XVI*, compiled by Alfredo Jiménez Núñez, 291–314. Seville: Universidad de Sevilla, 1997.

Julián, Amadeo. "La fuga de esclavos de la colonia francesa a la colonia española de Santo Domingo, la fundación del pueblo de los Minas, y la resistencia y solidaridad de los negros libres." *Clío* 87, no. 195 (January–June 2018): 35–91.

———. "Situación económica, demográfica y social de Santo Domingo en el siglo XVII." *Clío* 83, no. 187 (January–June 2014): 9–96.

Kagan, Richard L. *Students and Society in Early Modern Spain*. Baltimore: Johns Hopkins University Press, 1974.

Kamen, Henry. *Empire: How Spain Became a World Power*. New York: HarperCollins, 2003.

Kapitzke, Robert L. *Religion, Power, and Politics in Colonial St. Augustine*. Gainesville: University Press of Florida, 2001.

Klooster, Wim. *The Dutch Moment: War, Trade, and Settlement in the Seventeenth-Century Atlantic World*. Ithaca NY: Cornell University Press, 2016.

Kupperman, Karen Ordahl. *Providence Island, 1630–1641: The Other Puritan Colony*. Cambridge: Cambridge University Press, 1993.

Landers, Jane. "The Central African Presence in Spanish Maroon Communities." In *Central Africans and Cultural Transformations in the American Diaspora*, edited by Linda M. Heywood, 227–41. Cambridge: Cambridge University Press, 2002.

Lane, Kris E. *Pillaging the Empire: Piracy in the Americas, 1500–1750*. Armonk NY: M. E. Sharpe, 1998.

Llavador Mira, José. *La gobernación de Venezuela en el siglo XVII*. Caracas: Biblioteca de la Academia Nacional de la Historia, 1969.

Lockhart, James, and Stuart B. Schwartz. *Early Latin America: A History of Colonial Spanish America and Brazil*. Cambridge: Cambridge University Press, 1983.

López Beltrán, Clara. "La buena vecindad: Las mujeres de élite en la sociedad colonial del siglo XVI." *Colonial Latin American Review* 5, no. 2 (December 1996): 219–36.

López Cantos, Ángel. *Historia de Puerto Rico (1650–1700)*. Seville: Escuela de Estudios Hispano-Americanos, 1975.

Luque Talaván, Miguel. "La inmunidad del sagrado o el derecho de asilo eclesiástico a la luz de la legislación canónica y civil indiana." In *Los concilios provinciales en Nueva España: Reflexiones e influencias*, coordinated by María del Pilar Martínez López-Cano and Francisco Javier Cervantes Bello, 253–84. Mexico City: Universidad Nacional Autónoma de México, 2005.

Lynch, John. *The Hispanic World in Crisis and Change, 1598–1700*. Oxford: Basil Blackwell, 1992.

Macías Domínguez, Isabelo. *Cuba en la primera mitad del siglo XVII*. Seville: Escuela de Estudios Hispano-Americanos, 1978.

MacLachlan, Colin M. *Spain's Empire in the New World: The Role of Ideas in Institutional and Social Change*. Berkeley: University of California Press, 1988.

MacLeod, Murdo. "Self-Promotion: The *Relaciones de Méritos y Servicios* and Their Historical and Political Interpretation." *Colonial Latin American Historical Review* 7, no. 1 (Winter 1998): 25–42.

Malagón Barceló, Javier. *El distrito de la Audiencia de Santo Domingo en los siglos XVI a XIX*. 2nd ed. Santiago DR: Universidad Católica Madre y Maestre, 1977.

Malcolm, Alistair. *Royal Favouritism and the Governing Elite of the Spanish Monarchy, 1640–1655*. Oxford: Oxford University Press, 2017.

Marichal, Carlos, and Matilde Souto Mantecón. "Silver and Situados: New Spain and the Financing of the Spanish Empire in the Caribbean in the Eighteenth Century." *Hispanic American Historical Review* 74, no. 4 (November 1994): 587–613.

Martínez Torres, José Antonio. *Prisioneros de los infieles: Vida y rescate de los cautivos cristianos en el Mediterráneo musulmán (siglos XVI–XVII)*. Barcelona: Edicions Bellaterra, 2004.

Martiré, Eduardo. *Las Audiencias y la Administración de Justicia en Las Indias*. Madrid: Universidad Autónoma de Madrid, 2005.

Masters, Adrian. "A Thousand Invisible Architects: Vassals, the Petition and Response System, and the Creation of Spanish Imperial Caste Legislation." *Hispanic American Historical Review* 98, no. 3 (August 2018): 377–406.

Mathews, Thomas G. "The Spanish Domination of Saint Martin (1633–1648)." *Caribbean Studies* 9, no. 1 (April 1969): 3–23.

Matibag, Eugenio. *Haitian-Dominican Counterpoint: Nation, State, and Race on Hispaniola*. New York: Palgrave Macmillan, 2003.

Mawson, Stephanie J. "Convicts or *Conquistadores*? Spanish Soldiers in the Seventeenth-Century Pacific." *Past & Present* 232 (August 2016): 87–125.

Mayorga García, Fernando. *La Audiencia de Santafé en los siglos XVI y XVII*. Bogotá: Instituto Colombiano de Cultura Hispánica, 1991.

Mir, Pedro. *La noción de período en la historia dominicana*. 2nd ed. Vol. 1. Santo Domingo: Archivo General de la Nación, 2013.

Montemayor de Cuenca, Juan Francisco de. *Discurso político-histórico-jurídico del derecho y repartimiento de presas y despojos aprehendidos en justa guerra: Premios y castigos de los soldados*. Mexico City: Juan Ruiz, 1658.

Montoya Salas, Miguel. *Evolución político-territorial de Mérida (1558–1914)*. 2nd ed. Mérida, Venezuela: Universidad de los Andes, 2008.

Morales Padrón, Francisco. *Jamaica Española*. Seville: Escuela de Estudios Hispano-Americanos, 1952.

Moreno, Gabriel René. *La Audiencia de Charcas*. La Paz: Ministeria de Educación y Cultura, 1970.

Moreta Castillo, Américo. *La Real Audiencia de Santo Domingo (1511–1799): La Justicia en Santo Domingo de la época colonial*. Santo Domingo: Academia Dominicana de la Historia, 2010.

Morgan, William Thomas. "The British West Indies during King William's War (1689–97)." *Journal of Modern History* 2, no. 3 (September 1930): 378–409.

Moutoukias, Zacarías. *Contrabando y control colonial en el siglo XVII: Buenos Aires, el Atlántico, y el espacio peruano*. Buenos Aires: Centro editor de América Latina, 1988.

———. "Power, Corruption, and Commerce: The Making of the Local Administrative Structure in Seventeenth-Century Buenos Aires." *Hispanic American Historical Review* 68, no. 4 (November 1988): 771–801.

Moya Pons, Frank. "Evolución de la población dominicana, 1500–2010." In *Historia de la República Dominicana*, coordinated by Frank Moya Pons, 29–54. Madrid: Consejo Superior de Investigaciones Científicas, 2010.

———. *Historia colonial de Santo Domingo*. 3rd ed. Santiago DR: Universidad Católica Madre y Maestre, 1977.

———. *La otra historia dominicana*. Santo Domingo: Librería La Trinitaria, 2008.

Muro Romero, Fernando. *Las Presidencias-Gobernaciones en Indias (siglo XVI)*. Seville: Escuela de Estudios Hispano-Americanos, 1975.

Nesvig, Martin Austin. *Promiscuous Power: An Unorthodox History of New Spain*. Austin: University of Texas Press, 2018.

Nolasco, Flérida de. *Días de la colonia (Estudios Históricos)*. Ciudad Trujillo: Impresora Dominicana, 1952.

Nuzzo, Luigi. "Between America and Europe: The Strange Case of the *Derecho Indiano*." In *New Horizons in Spanish Colonial Law: Contributions to Transnational Early Modern Legal History*, edited by Thomas Duve and Heikki Pihlajamäki, 161–91. Frankfurt: Max Planck Institute for European Legal History, 2015. http://dx.doi.org/10.12946/gplh3.

Ortega y Pérez Gallardo, Ricardo. *Historia genealógica de las familias más antiguas de México*. 3rd ed. 3 vols. Mexico City: A. Carranza, 1908–10.

Ots Capdequi, José María. *El Estado español en las Indias*. 4th ed. Mexico City: Fondo de Cultura Económica, 1965.

Paredes Vera, María Isabel. "Ejército, milicias y sociedad en La Española (1650–1700)." In *Orbis incognitvs. Avisos y legajos del Nuevo Mundo: Homenaje al profesor Luis Navarro García*. Vol. 1, coordinated by Fernando Navarro Antolín, 397–420. Huelva, Spain: Universidad de Huelva, 2007.

———. "El cabildo de Santo Domingo en la segunda mitad del siglo XVII y creación del cabildo de San Carlos de Tenerife en La Española." *Boletín del Archivo General de la Nación* (Dominican Republic) 40, no. 142 (May–August 2015): 227–53.

———. "Justicia y gobierno en la Española durante el reinado de Carlos II (1665–1700). La Real Audiencia de Santo Domingo." *Boletín del Archivo General de la Nación* (Dominican Republic) 37, no. 133 (May–August 2012): 279–303.

———. "La decadencia de la población y de la economía de estancias hasta mediados del siglo XVII." In *Historia general del pueblo dominicano*. Vol. 2, *Configuración de la sociedad criolla: Siglos XVII y XVIII*, coordinated by Raymundo González de Peña, 91–146. Santo Domingo: Academia Dominicana de la Historia, 2018.

———. "'No hay más Ley ni más Rey que don Rodrigo Pimentel': De cómo un hombre manejó en su propio beneficio las riendas de la economía dominicana en el siglo XVII." *Clío* 92, no. 205 (January–June 2023): 365–416.

Parry, J. H. *The Audiencia of New Galicia in the Sixteenth Century: A Study in Spanish Colonial Government*. Cambridge: Cambridge University Press, 1948.

Pelorson, Jean-Marc. *Les "Letrados": Juristes castillans sous Philippe III; recherches sur leur place dans la société, la culture et l'état*. Poitiers, France: Université de Poitiers, 1980.

Peña Batlle, Manuel Arturo. *Historia de la cuestión fronteriza domínico-haitiana*. 3rd ed. Santo Domingo: Banreservas-Bibliófilos, 2012.

———. *La Isla de Tortuga: Plaza de Armas, Refugio, y Seminario de los Enemigos de España en Indias*. 3rd ed. Santo Domingo: Editora Taller, 1988.

Peña Pérez, Frank. *Antonio Osorio: Monopolio, contrabando, y despoblación*. Santiago DR: Universidad Católica Madre y Maestre, 1980.

———. *Cien años de miseria en Santo Domingo, 1600–1700*. Santo Domingo: Editorial CENAPEC, 1985.

Pérez Aínsua Méndez, Natalia. *De sellos, heráldica y alegorías: El papel sellado en España*. Seville: Universidad de Sevilla, 2014.

Pérez Collados, José María. *Una aproximación histórica al concepto jurídico de nacionalidad (La integración del Reino Aragón en la monarquía hispánica)*. Zaragoza: Institución "Fernando el Católico," 1993.

Pérez Memén, Fernando. *El Arzobispo Fernando Carvajal y Rivera: Un crítico de la política colonial española (y otros ensayos historicos)*. Santo Domingo: Universidad Nacional Pedro Henríquez Ureña, 1985.

Pérez Tostado, Igor. "'Buscando el amparo de los españoles': Participación irlandesa en la estructura militar hispana en el Caribe. Siglo XVII." In *Por fuerza de las armas: Ejercito e independiencias en Iberoamérica*, edited by Juan Marchena and Manuel Chust, 41–61. Castelló de la Plana: Universitat Jaume I, 2008.

Pestana, Carla Gardina. "Early English Jamaica without Pirates." *William and Mary Quarterly* 71, no. 3 (July 2014): 321–60.

———. *The English Conquest of Jamaica: Oliver Cromwell's Bid for Empire*. Cambridge MA: Belknap Press, 2017.

Phelan, John L. "Authority and Flexibility in the Spanish Imperial Bureaucracy." *Administrative Science Quarterly* 5, no. 1 (June 1960): 47–65.

———. *The Kingdom of Quito in the Seventeenth Century: Bureaucratic Politics in the Spanish Empire*. Madison: University of Wisconsin Press, 1967.

Phillips, Carla Rahn. *Six Galleons for the King of Spain: Imperial Defense in the Early Seventeenth Century*. Baltimore: Johns Hopkins University Press, 1986.

Pietschmann, Horst. *El estado y su evolución al principio de la colonización española de América*. Translated by Angelica Scherp. Mexico City: Fondo de Cultura Económica, 1989.

Pincus, Steven C. A. *Protestantism and Patriotism: Ideologies and the Making of English Foreign Policy, 1650–1668*. Cambridge: Cambridge University Press, 1996.

Planas Rosselló, Antonio. *La Real Audiencia de Mallorca en la época de los Austrias (1571–1715)*. Barcelona: Publicacions de la Universitat Pompeu Fabra, 2010.

Polo y La Borda, Adolfo. "Representando la experiencia: Imágenes e imaginarios en el Imperio español del siglo XVII." *Anuario de Historia de América Latina* 57 (2020): 52–86.

Ponce Vázquez, Juan José. "Atlantic Peripheries: Diplomacy, War, and Spanish-French Interactions in Hispaniola, 1660s–1690s." In *The Atlantic World*, edited by D'Maris Coffman, Adrian Leonard, and William O'Reilly, 300–318. London: Routledge, 2015.

———. "Casting Traitors and Villains: The Historiographical Memory of the 1605 Depopulations of Hispaniola." In *Sites of Memory in Spain and Latin America*, edited by Marina Llorente, Marcella Salvi, and Aida Díaz de León, 151–66. Lanham MD: Lexington, 2015.

———. "Colaboraciones fronterizas, diplomacia y guerra en La Española, 1660–1690." *Boletín del Archivo General de la Nación* (Dominican Republic) 40, no. 142 (May–August 2015): 255–83.

———. "Contrabandistas, piratas y diplomacia: Santo Domingo y el Caribe español a finales del siglo XVII." *Clío* 92, no. 205 (January–June 2023): 269–306.

———. *Islanders and Empire: Smuggling and Political Defiance in Hispaniola, 1580–1690*. Cambridge: Cambridge University Press, 2020.

———. "Unequal Partners in Crime: Masters, Slaves and Free People of Color in Santo Domingo, c. 1600–1650." *Slavery & Abolition* 37, no. 4 (2016): 704–23.

Prado, Estevan de. *Por Francisco Nuñez Melian Governador, y Capitan general, que fue de la provincia de Veneçuela, con Bartolome de Monesterio, vezino de la ciudad de Caracas* . . . ([Madrid?]: [1640?]). http://access.bl.uk/item/viewer/ark:/81055/vdc_100049668151.0x000001.

Pritchard, James. "The French West Indies during the Nine Years' War, 1688–1697: A Review and Reappraisal." *French Colonial History* 2 (2002): 45–59.

———. *In Search of Empire: The French in the Americas, 1670–1730*. Cambridge: Cambridge University Press, 2004.

Quiles García, Fernando. "Casos y cosas de la América hispana, desde Sevilla: Siglos XVII–XVIII." In *Arte y patrimonio en España y América*, edited by María de los Ángeles Fernández Valle, Francisco Ollero Lobato, and William Rey Ashfield, 141–59. Montevideo: Universidad de la República, 2014.

Rappaport, Joanne. *The Disappearing Mestizo: Configuring Difference in the Colonial New Kingdom of Granada*. Durham NC: Duke University Press, 2014.

Recopilación de leyes de los reynos de las Indias. 4 vols. Madrid: Julián de Paredes, 1681.

Reichert, Rafal. *Sobre las olas de un mar plateado: La política defensiva española y el financiamiento militar novohispano en la región del Gran Caribe, 1598–1700*. Mérida: Universidad Nacional Autónoma de México, 2013.

Rilova Pérez, Isaac. "De Sasamón a América: Don Diego de Osorio, capitán general y gobernador de Venezuela y presidente de la Real Audiencia de Santo Domingo (1552–1600)." *Boletín de la Institución Fernán González* 224 (2012): 73–93.

Rodríguez Demorizi, Emilio. "Familias Hispanoamericanas." *Boletín del Archivo General de la Nación* (Dominican Republic) 21, no. 95 (January–March 1958): 6–133.

Rodríguez Morel, Genaro, comp. *Cartas del cabildo de Santo Domingo en el siglo XVII*. Santo Domingo: Editora Búho, 2007.

———. "Las Devastaciones de Osorio y el surgimiento del criollo en Santo Domingo." *Clío* 85, no. 191 (January–June 2016): 279–330.

———. "The Sugar Economy of Española in the Sixteenth Century." In *Tropical Babylons: Sugar and the Making of the Atlantic World, 1450–1680*, edited by Stuart B. Schwartz, 85–114. Chapel Hill: University of North Carolina Press, 2004.

Rodríguez Ridao, Antonio Luis. "La administración del Real Situado en tiempos del gobernador Tomás Marín de Poveda: Corrupción en detrimento del Ejército de Chile (1692–1700)." *Revista Complutense de Historia de América* 43 (2017): 101–26.

Rodríguez-Sala, María Luisa, and Miguel B. de Erice. "Juan Francisco de Montemayor y Córdoba de Cuenca, abogado, oidor y recopilador del siglo XVII." *Anuario Mexicano de Historia del Derecho* 9 (1997): 193–233.

Rodríguez Souquet, Carlos Antonio. *El Concilio Provincial Dominicano (1622–1623): Un aporte para la historia de las Antillas y Venezuela*. Mexico City: Siglo Veintiuno Editores, 2003.

Rodríguez Vicente, María Encarnación. "El derecho de Media Anata." In *Poder y presión fiscal en la América española. Siglos XVI, XVII y XVIII: Trabajos del VI Congreso del Instituto Internacional de Historia del Derecho Indiano en homenaje al Dr. Alfonso García-Gallo*, 465–504. Valladolid: Universidad de Valladolid, 1986.

Rosenmüller, Christoph. *Corruption and Justice in Colonial Mexico, 1650–1755*. Cambridge: Cambridge University Press, 2019.

———. "Two Kingdoms in a Multi-tiered Empire: New Spain and New Galicia in the Mid-eighteenth Century." *Max Planck Institute for European Legal History Research Paper Series*, no. 2018-10 (2018): 1–29. http://doi.org/10.2139/ssrn.3272113.

Ruíz Guiñazú, Enrique. *La magistratura indiana*. Buenos Aires: Facultad de Derecho y Ciencias Sociales, 1916.

Rupert, Linda M. *Creolization and Contraband: Curaçao in the Early Modern Atlantic World*. Athens: University of Georgia Press, 2012.

Russell-Wood, A. J. R. "The Portuguese Atlantic, 1415–1808." In *Atlantic History: A Critical Appraisal*, edited by Jack P. Greene and Philip D. Morgan, 81–109. Oxford: Oxford University Press, 2009.

Sáez Ramo, José Luis. "La epidemia de viruelas en Santo Domingo, 1666–1674." *Clío* 86, no. 193 (January–June 2017): 67–88.

———, ed. *Libro de bautismos de esclavos (1636–1670)*. Santo Domingo: Archivo General de la Nación, 2008.

Sánchez Belén, Juan A. *La política fiscal en Castilla durante el reinado de Carlos II*. Madrid: Siglo XXI de España Editores, 1996.

Sánchez Bella, Ismael. *La organización financiera de las Indias (siglo XVI)*. Seville: Escuela de Estudios Hispano-Americanos, 1968.

———. "Las audiencias y el gobierno de las Indias (siglos XVI–XVII)." *Revista de Estudios Histórico-Jurídicos* 2 (1977): 159–86.

———. "Visitas a Indias (Siglos XVI–XVII)." In *Memoria del segundo congreso Venezolano de Historia, del 18 al 23 de noviembre de 1974*, vol. 3, 163–208. Caracas: Academia Nacional de la Historia, 1975.

Sánchez Lustrino, Gilberto. "Los Archivos Dominicanos." *Boletín del Archivo General de la Nación* (Dominican Republic) 1, no. 1 (March 1938): 3–13.

Santos Pérez, José Manuel. "La práctica del autogobierno en Centroamérica: Conflictos entre la Audiencia de Guatemala y el Cabildo de Santiago en el siglo XVIII." *Mesoamérica* 40 (December 2000): 69–94.

Sanz Morquecho, Pedro. *Practica quotidiana*. Frankfurt: Collegium Musarum Palthenianum, 1607.

Sanz Tapia, Ángel. *¿Corrupción o necesidad?: La venta de cargos de gobierno americanos bajo Carlos II (1674–1700)*. Madrid: Consejo Superior de Investigaciones Científicas, 2009.

———. “Provisión, beneficio y venta de oficios americanos de Hacienda (1632–1700).” *Revista Complutense de Historia de América* 37 (2011): 145–72.

Sarfatti, Magali. *Spanish Bureaucratic-Patrimonialism in America*. Berkeley: University of California Press, 1966.

Schäfer, Ernst. *El Consejo Real y Supremo de las Indias: Su historia, organización y labor administrativa hasta la terminación de la casa de Austria*. 2 vols. Seville: Imp. M. Carmona, 1935–47.

Schmidt, Benjamin. “The Dutch Atlantic: From Provincialism to Globalism.” In *Atlantic History: A Critical Appraisal*, edited by Jack P. Greene and Philip D. Morgan, 163–87. Oxford: Oxford University Press, 2009.

Schmitt, Casey. “Centering Spanish Jamaica: Regional Competition, Informal Trade, and the English Invasion, 1620–62.” *William and Mary Quarterly* 76, no. 4 (2019): 697–726.

Schwaller, Robert C. “Contested Conquests: African Maroons and the Incomplete Conquest of Hispaniola, 1519–1620.” *The Americas* 75, no. 4 (October 2018): 609–38.

Schwartz, Stuart B. *Sovereignty and Society in Colonial Brazil: The High Court of Bahia and Its Judges, 1609–1751*. Berkeley: University of California Press, 1973.

Seed, Patricia. *To Love, Honor, and Obey in Colonial Mexico: Conflicts over Marriage Choice, 1574–1821*. Stanford CA: Stanford University Press, 1988.

Serrano Mangas, Fernando. *La Encrucijada Portuguesa: Esplendor y quiebra de la unión ibérica en las Indias de Castilla (1600–1668)*. Badajoz, Spain: Diputación de Badajoz, 2001.

Sigüenza y Góngora, Carlos de. “Trofeo de la justicia española en el castigo de la alevosía francesa.” 1691. In *Seis obras*, edited by William G. Bryant, 49–92. Caracas: Biblioteca Ayacucho, 1984.

Silva i Molina, Abraham de. “Oidores de la Real Audiencia de Santiago de Chile durante el siglo XVII.” *Anales de la Universidad de Chile* 113 (July–December 1903): 5–75.

Sluiter, Engel. “Dutch-Spanish Rivalry in the Caribbean Area, 1594–1609.” *Hispanic American Historical Review* 28, no. 2 (May 1948): 165–96.

———. “The Word *Pechelingue*: Its Derivation and Meaning.” *Hispanic American Historical Review* 24, no. 4 (November 1944): 683–98.

Socolow, Susan Migden. *The Women of Colonial Latin America*. Cambridge: Cambridge University Press, 2000.

Solórzano Pereira, Juan. *Política Indiana*. 3 vols. Madrid: Diego Diaz de la Carrera, 1648.

Storrs, Christopher. *The Resilience of the Spanish Monarchy, 1665–1700*. Oxford: Oxford University Press, 2006.

Stradling, R. A. *Philip IV and the Government of Spain, 1621–1665*. Cambridge: Cambridge University Press, 2002.

Studnicki-Gizbert, Daviken. *A Nation upon the Ocean Sea: Portugal's Atlantic Diaspora and the Crisis of the Spanish Empire, 1492–1640*. Oxford: Oxford University Press, 2007.

Suárez, Santiago-Gerardo. *Las reales audiencias indianas: Fuentes y Bibliografía*. Caracas: Academia Nacional de la Historia, 1989.

Tau Anzoátegui, Victor. *El Jurista en el Nuevo Mundo. Pensamiento. Doctrina. Mentalidad*. Frankfurt: Max Planck Institute for European Legal History, 2016. http://doi.org/10.12946/gplh7.

———. "Entre leyes, glosas y comentos: El episodio de la Recopilación de Indias." In *El Jurista en el Nuevo Mundo. Pensamiento. Doctrina. Mentalidad*, 147–66. 1996. Reprint, Frankfurt: Max Planck Institute for European Legal History, 2016. http://doi.org/10.12946/gplh7.

———. "La idea de Derecho en la colonización española en América." In *El Jurista en el Nuevo Mundo. Pensamiento. Doctrina. Mentalidad*, 25–33. 1991. Reprint, Frankfurt: Max Planck Institute for European Legal History, 2016. http://doi.org/10.12946/gplh7.

———. "Provincial and Local Law of the Indies: A Research Program." In *New Horizons in Spanish Colonial Law: Contributions to Transnational Early Modern Legal History*, edited by Thomas Duve and Heikki Pihlajamäki, 235–55. Frankfurt: Max Planck Institute for European Legal History, 2015. http://dx.doi.org/10.12946/gplh3.

Taylor, S. A. G. *The Western Design: An Account of Cromwell's Expedition to the Caribbean*. 2nd ed. London: Solstice, 1969.

Torres Agudo, Ruth. "Élites y grupos de poder: Los hacendados de Santo Domingo (1750–1795)." PhD diss., Universidad de Salamanca, 2008.

———. "Los Campuzano-Polanco, una familia de la élite de la ciudad de Santo Domingo." *Nuevo Mundo Mundos Nuevos* 7 (2007). http://doi.org/10.4000/nuevomundo.3240.

Torres Ramírez, Bibiano. *La Armada de Barlovento*. Seville: Escuela de Estudios Hispano-Americanos, 1981.

Tortorici, Zeb. *Sins against Nature: Sex and Archives in Colonial New Spain*. Durham NC: Duke University Press, 2018.

Ugarte, María, *Estampas Coloniales*. 2 vols. Santo Domingo: Comisión Permanente de la Feria Nacional del Libro, 1998.

Utrera, Cipriano de. *Noticias históricas de Santo Domingo*. Edited by Emilio Rodríguez Demorizi. 5 vols. Santo Domingo: Editora Taller, 1978–82.

———. *Santo Domingo: Dilucidaciones históricas (I–II)*. 1927–29. Reprint, Santo Domingo: Secretaría de Estado de Educación, Bellas Artes y Cultos, 1995.

Vaccari San Miguel, Letizia. *Juicios de residencia en la provincia de Venezuela: Don Francisco Dávila Orejón Gastón (1673–1677)*. 3 vols. Caracas: Academia Nacional de la Historia, 1983.

———. *Sobre gobernadores y residencias en la Provincia de Venezuela (siglos XVI, XVII, XVIII)*. Caracas: Academia Nacional de la Historia, 1992.

Valenzuela Márquez, Jaime. *Las liturgias del poder: Celebraciones públicas y estrategias persuasivas en Chile colonial (1609–1709)*. Santiago, Chile: LOM, 2001.

Vega, Bernardo. *La derrota de Penn y Venables en Santo Domingo, 1655*. Santo Domingo: Academia Dominicana de la Historia, 2013.

Vega Boyrie, Wenceslao. "La Real Audiencia de Santo Domingo: Funciones y Procedimientos del Primer Tribunal de América." *eme eme: Estudios Dominicanos*, 4, no. 21 (November–December 1975): 91–104.

Veitia Linage, Joseph. *Norte de la Contratación de las Indias occidentales*. Seville: Juan Francisco de Blas, 1672.

Vila Vilar, Enriqueta. *Hispanoamérica y el comercio de esclavos: Los asientos portugueses*. Seville: Escuela de Estudios Hispano-Americanos, 1977.

———. *Historia de Puerto Rico (1600–1650)*. Seville: Escuela de Estudios Hispano-Americanos, 1974.

Wheat, David. *Atlantic Africa and the Spanish Caribbean, 1570–1640*. Chapel Hill: University of North Carolina Press, 2016.

Williams, Patrick. *The Great Favourite: The Duke of Lerma and the Court and Government of Philip III of Spain, 1598–1621*. Manchester: University of Manchester Press, 2006.

Wright, Irene A. "Rescates: With Special Reference to Cuba, 1599–1610." *Hispanic American Historical Review* 3, no. 3 (August 1920): 333–61.

Wright, L. P. "The Military Orders in Sixteenth- and Seventeenth-Century Spanish Society: The Institutional Embodiment of an Historical Tradition." *Past & Present* 43, no. 1 (May 1969): 34–70.

INDEX

Page numbers in *italics* refer to figures. Page numbers followed by *t* refer to tables.

www.ingramcontent.com/pod-product-compliance
Lightning Source LLC
Chambersburg PA
CBHW030812220625
28473CB00004B/5
9781496208378